T0190406

Demystifying Internet of Things Security

Successful IoT Device/Edge and Platform Security Deployment

Sunil Cheruvu
Anil Kumar
Ned Smith
David M. Wheeler

Demystifying Internet of Things Security: Successful IoT Device/Edge and Platform Security Deployment

Sunil Cheruvu
Chandler, AZ, USA

Anil Kumar
Chandler, AZ, USA

Ned Smith
Beaverton, OR, USA

David M. Wheeler
Gilbert, AZ, USA

ISBN-13 (pbk): 978-1-4842-2895-1
https://doi.org/10.1007/978-1-4842-2896-8

ISBN-13 (electronic): 978-1-4842-2896-8

Managing Director, Apress Media LLC: Welmoed Spahr
Acquisitions Editor: Natalie Pao
Development Editor: James Markham
Coordinating Editor: Jessica Vakili

Cover designed by eStudioCalamar

Cover image designed by Freepik (www.freepik.com)

Distributed to the book trade worldwide by Springer Science+Business Media New York, 233 Spring Street, 6th Floor, New York, NY 10013. Phone 1-800-SPRINGER, fax (201) 348-4505, e-mail orders-ny@springer-sbm.com, or visit www.springeronline.com. Apress Media, LLC is a California LLC and the sole member (owner) is Springer Science + Business Media Finance Inc (SSBM Finance Inc). SSBM Finance Inc is a **Delaware** corporation.

For information on translations, please e-mail rights@apress.com, or visit http://www.apress.com/rights-permissions.

Apress titles may be purchased in bulk for academic, corporate, or promotional use. eBook versions and licenses are also available for most titles. For more information, reference our Print and eBook Bulk Sales web page at http://www.apress.com/bulk-sales.

Any source code or other supplementary material referenced by the author in this book is available to readers on GitHub via the book's product page, located at www.apress.com/978-1-4842-2895-1. For more detailed information, please visit http://www.apress.com/source-code.

Printed on acid-free paper

Table of Contents

About the Authors

Sunil Cheruvu is a Principal Engineer in the Platform Engineering Division of Internet of Things Group (IOTG) at Intel Corporation and has been involved in architecting complex embedded systems involving HW/FW/SW for almost 27 years on Intel/ARM/MIPS/PowerPC architectures. At Intel, he is the chief IoT Security architect and leads the end-2-end security architecture for embedded devices including the scaling of security (from below Atom to Xeon products) on multiple operating systems including RTOS. He is the subject matter expert for IOTG security across Intel and industry. He frequently interacts with many customers in architect-2-architect capacity from multiple IoT segments including Industrial, Digital Surveillance Systems, Retail, Transportation, Medical/Healthcare, Gaming, Print Imaging, and Military/Aerospace/Government. Due to the uniqueness of IoT deice lifespan and the required robustness, he drives architectural initiatives such as Post Quantum readiness, physical & side-channel attack mitigations, and alternative/configurable roots of trust (via FPGA, ASIC/IP, etc.) for IOTG. In previous roles at Intel, he owned the content protection & system-level architecture of conditional access and trusted data path (end-to-end premium content protection within a SoC). He also lead the BIOS/UEFI development on IOTG's first SoC and programmed VBIOS/UEFI GOP & embedded pre-OS graphics drivers in embedded group.

At Microsoft as a SW Design Engineer, he was the tech lead for vehicle networking (CAN, KLINE, MOST) on ARM based platform involving the NDIS bus and protocol driver stacks. He took these stacks through the threat modeling and implemented the resolutions in what was released as the Windows Mobile for Automotive (WMfA) platform. At Conexant Systems as a senior SW staff engineer, he designed and implemented the code for SCDMA & secure NAND Flash driver in ARM based DOCSIS 2.x compliant Cable Modems. At 3com Corporation, as senior SW engineer, he implemented the code for Telco return NT kernel mode drivers, embedded ROM webserver, and Baseline Privacy security in DOCSIS 1.x compliant cable modems.

Anil Kumar is a Principal Engineer in the Platform Engineering Division of IOTG at Intel Corporation and is responsible for the Connectivity Platform Architecture across IOTG. In this role, he lead the effort with the planning team to create IOTG's first ever roadmap for connectivity solutions. He is currently driving platform and chip-level integration of several key connectivity and communication technologies which are critical for cyber-physical systems. Anil joined Intel in 2007 as a design engineer in Digital Home Group. He served as a Platform Architect for several Intel Architecture–based Media Processors for TV and Set-Top Box applications. As the Platform Architect in Intel Media Group, Anil has led several designs that resulted in award-winning consumer electronic device designs at CES. The world's first Google TV devices were based on reference design efforts led by Anil as well. Prior to joining Intel, Anil held design engineering positions at multinational companies such as Fujitsu and Alcatel. He was instrumental in taking several designs from concept to production throughout his career.

Ned Smith is a Principal Security Architect in Intel's Open Technology Center developing trusted edge computing technologies. He co-chairs the IETF Remote Attestation Procedures working group. He developed the Open Connectivity Foundation (OCF) security specification for IoT devices and was a security architect for Intel® vPro™ and related security technologies. He co-chaired the Trusted Computing Group's (TCG) Infrastructure and Trusted Network Communication (TNC) working groups. He developed the Common Data Security Architecture (CDSA) specification in The Open Group. He holds over 150 US patents. He received Intel's Top Inventor award in 2016 and was runner up for Intel's distinguished inventor award in 2018. His professional interests include trusted computing for cloud, edge, IoT and blockchain. His non-professional interests including scuba, motorcycles and genealogy.

David M. Wheeler is a Senior Principal Engineer in the Platform Security Division of IAGS at Intel Corporation and has 30 years' experience in software, security, and networking. In his current role, Dave is responsible for research and development of new cryptographic algorithms and protocols, security APIs, and libraries across Intel including for IoT platforms, performs security reviews on Intel's cryptographic implementations, and represents Intel at the IETF. Within the Internet of Things, Dave has contributed to Intel's Software-Defined Industrial Systems architecture and IOTG's Health Application Platform. Prior to Intel, Dave held various lead software and systems architecture positions at Motorola, Honeywell Bull, General Dynamics, as well as his own consulting firm. Dave has designed and built several hardware security engines, including a Type 2 security coprocessor for a software-defined radio and the Intel Wireless Trust Module, a hardware cryptographic coprocessor on the Intel XScale processor. He has implemented several cryptographic libraries and protocol layers, including an IPSec-type implementation for an SDR radio; header compression protocol layers for IP, TCP, and UDP over multicast; a connectionless network layer protocol; two-factor authentication verification over RADIUS for a firewall VPN, PPP for serial; an instant messaging protocol over Bluetooth; and many others. Dave has been a key contributor to other full-stack product implementations including Intel's Blue River Network appliance and several complete public Internet applications in PHP, JavaScript/Sails, and even VBScript. Dave has also worked on smartcard security for banking and gaming applications at a startup, Touch Technology. While at Motorola in 1992, Dave authored the "Security Association Management Protocol" for the National Security Agency and subsequently spoke nationally about key management and key management protocols. He has led clean-room implementations for ISAKMP, IKEv2, and a custom network-keying protocol. Dave's extensive experience in security, networking, software, and hardware is leveraged across a broad segment of Intel's Internet of Things to make Intel's products and software projects secure.

Acknowledgments

For a book such as this, one that covers a myriad of specialized topics, it is difficult to single out only a few people to appreciate because so many actually contributed to the content in both direct and indirect ways.

We would like to thank our Intel IOTG management, Michael R. Crews and Michael Carboni, for providing unconditional support throughout the process. And a special thanks must be given to Sunil, our lead author, for keeping us all on track and always inspiring us to keep working toward our goal.

Each of us as authors received support from many colleagues at Intel who provided information, reviewed content, and answered questions. Our special thanks to those who contributed significantly to this process including Mats Agerstam, Jody Booth, Vincent Cao, Geoffrey Cooper, Jan Krueger, Tony Martin, Srini Musti, Al Elizondo, Imran Desai, Maurice Ma, Mike Taborn, Anahit Tarkhanyan, Yu Wang, Matt Wood, Anthony Xu, Dave Zage, Anthony Chun, Todd Cramer, Mitchell Dzurick, and many others. We especially want to thank Geoffrey Cooper for reading, rereading, and then reading again too many drafts of our chapters and Mats Agerstam for his many insightful contributions.

We offer our sincere gratitude to numerous others across Intel Corporation who have shared their experiences and knowledge in various meetings, SAFE reviews, crypto reviews, and the countless presentations that we as authors are privileged to be a part. Your contributions have helped us comprehend security in various IoT domains and we learn more from you every day – Thank You!

ACKNOWLEDGMENTS

We also wish to thank many colleagues in our industry with whom we have worked to define and align our architectures, standards and open source contributions for the betterment of secure computing.

— Sunil Cheruvu

— Anil Kumar

— David M. Wheeler

— Ned Smith

Foreword

In 1989 I walked into the Distributed Systems Laboratory as an undergraduate in the Electrical Engineering department at University of Pennsylvania and it seemed as if I didn't leave that lab until I received a doctorate 6 years later. Combining compute and communications has been a professional passion ever since as I've lead a range of initiatives at Intel Corporation in protecting video and audio content, bring networks and digital technologies into the home, securing compute infrastructure, and preparing for a new generation of distributed applications popularly referred to as the Internet of Things (IoT).

IoT's connection and computerization is a pervasive trend transforming everything we do and the infrastructure which supports us. From smart cities and homes to Industry 4.0, enterprises, critical infrastructure, healthcare, retail, and wearables, vast flows of data, increasingly processed using machine learning algorithms, are altering our existence. This unprecedented scale, pervasiveness, and interconnectivity also creates an environment where the security and integrity of these applications becomes a paramount concern. One only has to look to the headlines where attacks on critical infrastructure such as power generation and distribution, vulnerabilities in our automobiles, and malware in the devices such as webcams, smartphones, and PCs which we bring into our homes, highlight our collective vulnerability. Given the extensive attack surfaces being created and the asymmetry between attackers needing to find a single vulnerability to exploit while defenders have to find and close all vulnerabilities, IoT creates an unmatched set of security challenges.

During my journey, I've had the pleasure of working with many experts in their respective fields. These authors are the best when it comes to offering practical guidance in addressing the IoT Security challenges. This timely book will build your knowledge about the IoT security challenges and remedies from the ground up, starting with the fundamental security building blocks and extending into available IoT frameworks and specific vertical applications. Please join us in the critical mission of securing IoT applications, and by extension, our future!

— Brendan Traw

Intel Senior Fellow

Hillsboro, Oregon

July 2019

Introduction

The Internet of Things (IoT) is a general term describing any device used to collect data from the world around us and then share that data across the Internet where the data can be intelligently processed to provide information and services. This definition can be extended to an industrial closed loop control system where data is acquired, coalesced with related data, transmitted to an intelligent station, analyzed, and then acted upon to influence the environment.

The technology consulting firm Gartner, Inc. forecasts that 20.4 billion connected things will be in use worldwide by 2020. The total spending on endpoints and services will reach nearly $3 trillion in 2020.[1] They also forecast that worldwide spending on IoT security[2] is expected to reach $3.1 billion by 2021. In a similar study, IDC Forecasts Worldwide Technology Spending on the Internet of Things will experience a compound annual growth rate (CAGR) of 13.6% over the 2017–2022 forecast period and reach $1.2 trillion in 2022.[3]

The authors believe that IoT is a ripe field for not just securing the IoT devices but also for innovations in secure system design, secure building block technologies, and secure hardware and software development practices that together turn the Internet of Things into the Secure Internet of Things.

---

[1]www.gartner.com/en/newsroom/press-releases/2017-02-07-gartner-says-8-billion-connected-things-will-be-in-use-in-2017-up-31-percent-from-2016

[2]www.gartner.com/newsroom/id/3869181

[3]www.idc.com/getdoc.jsp?containerId=prUS43994118

The IoT ecosystem is at an inflection point, and Intel has developed a roadmap of products and services which comprehend this growth and enables customers to participate in the IoT ecosystem transformation from a collection of disjointed, vertically integrated suppliers of embedded technologies into an ecosystem of interoperable and flexible building block technologies. This transformation has three evolutionary phases:

> Phase 1: Connect previously unconnected devices through a multitude of interfaces and gateways eventually converging on the Cloud.

> Phase 2: Make devices smarter and more secure where the connected devices are empowered to make more important decisions and become more aware of their environment and context, while security is resiliently maintained.

> Phase 3: Increase the degree of autonomous operation while maintaining security where the smart devices require less dependence on back-end services – to dictate policies and to make decisions, becoming devices that can dynamically join or leave a network, can resiliently recover from failures, proactively update system software, and even learn to optimize operational efficiency.

Up through calendar year 2018, the industry, largely, has experienced a transition to Phase 1. We're now seeing dramatic shifts toward Phases 2 and 3 throughout the industry. We anticipate the future will be all about making IoT systems secure as a prerequisite to paving the way for a smarter and more autonomous IoT. Some may argue that IoT isn't a new phenomenon, and some say it's revolutionizing the compute domain where compute happens from Edge networks to cloud services. Our perspective is that IoT is actually both evolutionary and revolutionary – IoT will advance and reshape the existing (brownfield) infrastructure while at the same time revolutionize and create new (greenfield) markets, processes, and ecosystems. IoT will disrupt some businesses, transform others, and create entirely new ones. That is both evolutionary and revolutionary!

In this expanding world of IoT, security becomes critical since the attack surface expands in intricate and profound ways when connecting billions of new and previously unconnected devices. Connecting devices that have not historically been part of the Internet world is a bit like throwing the innocent to the wolves. Security is a vital part of the IoT transformation to connectedness. The data[4] from the National Vulnerability Database (NVD) pertaining to "CVSS[5] Severity Distribution Over Time" shows that during 2016–2018, the number of vulnerabilities with medium severity tripled (3359 vs. 8912) and those with high severity doubled (2469 vs. 4317). During the same period, the total number of vulnerabilities almost tripled. A search[6] for IoT in the NVD from 2016 to 2018 resulted in 89 hits with several critical and high severity vulnerabilities in IIoT gateways and in other IoT devices. Therefore it is not enough to simply connect these devices; the imperative is that these devices authenticate mutually and authorize services all while protecting the confidentiality, integrity, and privacy of the data they collect and share between elements of the system. It is critical to have end-to-end security including each element along the data and control paths from sensor and actuator, to edge and gateway, all the way to the Cloud, protecting both the device and their associated data, interfaces, and software. Edge devices range from the lowest-power MCU-based devices to Intel Atom, all the way up to high-performance Intel Core/Xeon-based platforms.

---

[4]https://nvd.nist.gov/general/visualizations/
vulnerability-visualizations/cvss-severity-distribution-over-time

[5]Common Vulnerability Scoring System (CVSS): https://nvd.nist.gov/
vuln-metrics/cvss

[6]https://nvd.nist.gov/vuln/search/results?form_type=Basic&results_
type=overview&query=IoT&search_type=last3years

It is important to understand that the anatomy of IoT hacks is radically different from typical consumer or enterprise computing. Consider the example of a hypothetical shutdown of the electrical grid via a domestic, Wi-Fi-connected oven and a ransomware attack that encrypts the firmware in a connected oven rendering it unusable. In both cases the oven becomes inoperable. The difference is in how the device owner needs to respond to the outage. A systemic outage of the power grid marshals resources to address the issue fairly quickly as the impact is more broadly felt. This outage will garner attention from government and private sector professionals because of its broad indiscriminate impact. Consumers could overcome the outage by resorting to local power generation sources to keep appliances, lights, and local networks running. Conversely, a localized malware compromise of a single oven requires the home owner themselves to be the first to respond and diagnose. If the malware is virulent, and noticed by network operators, the home network may be quarantined to prevent further spreading. The home network owner may be required to prove to network operators that the home network is free from malware before being reconnected. This is a significant burden to most appliance owners – a burden many do not have the skills to adequately carry. The IoT phenomenon brings an important paradigm shift where the focus of our attention turns from tactile devices like a smartphone to a network-of-networks and a system-of-systems where the misbehavior of a few devices may have systemic consequences. And at times those consequences may be broadly felt, while at other times fall fully on an unsuspecting and unprepared few.

Nevertheless, the IoT paradigm shift doesn't seem to fully persuade security practitioners to carefully regard the security design of every connected device. Some even ask: What is so unique about IoT that it requires unique security knowledge or expertise? How is it different from say PCs and servers? What devices qualify as purely or only IoT things? Any CPU spanning from MCU class to Atom to Core to Xeon to Xeon-SP can be a "thing" that is connected to the Internet. So what's unique? From our perspective, the challenge in IoT can be framed as follows:

- The Device Lifecycle is unique since IoT devices often have a much longer replacement cycle than PCs and smartphones (sometimes up to 30 years). Few of us are still using their 10-year-old PC, but many of us can identify components in our offices, public buildings, transportation systems, HVAC systems, water treatment systems, and factories that may be much older. Long replacement cycles imply embedded systems with security vulnerabilities have embedded attack vectors.

- Security objectives and robustness rules vary greatly across multiple verticals/domains. Here are a few examples: AutoSAR and the numerous standards impacting the automotive domain – Automotive E-safety Vehicle Intrusion proTected Applications (EVITA)/Secure Hardware Extension (SHE)/ AUTomotive Open System Architecture, Retail Payment Card Industry (PCI), Medical Health Insurance Portability and Accountability Act (HIPAA), naming only a few.

- Multiple Operating Systems must be considered in IoT systems to address diverse operational requirements. Some examples include Linux-Yocto, Wind River Linux, Android, Windows IoT/Enterprise/Client, VxWorks, QNX, and many other proprietary implementations. Interoperability and consistency in service operations, system update capabilities, and driver support are only a few of the obstacles encountered in supporting such a diverse field of operating systems on a single hardware platform.

- System on Chip (SoC) and CPU with embedded security capabilities and features can vary significantly across vendors' MCU products and even within the same vendors' products including Intel Atom, Core, Xeon, and Xeon-SP architectures, making design of end-to-end services and security more challenging.

- There are multiple pre-OS boot loaders and platform initialization software, for example, Firmware Support Package (FSP) + Coreboot, Intel Slim Bootloader, UEFI, Legacy BIOS, Deep Embedded, and other types of firmware that are used across the various IoT segments, all of which complicate IoT platform design and field support. Inadequate field update mechanism would result in attacks on initialization software implying that attackers are able to load and configure malware.

- The stakeholders are many and scattered – independent BIOS/boot loader vendors, board vendors, independent maker community design and integration shops, OEM/ODM, tiered SW/HW System Integrators, and Middleware providers. Producing a coalesced platform with consistent and interoperable features and services in such a diverse ecosystem is formidable. This implies security processes such as incident response, forensics, compliance, and system design must maintain healthy ecosystem interactions to prevent security issues from falling into the "cracks."

- Hypervisors are a critical part of the security equation since they provide needed isolation and protection. Some of these include Wind River Virtualization Profile,

Xen, VMWare, RTS, and ACRN. However, hypervisors also add system complexity as they impact operating systems, device drivers, and platform firmware.

- Managing these devices on heterogeneous networks is a huge challenge that requires a cradle-to-grave lifecycle approach; this includes provisioning, commissioning, decommissioning, software update, and other operational management tasks. Safety and regulatory aspects of security are also inherently present.

Security is not just a single step but instead a journey since what is secured this minute may not be secure the next minute and also because security has to be comprehended in all phases of the IoT device lifecycle. This book aims to diverge from a generic discussion of technologies presented by existing literature. It instead strives to inform readers of the methodology and intuition associated with implementing secure systems that were designed to be secure and presents focused insights gathered from the authors' years of experience in the security domain.

While this book represents a snapshot in time, the IoT ecosystem is not stationary. The anatomy of threats is dynamic, and more applications are being designed and deployed every day. The National Vulnerability Database (NVD) mining reveals that the threats are consistently moving down the stack, and they are now at the firmware and hardware level. This makes constant improvement through security by design critical, and security design cannot start with the application developer, but must begin at the silicon design and manufacturing phase and continue through platform development, software design, system installation, and sustaining operations. This is where a partnership with Intel begins to pay out enormous benefits that continue long into the system lifecycle.

Design of IoT devices cannot consider only their own security. IoT devices that are designed for security must still interoperate with other devices and systems that may not be built with the same security measures. Interoperability requires commonly accepted standards and regulations that help ensure behavior of the singleton as well as a system of devices is consistent from vendor to vendor and from product to product. More standards are being created and regulations are being enacted to address many of the IoT security concerns, including protecting the user's data, identity, and other valuable assets.

Managing risk in an IoT environment is inherently a formidable task. As Mike Crews, Director of Architecture in Intel Corporation's Internet of Things Group (IoTG) – a staunch believer in Security – opines, "Every vertical domain – whether it is Retail, or Industrial, or Digital Surveillance System – is just one 'Jeep Hack' incident[7] away from encountering the potential risks in not deploying and managing the security lifecycle of the IoT Devices." His opinion is vertical domain business owners have to be well informed, feel responsible, and must judiciously invest in securing their own assets as well as the assets of their customers.

The authors believe there are three principles that support security by design which we have interwoven throughout this book. They are by no means trivial to achieve in real systems, and instead require a lot of commitment from all participants in the IoT ecosystem. The principles to evaluate features that are secure by design include

- **Simple to Implement** by leveraging relevant standard Application Programming Interface (API), frameworks, and Software Development Kits (SDK) to develop the IoT device

---

[7]www.wired.com/2015/07/hackers-remotely-kill-jeep-highway/

- **Seamless to Deploy** by leveraging relevant standard and scalable provisioning tools and associated collateral to deploy IoT devices in the field

- **Easy to Manage** by leveraging the standard management technologies, tools, and associated collateral to manage the IoT device lifecycle

After reading this book, we anticipate readers will be empowered with the knowledge and tools needed to recognize security trade-offs in IoT system design and software architecture and to identify the relevant hardware building block ingredients that underpin secure IoT deployments. We believe the solutions presented here provide reasonable security trade-offs and follow the secure by design principles. The chapters of this book aim to enlighten the reader's understanding to address the following:

- Chapter 1: How the IoT ecosystem differs from the PC and data center ecosystem and how those differences impact security.

- Chapter 2: What are IoT frameworks and how design choices in different frameworks affect security, interoperability, and usability trade-offs.

- Chapter 3: What are the relevant hardware security features and building block technologies – as the authors believe, hardware security is the last line of defense.

- Chapter 4: How to approach building secure firmware, system software, and applications that leverage hardware security capabilities.

- Chapter 5: Which security properties affect IoT connectivity and what impact do they have on network and system designs given the IoT paradigm shift toward Network of Networks (NoN) and system of systems.

- Chapter 6: What other requirements affecting IoT verticals are relevant to security and why security is not a simple blanket but instead must be designed from the beginning with a foundational layer common across all verticals and then built up using vertical-specific stack components and application services. We also discuss key standards impacting some of the IoT verticals.

From this book, readers will gather an overview of the different security building blocks available in Intel Architecture (IA)–based IoT platforms. Readers will also be able to understand the threat pyramid, secure boot, chain of trust, and the SW stack leading up to defense in depth. Readers will also be able to comprehend the connectivity interfaces with security implications and IoT verticals with their unique security requirements and associated standards and regulations.

We invite you to join us on our journey demystifying IoT security!

CHAPTER 1

Conceptualizing the Secure Internet of Things

In this chapter we relate several iconic attacks on cyber-physical IoT systems to illustrate the clever ways attackers are able to achieve their objectives. The physicality of cyber-physical systems and resource limitations of constrained IoT devices present new challenges, both for attackers and systems designers. This chapter explores security trade-off consequences resulting from design decisions aimed at reducing device cost. We advocate more enlightened perspectives that consider the value of the device in terms of the broader network and system value. The security front line often is a constrained device requiring world-class security capabilities such as hardware underpinnings for cryptography, integrity protection, storage, and attestation. Devices that don't provide the basic building blocks of security are the *weak links* in the system – which systems designers aim to quarantine.

© The Author(s) 2020
S. Cheruvu et al., *Demystifying Internet of Things Security*,
https://doi.org/10.1007/978-1-4842-2896-8_1

The BadUSB Thumb Drive

In 2014 Karsten Nohl and Jacob Lell presented proof-of-concept malicious software at Black Hat USA 2014[1] that demonstrated how USB is fundamentally broken. The malware infects USB firmware rather than simply placing malicious applications on the storage area. USB firmware is trusted by most every USB controller to behave properly, as defined by the USB Consortium specifications.[2] However, as long as USB firmware works within the framework defined by the standard, malware can cause the USB controller to give the USB firmware unintended access to the host computer. This is unfortunate as the lack of attention given to security implies a potential for exploits that includes key-logging, privilege escalation, data exfiltration, identity and access misdirection, session hijacking, and denial-of-service.

Karsten and Jacob not only published their findings but also published the malware on an open source repository known as GitHub.[3] This means virtually anyone can construct their own USB attack device and even improve upon the original design. There have even been "how-to" publications[4] that step the reader through the process, making it easier than ever for even those without prior knowledge of USB architecture and implementation to successfully build an attack device.

Subsequently, the "maker community"[5] has picked up on BadUSB by creating a business around hardware platforms that have BadUSB preintegrated called "MalDuino"[6] – a play on words involving a popular

---

[1]www.blackhat.com/us-14/speakers/Karsten-Nohl.html
[2]www.usb.org/home
[3]https://github.com/brandonlw/Psychson
[4]https://null-byte.wonderhowto.com/how-to/make-your-own-bad-usb-0165419/
[5]https://en.wikipedia.org/wiki/Maker_culture
[6]www.indiegogo.com/projects/malduino-badusb-arduino-usb#/

"maker" platform named Arduino.[7] Using MalDuino as a development platform, it is possible for attackers to integrate other interesting malware designed to further infiltrate the victim computer or network. Often an attacker exploits a vulnerability in order to stage an attack on another vulnerability. Attack lethality can be amplified by linking several exploits that expose larger attack surfaces and allow the attacker to marshal more resources for the next attack. An attack that began as a compromise of something without network connectivity may morph into a compromise of resources with network connectivity – that broadens the attacker's reach and lethality.

Air-Gap Security

Some of the most secure networks rely on "air-gap" security as a way to prevent the spread of malware through interconnected networks. Air-gap is an isolation technique that ensures there are no wired or wireless connections between a highly sensitive network and one that is commonly accessible to everyone, such as the Internet. The security principle behind air-gapping is to establish physical isolation such that in order to move information back and forth between the secure network and other networks, there needs to be a mechanical system in place – euphemistically termed a "sneaker-net." The idea is that only trustworthy people would have physical access to the air-gap and would follow appropriate security practices and procedures that ensure sensitive networks do not fall victim to the many attack scenarios found on public networks.

However, air-gaps rely on the use of electronic media to "sneaker-net" information to and from air-gapped networks. This often involves the use of USB connected peripherals. The assumption is that a device that isn't

---

[7]www.arduino.cc

capable of sending or receiving electromagnetic emanations is safe to cross an air-gap. The fallacy of this assumption, of course, is they are not safe as evidenced by BadUSB.

Air-gap security has a significant usability downside in that it is costly to deploy, doesn't scale well, and isn't forward looking. The next generation of industrial IoT looks to other network security mechanisms such as VLANs that segment networks that isolate manufacturing equipment behind routers, static/dynamic whitelisting, and zoning/quarantining using network firewalls.

The lesson learned by air-gap security is that attention to usability cannot be ignored. Security mechanisms must be designed with all other system requirements taken into consideration to find the security mechanisms that optimize trade-offs.

Stuxnet

"Stuxnet"[8] is the name given to a malware found to have successfully infiltrated a top security nuclear research facility in Iran in June 2010. The Natanz uranium enrichment facility employed air-gap security mechanisms due to the safety critical aspect of the uranium enrichment process. Furthermore, uranium enrichment processes rely on SCADA (Supervisory Control And Data Acquisition) systems that are commonly used for industrial control because of their ability to precisely control physical machinery and remain resilient in the face of physical system failures, but also incorporate popular information messaging protocols such as MQTT (Message Queuing Telemetry Transport), AMQP (Advanced Message Queuing Protocol), and DDS (Data Distribution Service).

---

[8]www2.cs.arizona.edu/~collberg/Teaching/466-566/2012/Resources/presentations/2012/topic9-final/report.pdf

SCADA systems may use programmable logic controllers (PLCs) and a variety of other sensors and actuators that can be customized to suit the needs of the particular mechanical operations in a plant or factory. PLCs often have USB interfaces for uploading the control logic executed by the PLC, but also support serial bus interfaces and protocols such as Modbus or 4-20mA current loops that transfer information reliably and with less wiring and setup. Unfortunately, these techniques did not anticipate security or are simply incapable of stopping attackers who have physical access.

Stuxnet employed a variety of techniques, some seemingly designed as alternative attack strategies in case some other strategy failed to pan out. Among them included a strategy to propagate the Stuxnet malware using Internet "Futbol"–themed web sites. Ultimately, Stuxnet found a way to program USB thumb drives that were used to update PLCs used for uranium enrichment centrifuges.

Stuxnet ultimately was able to cause physical damage to centrifuges by working within the tolerance specifications of the control system, but stealthily controlling the centrifuges to spin faster than usual for longer than usual or to adjust the rate of acceleration and deceleration in ways that exceeded the mechanical designer's expected use case scenarios.

Although there still remains controversy over who created Stuxnet and whether it was targeting Iranian nuclear enrichment or not, statistics gathered by Symantec[9] suggest there were unintended consequences in the form of compromise to "friendly" or untargeted installations. While the majority of infections, 58.85%, occurred in Iran, the remaining 41.15% affected other countries; 8.31% occurred in India, 18.22% in Indonesia, and 1.56% in the United States. 13.05% occurred in other parts of the world.

Stuxnet is interesting because it demonstrates the possibility for information systems to cross over to operational systems in such a way that physical systems, infrastructure, the environment, and ultimately human

---

[9]"W32.StuxNet". Symantec. 17 September 2010. Retrieved 2 March 2011.

life can be harmed using only commonly available inexpensive electronics and software.

It marks the fusion of Information Technology (IT) with Operational Technology (OT). The acronym Internet of Things (IoT) takes on an additional and apropos meaning of Informational and Operational Technology (IOT).

Designing Safe and Secure Cyber-Physical Systems

The preceding attack scenarios suggest we need to revisit past assumptions that electronic equipment is "secure" because of physical and air-gap isolation is incorrect. The presence of electronic "things" may be sufficient for some form of "networking" to be implemented involving the exchange of electronic things and therefore the exchange of malware that can transform to take advantage of different attack vectors. A more enlightened view of IoT may be the idea that the interconnection of all networks – including the exchange of physical things containing information – is the Internet.

Applying this view of the Internet, there are two additional layers to classes of computers[10] that historically fit into three categories: (1) cloud servers largely composed of mainframes and super computers; (2) mini computers such as workstations and department or team servers; (3) microcomputers such as PCs, laptops, tablets, and smartphones.

IoT more commonly refers to a fourth layer consisting of smart cars, drones, wearable computing, and pervasive computing. However, a fifth layer consists of everything else that is electronic including USB thumb drives, cameras, MEMS,[11] smart construction materials, and "Smartdust."[12]

---

[10]https://en.wikipedia.org/wiki/Classes_of_computers
[11]https://en.wikipedia.org/wiki/Microelectromechanical_systems
[12]https://en.wikipedia.org/wiki/Smartdust

The layering of technology has many non-security related benefits, but technology layers can present new security challenges. The interaction between layers is often not well understood or clearly specified. This can result in exploitable security weaknesses. Security analysis and design scope should therefore be expanded to include these other layers. Another aspect of security analysis is to determine the "attack surface"[13] – the environment or sum of all points where an unauthorized user can try to extract information or inject control not anticipated by system designers. A basic tenant of security design is to keep attack surface small to limit the potential for unanticipated interactions.

The attack surface of IoT can be viewed as a pyramid (Figure 1-1) where the number of possible interactions is a function of the number of possible "things." Although cloud servers process large workloads, there are only a few cloud servers in terms of possible points of interaction. Cloud servers expose commonly used web interfaces that do largely a small set of things, but in large volumes.

The IoT pyramid also illustrates the importance of defense in depth as nodes at opposite ends of the pyramid tend to be separated by routers, gateways, and other networking equipment that can be repurposed as security enforcement. Network segmentation reduces the effective attack surface by artificially isolating IoT nodes.

Intel predicts there will be 200 billion "objects" by the year 2020.[14] An object is anything that is "smart" – that is anything that has a microcontroller of some kind. If we consider relative population of objects across a five-layer IoT pyramid, the number of objects is roughly exponentially larger in the layer below and the layer above is exponentially smaller. A simple calculation showing exponential distribution across five layers reveals approximately 1.4B objects at the top layer, 1.9B objects at

---

[13]https://en.wikipedia.org/wiki/Attack_surface

[14]www.intel.com/content/www/us/en/internet-of-things/infographics/
  guide-to-iot.html

the second layer, 3.6B objects at the third layer, 13.4B objects at the fourth layer, and an amazing 179B objects at the fifth layer.

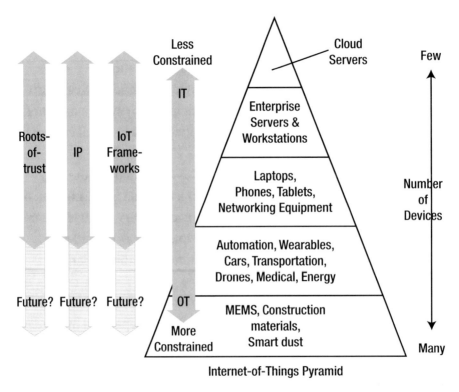

Figure 1-1. *Internet of Things pyramid*

Amazon had around 2M cloud servers and 1M customers in 2014.[15] Alibaba had 765,000 customers in June 2017.[16] Microsoft, IBM, Google, and others also have cloud service offerings that contribute to an estimate in terms of number of cloud server objects that could very well be in the 1B range by 2020.

---

[15]www.bloomberg.com/news/2014-11-14/5-numbers-that-illustrate-the-mind-bending-size-of-amazon-s-cloud.html

[16]https://intl.aliyun.com/about

In 2015, it was estimated there were 2.6B smartphones[17] and predicted to be 6.1B by 2020. There were about 2B PCs and laptops in 2014.[18] Our simple calculation suggests there would be 3.6B objects at layer 3 – off by a factor of 1.5 or 2, but still in the ballpark.

Even with conservative estimates, these account for only 10B of the 200B forecasted. If layer 4 accounts for 15B objects, that leaves 175B objects unaccounted for at layers 1–4. These estimates suggest, by far, that layer 5 represents the largest attack surface. That suggests there will be many more "Stuxnet"-like attack scenarios going forward. It also suggests mitigation of these attacks will be countered by additional security capabilities being applied to layer 4 and layer 5 objects.

Security capabilities often are required across a spectrum of technologies ranging from hardware to system software to application layers. IoT security also embraces network security and distributed computing security techniques. The potential exists to substantially increase the overall cost and complexity of security functionality for IoT systems. As security professionals anticipate the role security should play given an Internet of 200B connected things, security interoperability and standards are increasingly needed at layers 4 and 5 of the IoT pyramid. This includes the need for hardware-roots-of-trust (specially hardened components in hardware that resist many common vulnerabilities), common networking layers, and common IoT framework and object models. Consolidation of technology choices has a desirable consequence of allowing more security functionality to fit into constrained computing environments.

Constrained Computing and Moore's Law

In 1965 Gordon Moore made a prediction that computing would dramatically increase in power, and decrease in relative cost, at an exponential pace.[19] The computing industry perspective historically has been one that continually looks for "power-hungry" applications that can soak up the predicted CPU cycles. Ironically, that pursuit has led the computing industry to push the IoT pyramid higher and wider, but only recently has realized a frontier in the form of many (billions) chips that are power constrained. In constrained computing environment, the application that runs on a chip is quite small and functionally is relatively simple. The path to realizing Moore's Law is through the number of chips – increasing in number exponentially.

Rather than consolidating more workloads on increasingly more powerful computers, constrained computing is about distributing workloads across hundreds, thousands, and even millions of nodes. Distributed applications are described more in terms of conceptual notions of computing such as "pervasive," "mobile," "intelligent," "autonomous," "perceptual," "virtual," "emotional," and "augmented." These adjectives describe properties of computation that are realized in large part due to distributed computing that bridges the five layers of the IoT pyramid.

Constrained computing dynamics optimizes the computing environment to fit specialized functions. The function is unique to sensor/ actuator capability. Hence, enhancing a distributed application may be realized by adding constrained nodes as well as by adding more powerful nodes or by moving compute-intensive operations to edge servers.

These dynamics aim to provide more flexibility at the lower layers of the technology stack by using, for example, virtualized PLCs where manufacturing equipment can be consolidated into more powerful gateways running multiple, redundant servers that are less expensive to

---

[19]www.intel.com/content/www/us/en/silicon-innovations/moores-law-technology.html

operate than deployments of multiple less powerful devices. Non-mission critical sensing over wireless technologies is an important trend where the cost driver is low-power sensing solutions (sometimes retrofitted with brownfield sensors and actuators) designed to operate without replacement over many years. Deployment models such as this don't anticipate having extra watts for security processing.

Security however follows a counterintuitive cost model (Figure 1-2) where the motivation is to make nodes more powerful – so they can perform security processing that applies security consistently across all nodes. Workload consolidation, data consolidation, and redundancy result in the deployment of additional nodes or more powerful nodes – all requiring consistently strong security capabilities and hardening.

In the Stuxnet scenario, attackers were able to connect USB thumb drives to air-gapped process control networks because the USB thumb drive didn't have strong cryptography and authentication protections built into the IO control subsystem. Such sophisticated security operations are often determined to be "too costly" to justify bills-of-material cost constraints typically expected in "mass market" products.

Security functionality overhead for layer 1–3 systems typically is expected to be 10–15% of the total system cost. These environments are often very capable of supporting a common set of security features, algorithms, and operations such that the goal of having a network of equivalently protected computers is achieved. However, when moving compute into constrained environments, even with the dynamics of Moore's Law, computing power remains constrained. As such, the percentage of overall functionality that is security related vs. non-security related increases. Our estimates suggest that as much as 60% of a constrained environment computer could be focused on performing security-related computation, leaving 40% for application-specific computing. In other words, the "tinification" (the process of removing unused functionality not needed by purpose-built embedded systems) of an application to fit into constrained environments results in the need to preserve more of the security functionality than the non-security functionality. This leads business decision makers to question the viability of profits in constrained environments. Often these trade-off decisions lead to justification for weaker security, lack of firmware update capability, and no support for hardware root-of-trust architectures. These economic dynamics have led leading security thinkers to suggest the only resolution is through regulation.[20] However, regulation aimed at even the most insignificant of IoT platforms would affect over 170B things – 85% of everything! If regulation happens to have inefficiencies, those inefficiencies would be multiplied 170B times – a cost that could outweigh the cost of smartly applied security.

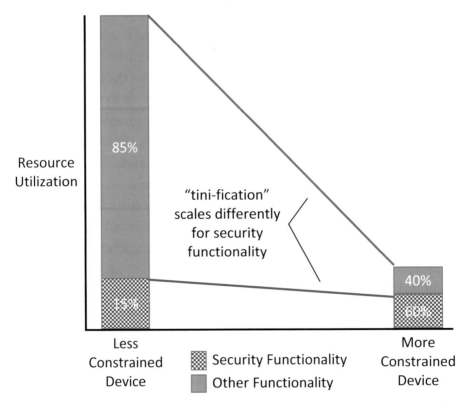

Figure 1-2. Nonlinear "tinification" of security vs. other functionality

---

[20]www.schneier.com/blog/archives/2017/02/security_and_th.html

Trusted IoT Networks and the Network Edge

The Internet of Things is a new term to describe an old concept – connected embedded computing. For as long as there has been electronic control, there has been connected embedded computing. Every dimension of process control and automation is characterized by a flavor of connected embedded control technology.[21] In most cases, process control networks were connected using wires. This is no different a phenomenon for IP networks that first began as Ethernet[22] cable. More recently wireless communications dominate applications where mobility or deployment considerations make using wires infeasible. Nevertheless, the array of wireless networking standards[23] has evolved to take the place of wired equivalents. However, convergence toward a single network protocol remains a promise of IoT which anticipates that IPv6 (Internet Protocol)[24] will become the foundation of IoT networks – and by extension the entire Internet. Nevertheless, there are non-IP protocols that sometimes are included under the umbrella of the IoT buzz word such as Bluetooth[25] and Zigbee.[26] Although these are not technically IP, there are strategies to encapsulate IP over non-IP networks using 6LoWPAN[27] to support larger payloads, compression, and framing that otherwise would not be feasible. IPv6 encapsulation is currently supported with Bluetooth Low Energy (BLE) 5, IEEE 802.15.4, and ZigBee.

The interesting security challenge for encapsulated or bridged networks (Figure 1-3) is the expectation of end-to-end security is often

---

[21]https://en.wikipedia.org/wiki/List_of_automation_protocols

[22]www.safaribooksonline.com/library/view/ethernet-the-definitive/1565926609/ch01.html

[23]https://en.wikipedia.org/wiki/Comparison_of_wireless_data_standards

[24]www.ietf.org/rfc/rfc2460.txt

[25]www.bluetooth.com/specifications/bluetooth-core-specification

[26]www.zigbee.org/zigbee-for-developers/network-specifications/

[27]https://tools.ietf.org/html/rfc4944

not possible since security applied within one suite of IoT network technology must be mapped, in the clear, to an Internet-based protocol suite. This creates the need for a security appliance, such as a firewall, that maps not only distributed application data but also security semantics and operations. We show a simple security appliance example here. Subsequent chapters provide additional insights into network partitioning, monitoring, and responses facilitated by security appliances.

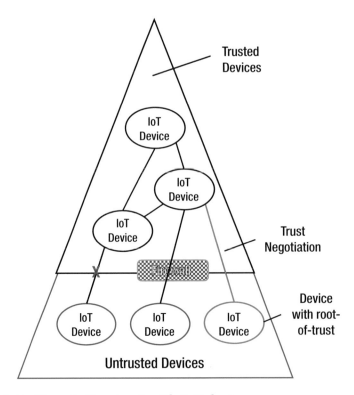

Figure 1-3. *Negotiating trust with IoT devices*

IoT networks are in a constant state of flux forming and re-forming coalitions of devices needed to implement a variety of distributed applications. We use the term "onboarding" to refer to this dynamic. Devices not yet recognized as members of a coalition are considered "untrusted," while devices already part of the coalition are considered "trusted." Membership in the coalition involves trust negotiation where the device presents evidence of trustworthiness; for example, the device may be equipped with a "root-of-trust" hardened environment containing a manufacturer embedded attestation key. The root-of-trust is designed to meet a set of security features and assurances as a basis for trust. Secure key storage and secure cryptographic operations are important capabilities of a root-of-trust that can be used to implement attestation.

Attestation protocols (Figure 1-4) allow the root-of-trust to prove to a verifier that it is capable of protecting secrets, identities, and data. When an untrusted device is onboarded into a coalition, it first attests to its level of trustworthiness. This allows the attestation verifier to determine if the desired coalition is appropriate or if some other coalition is more appropriate. For example, a coalition of medical devices might expect all coalition member devices to have been approved by a quality control agency and receive a statement of approval that could be included with the attestation exchange at onboarding. If omitted, the verifier might conclude the device hasn't been vetted by the agency and recommend it join a coalition of personal health fitness devices (that don't require agency vetting).

The attestation verifier is a process that operates at a border that separates trusted and untrusted. In practice, these borders are nondescript. They may not align with geographic, topologic, social, or political boundaries. Likewise, such boundary criteria could also be asserted as part of attestation (if combined with additional contextual information), making enforcement of such bounding criteria eminently possible.

Attestation is a form of operational integrity checking that can be pervasive. IoT nodes should respond to changes that might invalidate recent checks and respond proactively by updating integrity profiles and rechecking. If an attack is successful, the attestation check can detect it and respond appropriately.

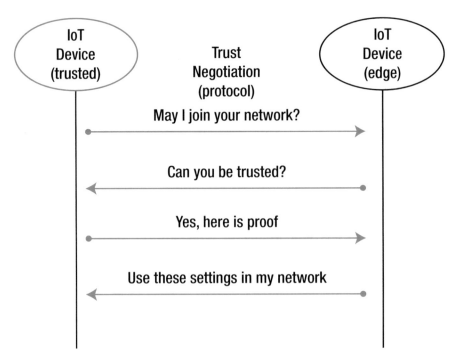

Figure 1-4. *Attestation protocol*

IoT can therefore be thought of as a connectivity graph where certain nodes are simultaneously connected to multiple other coalitions of connected nodes. The connectivity graph reveals relative importance of certain nodes but also relative security and safety risk as more highly connected nodes represent a greater potential for doing harm if compromised or malfunctioning.

Attestation therefore can be thought of as a fundamental capability for anything that is connected. It provides a first-order filter that categorizes IoT devices according to the risk they bring to the established coalition. If we consider all ventures as being composed of a collection of IoT devices, whether they be Smartdust or whether they are cloud servers, the value of the venture is collectively held by the coalition. The introduction of a new IoT device that may have the potential to nullify that value creates the basis for risk-based management approach that relies primarily on attestation and root-of-trust as the primary tools for value preservation and risk management.

An IoT root-of-trust (Figure 1-5) can be constructed in a variety of ways and can vary dramatically in terms of implementation and deployment costs. However, all root-of-trust designs have several minimum capabilities. First the IoT device is partitioned into trusted and traditional functionality. Traditional functionality is everything that isn't essential to satisfying coalition onboarding requirements. An IoT device that can't satisfy onboarding is simply an embedded or stand-alone device. It isn't a "connected" device – at least not a trusted connected device. Trusted functionality is everything else that is needed to satisfy coalition onboarding and is trusted to work correctly.

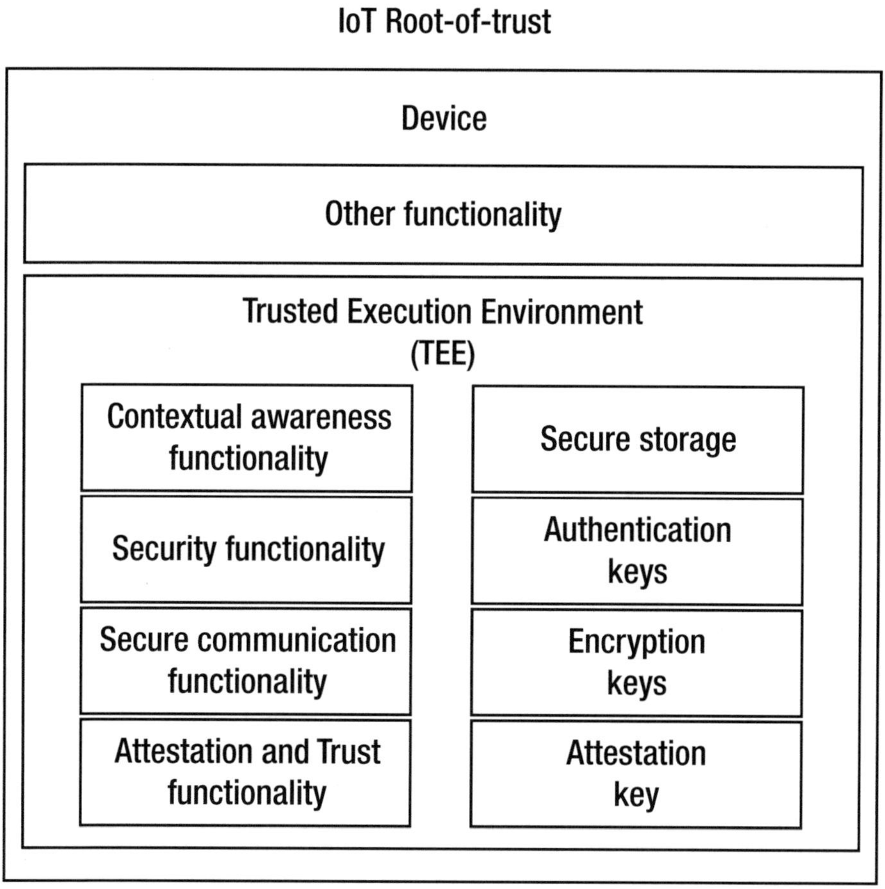

IoT Root-of-trust

Figure 1-5. *Root-of-trust architecture*

Trusted computing is defined by TechTarget[28] as "Trusted computing is a broad term that refers to technologies and proposals for resolving computer security problems through hardware enhancements and associated software modifications." Wikipedia[29] defines a trusted system as "... a system that is relied upon to a specified extent to enforce a specified security policy. This is equivalent to saying that a trusted system is one whose failure would break a security policy (if a policy exists that the trusted system is trusted to enforce)."

The most essential elements of a trusted system are its trusted computing base (TCB). The TCB of a computer system is the set of all hardware, firmware, and/or software components that are critical to its security, in the sense that bugs or vulnerabilities occurring inside the TCB might jeopardize the security properties of the entire system.

Some devices have a Trusted Execution Environment (TEE) for executing trusted application code. The TCB and TEE cooperate to ensure embedded security functionality can be accessed from within the TEE without a significant security risk. Bugs and vulnerability in these components jeopardize the security properties of the device. The TEE may be effective at detecting, preventing, or countering security events occurring in other parts of the system. It is therefore extremely important that every IoT device have a *trustworthy* TCB!

The authors suggest every TCB for IoT should contain the following:

(A)   Attestation key: An asymmetric key supplied by the device manufacturer that establishes device origin authenticity. The Enhanced Privacy Identifier (EPID)[30] can be used to attest device origin without

---

[28]http://searchsecurity.techtarget.com/definition/trusted-computing
[29]https://en.wikipedia.org/wiki/Trusted_system
[30]Proceedings: WPES '07 Proceedings of the 2007 ACM workshop on Privacy in electronic society, pp 21-30, Alexandria, Virginia, USA – October 29, 2007, ACM New York, NY, USA ©2007, ISBN: 978-1-59593-883-1 doi> https://doi.org/10.1145/1314333.1314337

introducing a trackable identifier that violates privacy.

(B)   Attestation functionality: Trusted code that implements attestation and attestation verification logic.

(C)   Encryption keys: Symmetric and asymmetric keys used to protect device-device and device-human interactions that may occur in the context of a coalition.

(D)   Secure communication: Trusted code that implements cryptographic algorithms used to protect the confidentiality and integrity of information exchanged between devices and TCB peers. It contains support for key management protocols such as Kerberos,[31] PKI,[32] and Fluffy.[33]

(E)   Authentication keys: Symmetric and asymmetric keys used to authenticate the originators of messages exchanged device-device and device-human, also in the context of a coalition.

(F)   Authentication functionality: Trusted code that implements identity and authentication primitives including support for distributed authentication protocols such as OAuth2[34] and OpenID Connect.[35]

---

[31]https://web.mit.edu/kerberos/
[32]www.ietf.org/rfc/rfc5280.txt
[33]https://datatracker.ietf.org/doc/draft-hardjono-ace-fluffy/
[34]https://tools.ietf.org/html/rfc6749
[35]http://openid.net/connect/

(G)   Secure storage: The ability to store keys, integrity measurements (cryptographic hash), whitelists, settings, and contextual information that if modified or deleted could result in failure of the TCB to correctly apply a security objective.

(H)   Contextual awareness functionality: Trusted code that can encrypt and authenticate stored data securely even if the attacker has physical access to the storage resource. The ability to sense and collect security relevant context such as time, location, biometrics, and other context.

(I)   Trusted execution environment functionality: Trusted code that correctly implements the TEE environment such that the TEE firmware can be updated securely and computing interfaces into the TEE are resistant to attack.

These security "building blocks" provide the core set of hardened functionalities that enables an IoT device to establish itself as a trustworthy node suitable for inclusion in one or more coalition groups of IoT devices. Once a member of a coalition group, a distributed application can be deployed securely.

Conclusion

The Internet of Things can be described as a dynamic set of distributed computing coalition groups that come into existence seemingly on their own, without a presumption of central control or orchestration. Coalition groups may just as easily disappear, but IoT networks persist as a set of protocols, data structures, and capabilities that enable these dynamics. A secure IoT network is essential to a sustainable and automated distributed computing on a massive scale where the tiniest of computing nodes needs to support a set of security capabilities that is common to all other nodes in the Internet including the largest cloud servers. Coalitions of devices will work together to manage risk and to preserve the value inherent in the distributed computing venture by vetting coalition memberships. Failure to enforce membership integrity places at risk the value of the coalition. These economic dynamics, once properly understood, motivate proper investment in security capabilities, even among the simplest of IoT devices. This leads to a rethinking for conventional practices that assume security functionality should be less than 15–10% of total system cost. Rather, we think an enlightened approach considers the value of the network is greater than the sum of its constrained endpoints. The cost of security is weighed against the larger value where the percentage investment in security technology, standards, and business practices is aligned. Such a perspective will make it more feasible for most relevant IoT security technology to exist at the right layers of the IoT pyramid.

CHAPTER 2

IoT Frameworks and Complexity

The complexity of things – the things within things – just seems to be endless. I mean nothing is easy, nothing is simple.

—Alice Munro[1]

Introduction

In Chapter 1 we explored device cost dynamics when security is built-in from the beginning. Either the cost of the device increases or the ratio of device resources attributed to non-security-related functionality decreases. However, ignoring security results in the IoT device becoming the "weak link." This chapter surveys IoT frameworks. We categorized them according to a consumer, industrial, or manageability focus though many seek broader relevance. IoT frameworks hide a lot of underlying complexity as the industry wrestles with embracing newer Internet protocols while maintaining backward compatibility. A plethora of standards setting groups have come to the rescue offering

---

[1]www.brainyquote.com/quotes/alice_munro_176434

© The Author(s) 2020
S. Cheruvu et al., *Demystifying Internet of Things Security*,
https://doi.org/10.1007/978-1-4842-2896-8_2

insightful perspectives on framework design to accommodate broader interoperability goals. But this may be too much of a good thing as framework interoperability has become yet another interoperability challenge. Framework designs often emphasize differing objectives, interoperability, adaptability, performance, and manageability. We offer an idealized framework that focuses on security to add contrast to what the industry already has considered. This chapter is lengthy relative to the other chapters in part because there are many IoT framework standards available and each takes a different perspective. Each has merit but ultimately the IoT ecosystem is likely to reduce the number of viable frameworks. We nevertheless encourage continued IoT framework evolution that removes unnecessary complexity and places security by design at the center.

Historical Background to IoT

Before the "Internet of Things" became a commonly used term, embedded control networks used for real-time distributed control were known as process automation protocols, also referred to as fieldbuses. Fieldbuses are commonly used to implement SCADA (Supervisory Control and Data Acquisition) networks, building automation, industrial process control, and manufacturing control networks. These systems tend to be extremely complex and difficult to manage, especially over time as the number of system endpoints grows and the usages demanded of these systems increase. SCADA systems often involve connecting programmable logic controllers (PLCs), proportional-integral-derivative (PID) controllers, sensors, actuators, and supervisory management consoles, all connected through fieldbus protocols. But fieldbus technology isn't limited to a single protocol or even a small number of protocols. There have been more than a hundred fieldbus protocols entering industrial automation markets in the last 20 years. The IEC-61158-1[2] and related standards describing fieldbus technologies contain over 18 families of fieldbus protocols. Some of these include CAN bus, BACnet, EtherCAT, Modbus, MTConnect, LonTalk, and ProfiNet. Wikipedia also has a fairly complete listing.[3] The Complexity can skyrocket when multiple fieldbus protocols are used to create an interconnected system. Then, with the birth of IoT, these fieldbus protocols are required to interconnect with Internet protocols, in some cases by replacing a fieldbus layer with an IP layer, which adds further complexity. When IoT systems are built to integrate with existing systems, based on fieldbus protocols, IoT systems are sometimes referred to as *brownfield* IoT because they represent use cases, ecosystems, and solutions that existed before the introduction of Internet technologies. Looking forward, industrial process automation and control, building automation, electrical grid automation, and automobile automation might continue using brownfield IoT nomenclature even though Internet technology integration is taking place.

Nevertheless, existing brownfield systems are highly proprietary and vertically integrated solutions, while Internet protocols historically have been more open and layered and support a richer ecosystem of vendors and value-added suppliers. Reducing fragmentation of brownfield networks through IT/OT convergence is a key motivation for IoT. Possibly it is this openness and richness of the Internet that drives the OT industry toward an "Internet of Things." Additionally, with respect to security, IT priorities have focused on CIA (confidentiality, integrity, and availability), in that order, while OT has prioritized availability and integrity above confidentiality. The tension between CIA trade-offs is an important consideration as the IT and OT come closer together.

---

[2]IEC 61158-1:2019 "Industrial communication networks - Fieldbus specifications - Part 1: Overview and guidance for the IEC 61158 and IEC 61784 series", International Standard, Ed. 2.0, 2019-04-10. Available at: https://webstore.iec.ch/publication/59890

[3]https://en.wikipedia.org/wiki/List_of_automation_protocols

Instead of using existing system as the starting point, the Internet of Things can bring a fresh perspective. Extending Internet connectivity beyond desktops, laptops, smartphones, data centers, cloud computing, and enterprise computing to agricultural, industrial, energy, health, transportation, public sector, and critical infrastructure seems a reasonable context for understanding the momentum behind the Internet of Things (IoT) evolution. The use of IoT technology to implement a completely new IoT system spawns unique applications for operational automation; building such a system with wholly new technology and protocols is sometimes referred to as *greenfield* IoT technology. Some examples may include drone control, self-driving cars, smart cities, supply chain automation, and machine learning. Greenfield IoT is riding the Internet wave of less-proprietary, lower-cost, and increasingly ubiquitous network technology that revolutionized PC, data center, and mobile device networks in the 1990s and 2000s. IoT may also benefit from the wave of microprocessor, memory, power, and storage innovations in mobile computing that results in lower-cost but highly capable computing platforms.

Whether the system is a brownfield system tying existing industrial or manufacturing automation control system with Internet technology or a greenfield system using completely new protocols and devices, both instances of IoT systems bring a level of intricacy that necessitates some abstractions to improve application development efficiency and to make management of these systems feasible.

But it isn't just the protocols that generate complexity in IoT systems. Industrial IoT systems may have multiple layers of networks connected through gateways. IoT systems may best be categorized as a *system of systems*. As security practitioners contemplating the prospect of securing a complex system of systems, we must take every opportunity to ask whether the complexity is justified because we, like other security practitioners, believe complexity is the enemy of security.[4]

IoT Ecosystem

The IoT ecosystem is extremely complicated, fragmented, and evolving. It evolves at different rates depending on many factors, one of which is the replacement cycle for a given solution or industry. The replacement cycle for business PCs is 3–5 years, smartphone replacement is 1–3 years. Contrast this with building automation where an HVAC system replacement cycle is 15–20 years or nuclear power generation facilities that must replace failing parts with identical replacement parts – leaving no room for the introduction of innovative or more secure technologies. These refresh rates either speed adoption of new technologies or restrict, even inhibit, the adoption of technologies that might improve operations, reduce costs, or even protect lives.

Due to the many differences in various sectors of the IoT ecosystem (e.g., health, public, transportation, industrial, energy), the sectors appear to embrace Internet technology differently – in silos (refer to Figure 2-1). However, the market forces keeping the silos defined are due in part to the technical requirements unique to the usages and applications that drive internal market cohesion. Brownfield solutions may have benefitted from proprietary or vertically integrated solutions, aided by these cohesive market forces, long replacement cycles, and costly specialized hardware components. But that is unlikely to persist as IoT innovations continue to find technology adjacencies that spill over silo barriers causing technological disruptive innovation. Generally, this is a good thing. However, these disruptive forces breaking down the proprietary silos also brings new challenges that impacts security in the form of increased complexity, new business models and unanticipated interactions.

---

[4]Tom Gillis, Contributor, Network World, "Complexity is the enemy of security," Aug 8, 2016. www.networkworld.com/article/3103474/security/complexity-is-the-enemy-of-security.html

Just as the changes in Internet protocols brought more complexity to PC networks in the 1990's, Internet of Things technologies promise more complexity (at least initially) for industrial, control and automation systems.

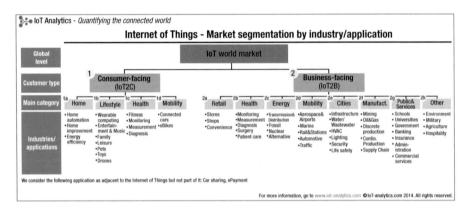

Figure 2-1. *IoT market segmentation by industry/application[5]*

   The IoT ecosystem (referring to Figure 2-2) can be understood in terms of concentric rings of technology used to connect distributed physical and logical components. The technology within a particular ecosystem is specialized for that ecosystem, its business models, as well as the producers and consumers in that market. Ecosystem-specific components are specialized for different aspects of an ecosystem's distributed applications, resulting in unique devices that coordinate sensing, actuation, control, data collection, data aggregation, data analysis, risk management, and operations. IoT system components may be distributed because of physicality of sensing and actuating, or due to efficiency requirements that result in specialized computation. A potential unifying factor in all this is an interoperable, low-cost networking capability that makes distributed IoT possible. But satisfying the myriad needs canvasing multiple IoT segments using a single IoT technology seems improbable if not impossible.

---

[5]IoT Analytics, Knud Lasse Lueth, "IoT market segments – Biggest opportunities in industrial manufacturing," Oct 31, 2014. https://iot-analytics.com/iot-market-segments-analysis/

Connectivity Technology

Network and connectivity are nevertheless of paramount importance. IoT systems must enable connections over short-, medium-, and long-range distances. IoT solutions often must satisfy a wide range of transmission quality requirements that may also need optimizations for low latency, isochronous, asynchronous, store-and-forward, mobility, or streaming. IoT systems must consider environmental disturbances such as radio interference or emissions from other electronic equipment, low-power conditions, congestion, and resource starvation scenarios. Guaranteed service levels also add to the mix of requirements.

Additionally, trade-off decisions impact safety, reliability, resiliency, security, and availability. A variety of network technologies have emerged to address the multifaceted needs of IoT such as Zigbee, Industrial Ethernet, LoRa, LPWAN, Modbus, and TSN – to name a few. Some are highly specialized to a specific application context such as the Control Area Networks (CAN), which uniquely addresses the safety critical automated braking systems found in many automobiles. Fieldbus protocols, such as Modbus, use a synchronized communications bus to ensure each PLC (programmable logic controller) receives the messages directed at it.

While others are more general purpose such as Wi-Fi, Bluetooth, 5G, and Ethernet that accommodates information networks, streaming media, as well as control network applications. Industrial Ethernet operating at very high data rates can accommodate industrial real-time control requirements by ensuring network utilization remains below about 10%. Chapter 5 will dive deeper into details of different connectivity interfaces and considerations facing consumer and industrial IoT.

Messaging Technology

IoT frameworks are exposed to IoT applications using a data model abstraction. The framework data model describes a view of the network where nodes appear as flat or nested data structures, and updates to data values may result in actuation of various controllable elements. The data model abstraction allows the applications to focus on capturing semantic richness and less on moving data from node to node. Data are represented as structured markup that easily maps to messaging transport technologies.

Messaging technology determines how messages flow between network nodes. It also facilitates the building of IoT systems that collect data from various nodes using disparate protocols at the expense of creating additional complexity in the messaging layer. Simple messaging is request-response based such as REST (Representational State Transfer). HTTP (Hypertext Transfer Protocol) and CoAP (Constrained Application Protocol) follow the REST methodology. Publish-subscribe messaging allows multiple nodes to register for notifications when a change is detected in a variable on a peer node. MQTT (Message Queuing Telemetry Transport) is a popular example of a publish-subscribe messaging system. Broadcast and multicast can make publish-subscribe more efficient, which may be used in some IP-based networks. Different protocols are useful in different environments, and the whole communication stack even down to the availability of broadcast at the network physical layer must be considered when developing services in an IoT system. This complexity is difficult for the system designer but becomes overwhelming to the IoT developer. This complexity becomes most evident when designing an IoT platform, especially when designing an IoT platform intended to service multiple ecosystems. Platforms manage this complexity through the use of IoT frameworks.

Platform Technology

IoT platforms host applications, resources, and data useful to an IoT distributed application. Platforms are specialized to the type of work each performs. Constrained IoT platforms may optimize for connectivity, latency, and small footprint, while less constrained platforms at the OT network edge may optimize for device offload and bridging across control domains. Cloud platforms optimize for compute, scalability, capacity, and analytics. IoT frameworks are used in platforms because they facilitate interoperability and connectivity by combining appropriate networking, protocol, and platform ingredients in ways that allow application portability regardless of the node's native specialization characteristics.

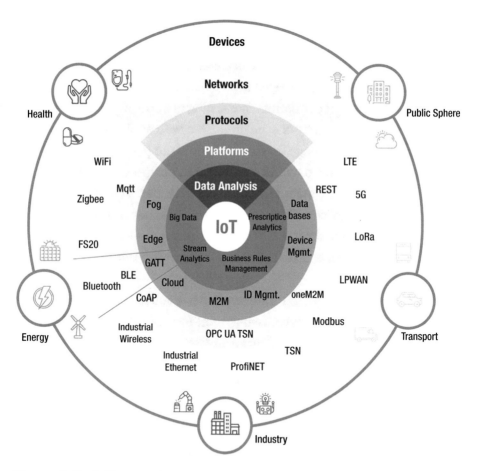

Figure 2-2. *IoT ecosystem*

Elements of an IoT System

This section describes the elements of an IoT system focusing on device architecture, network architecture (an interconnected collection of devices), system management architecture, and lastly framework architecture.

IoT Device

The term "device" can be confusing because it means different things in different contexts. When viewed from a manufacturing perspective, the device is a physical component consisting of hardware, firmware, and system software. It may also be preloaded with application software compiled into a single image that is embedded into persistent memory.

When viewed from a network management perspective, a device is a node that has a network address and could be part of a collection of interconnected devices. There could be multiple network endpoint addresses per physical device. Furthermore, given multiple network interfaces, the same physical device could appear as multiple nodes to other devices.

When viewed from an IoT framework perspective, a device is a logical context that exposes message passing interfaces. Interfaces are used to exchange data that is structured according to an interface definition. The actual data structure as viewed from within the framework may differ depending on the network protocols, message passing technology, or system usage. A logical device may have multiple interfaces to the network giving the impression to peer nodes there are multiple physical devices. This can be confusing if network address is the only way to disambiguate IoT devices. IoT frameworks expose a logical IoT device whose identity is independent of the underlying connectivity layer. However, security challenges can arise when a single networking interface exposes shared data or control surfaces with multiple logical devices. This creates an opportunity for an attacker to exfiltrate data, perform side-channel analysis, or maliciously control logical devices. Consequently, the security design should incorporate endpoint protection technology deeper into the system – at the logical device level.

When viewed from an application perspective, the IoT framework data abstractions can make it difficult for application code to tell when a physical device boundary is crossed. A single application may interact with multiple IoT framework "devices" not knowing if they are geographically local or remote. This is relevant to security practitioners because device physicality is often what defines a security boundary. Obscured security boundaries make it more difficult for applications to effectively apply security protections.

To avoid confusion, the authors try to provide clarifying context whenever "device" terminology is used.

IoT Device Architectural Goals

Unlike smartphones, PCs, laptops, and servers, the device bill of materials (BOM) for constrained IoT devices is often under significant cost pressure. In addition to the expected processing requirements, IoT devices often must accommodate hostile operating conditions that include extreme temperatures, vibration, humidity, and ultraviolet radiation. Meeting BOM constraints implies every ingredient is scrutinized to identify the minimum viable hardware, firmware, and software configuration while still satisfying product requirements. Part substitutions may be made over the course of a product's lifetime to lower production costs.[6] The IoT supply chain competes to be the low-cost supplier, and device vendors want to foster this competition to drive component costs even lower. Common interfaces facilitate interoperability and the integration of specialized hardware with

---

[6]Vendors often qualify multiple suppliers for hardware components that perform essentially the same function but allow production lines to keep producing if one supplier's supply chain happen to be disrupted.

general purpose hardware, sensor, accelerator, and Field Programmable
Gate Array (FPGA) processor integration traditionally is done by a device
manufacturer, but increasingly, specialized functionality is exposed to the
network as a service. Software layers create logical devices that may be
dynamically defined. Software defined devices offers greater flexibility for
tailoring IoT solutions that meet customer need. Securing software defined
devices requires a trusted execution environment that creates trustworthy
hardware isolation and exposes security roots of trust to the soft device.

Interoperability

Architecting a device to be interoperable with other devices or infrastructure
already, or soon to be, on the market is of paramount importance for IoT,
especially given the enormity of different devices in large IoT systems. Web-
based validation suites allow device vendors to verify their products will
interoperate with a wide variety of other vendors' products, which would
be too numerous to exhaustively validate using direct interactions from
device to device. Testing for interoperability with an actual device that has
not completed development or is not yet released to market is simply not
possible. However, web validation suites allow testing for interoperability
with standard protocols and frameworks, ensuring compatibility with peer
IoT devices that have not yet completed development.

Nevertheless, interoperability gaps are likely to exist. For example, data
models developed by competing standards may have syntactic differences
even though semantics are similar. Standard protocols may not fully
interoperate if certification testing is missing or is not comprehensive.
Simulation tools that virtually deploy customer-specific configurations can
be helpful. Simulations help expose interoperability gaps in specifications
and validation suites relating to software behavior and data definitions.
Trial deployments and test beds are another technique for finding gaps.
This helps find hardware-dependent incompatibilities. Trial deployments
go live once the gaps can be corrected. Test beds can be used for

longer-term evolution of products with sequenced rollout of increasing capabilities and features while ensuring that interoperability or backward compatibility problems do not creep in.

It is prudent for IoT system designs to anticipate having to work around incompatibilities and building specific features into their design to compensate for such issues. Postdeployment reconfigurable layers between applications and embedded components give systems architects the ability to make corrections during simulation and trial deployment. Less constrained devices such as hub controllers, bridges, and gateways more easily accommodate reconfigurable layers as they often support a wider variety of network interfaces and have more computing resources and storage to draw upon. Nevertheless, reconfigurability comes with a security cost. Malware might more easily exploit reconfigurability features that compromise embedded system components.

Security

Security consists of both functionality and assurance disciplines. Security functionality typically deals with secure boot, secure key storage, and cryptographic algorithm acceleration, while security assurance typically deals with ensuring security functions work the way they are intended. Trusted computing technology combines security functionality with security assurance mechanisms so that security compromise isn't catastrophic. Trusted computing components are called upon to perform recovery steps. All devices contain some set of trusted functionalities, upon which all other parts of the system assume is trustworthy and has not been compromised; this is called the *root of trust* for the device. The root of trust is normally involved in the secure booting of the device, holding the device's identity credentials, and presenting cryptographic evidence of device claims, called attestation. Depending on the device, the quality of the root-of-trust may vary.

In less constrained environments, a root-of-trust could be a security subsystem such as a Trusted Computing Group (TCG) Trusted Platform

Module (TPM) or a secure storage module such as Replay Protected Memory Block (RPMB). It could be a secure coprocessor such as ARM TrustZone or a security mode of a CPU such as Intel Software Guard Extensions (SGX). All other software and hardware components depend on the root-of-trust components in some way for their security.

Typically, less constrained systems make use of multiple roots-of-trust and multiple trusted execution environments. For example, trusted boot may rely on a root-of-trust for measurement in the form of a boot ROM that computes an integrity value for software images loaded during boot-up. These integrity values are stored in another root-of-trust for storage that protects them until they're queried by a remote device that verifies boot integrity. The remote device expects to receive an attestation report that is signed by a trustworthy signing key protected by a root-of-trust for reporting. The TPM is an example of a discrete processor that combines roots-of-trust for storage and reporting.

Roots-of-trust can protect application code while it executes using Trusted Execution Environment (TEE) technology such as Intel SGX. Application developers partition application functionality according to the functions that are security relevant and those that aren't. Less constrained environments allow multiple TEE instances. Managing and deploying multiple trusted environments and roots of trust adds cost and complexity.

In more constrained devices, these costs may be too high. Instead, devices must be designed with layered trusted computing. The Trusted Computing Group (TCG) proposed an approach for secure constrained device boot, secure device identity creation, and device attestation (Figure 2-3) that doesn't depend on a security coprocessor called Device Identity Composition Engine (DICE).

Using a DICE strategy, the root-of-trust elements are those that operate first when the device is reset or when it resumes from a nonoperational state. The DICE architecture defines a Unique Device Secret (UDS) that is a circuit that produces a unique number when the platform undergoes power reset. The UDS circuit reads low-level device firmware that is used to boot and possibly operate the device once booted. Firmware is cryptographically hashed with the UDS that is then fed into a cryptographic key generation circuit to produce a device identifier. Cryptographic hash is a one-way function that ensures input data can't be discovered by analyzing the output value. If a different firmware image is hashed, it will produce a different hash output value. This will cause the key generation circuit to produce a different device identifier than what results from the first firmware image. If the device identity changes from what the IoT network expects, the changed device identity is no longer trusted and must be revetted and onboarded into the network.

The device identifier is unique to the UDS secret and the firmware installed. The secret is immutable because it is hardware. If the firmware is updated, a different device identity key is generated. A controller, bridge, gateway, or other IoT nodes can determine if firmware changes because it will no longer recognize the device identifier or be able to verify its digital signature. If malware corrupts device firmware then resetting the device sill return it to a secure operational state. The UDS and DeviceID derivation functionality form a root of trust that is simpler than a traditional Trusted Platform Module (TPM), secure co-processor or TEE. This is better suited for cost constrained IoT devices, but also benefits TCB design by tailoring TCB functionality that is most appropriate for special purpose IoT devices.

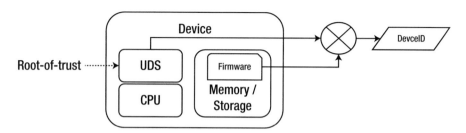

Figure 2-3. *Device Identity Composition Engine*

IoT Network

When multiple IoT devices are connected together, they form an IoT network. However, connectivity alone isn't very interesting. IoT devices should interoperate as a distributed application. One expects IoT nodes will cooperate to achieve a common objective. To do this, devices need a few basic behaviors: (a) the ability to discover peer nodes, something about their function or role and interfaces they support; (b) the ability to connect, which may involve authenticating and constructing a secure channel or cryptographic association; and (c) the ability to send and receive formatted data, parse it, and process it according to application-specific semantics.

Core to IoT design is the idea of an hourglass network layering model (Figure 2-4) that seeks to simplify the possible choices of network layer protocols to Internet Protocols (IPv4 and IPv6) while permitting legacy SCADA, fieldbus, and embedded control physical and data link layer technologies to remain available either through gateways or through encapsulation, such as 6LoWPAN[7] (IPv6 over Low-Power Wireless Personal Area Networks).

The top half of the hourglass hosts existing and evolving IP transport layer technologies, for example, the Constrained Application Protocol (CoAP)[8] supports an HTTP-like RESTful message exchange without the overhead required to support HTTP and TCP. The Datagram Transport Layer Security (DTLS)[9] applies TLS-like security to CoAP. An impressive array of emerging protocols designed for IoT are being developed by the IETF Constrained RESTful Environments (CORE)[10] working group. DTLS may be appropriate in cases where reliability and in-order guarantees are not needed.

---

[7]https://tools.ietf.org/html/rfc4944
[8]https://datatracker.ietf.org/doc/rfc7252/
[9]https://datatracker.ietf.org/doc/rfc6347/
[10]https://datatracker.ietf.org/wg/core/documents/

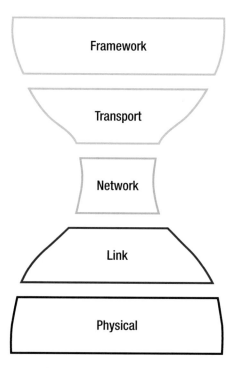

Figure 2-4. *IoT network layering*

The framework layer sits atop the hourglass consisting of a dizzying mix of technologies that predate IoT or have emerged as a result of it. Most interestingly a flurry of new standards organizations has emerged that seem to have insightful perspectives on how best to define IoT frameworks. The authors believe that much of the IoT ecosystem will coalesce around a common set of Internet-based technologies forming an hourglass shape.

IoT System Management

IoT system management comprehends manageability goals for both IT (Information Technology) and OT (Operational Technology). Device lifecycle management is common to both IT and OT disciplines covering the full spectrum beginning with manufacturing and supply chain through all phases of operation, including decommissioning and retirement. Management services support device lifecycle management. These include security services for managing roles, access control policies, and cryptographic keys and certificates; software update services for distribution and installation of firmware, software, and security patches; orchestration services for coordinating distributed application behavior, simulation, and for handling graceful failover, resiliency, load balancing, and redundancy; and telemetry services report on a variety of operational, security, safety, and behavior components of an IoT system that may be used further by IoT analytics and business management.

A challenge facing IoT systems is finding a uniform and consistent approach to manageability given the deeply fragmented brownfield and greenfield IoT solutions. Proprietary and vertically integrated solutions often don't interoperate with horizontal IoT framework approaches, and framework manageability is quite often rudimentary lacking deep integration.

Lack of a uniform approach to security manageability has potentially significant IT and OT impact. For example, application of a security patch in an industrial IoT deployment may require multiple security consoles with labor-intensive checklists that verify all nodes are patched properly. Access control policies may not be consistently expressed across disparate IoT systems where role names and syntax may differ, access enforcement conventions may differ and be inconsistent, or key management capabilities may differ and may lack scalability or equivalent security strengths. Security gateways may be considered as a way to address some of these issues, but they may require deployment of new trusted nodes in situations where trust semantics don't normally expect or allow a universally trusted gateway system. For example, a security gateway node that links an industrial process automation network to a business analytics server might be located at a base station in a wireless edge environment that has limited physical security, but nevertheless must operate with full security privileges of both networks.

Device Lifecycle

Trust in logical IoT devices is (or should be) tied to trust in the physical layer that hosts it. In an enterprise deployment scenario, servers, PCs, and even smartphones can undergo a rigorous manual inspection and configuration step by trained security professionals. However, the scale at which IoT devices are deployed is seldom feasible to apply the same rigorous manual processes. Instead, onboarding techniques that require minimal or no touch are needed. IoT platforms and devices follow a lifecycle (Figure 2-5) that may begin during manufacturing and ends when the device is decommissioned or waterfalled to another owner for redeployment starting another lifecycle.

Figure 2-5. *IoT device/platform lifecycle model*

Attackers may target vulnerabilities earlier in the lifecycle in order to avoid detection and circumvent mitigation strategies that presume manufacturing, supply chain, and onboarding steps are free from compromise.

IoT frameworks make assumptions about where along the device lifecycle continuum the framework abstraction models begin to apply. Early in the lifecycle, only physical devices exist. Even if logical devices come into being early in the supply chain, it may still be possible for additional logical devices to appear subsequent to initial onboarding or may disappear prior to a final decommissioning step. Security of the IoT system may depend on how well the IoT framework layer integrates with the platform lifecycle.

Manufacturing

Manufacturing processes are critical toward the establishment of hardware-roots-of-trust which is a term used to describe security building blocks having to do with establishing platform/device identities, protecting cryptographic keys and algorithms, and creating hardened execution environments and system bootstrap procedures that resist attacks. Features may include hardware random number generation, cryptographic algorithms in ASICs (Application-Specific Integrated Circuit), FPGA (Field Programmable Gate Array) or instructions, hardware fuses that seed random number generation, boot ROM, replay protected memory, and others.

Supply Chain

Supply chain processes protect platforms and devices as they make their way from manufacturers to retailers to customer first deployment. Supply chain participants may have physical access to hardware components that if replaced by malicious components could result in undetectable attack scenarios. Tracking platform and devices through the supply chain may involve the use of RFID (Radio-Frequency Identification) tags, supply chain UUIDs (Universally Unique Identifiers), or cryptographic device identifiers. Privacy may become a challenge however as tracking capabilities could be misused in ways that violate privacy goals. Privacy requirements need to be anticipated as part of supply chain tracking mechanisms.

Deployment

Deployment is concerned with initial power up, customer-specific configuration, and establishment of the platform/device owner. Then the entity responsible for adding IoT devices to their network is sometimes called the "owner" which implies a change of ownership and establishment of a "local" identity that differs from a manufacturer or supply chain supplied identity. The owner operates onboarding services that facilitate ownership transfer, verification of supply chain provenance, attestation of security properties and roots of trust, issuance of credentials, security associations, roles, and access control policies. Taking ownership of many devices can be challenging given limited human resources and large numbers of devices. Zero-touch commissioning is immensely important and difficult to get right given the diversity in supply chain and given the spectrum of customer security and privacy expectations.

Normal Operation and Monitoring

Normal operation refers to operational states where IoT functions are fully enabled and ready for use. Security monitoring ensures devices and networks continue to function securely. IoT frameworks may choose to hide security monitoring operations from IoT application-level abstractions, but they should consider how to fail gracefully when security conditions require service disruption.

Manage

IoT devices require periodic management, tuning, and adjustment. Some management functions can occur while devices are operating normally. For example, addition of security credentials for dynamically added devices may not need to interrupt activity with existing devices. Other management tasks may require disruption of normal operations. For example, an uncalibrated actuator may result in device, process, or system failures if asked to operate outside its design constraints. Frameworks can facilitate communication of device status and availability to enable periodic maintenance without major disruption to peer nodes. This management implementation could be in-band (within the OS/FW control) and/or out-of-band (outside of OS/FW control).

Update

Software and firmware updates are arguably a subset of device management commonly known as Software Over-the-Air (SOTA) and Firmware Over-the-Air (FOTA) updates. Software update management must consider trade-offs of propagating large image files over networks optimized for small messages that may be latency sensitive. IoT networks may have "sleepy" nodes that are not available to receive an update in a timely manner.

Nevertheless, software and firmware updates are essential to secure operation. It is inevitable that security weaknesses will exist in most firmware and software images. Hence, when weaknesses are found, they should be fixed quickly to avoid possible exploit.

Decommissioning

Decommissioning is the process of undoing onboarding, commissioning, and provisioning that were applied previously. Although it is expected that devices and frameworks will anticipate scenarios involving devices that don't go through a decommissioning process to handle it gracefully, applying decommissioning steps helps ensure privacy objectives are met by removing trackable personally identifiable information (PII) or privacy-sensitive information before it falls into other hands. Decommissioning also ensures security-sensitive data, credentials, keys, and access tokens are removed so they aren't used to later attack other nodes. Frameworks can facilitate decommissioning by orchestrating the nodes removal in a coordinated way. Sometimes decommissioning could entail replacing the device under consideration with another device consisting of the same persona.

Automation of the IoT device lifecycle is an important security capability as it helps ensure the device never enters an insecure state and minimizes opportunities for attacker exploit by ensuring secure lifecycle practices are consistently applied.

IoT Framework

An IoT framework is a middleware layer beneath one or more IoT applications that presents a network-facing application interface through which peer framework nodes interact. Frameworks often support multiple communication technologies and message passing techniques. IoT frameworks also expose security capabilities including hardware-roots-of-trust to applications and peer framework nodes.

IoT Framework Design Goals

IoT frameworks have four primary design goals: (1) reduce development time and bring IoT solutions to market sooner; (2) reduce apparent complexity of deploying and operating an IoT network; (3) improve application portability and interoperability; and (4) improve serviceability, reliability, and maintainability. Given the vast range of existing and emerging communication technology choices, it is untenable for applications to manage the combinations of possible ways to connect. Frameworks hide connectivity complexity beneath a higher-level message passing abstraction like REST and publish-subscribe. Standards organizations help achieve these goals through standardization of the framework layer interconnect, message passing interface definition, and data definitions leveraged by applications. Standards groups also document IoT system design principles, architecture, and interconnect options. Standards organizations and industry consortia may assist developers by supplying and certifying reference implementations that include source code. Reference code helps streamline development by providing implementations that pass compliance tests and correctly interprets standards specifications. Reference codebases are easier to maintain benefiting from a large diverse community of open source developers who cooperate by actively developing code and improving the codebase.

Frameworks simplify IoT networks by creating an abstraction of the IoT device networks that hides much of the underlying complexity while exposing data, interfaces, and functions that facilitate interoperation. All it should take to develop an IoT application is to create an application in a high-level language such as Node.js that utilizes framework APIs. The framework provides a semantically rich description of IoT nodes, objects, and interactions that allow IoT network designers to focus only on node interaction semantics rather than on the details of connectivity.

Frameworks facilitate improved application portability. This can be achieved at different levels. The bottom layer of the framework is operating system specific. The top layer of the framework is IoT use case specific in that it exposes a data model abstraction that reinforces an IoT usage context. Some examples include lighting control, home automation, health monitoring, entertainment, process automation, industrial control, and autonomous control. IoT applications can be developed once given the framework abstraction and can execute on any OS the framework is ported to. The details of dissimilar OSs and platforms can be hidden where porting of framework code to another OS (source code–level compatibility) can happen independently of application development. Binary compatible platforms can migrate compiled framework code across platforms using the same binary. Platforms that are not binary compatible may rely on virtualization to host framework images or may rely on device management services that hide the complexity associated with paring and installing the right framework with the correct platform.

Frameworks enable interoperable devices in heterogeneous environments. Consider a hypothetical scenario where devices are running different OSs and HW platforms. These devices could be built by different platform vendors using silicon from multiple vendors running different OSs such as Windows IoT Embedded and VxWorks running different middleware stacks. This is a perfect storm scenario for an IoT network deployment where there are too many possible combinations of connectivity and message exchange options to expect speedy deployments. IoT frameworks come to the rescue by building the connectivity intelligence into the framework – hidden from application view and simplified from the device and network management view.

Frameworks also facilitate seamless manageability and serviceability by leveraging the framework's infrastructure to expose platform status information through the framework layer in accordance with the framework's data model abstraction. For example, a firmware update availability notification may be easily propagated across an IoT network. If the framework supports applying a firmware update, either push or pull, the firmware update images may be distributed over the air using the connectivity solution worked out by the framework.

IoT Data Model and System Abstractions

IoT frameworks define an application layer abstraction so that applications interact directly with framework data. For example, a temperature sensor might show the current temperature (*currTemp)* and the average temperature over the course of 24 hours (*aveTemp)*. Temperature values might be shown in Fahrenheit and Centigrade. Consequently, a data model description might be as follows:

```
{
    "tempSensor" = "/myTempSensor",
    {
        "currTemp"="85",
        "aveTemp"="70",
        "degrees"="Centigrade"
    }
}
```

Data modeling languages are used to richly describe framework objects according to a schema definition. Examples of data modeling languages include XML (eXtensible Markup Language), JSON (JavaScript

Object Notation), CBOR (Concise Binary Object Representation), and YANG (Yet Another Next Generation language) – just to name a few.

Data structures are accessed through well-defined network interfaces. For example, CoAP is a REST model interface that uses four methods: GET, PUT, POST, and DELETE to interact with framework data. A couple RESTful interface definition languages include RAML (Restful API Modeling Language) and Swagger.[11]

A framework node may consist of several objects such as a temperature sensor, camera, and light bulb. A *deviceId* may disambiguate multiple instances of a framework node. For example:

```
{
    "nodeType"="myDeviceType",
    "deviceID"="<UUID>",
    {
        "tempSensor" = "/myTempSensor",
        "ptzCamera" = "/myPtzCamera",
        "lightBulb" = "/myLight"
    }
}
```

Using these simple but powerful data modeling tools, IoT frameworks can describe elaborate IoT systems while hiding much of the network complexity that underlies connection establishment, routing, packet transmission, network address translation, and so on.

To a certain extent, IoT frameworks can be compared with Information-Centric Networking (ICN).[12] ICN rethinks the network where named information is the centerpiece of network architecture. Rather

---

[11]https://swagger.io/
[12]https://irtf.org/icnrg

than focusing on nodes, network topology, and protocol layering, ICN focuses on end-to-end data interactions. Data doesn't necessarily *reside on endpoints* but may be cached and replicated anywhere in the network. Like ICNs, the upper layer of IoT frameworks presents a data-centric view of the network. However, unlike ICNs existing protocol layering is retained. Arguably, this adds additional complexity but offers greater interoperability. Indeed, an ICN connectivity plugin to an IoT framework is a reasonable approach to bridge ICN with legacy networks.

Securing IoT messages must take an end-to-end view so that authentication, confidentiality, privacy, and authorization goals may be realized. Otherwise, the benefits of hiding complexity beneath an IoT framework may instead be hiding security gaps. The IoT application using an IoT framework may not be aware when security is managed using system layer interfaces. Internet protocols often have a secure alternative such as *https* for *http* and *coaps* for *coap*, where the "s" means security. A REST GET message works the same over *coaps* as it does for *coap*. The main difference is the Transport Layer Security (TLS) binding to the REST messaging protocol negotiates a secure session using credentials (keys and certificates) that may have been provisioned directly into the TLS subsystem without coordination through the framework layer. The framework layer may not be aware of the impact to authorization which can result in the framework misrepresenting actual security posture to IoT applications. IoT frameworks can differ significantly in their design and implementation attention to end-to-end security. We hope to illustrate this point more profoundly as we walk through a variety of IoT frameworks later in this chapter.

IoT Node

IoT frameworks define a *device* abstraction that is a logical representation of a physical device. This chapter uses the term IoT *node* to refer to the logical abstraction to avoid confusion regarding the physical device. Frameworks can create some interesting properties regarding IoT nodes:

- They may expose multiple nodes per framework to give the appearance of many nodes having the same IP address.

- They may consolidate multiple network addresses terminating into a common framework node.

- They may host services and capabilities that are dynamic – being created and deleted according to RESTful messages.

- They may impose system partitioning semantics such as dividing nodes into domains, groups, rooms, or some other semantic overlay.

Nevertheless, security semantics must remain true despite the framework abstraction. For example, if the node describes the endpoint where access is controlled, data is encrypted and decrypted. Then protection of the physical endpoint resources should strongly correlate with protection of the framework node.

IoT Operations Abstraction

IoT operations consist of several node interactions facilitated by frameworks. These include discovery, message exchange, event registration, and asynchronous notification. IoT nodes typically are not preconfigured to recognize other nodes. They must instead be discovered.

Discovery allows other framework nodes to inquire regarding supported interfaces and data structures essential to interoperability. Discovery can take many forms. For example, multicast and broadcast networking supports unsolicited discoveries. Nodes monitoring the broadcast may be required to disposition discovery events even if there is no action needed. Devices with limited battery capacity may have shorter life expectancies if deployed in highly dynamic networks. Alternatively, discovery may be accomplished by sending discovery requests to discovery interfaces for specific nodes querying the relevant information. This approach minimizes unnecessary activity on nodes that wouldn't otherwise need to participate. However, this approach may require multiple "drill down" discovery requests before finding the data or interface needed. Passive discovery employs directories or less constrained nodes that respond in place of other nodes that may disregard all discovery requests while in a low-power mode. The directory nodes satisfy the discovery phase so that power-constrained nodes only process the functions that they uniquely provide.

Discovery conventions:

- Consulting a directory of framework devices to learn device identities and how to connect – conceptually similar to LDAP (Lightweight Directory Access Protocol) commonly used by PCs in IT networks to accomplish a similar objective

- Inspecting a schema describing interfaces to learn which REST, publish/subscribe, and asynchronous notification messages can be used

- Querying the device directly to introspect its current state and configuration

Note   An anonymous entity may learn a tremendous amount about how an IoT network functions, the type of nodes involved, what work they're capable of performing, and typical interaction patterns simply by using available discovery mechanisms. Given a small amount of additional information that links actual devices or users to the observable network, it may be relatively easy for an attacker to obtain or infer knowledge that otherwise is expected to be privacy sensitive.

Message exchange conventions:

- Preparing a message body whose syntax satisfies a recognized (standardized) data model schema

- Protecting the message using the appropriate security credentials

- Sending the message following the interface definition schema for the target node

- Collecting and processing the response message that similarly follows these conventions

Event handling conventions:

- Identifying objects and attributes available for participating in asynchronous events and conditions to be met that result in notifications.

- Preparing and sending a registration/subscription message following messaging exchange conventions.

- Maintaining context for processing asynchronous notifications.

- Nodes managing registrations/subscriptions must maintain context for secure delivery of the notification message(s) potentially involving many subscribers. Asynchronous message delivery may involve different security associations and context from those used to process registrations/subscriptions.

Connectivity Elements

IoT frameworks facilitate connectivity, gatewaying, and bridging. The following briefly summarizes how each is facilitated:

- Connectivity: Framework endpoint abstractions are mapped to network layer addresses and protocols where framework message exchange abstractions map to protocol specifics such as MTU (Maximum Transmission Unit) framing, multicasting, broadcasting, and packet delivery mechanisms.

- Gatewaying: Framework domain abstractions impose operational context for domain-specific filtering (hiding) traffic and performance of administrative duties.

- Bridging: Due to the proliferation of framework solutions, it is often necessary to translate from one framework environment to another. Framework bridging may have side effects where objects, interfaces, or semantics in one environment don't exactly translate to a second.

Manageability Elements

IoT frameworks may expose manageability elements through the framework object abstraction layer as a way for other framework objects and resources to better manage and respond to change resulting from management activity. However, this is more the exception than the rule. Even among horizontal open standard frameworks, there are many examples of device vendors wishing to retain proprietary or exclusive control over firmware/software update, onboarding, and cloud access capabilities. Nevertheless, frameworks can facilitate updates occurring outside the IoT framework by informing other nodes regarding pending updates or notifying regarding changes to version information. Additionally, IoT frameworks may not allow the framework itself to be updated from within an IoT framework context.

Security Elements

IoT frameworks need to accommodate security by ensuring endpoint nodes and their physical equivalents (i.e., device, process, virtual machine, enclave) have a secured identity, protected cryptographic keys and appropriately provisioned roles, credentials, and access policies. Endpoint security capabilities should protect sensitive data that is stored, transmitted, or manipulated locally outside of the IoT framework. Software and firmware should be protected when transmitted, installed, stored, and loaded for execution. Framework processing of encrypted data, access control decisions, and identities should be protected within an appropriately hardened Trusted Execution Environment (TEE) or isolated from non-framework aware services and interfaces. IoT device roots of trust should be used to protect device identities and ensure the appropriate firmware and software is loaded and executed.

Inherent to distributed systems is added risk associated with a dependence on multiple peer nodes that contribute data, processing, and administration to an overarching distributed application. Nodes largely trust peer nodes to be in a correct operational state. However, this assumption of trust may not be justifiable without taking additional precautions to prove and verify the hardware, firmware, software, and operational state to peer nodes. Attestation is a security concept that addresses this concern but only if it is correctly implemented and integrated.

Consider the Cost of Cryptography

IoT systems are inherently distributed. Cryptography is an essential security building block technology for distributed systems. Nevertheless, cryptography imposes additional overhead in terms of computation, memory, storage, network bandwidth, and hardening. Symmetric cryptography generally speaking is lighter weight than asymmetric cryptography, and asymmetric cryptography is lighter weight than certificate-based asymmetric cryptography. IoT devices typically are designed with cost targets that may impact device cryptographic capabilities. Since these choices also impact interoperability, IoT frameworks must anticipate common cryptographic algorithms, key sizes, and key management infrastructures. Asymmetric cryptography is dominated by at least two algorithms: elliptic curve cryptography[13] (ECC) and Rivest-Shamir-Adelman (RSA)[14] algorithms. ECC has smaller key sizes than the RSA. ECC can accomplish the same level of security as RSA with key sizes that are 10–15% smaller. Key size is an important factor for constrained platforms as such many IoT standards require ECC.

Table 2-1 details some of the trade-offs associated with cryptography.

---

[13]https://tools.ietf.org/html/rfc6090
[14]https://tools.ietf.org/html/rfc8017

Table 2-1. *Trade-Offs Associated with the Type of Cryptography Used*

Criteria	Symmetric (Preshared Secrets)	Asymmetric (Raw Public/ Private Keys)	Asymmetric (Certified Public/ Private Keys)
Hardware Acceleration	Not Required	Required	Required
Memory Size	Small	Medium	Large (certificates)
Code Size	Small	Medium	Large (certificate parsing)
Message Size	Small	Medium	Large (certificates)
Persistent Storage Size	Small–Medium (depends on network size)	Medium–Large (depends on network size)	Medium (depends on caching algorithms)
Security – Perfect Forward Secrecy (PFS)	No	Yes	Yes
Security – Impersonation Risk	High (keys are shared, no detection of misuse, no common trusted infrastructure, depends on secure storage)	Medium (no common trusted infrastructure, depends on secure storage)	Low (depends on secure storage)
Constrained Environment	Optimized for Verification (benefits constrained servers)	Balanced	Optimized for Signing (benefits constrained clients)
Scalability (number of nodes interacting)	Low	Medium	High

Quantum computers[15] present new threats to existing cryptographic solutions because they are more effective at solving certain types of mathematical problems such as the integer factorization[16] problem, the discrete logarithmic problem,[17] or the elliptic curve discrete logarithm problem.[18] Current asymmetric cryptography algorithms reduce to one of these mathematical problems which are known to be solved by quantum computing more easily than traditional computers. Cryptographic algorithms are being designed that are thought to be secure against quantum computers are called *post-quantum* safe algorithms and has led to a new branch of cryptography study called post-quantum cryptography. Since asymmetric cryptography is most threatened by quantum computing, post-quantum asymmetric algorithm design is receiving a lot of attention currently. In contrast, symmetric key cryptography and hash functions are relatively secure against attacks using quantum computers. It is believed doubling the key size (e.g., from 128-bits to 256-bits) adequately protects against quantum computer attacks on symmetric algorithms.[19]

It is still too early to tell which quantum-safe algorithms will become an industry favorite for IoT given cost, power, and size constraints. However, it seems clear that where symmetric cryptography is already acceptable for IoT, it should continue to remain acceptable given a doubling of key size is the most economical quantum-safe solution. Quantum-safe asymmetric algorithms have much larger key size requirements or computation trade-offs, both of which apply to typical IoT platforms.

---

[15]https://en.wikipedia.org/wiki/Quantum_computing
[16]https://en.wikipedia.org/wiki/Integer_factorization
[17]https://en.wikipedia.org/wiki/Discrete_logarithm
[18]https://en.wikipedia.org/wiki/Elliptic-curve_cryptography
[19]Daniel J. Bernstein (2010-03-03). "Grover vs. McEliece" (PDF).

Summary IoT Framework Considerations

IoT frameworks came into being as a way to simplify development and deployment of IoT networks. The reality is IoT networks are inherently complex and, in many cases, necessarily so. IoT frameworks offer value because they create a data model abstraction that is simpler than applications having to deal with a myriad of message exchange options and dissimilar data definition. By allowing applications to focus only on the semantics of IoT node behavior and node interactions, interoperability improves. By hiding the complexity of connection establishment, bridging, gatewaying, and deployment of heterogeneous platforms, efficiency optimizations can be applied more uniformly. Although frameworks may increase complexity for simple deployment situations, they scale as deployments grow resulting in a simpler IoT system overall. Frameworks have other advantages, namely, they enable multiple views of the IoT system so manageability, resiliency, interoperability, security, safety, and usability perspectives can be represented. Complexity in any form, however, is a security consideration because vulnerabilities and security weaknesses can hide within the corners of complexity. Security practitioners should ask whether the framework is more complex than needed in order to realize the expected benefits, but also avoid workarounds that expose new attack surfaces.

IoT Framework Architecture

This section explores IoT framework layers in more detail. A following section looks at specific framework architectures that may be compared and contrasted. The majority of IoT framework architectures define three layers: (1) Data Object layer, (2) Node Interaction layer, and (3) Connectivity and Hardware Abstraction layer. This section also considers the Hardware layer, though it typically isn't considered part of an IoT framework. However, because security necessarily should have ties to hardware, we've included a Hardware layer discussion. Security is integral to IoT framework layers revealing additional security insights relating to each layer (see Figure 2-6). This section explores each framework layer in detail with an emphasis on security.

Data Object Layer

The Data Object layer defines data structures that expose the "nodes" and their capabilities using a data definition language such as JSON.[20] One or more nodes may be hosted in the framework where one or more applications may interact with framework nodes via a framework API. Data objects are a set of attribute encapsulations. Some framework object models allow nested encapsulation with unlimited depth. Other frameworks limit nesting depth. The outermost encapsulation is the node. Since nodes logically correspond to an IoT network endpoint, it is given an identifier, NodeID, such as a Universally Unique Identifier (UUID) which is easy to generate dynamically given framework nodes may be transient. NodeID differs from DeviceID in that DeviceID is fixed in hardware. It is created during manufacturing and is used to facilitate device onboarding. NodeID typically is created in response to successful onboarding. Very constrained devices may use the DeviceID as the NodeID if the manufacturer has prevented the framework from supporting additional nodes.

The Data Object layer may define security objects such as access control lists (ACLs), credentials, and other device status information useful to management consoles and other nodes. Exposing security objects using the framework object model allows device and security management using the IoT framework infrastructure. The framework connectivity and interoperability properties make it a desirable ingredient for manageability. Security objects may expose values that are specific to a

---

[20]www.json.org

node such as credentials, ACLs, and NodeID or may expose values that are node independent or shared such as DeviceID, firmware, and hardware configuration.

The Security Objects in Figure 2-6 are useful for intranetwork and intradomain interactions. More sophisticated internetwork and interdomain interactions require an additional security layer that may be helpful for gateway operations. The gateway application contains control and management logic to present nodes to a peer IoT network that shadow actual nodes existing deeper inside the local IoT network. Gateway applications might even be used to bridge non-interoperable IoT frameworks. A following section explores interdomain security and framework gateways in more detail.

Node Interaction Layer

The Node Interaction layer contains messaging semantics and defines interfaces used for peer node interaction. Interface definition languages such as RAML and Swagger may be used to create machine- and human-readable interface definitions. A framework instance may support one or more messaging models, such as REST, publish-subscribe, and MESH. This layer ensures messages are formatted correctly, parses message contents, performs data consistency checks, and ensures messages are sent, queued, resent, or received properly.

Messages may require encryption and integrity protections. This layer maintains security associations between the local and peer nodes. Security associations identify the nodes, ACLs, privacy policies, and credentials (used to authenticate, authorize, and protect message contents). They may also define the security context from which to perform various security relevant operations such as encryption, decryption, signing, verifying signatures, enforcing access control, and so forth. The security context defines what is (or should be) the correct way to terminate the data exchange with peer nodes.

There are implementation challenges associated with security endpoint definition due to network layering. For example, a TLS or IP Security (IPSec) secured channel may be shared across multiple locally hosted nodes, implying nodes must use shared credentials, something frowned upon by most security practitioners. Alternatively, acceleration hardware may offload packet processing which may include offloading security operations too.

Ideally, the *Security Endpoint Context* is the central point of enforcement where the flow of data between the Data Object layer and the Connectivity layer can be inspected and controlled.

Platform Abstraction Layer

The Platform Abstraction layer defines the logical connection points available to framework nodes. Connection points support the messaging models available to the Node Interaction layer regardless of the capabilities of the underlying network stack. The Connectivity layer typically supports multiple connection points – one for each unique network stack. For example, the connection point, Conn-A, has a network stack consisting of HTTP, TCP, IP(v4 or v6), and Ethernet (Figure 2-6). A second connection point, Conn-B, has a network stack consisting of MQTT, TCP/UDP, IPv6, 6LoWPAN, and IEEE802.15.4. Connection points may be dynamically added or removed on more sophisticated platforms, while constrained platforms may embed a single connection point and network stack.

In some cases, the network stack includes message security technology such as IPSEC and TLS. The Connectivity layer depends on the Device Interaction layer for security associations specific to the node-to-node interaction semantics. This potentially divides the security enforcement point between the security side and the networking side. Some platforms are equipped with isolated execution technology that enables security processing within a network stack to be offloaded to a resource-isolated environment here referred to as a *container*. An alternative approach is to move data protection into the Node Interaction layer. For example, OSCORE[21] defines a standard format for encrypting CoAP payloads before being given to the CoAP layer. This approach allows the security endpoint to move out of the protocol stack into the Node Interaction layer potentially simplifying implementation.

The basic idea is that the security endpoint context, data packets, and node-to-node security associations should exist within a suitably hardened container as a prerequisite for performing security relevant operations. Otherwise, there is opportunity for clever attackers to intercept, modify, view, or replace node objects.

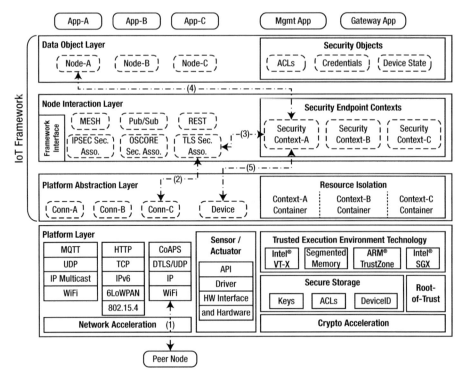

Figure 2-6. *IoT framework layers*

---

[21]https://core-wg.github.io/oscoap/draft-ietf-core-object-security.html

Platform Layer

The Platform layer beneath IoT frameworks can be divided into three categories: (1) networking, (2) sensor and actuator, and (3) security. The network layer focus is on efficient processing of network packets, quality of service, and power optimization. It also addresses network security threats related to malicious manipulation of network protocols. A common denial-of-service attack might flood the network with unexpectedly high volume of discovery packets. Discovery (aka *ping*) packets may not require prior authorization since the goal of discovery often implies finding out which credentials are most appropriate to use. Well-known attack mitigation techniques often are part of network hardware implementations, allowing the mitigation technique to be applied efficiently.

The sensor and actuator focus is on implementation of the main processing function of the IoT node which often represents the transition from IT to OT as native interactions are applied to the physical world. Otherwise, the node would just be manipulating data and couldn't be considered a *cyber-physical* system. The device driver and API are most often proprietary and specific to the vendor and model of the sensor or actuator. Vendor-specific behavior multiplied by the already large and expanding collection of IoT devices multiplies the complexities associated with multivendor interoperability. Hiding this complexity behind a common data object model is a primary reason for IoT frameworks.

The security focus is on hardening security-sensitive IoT functions. Trusted Execution Environment (TEE) technology isolates computing resources according to the various system tenants. IoT frameworks allow multiple tenants in the form of IoT nodes – nodes that may have different identities, security credentials, access policies, and configurations. Even in constrained environments where a single node is supported, there are security and device management scenarios that require tenant isolation for nodes performing administrative duties. The industry has a variety of TEE technologies that could be leveraged to harden IoT workloads that include Intel SGX, Intel VT-x (virtualization technology), ARM TrustZone, and hardware memory managers that physically partition memory and other compute resources.

Secure storage is an essential element in IoT devices in that cryptographic keys, trust anchors, access control lists, and other policies need to be stored in ways that resist software attacks and ideally resist attackers who have physical access to the device. Replay protected memory is helpful toward preventing attacks on key exchange protocols, memory replacement, firmware update, and timing attacks.

Root-of-trust hardware is essential to the creation and protection of device identities that may be used to attest device security properties to a peer node and to security boot the device. Crypto acceleration hardware may offer additional protections as offloading encryption and signing operations may involve the use of a hardened coprocessor or ASIC (Application-Specific Integrated Circuit). Root-of-trust hardware or crypto offload hardware often includes a source of entropy necessary for generating encryption keys and trustworthy identifiers.

Security Challenges with IoT Frameworks

Security challenges are a reoccurring theme as we explore various IoT frameworks. Though they may have been designed with a wide range of security and privacy requirements, there are a few areas that are consistently problematic. IoT framework nodes are the logical endpoints in IoT networks, but the network layer context is often out of scope when operating at the framework Data Object layer (Figure 2-7).

In IP networks, endpoint nodes are identified by IP addresses, and routing logic is expressed in terms of IP addresses. Network layer identifiers are insufficient as IoT framework node identifiers. In IoT frameworks, nodes are logical and hence may share the same IP address but have different node identifiers. Linking encryption keys, authentication credentials, and access control policies to IP address means security will not be granular enough and can't be consistently applied.

Uniform Resource Identifiers (URIs) and object identifiers such as Universally Unique Identifier (UUID) may be used to reference the framework's device nodes. For example, a URI might identify the framework context followed by an object identifier that is specific to the logical device instance – "href" : "oic://<Base64_encoded_UUID>/oic/d".

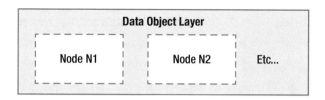

Figure 2-7. *IoT framework nodes are the logical endpoints in IoT networks*

The IoT framework node presents a security context where the security endpoint is an IP multicast address; using IPSEC implies the data protection ends at the network interface card or possibly inside a networking driver in an operating system. This leaves data exposed before it reaches the IoT framework's enforcement point where the decision is made to which node the data belongs.

A similar concern exists using Transport Layer Security (TLS) where data protections end within the operating system or within a network connection provider service. Connection services often expose APIs that a variety of applications may utilize. If the service isn't exclusive to the IoT framework, it is possible the cryptographic protections intended to terminate within the logical IoT device terminate within the service instead. Other applications serviced by the connection provider are at risk of becoming targets for attack because of the special access unwittingly given to them by the service. Care must be taken to ensure data carried over communication channels and messaging systems are protected by trusted execution environments that correspond to the expected logical device endpoint.

If data is protected using message-oriented techniques such as JSON Web Token (JWT), data protection may be extended into the IoT framework data abstraction layer, but there may be secure messaging library that is shared by all the logical device instances. A man-in-the-middle (MITM) attack could be successful if malware found a way to intercept the data after the data protection module is finished but before the logical device context is in place.

An IoT framework access path is depicted in Figure 2-6 where in step (1) a peer node accesses the IoT device through a Wi-Fi networking stack at connection Conn-C. In step (2) the Conn-C access path finds the TLS security association and the Security Context-A in the Security Endpoint Contexts. In step (3) access to decryption keys, ACLs, and role credentials is checked. The Security Context-A is a fulcrum point in the framework that uniformly applies an IoT network security policy involving the peer nodes and Node-A. Ideally, the security context operations are performed in a TEE that resists *man-in-the-box* attacks. If access is permitted, in step (4) the sensor/actuator hardware may be exposed to the peer node through Node-A data objects at step (5). Ideally, the entire access path will be isolated from the other nodes and operations occurring on the same device as the other tenants present security threats from within the device.

Consumer IoT Framework Standards

In this section, we explore several IoT framework architectures highlighting similarities and differences. In some cases, differences exist because different frameworks intend to address different requirements and use cases. In other cases, significant overlap of features and capabilities appears to exist because they address similar requirements but do so differently. This is unfortunate because it creates opportunities for incompatibilities. Such differences may be benign when used in isolated deployments but add significant complexity when interoperability across multiple deployments is desired.

Open Connectivity Foundation (OCF)

The Open Connectivity Foundation (OCF) was originally formed under the name Open Interconnect Consortium (OIC). Broadcom, Intel, and Samsung were among the initial founders of OIC and were later joined by Electrolux, Microsoft, and Qualcomm. IoTivity is the open source reference implementation of both OIC and OCF specifications. The OIC later became OCF when the AllSeen Alliance and OIC merged in October of 2016. The AllSeen Alliance is discussed in more detail in a following section.

The OCF framework (Figure 2-8) consists of three layers, Transports, Core Framework, and Profiles. The transport layer is a plugin interface that supports any number of transport plugin modules. Although the architecture refers to them as transports, the remaining networking layers (network, data link, and physical) are presumed to be provided as well. The OCF specifications do not prescribe how the layers are implemented, but the IoTivity reference implementation (see `https://iotivity.org/downloads`) may offer guidance. Support for various wired and wireless transports in IoTivity continues to grow. At the time of this writing, there was support for CoAP (UDP) over IPv4, IPv6, Ethernet, Wi-Fi, and Bluetooth LE. At the time of this writing, an Object Security for Constrained RESTful Environments (OSCORE) draft specification[22] defines a REST message binding to CoAP and HTTP. OSCORE supports connections originating in IoT networks based on a UDP transport that terminates in cloud services environments or remote access gateways that are based on a TCP transport.

OCF transport plugin module interface is transport agnostic, making it possible to define transport plugin modules that implement REST (Representational State Transfer) semantics. This implies OCF transport plugins could implement message queuing techniques such as MQTT (Message Queuing Telemetry Transport) or XMPP (eXtensible Messaging and Presence Protocol) without structural modifications to the framework.

---

[22]`https://datatracker.ietf.org/doc/draft-ietf-core-object-security/`

The transport interface interaction model roughly follows an object lifecycle pattern called CRUDN – Create, Retrieve, Update, Delete, and Notify. RESTful interaction semantics easily map to a series of request-response exchanges for each interaction – for example, Send Create_Request message followed by Receive Create_Response message. OCF interface semantics are typically defined using RAML[23] (RESTful API Modeling Language), although there is interest in migrating to Swagger[24] which complies with the OpenAPI specification. The OpenAPI specification[25] is an open source community effort aimed at defining robust data modeling languages and tools.

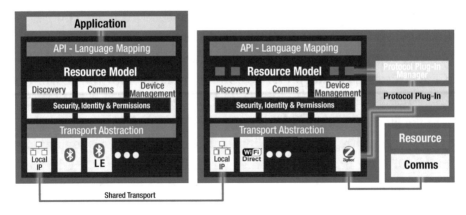

Figure 2-8. *OCF conceptual framework*

OCF Core Framework Layer

The Core Framework lies at the center of the OCF architecture. It defines the "resource" abstraction model which is arguably its most fundamental building block concept and the characteristic that most distinguishes it from other frameworks. An OCF *resource* is primarily a sequence of

---

[23]https://Raml.org

[24]https://swagger.io/

[25]https://github.com/OAI/OpenAPI-Specification

tag-value pairs but can have nested sequences as well. Resources are typically described using JSON. The OCF *resource model* approach to IoT networking presumes all aspects of the network can be represented declaratively, as a set of resource data structures having CRUDN interaction semantics. The traditional notion of a network topology consisting of nodes having routable IP addresses is hidden behind the resource abstraction.

Resources have several built-in properties (tags) that are common to all resources such as name, resource type, interface type, and whether or not it is discoverable and observable. Resource names are a URI (Universal Resource Identifier). Property names and name prefixes that are common to all are reserved by the OCF specification.

For example, "rt" refers to the resource type property, "if" refers to resource interface type property, "uri" is the resource name property if expressed as a URI, and "n" refers to a resource by its friendly name. Resource names prefixed with "/oic" are reserved for OCF use.

Additional properties may be appended that further specialize the resource. For example, it might define a property representing an operational state such as "on-off-state" where the accepted values are either ON or OFF. It might have another property "dim-level" with values in a range from 0 to 100, representing a light's brightness level.

This is a JSON schema representation of a simple resource:

```
"oic.r.switch.binary": {
    "type": "object",
        "properties": {
            "value": {
                "type": "boolean",
                "description": "Status of the switch"
            }
        }
}
```

This is a RAML representation of a CRUDN RETRIEVE interface definition:

```
get:
responses :
200: body:
            application/json:
                schema: |
                    { }
```

The point behind using interface and data modeling languages such as JSON and RAML is to enable the use of automated tools for generating code, tests, and even human-readable documentation that makes it easier to develop applications that not only interoperate but also can be adapted, updated, or modified at various operational stages.

The Core Framework layer defines several built-in resources used to implement several of the services and capabilities offered by the core layer. These include resource discovery, data transmission, data management, device management, security, identity, and permissions. Several built-in resources are listed in Table 2-2.

Table 2-2. *A Few Resources Built into an OCF Core Framework Layer*

Resource Name	Description	Functional Area
/oic/res	A resource that lists all discoverable resources known to the current network	Discovery
/oic/p	A resource that reveals details about the platform that hosts the OCF device	Discovery
/oic/rts	A resource that lists the resource type information for all discoverable resources	Discovery

(continued)

Table 2-2. (*continued*)

Resource Name	Description	Functional Area
/oic/ifs	A resource that lists the resource interface information for all discoverable resources	Discovery
/oic/mon	A resource that reveals observable resources	Device Management
/oic/sec/cred	A resource that lists the credentials this device has configured	Security Management
/oic/sec/acl2	A resource that lists the access control restrictions for this device	Security Management
/oic/sec/dots	A resource that facilitates device onboarding	Device and Security Management

A JSON representation of the /oic/p resource might appear as follows. Note this example includes comments denoted by double slash "//" which isn't defined by JSON:

```
/oic/p {
"rt": "oic.wk.p",
"if": ["oic.if.r"],
"pi": "ABCD123...",        //platform identifier UUID
"mnmn": "acme.org",      //platform manufacturer
"mnmo": "widget X",      //platform model number
"mnpv": "v1.0",          //platform version number
}
```

All properties of the /oic/p resource are read-only to support discovery use cases. A device management resource would likely allow update so a management console could configure the resource according to management goals.

The Core Framework specifications also define helpful building block resources that other resource designers may find useful such as *Links* and *Collections*. Links are a structure for defining a static connection between multiple resources. It consists of at least three parts: (1) the Context, (2) the Relationship, and (3) the Target and (4) additional parameters.

For example:

```
{
    "anchor": "/my/room/1",     //the Context
    "rel": "contains",          //the Relation
    "href": "/the/light/1",     //the Target
    "rt": "acme.light",         //the resource type
    "if": "oic.if.a"            //the interface type
}
```

The Collection resource is a bit like a Link resource only it contains an array of static connections to other resources.

For example:

```
/my/room/1 {
"rt": "acme.room",
"if": ["oic.if.r", "oic.if.rw"],
"color": "blue",
"dimension": "15bx15wx10h",
"links": [
    {"href":"/the/light/1", "rel":"contains", "rt":"acme.
    light",    "if":["oic.if.a", "oic.if.baseline"]},
    {"href":"/the/light/2", "rel":"contains", "rt"="mycorp.
    light", "if":["oic.if.s" , "oic.if.baseline"]},
    {"href":"/the/fan/1", "rel":"contains", "rt":"hiscorp.fan",
    "if":["oic.if.baseline"]}
    ]
}
```

OCF Profiles Framework Layer

OCF Profiles are libraries of resources containing common functionality (e.g., light bulb, pan-tilt-zoom camera). Profiles are grouped according to a target deployment context such as consumer, enterprise, industrial, auto, education, and health. Profiles are extensible. JSON validation ignores content not matching a schema target. OCF makes use of this behavior by allowing vendors to customize in any way they choose. We have mixed opinions regarding the use of this extensibility mechanism because, although it allows for post deployment customization, it also encourages the use of non-interoperable profiles.

The OCF data model supports resource introspection. Introspection can be used by a client to obtain a machine-readable description of all the resources, properties, and interface definition syntax. Introspection may be useful for systems that can learn how to interact with resources without prior programming.

The OCF Device Abstraction

OCF uses Universally Unique Identifiers (UUIDs) to identify OCF devices. The OCF device is like an OCF resource in that it has nested OCF defined Core and Profile resources. Core resources facilitate discovery, manageability, security, and connectivity. Profile resources define device type–specific data and behavior.

Access to OCF resources is accomplished using URIs. The OCF URI contains a device identifier in the form of a UUID followed by a reference to its resources. A client interacts with an OCF device by issuing a discovery message to identify available OCF server devices. This is followed by a RESTful message targeted at the device with interesting capabilities. The device's introspection resource may be used to gain additional insight regarding device capabilities and may be used to fine-tune subsequent interactions.

The OCF device abstraction logically defines a security boundary. OCF resource accesses follow CRUDN (Create, Retrieve, Update, Delete, Notify) interaction semantics that are part of the RESTful interface definition (e.g., PUT, GET, POST, DELETE). Access control policies use CRUDN privileges that are applied prior to returning resource data.

There can be multiple OCF devices hosted on the same physical platform. Logical devices are identified independently of the physical platform that hosts them. This means, from the perspective of the OCF device, it is not possible to distinguish whether a peer OCF device is geographically local or remote.

OCF Security

OCF security is exposed to devices through OCF resources. This is a simple yet powerful idea as all security interactions can be accomplished using the OCF framework. OCF security architecture has three main aspects: (1) access control, (2) message encryption, and (3) device lifecycle management. Access control is applied at the OCF device and resource-level granularity. It's worth noting that access control is not applied at the property level (although there are some exceptions). Access control list (ACL) policy is configured using the /oic/sec/acl2 resource. This resource is an array of ACL entries where each entry may be used to match the resource requestor to the requested resources so that an access restriction, expressed as CRUDN, can be applied before the requested resource is returned to the requestor.

```
/oic/sec/acl2 {
"aclist2": [
                "subject": ...,
                "resources": [...],
                "permission": CRUDN,
```

```
        "validity": ...,
        "aceid": INTEGER
    ]
}
```

The subject property is used to match the requestor. There are three ways this could be accomplished. One method uses the OCF device ID, which is a UUID. If the requesting device authenticates with a credential known to the local device, then the requesting device's ID is known. Another method is by role name. A role certificate may be presented at any time by the requestor during a session. If a role is asserted, then ACL entries that specify a role name could be used to match the requestor. A third method is by connection type. OCF connectivity options allow for anonymous (unauthenticated) and/or encrypted message payloads. It may be appropriate to supply a blanket ACL entry for anonymous requestors that is highly restrictive and only lessen restrictions when requestor is authenticated. Unencrypted data similarly may require a blanket ACL rule.

OCF supports a variety of cryptographic algorithms and key types including symmetric, raw asymmetric, and certified asymmetric. OCF devices must support symmetric keys and related algorithms. Security profiles may require support for raw asymmetric keys or keys with certificates.

Message encryption is applied by the transport layer (e.g., DTLS applied to CoAP messages). The use of TLS (Transport Layer Security) implies the endpoint where data is no longer protected by cryptography is somewhere in the framework but not necessarily in the OCF device context. The use of TLS also implies there are deployment cases where the TLS endpoint is actually a gateway, proxy, or firewall or another intermediate node that isn't the originating OCF device. Consequently, the use of TLS alone can't guarantee end-to-end data protection. To handle these, one of four options may be tried: the intermediary obtains a copy of the OCF device's credential, the intermediary presents its own OCF credential (masking the true OCF device originating the request), the intermediary uses its own credential but supplies a role credential that is common to the originating device, or the intermediary remains anonymous.

While there may be several ways for an intermediary to establish a connection legitimately, the credentials used may not adequately enable the original requestor the appropriate access rights. Lack of end-to-end message protections can complicate management and deployment of proper security controls. Adding this complexity runs counter to the philosophy of simplifying apparent complexity while hiding actual complexity.

OCF has a device lifecycle management model that incorporates device lifecycle state into the device resource model. The /oic/sec/pstat resource includes a property named Device Onboarding State or "dos." There are five states:

- RESET: Device transitions to its default state prior to onboarding.

- RFOTM: Device transitions to a state ready for onboarding into a new network.

- RFPRO: Device transitions to a state ready for provisioning resources.

- RFNOP: Device transitions to a state suitable for normal operations.

- SRESET: Device transitions to a state subsequent to onboarding, but where the device may be recommissioned or reconfigured with other options normally established only at onboarding.

The device is guaranteed to be in one of these five states throughout its deployment. These states map to elements of an IoT platform lifecycle model (see Figure 2-5). For example, a device may be in the RESET state during manufacturing and supply chain phases then transition to RFOTM in order to enter the deployment phase. It may transition to RFPRO as part of onboarding and initial commissioning then transition to RFNOP while in normal operation and monitoring phase. Management and update phases may or may not require a transition to RFPRO depending on how impactful the changes may be to the framework's resources. Hardware or low-level system changes may require transitioning to SRESET in order to change resources and properties the framework expects are immutable. Decommissioning implies a transition to RESET.

OCF "dos" states can have beneficial security impact because the device model at the framework layer enforces restrictions that could otherwise be ignored (potentially resulting in security incidents) by other resources and applications. For example, the /oic/sec/dots contains a property "owned" that is only updatable when the device is onboarded into a network for the first time. It is read-only thereafter. If an attacker tries to update it in some way to force an ownership change, the device state model prevents it.

OCF onboarding accommodates secure supply chains. Owner Transfer Methods (OTMs) are secure protocols designed to work with platform embedded credentials such as a manufacturer's certificate. OTMs rely on participation from platform vendors to establish platform provenance at manufacturing and through the supply chain. A variety of OTMs are supported having various levels of provability of supply chain provenance. The OTM interface is extensible, allowing improved OTM adoption over time.

A security challenge facing OCF frameworks is the binding between the lower framework layer to the platform and its security capabilities isn't defined by the specification. Implementers are free to make trade-off decisions that likely differ from product to product and vendor to vendor.

The OCF resource model tolerates complexity in that it supports any data structure representable by JSON. OCF standardized structures, Links and Collections, can be used to create complex relationships between resources enabling, for example, unlimited layers of nested resources that are difficult to define meaningful ACL rules. Resources can contain links to resources hosted on remote devices resulting in a chain of interactions not bounded by an end-to-end ACL policy. Encryption is achieved using TLS. TLS endpoints occur in the communication layer resulting in hop-by-hop confidentiality protection semantics. Although the OCF resource model complexity may be justified, its flexibility shouldn't reach beyond the security mechanisms protecting it.

AllSeen Alliance/AllJoyn

The AllSeen Alliance began in 2013 as an open source Linux Foundation project that defined an IoT framework aimed at consumer class home and small office automation use cases. AllJoyn is the open source reference implementation that first became available in 2016. AllSeen Alliance member companies included Affinegy, Arçelik, Canary, Cisco, Changhong, doubleTwist, Electrolux, Fon, Haier, Harman, HTC, LIFX, Liteon, LG, Microsoft, Muzzley, Onbiron, Panasonic, Sears, Sharp, Silicon Image, Sproutling, Sony, TP-Link, Two Bulls, and Wilocity. The AllSeen Alliance merged with the Open Connectivity Foundation in October of 2016. IoTivity 1.3 released in June 2017 contained support for an IoTivity to AllJoyn bridge.[26] AllSeen deployments exist primarily as legacy networks as development resources have turned elsewhere.

AllJoyn architecture (Figure 2-9) consists of three classes of node, leaf nodes, router nodes, and bridges. Leaf nodes contain application code and are primarily responsible for authentication and encryption. Router nodes host leaf nodes – no direct application to application

---

[26]https://iotivity.org/downloads/iotivity-1.3.0

interaction is permitted unless brokered by a D-Bus (Desktop Bus) agent – though application nodes may embed router node functionality giving the impression of direct application connectivity. Router nodes are responsible for message exchange that includes request-response and publish-subscribe support. It handles discovery, advertising, presence, and session management. The messaging transport is provided by D-Bus[27] technology. D-Bus is a point-to-point communications protocol built on top of IPS (inter-process communication) or through TCP sockets. A daemon process monitors bus activity processing messages on behalf of its connected applications. D-Bus channels are named using UNIX filesystem objects. An application must know which transport protocol to use and an appropriate D-Bus name when attempting to connect to a peer leaf node known as the "bus address." D-Bus supports several status and discovery commands that may be helpful in determining the health of D-Bus daemon processes:

- Org.freedesktop.DBus.Peer is used to determine if a peer is alive.

- Org.freedesktop.DBus.Introspectable is used to obtain an XML description of the interfaces, methods, and signals the device implements.

- Org.freedesktop.DBus.Properties is used to expose native properties and attributes of connected devices or to simulate them if they don't exist.

- Org.freedesktop.DBus.ObjectManager is used to query subobjects under its path when device objects are organized hierarchically.

---

[27]https://cgit.freedesktop.org/dbus/dbus/tree/NEWS?h=dbus-1.12

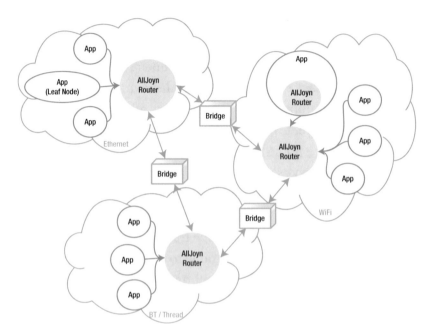

Figure 2-9. *Example AllJoyn network topology*

AllJoyn leaf node layers (Figure 2-10) consist of the AllJoyn Core
that handles discovery, security, connection management, and network
management. The AllJoyn Thin Client is an optimized subset of the AllJoyn
Core targeting ultra-constrained environments. Message authentication
and encryption protects the service framework and application data end-
to-end. However, AllJoyn Thin Client nevertheless requires at least one
routing node to complete an end-to-end connection.

The AllJoyn Service Framework implements device services.
Onboarding, control panel, and notification services are common to all
devices. Application-specific services are added as needed to expose
device-specific specializations.

The AllJoyn router nodes contain an AllJoyn Core layer that contains
message routing capabilities. However, routing nodes can be configured
to protect all D-Bus traffic between cooperating D-Bus daemon processes
using a common shared key. AllJoyn Management Functions perform
advertising and discovery functions on behalf of leaf nodes. Routers

maintain context regarding leaf node presence and maintain a session for each attached leaf node. Messages involved in publish-subscribe messaging may have fan-out semantics requiring platform-level optimization support. For example, IP multicast may be an efficient way to deliver the same message to multiple recipients. Subscription registrations are maintained here as well. Message filtering can be applied by AllJoyn routers where the aim is congestion control given requests containing a query string.

AllJoyn bridges perform network and link layer translations when AllJoyn nodes are physically separated or when AllJoyn framework-level objects are gatewayed to a different IoT framework environment. For example, framework bridges may support IoTivity or OneM2M mappings.

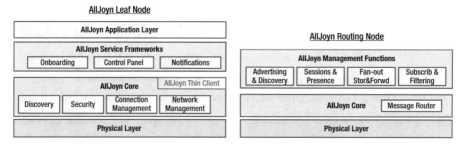

Figure 2-10. *AllJoyn leaf and router nodes layering*

AllJoyn Security

AllJoyn security rests with the AllJoyn leaf node and with the application layer. Such an approach encourages end-to-end protection of data. Effective data-level protection at the application layer requires data formatting and encapsulation technology that is part of its data model. AllJoyn data objects are described using XML and rely on XML Security[28] for secure encapsulation. Although D-Bus can support security at the IP layer, it relies on the application endpoint for end-to-end data protection.

---

[28]www.w3.org/standards/xml/security

When the Open Connectivity Foundation and the AllSeen Alliance merged, they defined a bridging specification that allows OCF and AllJoyn devices to interact; however the OCF bridging specifications do not define security interoperability.

Universal Plug and Play

Universal Plug and Play (UPnP) was originally designed for consumer electronics, mobile devices, home automation, and personal computer networks emphasizing *zero configuration networking* – the idea that setting up a service doesn't require any manual configuration. It includes automatic assignment of network addresses, automatic distribution of hostnames, and automatic discovery of network services. Although UPnP envisioned interoperation with consumer electronics and home automation, its first international specification published in 2008 by ISO/IEC[29] before the *Internet of Things* became a popular buzz word.

The UPnP set of standards has evolved to better support audio/video equipment, remote user interfaces, quality of service, and remote access from the Web. As recently as 2015, the UPnP Forum published the *UPnP Device Architecture 2.0*[30] specification that extends into the Web through XMPP integration. The *IoT Management and Control Architecture*[31] published September 10, 2013, addresses more directly home automation requirements with the inclusion of sensor management.

---

[29]"ISO/IEC standard on UPnP device architecture makes networking simple and easy." International Organization for Standardization. 10 December 2008. Retrieved 11 September 2014.

[30]www.upnp.org/specs/arch/UPnP-arch-DeviceArchitecture-v2.0.pdf

[31]http://upnp.org/specs/iotmc/UPnP-iotmc-IoTManagementAndControl-Architecture-Overview-v1.pdf

The UPnP protocol stack (Figure 2-11) may be regarded as IoT frameworks, though loosely as UPnP is tightly bound to IP and the network services built around IP such as DHCP, DNS, IP multicast, and so on. UPnP network topologies parallel that of IP network topologies.

The UPnP Device Architecture layer consists of a discovery service named Simple Service Discovery Protocol (SSDP) that supports passive discovery request-response as well as active service availability notification and unsolicited advertisements using local multicast addressing. The General Event Notification Architecture (GENA) handles the details of registering notification events and sending notification messages when events are triggered. The Simple Object Access Protocol (SOAP) uses XML-formatted messages that are delivered using RESTful HTTP request-response exchanges. UPnP also supports IP multicast events for simple messages that need to be broadcast to multiple UPnP nodes.

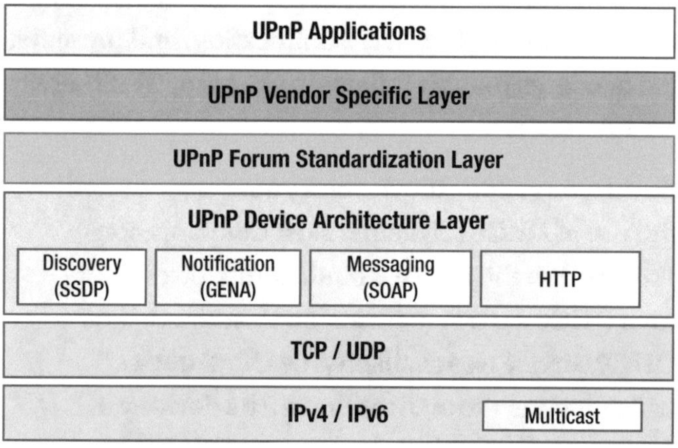

Figure 2-11. *UPnP protocol stack*

UPnP networks (Figure 2-12) consist of two node types, control points and Devices. Devices host Services. Device nesting is supported; the top-level Device is known as the Root Device. Devices are conceptual objects but are identified using IP addresses. Control points contain code that controls devices or otherwise interacts with services.

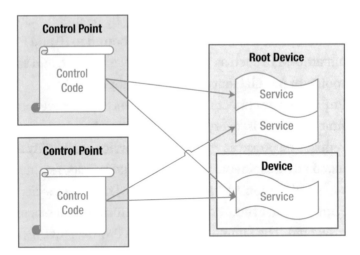

Figure 2-12. *UPnP network nodes consist of control points and Devices that host Services*

UPnP can be divided into six architectural elements: addressing, discovery, description, control, event notification, and presentation. Architectural elements roughly follow six phases of UPnP service and control point interactions:

I.   **Addressing**: Zero-touch configuration motivated the use of DHCP (Dynamic Host Configuration Protocol) so the device would automatically look for a DHCP service to obtain an IP address. If no DHCP service was available, the UPnP device will autogenerate an IP address. The device can automatically obtain a DNS name using DNS forwarding. Secure device and control point identity was not a major focus.

II. **Discovery**: Service discovery automation is achieved through proactive "alive" messages that are broadcast periodically to listening control points. Control points can send discovery messages with filters for the class of interesting service. This approach removes the need for statically configured services enabling dynamic services (that can go online or go offline easily). Control points rely on SSDP notifications to keep them appraised of service online status. Service name URLs are public which could have privacy implications. Secure discovery was not a major focus.

III. **Description**: Discovery reveals the existence of UPnP devices and services, but control points may require more context to determine if they are relevant to control point applications. Device description allows introspection using an XML description of the device structure. It includes the following information:

- Vendor-specific details include manufacturer name, model, version, serial number, and URLs to vendor-specific web sites.

- Service details include URLs for control, event notification, and service description. Service commands and their parameters are detailed.

- Variables that describe Runtime state are described in terms of data type, expected range, and event characteristics.

IV. **Control**: Control point code is expected to identify which commands and data objects are supported by the service to construct a program sequence that uses them to achieve application objectives. Command formatting is specified using SOAP protocol following the request-response pattern.

V. **Event Notification**: Services built around sensors and physical devices may change internal state autonomously. Control points seeking to be appraised of service and variable state changes can register for asynchronous notifications when things change. Notification messages are small; if the control point needs more information than is available in the notification message, it may need to follow the notification with a request-response interaction. UPnP event notification capability is referred to as the General Event Notification Architecture (GENA).

VI. **Presentation**: Normally, UPnP nodes operate as headless entities. Nevertheless, users may need to monitor and control things. UPnP services can support web browser user interfaces by returning a URL to a web page markup (HTML) that exposes service variables and control widgets.

UPnP Security

Initially, UPnP architecture did not comprehend security. It was thought to be addressed in the layers beneath (network) or above (application). More recently The IoT Management and Control Architecture[32] was added which included access control features for sensors was facilitated by roles and sensor permissions. Sensor permissions include

- ReadSensor: Control points can issue ReadSensor() actions to sensor objects.

- WriteSensor: Control points can issue WriteSensor() actions to sensor objects.

---

[32]http://upnp.org/specs/iotmc/UPnP-iotmc-IoTManagementAndControl-Architecture-Overview-v1.pdf

- ConnectSensor: Control points can issue
  ConnectSensor() and DisconnectSensor() actions to
  sensor objects.

- CommandSensor: Control points can modify
  IoTManagementAndControl properties in the
  data model (which is a data repository object).

- ViewSensor: Control points can read
  IoTManagementAndControl properties in the
  data model.

UPnP sensor objects expect control point operates with a particular role where permissions are assigned based on the set of behaviors each role is expected to follow.

UPnP control points must possess one of three UPnP defined roles:

- Admin: Role can read, write, connect, command, or
  view any sensor object.

- Public: Role can read or write specific sensor objects
  (e.g., those supporting the Public role).

- Basic: Role can read or write specific sensor objects
  (e.g., those supporting the Basic role).

A group of sensors form an object that can respond to control point accesses. Sensor groups have their own permission classification denoted by a sensor command name followed by the group name (e.g., smgt:ReadS ensor()#[SensorGroupName]). There are four permissions for Read, Write, Command, and View. ConnectSensor isn't supported. Sensors inherit the group permissions upon joining the sensor group. Control points acquire the "group" access by joining the sensor group as a Control point. Interestingly the UPnP specification refers to group permissions as group roles.

UPnP security features are optional to implement, making it difficult to force the ecosystem to deploy UPnP with security.

The Open Connectivity Foundation and the UPnP Forum merged in 2016. They defined a bridging specification that allows OCF and UPnP devices to interact; however the OCF bridging specifications do not define security interoperability.

Lightweight Machine 2 Machine (LWM2M)

The Open Mobile Alliance (OMA) defined the Lightweight Machine 2 Machine (LWM2M)[33] specification to address IoT device management. We have included it at the end of the section summarizing consumer class IoT frameworks, but it could just as easily be classified as an IoT manageability framework. However, the Internet Protocol for Smart Objects (IPSO) Alliance extended LWM2M such that it can be used to describe a variety of consumer class IoT devices referred to as "smart objects" borrowing terminology from the LWM2M "object" model. OMA and IPSO Alliance merged in March 27, 2018,[34] forming new committees within OMA organization to continue its evolution as both an IoT manageability framework and a general-purpose IoT framework.

LWM2M Architecture

LWM2M architecture (Figure 2-13) utilizes a LWM2M Server node to host device management and other applications that interact with LWM2M client nodes hosting one or more LWM2M objects. Servers use RESTful CoAP commands (GET, POST, PUT, DELETE) to read and update the objects. Secure access is achieved using DTLS layer of CoAPs. CoAP and DTLS use UDP/IP and SMS transport protocols.

---

[33]www.openmobilealliance.org/release/LightweightM2M/

[34]www.omaspecworks.org/ipso-alliance-merges-with-open-mobile-alliance-to-form-oma-specworks/

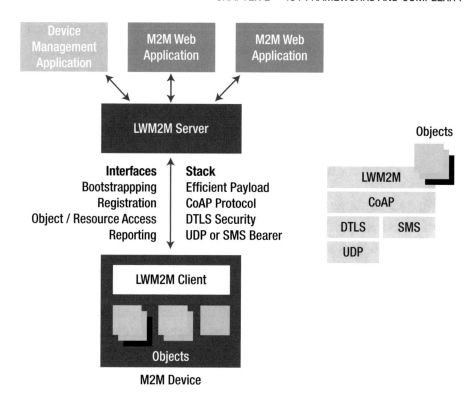

Figure 2-13. *LWM2M architecture showing client node with objects being managed by a Server node hosting device management and various web applications*

The LWM2M object model (Figure 2-14) is a simple but powerful abstraction of IoT devices. The LWM2M client is the managed node and corresponds to a sensor/actuator device. LWM2M nodes describe a set of network exposed variables called objects. A LWM2M Server may reference an object using a URI string that names the object plus its resources. For example, a LWM2M URI might appear as "/0/1" where "0" is the object identifier and "1" is the resource identifier. Objects contain one or more resources, but resources may not contain objects; in other words, nesting of objects is not supported. Friendly names are not supported since doing so was thought to make URIs unnecessarily verbose. Instead objects and resources are numeric values. It is possible to have an array of objects of the same type using same object identifier. An Object Instance Identifier is added between the object ID and the resource ID to qualify the object instance. The URI format has the following form:

```
/ <ObjectID> / <ObjectInstanceID> /
<ResourceID>
```

Figure 2-14 shows an example object configuration consisting of two objects. The first contains a single object instance with three resources. The URI path begins with a leading slash "/" followed by the ObjectID referencing the first object (denoted by red arrow). It is followed by a second slash then the ResourceID referencing the third resource in the first object (denoted by a green arrow). The second object contains two instances of Object 2 where each instance consists of six resources. The URI path examples have three elements, the middle being the Object Instance Identifier (denoted by a blue arrow). One URI path shows an Object Instance Identifier with the value 1 that references the first object instance and the first resource instance within it. The other URI path references the second object instance and the sixth resource within it.

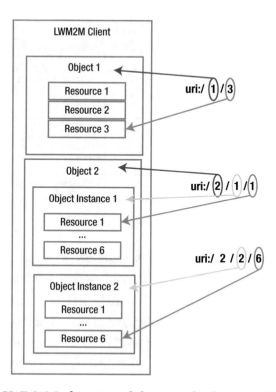

Figure 2-14. *LWM2M object model example showing URI references to data values*

The LWM2M object model expects IoT devices can be described relatively simply. The object model abstraction may hide significant actual complexity requiring the object model designer to think carefully about which device attributes need to be exposed and how best to map actual complexity to a simpler apparent complexity.

The example object in Figure 2-15 reveals six resources. The chart describes additional metadata regarding the resource including the type of access allowed (read vs. read/update), if it is a multi-instance object, the resource data type, the allowable range of data values, and the units in which the data is expressed.

Resource Name	ID	Access Type	Multiple Instances?	Type	Range	Units	Descriptions
Latitude	0	R	NO	Decimal		Deg	The decimal notation of latitude, e.g. -43.5723 [World Geodetic System 1984]
Longitude	1	R	NO	Decimal		Deg	The decimal notation of longitude, e.g. 153.21760 [World Geodetic System 1984]
Altitude	2	R	NO	Decimal		m	The decimal notation of Altitude in meters above sea level.
Uncertainty	3	R	NO	Decimal		m	The accuracy of the position in meters.
Velocity	4	R	NO	Refers to 3GPP GAD specs		Refers to 3GPP GAD specs	The velocity of the device as defined in 3GPP 23.032 GAD specification. This set of values may not be available if the device is static.
Timestamp	5	R	NO	Time			The timestamp of when the location measurement was performed.

Figure 2-15. *Example LWM2M location object*

The object namespace needs to be managed to avoid confusion when servers access client objects. The OMA reserved object identifiers 0–1023 for OMA defined objects. 1024–2047 are reserved for future use. 2048–10240 are allocated for third-party defined objects. For example, the IPSO Alliance object definitions are allocated from this range. 10241–32768 are assigned to public entities, vendors, or individuals for proprietary use.

Introspection is not supported except through the use of a separately defined introspection service – something that wasn't defined at the time of this writing.

LWM2M Device Management

LWM2M defines five device management services:

- Bootstrapping: Configures symmetric secrets, raw public keys, and certificates clients and service will use to establish DTLS sessions. LWM2M Services may be configured. Access control lists may also be configured.

- Remote Management: Updates operational settings as defined by device profiles. Triggers for controlling actuation may also be configured or reset as part of normal operation.

- Firmware Update: Client nodes report firmware version
  and firmware packages can be installed through the
  firmware update object.

- Fault Management: Device errors can be exposed
  through the fault reporting objects. These may be
  viewed by other nodes querying operational status.

- Reporting: Notification of changing sensor values
  can be configured for multiple recipients. Status of
  the notification can be monitored and configuration
  changes applied when needed.

The LWM2M architecture model reverses client and server roles
(Figure 2-16) in comparison to other frameworks such as OCF, UPnP, and
AllJoyn. This seems reasonable since the primary goal of LWM2M is device
management where the device utilizes management service providers
that bootstrap and configure the client. LWM2M supports both client- and
server-initiated bootstrapping. Once the client device is configured, it may
interact with other IoT nodes as an IoT service such as a sensor or actuator.

It may be reasonable to combine LWM2M for device management with
a different IoT framework that doesn't support device management since
LWM2M can operate alongside it provided the other IoT framework device
lifecycle states are aligned with the LWM2M device state model.

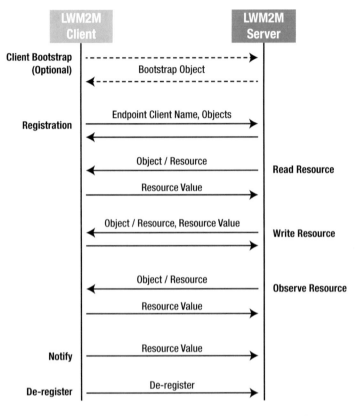

Figure 2-16. *LWM2M example device management lifecycle scenario*

LWM2M Security

LWM2M security has two main components, DTLS secured messages and access control lists (ACLs) for LWM2M objects (Figure 2-17). DTLS supports shared secrets (symmetric) using cipher suites for preshared keys (PSK), raw public keys (asymmetric) using cipher suites that perform ephemeral Diffie-Hellman key exchange that supports perfect forward secrecy (PFS), and certificates (asymmetric) using cipher suites that support popular certificate signing algorithms such as elliptic curve cryptography and RSA.

ACL support is achieved using the Bootstrap server to provision access control resources to LWM2M clients seeking access to LWM2M servers. In the following example, the Bootstrap server provisions the security object in Client 1 with the ACL object with read and write access to Server 1 (e.g., ACL:<Server 1, RW>). It also provisions Client 3 with read and write access to Server 2 (e.g., ACL:<Server 2, RW>).

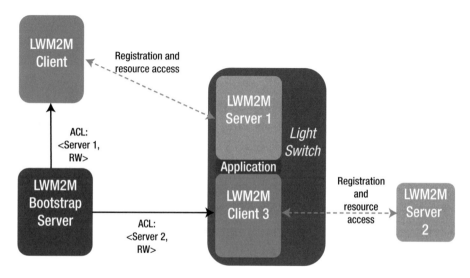

Figure 2-17. *LWM2M access control list configuration*

Provisioning credentials to each of the clients to allow the Bootstrap server access to their security objects is part of initial device setup, but LWM2M doesn't (at the time of this writing) implement onboarding (see the section "Deployment"). The method for establishing trust in the Bootstrap server by devices is vendor specific.

One Machine to Machine (OneM2M)

Eight global standards organizations [ARIB (Japan), ATIS (United States), CCSA (China), ETSI (Europe), TIA (United States), TSDSI (India), TTA (Korea), and TTC (Japan)] and six other industry fora, consortia, or standards bodies (Broadband Forum, CEN, CENELEC, GlobalPlatform, Next Generation M2M Consortium, OMA) collaborated to develop the OneM2M standard. The group, known as OneM2M,[35] was formed in July 2012. OneM2M produced the OneM2M technical specification in February 2016.[36]

OneM2M is an architecturally complete IoT framework (Figure 2-18) that consists of three basic layers: (1) Application layer, (2) Common Services layer, and (3) Network Services layer. An instantiation of a layered module is called an entity. An application is therefore an *application entity (AE)*, a service is a *common services entity (CSE),* and a network module is a *network services entity (NSE)*. Interfaces facilitate communication between entities known as *Reference Points*. A OneM2M reference point uses the nomenclature "Mc-" meaning M2M communication to the entity "-" – where the dash is a placeholder for the first letter of the entity name. For example, Mca describes a reference point connecting an Application Entity and a Common Services Entity. Mcn describes a reference point connecting a Network Services Entity to a CSE. Mcc describes a CSE to CSE reference point.

---

[35]http://onem2m.org/

[36]OneM2M Technical Specification, TS-0001-V1.13.1, Functional Architecture, 2016- February-29

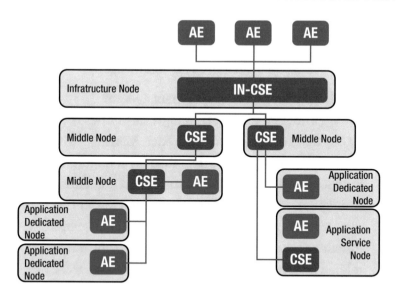

Figure 2-18. *OneM2M node topology architecture*

Deployment scenarios may have stereotyped nodes, according to
a logical or functional network topology. For example, Application and
Common Services entities may cooperate to provide infrastructure
capabilities such as manageability services, message logging, telemetry,
and so on. OneM2M refers to these nodes as infrastructure nodes (IN).
Other nodes may cooperate to implement an application, for example,
HVAC control, called Application Dedicated Node (ADN) or Application
Service Node (ASN). Nodes deployed to connect ADNs to INs or other
ADNs are called middle nodes (MN). Bridging non-OneM2M nodes are
given the acronym NoDN.

Nodes may contain programs that control resources on other nodes.
Resources are composed of a set of attributes. Resources can be nested,
called a *child* resource.

Nodes are identified with a globally unique identifier that is assigned
when the node registers with a registration node hosting a registration
common services function. Physical devices host OneM2M nodes.

Entity layers are subdivided into *functions*. The Common Services Entity (Figure 2-19) defines a handful of common services functions (CSF) that manage device lifecycle including the following:

- Application and service layer management (ASM): The ASM function manages all entities hosted by any node excluding NoDN nodes. Management functions consist of two categories: (1) configuration functions and (2) software management functions. Configuration CRUDN functions expose resources used to manage entities, while software management functions are concerned with managing software and related artifacts associated with a software lifecycle.

- Communication management and (message) delivery handling: These functions manage delivery, temporary storage, and caching of messages. It also manages policies related to configuration and tuning of message delivery infrastructure.

- Data management and repository handling: These functions manage data repositories. They are concerned with the collection, aggregation, mediation, storage, and preparation for analytics and semantic processing.

- Device management: These functions address device management capabilities associated with OneM2M nodes and can use existing IoT device management frameworks such as TR-069 and LWM2M or may define new functions. Device management functions translate data, protocol, and semantics from one management node to another using a *Management adapter* module. Management gateways, proxies, and bridging functions fall within the scope of device management functions. Device management functions perform device configuration, device diagnostics, monitoring, firmware management, and topology management.

- Discovery: Nodes, resources, and attributes can be discovered using a discovery CSF. Typically, the invoker supplies a query value that selects a subset of available possible matches. Filter criteria are expressed in terms of identifiers, keywords, location, and other semantic information.

- Group management: Nodes can be organized into groups. The group management CSF must validate group membership and whether the group member is capable of performing functions meaningful to the group. Groups are used to coordinate publication, broadcasts, or multicasts to multiple nodes and to define roles for access control.

- Location: The location CSF senses and publishes location information for the node. Location coordinates can be more than latitude-longitude coordinates but require knowledge of location extension semantics.

- Network service exposure: The network service exposure, service execution, and triggering (NSSE) CSF manages exposure of underlying networks and communication layers through Mcn reference points and NSE modules.

- Registration: Entity services must register with a registrar CSF in order to make their services available for use. The registration CSF supplies a requestor with the node identifier where the service can be reached, a schedule for when it can be reached, and details for accessing the service.

- Security: The security CSF handles identity management, access control, authorization, authentication, security associations, data confidentiality, data integrity, and security system management. Access control list subjects can group nodes that enforce read or write permissions. ACLs are associated with resources, entities, and repositories. Access control can be applied to discovery resources but requires subject authentication and authorization – though an "anonymous" group could be defined that corresponds to an ACL entry matching unauthenticated subjects.

- Service charging and accounting: The SCA CSF manages telemetry generation and collection used to charge for services, events, information, and real-time credit control.

- Subscription and notification: The subscription CSF manages subscription operations and notification message delivery to subscribers when the subscription condition is met. Subscriptions are registered with a resource or group of resources following an access control check. Changes to resources are tracked at attribute granularity. Changes to subresources are also tracked but not attributes of subresources.

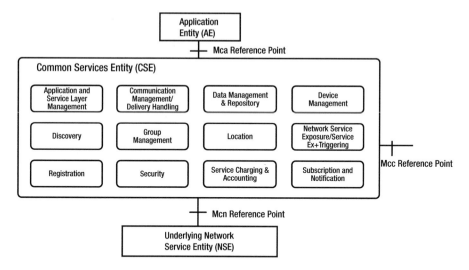

Figure 2-19. *OneM2M layering with entities and Common Services Entity functional modules*

IoT networks are sometimes partitioned into enclaves of subnetworks called *domains* (Figure 2-20) to improve isolation for safety, reliability, and security reasons. OneM2M reference point architecture envisages network enclaves by allowing multiple AE + CSE + NSE verticals connected through peer Mcc and Mca reference points. For example, a fieldbus domain may contain a network of closed-loop sensors and actuators running at real time or near real time, while an infrastructure domain may contain accounting, telemetry, firmware update, and other services based on restful client-server interactions. Still another domain may offload complex analytics to a data center or Cloud.

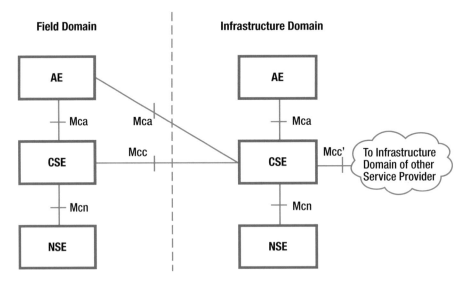

Figure 2-20. *OneM2M domain architecture allows network enclave isolation*

OneM2M device management is built from an open-ended set of common services functions that may be tailored toward any number of existing industry standard and nonstandard device management solutions including TR-069,[37] OMA-DM,[38] and LWM2M. As such, OneM2M can be thought of as a framework of frameworks.

OneM2M architecture allows extremely flexible configuration of functional modules and extensibility options. This flexibility may be helpful when tailoring a solution for constrained embedded devices seeking to minimize resource footprint or when designing gateways, bridges, and framework service nodes that are scattered throughout a complex IoT network. However, flexibility may come with a cost as

---

[37]Broadband Forum Technical Report, "TR-069 CPE WAN Management Protocol," Issue: 1 Amendment 6, Version 1.4, March 2018. www.broadband-forum.org/technical/download/TR-069.pdf

[38]www.openmobilealliance.org/wp/overviews/dm_overview.html

network latencies, routing, network security, and network management overhead may be incurred. Hiding this complexity from system designers may have undesirable consequences, while exposing the flexibility (having simplified apparent complexity) to applications and users may also have undesirable consequences.

OneM2M Security

OneM2M security design comprehends identity, authentication, authorization, access control, data protection, and privacy. That is to say, each of these security requirements was considered and addressed to a certain extent. However, the test determining adequacy largely depends on how completely the industry implements the standard and how effective the security mechanisms defined address the threats facing IoT networks.

OneM2M security administration begins with the provisioning of *master credentials* that enables the security CSF functions to be applied. Master credentials can be post-provisioned (subsequent to initial deployment of a CSE containing security CSFs) or pre-provisioned with cooperation from a device manufacturer – though the exact operation of onboarding protocols for pre-provisioning is out of scope.

OneM2M framework architecture abstracts away (hides) physical (device) boundaries. An Mcc reference point may or may not cross a device boundary. The same is true for Mca reference points as well. Intuitively, one might conclude that the use of an Mcn reference point does cross a physical boundary, but with IP loopback, shared memory, and other interprocess communication and overlay network mechanisms, Mcn also doesn't describe physical boundary crossing semantics. This is relevant to security because attack points often occur at boundary crossings. Although the specification intends security CSF functionality will "protect" security-sensitive information, there are a wide variety of hardware and software mechanisms to draw from – each having differing security and privacy properties.

Industrial IoT Framework Standards

The IoT framework standards discussed up to this point primarily address consumer grade IoT applications and deployments. That doesn't mean the standards organizations and member companies could not extend their architectures to accommodate requirements typically associated with industrial IoT. This section considers IoT frameworks that were designed specifically to address industrial control system requirements. Industrial control systems predate the Internet of Things and even predate the Internet. Fieldbus technology is the foundation of process automation, building automation, and automated manufacturing. This section doesn't survey the vast expanse of "brownfield" fieldbus technology.[39] Instead, it focuses on Industrial IoT (IIoT) standards that aim to improve interoperability through appropriate use of inexpensive, ubiquitous Internet technologies and are supported by a rich ecosystem.

Industrial Internet Control Systems (or just Industrial Internet Systems – IIS) may be a more appropriate terminology than IoT because at their core are complex semiautonomous and fully autonomous process automation systems that operate at a level of sophistication that clearly goes beyond consumer IoT. They pay close attention to Quality of Service (QoS), Quality of Experience (QoE), and safety requirements.

The architectural principles defined by the IIC reference architecture serves as a reference point for evaluating the merits and demerits of IIS framework solutions. The next section highlights important elements of industrial IoT system architecture as defined by the Industrial Internet of Things Consortium (IIC). In subsequent sections, we also highlight the Open Platform Communications-Unified Architecture (OPC-UA) and Data Distribution Services (DDS) open source IIS frameworks.

---

[39]<tbd Reference to industrial control systems>

Industrial Internet of Things Consortium (IIC) and OpenFog Consortium

The Industrial Internet of Things Consortium (IIC) was formed by AT&T, Cisco, IBM, Intel, and General Electric in November of 2016. The IIC created a reference architecture[40] for IIS that considers common needs and challenges pertaining to control systems in energy, healthcare, manufacturing, public sector, transportation, and factory automation.

In December 2018, the IIC and OpenFog Consortium agreed to join forces under the name IIC.[41] The OpenFog Consortium was founded by ARM Holdings, Cisco, Dell, Intel, Princeton University, and Microsoft in 2015. OpenFog Consortium and IIC both focused heavily on industrial IoT architecture.

Industrial Internet Systems bring new levels of performance, scalability, interoperability, reliability, assurance, and efficiency to the forefront. As such, the IIC determined it should produce a reference architecture first (and not an IoT framework[42] and a reference implementation). IIS systems often operate in mission critical environments that require real-time or near real-time responses and are "smart" through increased integration with higher-level networks that include enterprise resource planning, information technology administration, analytics, and big data correlation engines.

One aspect of the IIC architecture helps us understand the implications of transforming the largely isolated brownfield embedded control systems and technology into something that benefits from

---

[40]The Industrial Internet of Things Volume G1: Reference Architecture IIC:PUB:g1:V1.80:20170131 https://www.iiconsortium.org/IIC_PUB_G1_V1.80_2017-01-31.pdf

[41]www.smartindustry.com/industrynews/2018/iic-and-openfog-consortium-join-forces/

[42]Note to reader: The IIC specification refers to sub-architecture sections as "frameworks" not to be confused with our usage.

the Internet economies of scale and its robust ecosystem. Industrial embedded control systems have existed before the popular Internet and have evolved alongside it for several years. Its evolution into the IIoT seems inevitable, but doing so creates a complex problem for interoperability given the existing brownfield systems will likely continue for many years.

It is not our objective to deeply explore the IIC reference architecture here. However, the reader might appreciate the role of a reference architecture when evaluating IoT frameworks as building blocks of IIS systems. Different parts of an IIS ecosystem bring different viewpoints (Figure 2-21) of the system. The IIC reference architecture explores IIS from four viewpoints:

- Business viewpoint: Identifies stakeholders, business objectives, values, vision, and related regulatory context and comprehends business-oriented concerns.

- Usage viewpoint: Represents the activities, sequences, and functionality involving human or logical users. It ultimately establishes whether the IIS achieves value from the user's perspective.

- Functional viewpoint: Identifies functional components, structures, interfaces, interactions, and relationships. It considers trade-offs associated with the interests of systems architects, component architects, developers, and integrators.

- Implementation viewpoint: Considers challenges and implications of functional components, their communication, and lifecycle procedures and dependencies.

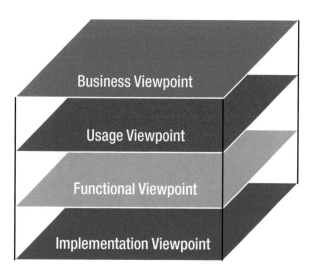

Figure 2-21. *IIC reference viewpoints*

Although multiple viewpoints exist, security objectives can be frustrated if a perspective somehow becomes hidden from the others in the context of continuous security monitoring, threat detection, decision making, and response management. For example, security return on investment value may be weighed against performance or consumer satisfaction value. The user benefits of autonomous operation (without users) may be compared to perceived and actual benefits of user involvement in setting and evaluating security relevant decisions. Security functional viewpoint defines points where security-related enforcement and decision making may impact other functional goals. The implementation viewpoint applies security technologies involving patterns and system components in ways that are correctly implemented and easy to maintain and ensure correct operation of security functions, algorithms, and hardening.

The IIC functional viewpoint reference architecture (Figure 2-22) recognizes an important understanding of IIS systems having five functional domains that must coexist as interoperable subsystems while ensuring appropriate isolation mechanisms prevent the goals of each domain from being compromised given failure or compromise in a peer domain.

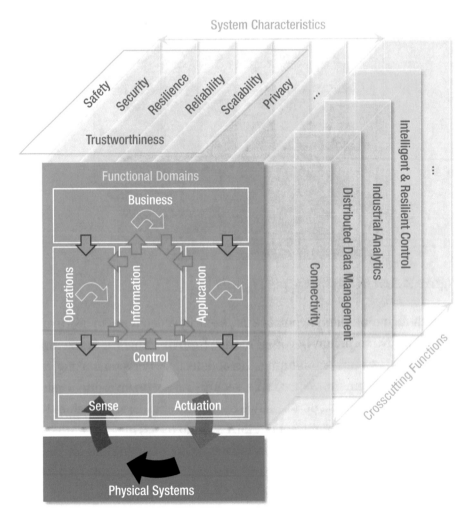

Figure 2-22. *IIC functional viewpoint reference architecture showing various functional domains*

The business domain functions as a layer on top of operations, information, and application domains that interact with the control domain. The control domain consists of a separation between cyber and physical systems brokered by sensing and actuation functions. User interactions may occur at each domain according to domain-specific

Quality of Experience objectives. Cross-domain interactions should carry the appropriate level of domain-specific context to ensure peer domain functions do not, in some way, misinterpret the semantics of command interaction, control flow, and data representation as this can result in failures and security vulnerabilities.

The IIC implementation viewpoint reference architecture (Figure 2-23) captures an important three-tier network topology structure that recognizes an Edge Tier network consisting of sensor, actuator, and controller nodes that may share latency, resiliency, and QoS requirements that typically are met by Edge-class technologies. These differ from Platform Tier technologies used to implement scalable, reliable, available systems for data analytics, operations, and data transformation. Similarly, the Enterprise Tier consists of technologies tuned for system maintenance, management, and system-level controls. Inter-Tier interactions are held in check through bridging, gatewaying, and proxying technologies aimed at preserving the correct context of the peer Tier when performing control operations or when moving data between Tiers.

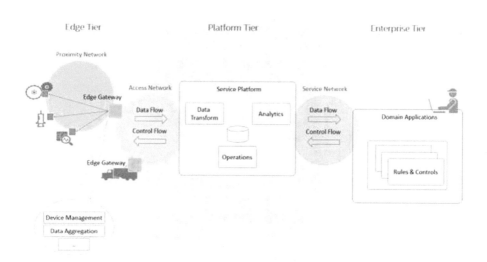

Figure 2-23. *IIC implementation viewpoint reference architecture showing a three-tier network*

Multiple viewpoints can be combined to reveal additional insights regarding an IIS system. For example, Figure 2-24 shows the functional viewpoint architecture overlaid with the implementation viewpoint architecture. The Control Domain exists in the Edge Tier which contains the Proximity Network consisting of sensors, actuators, controllers, and gateways to Platform Tier. The Information and Operations Domains exist in the Platform Tier bridging the Access and the Service Networks. The Platform Tier contains data service and platform management, data distribution, persistence, streaming, aggregation, and transformation. The Operations Domain is concerned with provisioning, deployment, metadata, monitoring, telemetry, optimization, and access control. The Application and Business Domains exist in the Enterprise Tier extending the Service Network with business analytics, CRM, DSS, BSS, and so on and enterprise applications, APIs, portals, and enterprise rules.

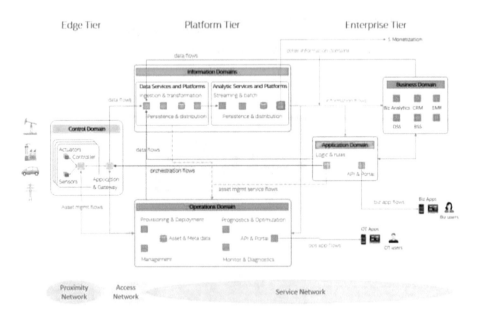

Figure 2-24. *Architectural overlay of functional and implementation viewpoints*

Open Platform Communications-Unified Architecture (OPC-UA)

Object Linking and Embedding (OLE) is a Microsoft technology aimed at office automation largely based on Windows operating systems. The Open Platform Communications (OPC) task force extended OLE for machine-to-machine control and industrial automation. The task force formed the OPC Foundation[43] in 1996 to maintain the OPC standard. OPC originally was based on Microsoft Windows-only COM/DCOM technology which was integrated with the existing OPC communications framework, resulting in a unified architecture called OPC-UA.

An industrial IoT network is really a layering of multiple networks customized to address a particular aspect of industrial operations. A typical IIoT system will consist of a four-layer system of networks (Figure 2-25). The device-level network consists of sensor-actuator devices with real-time control of physical world processes, logistics, and mechanics. The protocols linking nodes at this layer are typically traditional brownfield technologies such as ProfiNet, EtherCAT, and Modbus. These systems are designed to operate autonomously taking into consideration safety and reliability.

The control-level network consists of shop floor controllers that coordinate the end-to-end flow of the industrial system. The output of one shop floor device may be consumed as input to another shop floor device. Shop floor controllers orchestrate the hand off the work item, whether physical, informational, or both. OPC-UA is a framework for shop floor machine control. Controllers host multiple device nodes, run real-time or near real-time operating systems, and support both fieldbus and a traditional Internet protocol stack based on IP and TCP.

---

[43]www.opcfoundation.org/

The third level is the Manufacturing Execution System (MES) that provides plant-, site-, or factory-level coordination of various shop floor networks. This network consists of PCs and servers networked using traditional IP networks. The fourth level focuses on Enterprise Resource Planning (ERP) functions that filter data from the MES level for deeper analytics relating to process improvement, cost optimization, and operational efficiency improvement. ERP applications may be hosted in an enterprise data center or a cloud hosting environment such as Microsoft Azure.

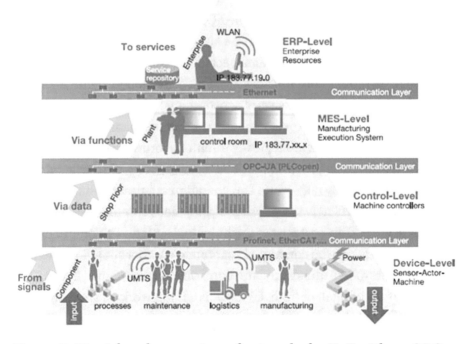

Figure 2-25. *A four-layer system of networks for IIoT with an OPC-UA layer*

OPC-UA is a device-centric technology that connects sensor, actuator, and PLC (programmable logic controller) devices to each other and to a larger system of PC and server class platforms. It aims to ensure device-level interoperability.

The basic structure of an OPC-UA network consists of an OPC-Client connected to an OPC-Server. The OPC-Server connects to sensor, actuator, and PLC devices. The OPC-Client to OPC-Server connection is typically based on IP networking. The OPC-Server to control devices is typically based on a fieldbus technology.

OPC-UA Framework Architecture

The OPC-UA design goals aim for platform independence, functional equivalence, and data interoperability through information modeling, extensibility, and security. Platform independence is achieved by porting the OPC-UA framework layer to multiple operating systems (e.g., Microsoft Windows, Apple OSX, Android, Linux) and hardware platforms based on X86, ARM, PLC, and others. As long as there is a framework instance that runs on the OS and hardware of interest, IIoT device interoperability exists.

Functional equivalence is the idea that OPC-UA applications operate consistently regardless of which operating system and hardware platform was used. There are six areas of functional equivalence defined:

(1)   Discovery: Devices search for peer devices, servers, and networks the OPC-UA application needs to perform its function. Plug-and-play behavior can be supported but requires application involvement to anticipate the type of objects and operations needed.

(2)   Address space layout: Devices implement a hierarchical object model where files and folders contain data that can be read/written across the network from one node to another.

(3)   Access control: Data objects have access control policies that control reading and writing on a per node basis.

(4)   Subscriptions: Client nodes can subscribe to data objects monitoring and receiving updates to data that changes. Client nodes may specify filtering criteria that are applied to monitored data values when determining when it is appropriate to notify the client.

(5)   Events: Client nodes can receive asynchronous responses when data values satisfy a specified criterion.

(6)   Methods: Client nodes execute subroutines based on server-defined criteria.

Information models define data access semantics. Each information model is independent from other information models, meaning each model has different access control, state, and quality contexts. The OPC-UA framework has several built-in information models (Figure 2-26): Data Access (DA), Alarms and Conditions (AC), Historical Access (HA), and Programmable state machines (Prog). The Data Access model supports live (near real-time) access to sensor data. Each data element has a *name* and *value*. There is also a *timestamp* to indicate when the data was read and a *quality* component that determines if the data is valid.

Historical Access (HA) data is not real-time data, and there could be a deep history of values stored. SCADA and other systems support devices that monitor sensor readings over a longer period of time. HA objects can transfer historical data from sensor to framework node easily. Framework application may apply analytics to HA data to gain additional insights into operations over a period of time.

Alarms and Conditions (AC) data doesn't have a current value. Rather it maintains subscriptions to other data where subscribers may specify conditions in which to send notifications and updates. Notifications have a *timestamp* but do not have *name* and *quality* attributes.

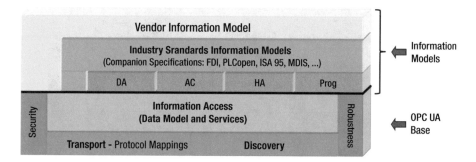

Figure 2-26. *OPC-UA information modeling framework*

Extensibility is achieved through a multilayered information model that supports vendor-specific, industry standard data models and native OPC-UA defined data models. Companion specifications define what information is exchanged, while OPC-UA Information Access layer defines how information is exchanged.

OPC-UA Security

Security is built around two framework layers (Figure 2-27). The **session layer** addresses user authorization, authentication, and access control based on role and permissions. The **secure channel layer** provides message encryption and integrity protection when exchanged between nodes. It also can be used to authenticate applications that connect with the OPC-UA framework. The security channel layer relies on TLS (Transport Layer Security) using HTTPS. Though HTTP is also supported. OPC-UA relies exclusively on X.509v3 certificates to authenticate and authorize users and applications.

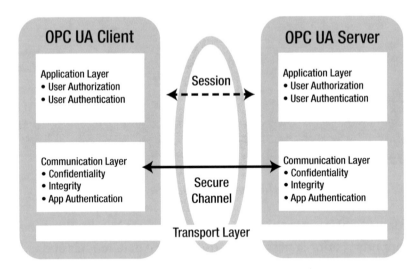

Figure 2-27. *OPC-UA secure communications*

Auditing is also supported in OPC-UA security supporting forensic investigation.

OPC-UA applications undergo a two-step access process where they first access servers and second access data. Authentication policy is expressed in terms of server or client identity, while data access is expressed in terms of read/write permissions on data objects.

The German government BSI (Bundesamt für Sicherheit in der Informationstechnik) did an extensive security evaluation of OPC-UA to determine if it is safe for using in German industry. Their conclusion was that it was designed with a focus on security and does not contain systemic security vulnerabilities. This is an important observation because, unlike other framework approaches we've reviewed, security was integral to the framework design.

However, the way in which hardware security capabilities such as secure storage, cryptographic algorithm implementation, and trusted execution environment enforcement are left as an exercise to implementers. Given the platform independence design goal, it is possible if not likely different platforms hosting OPC-UA frameworks could have very different attack resistance properties. At the time of this writing, OPC-UA did not implement attestation mechanisms that describe implementation choices linking framework security to hardware and platform security.

Data Distribution Service (DDS)

The Data Distribution Service[44] (DDS) is a connectivity framework designed for industrial process control. It is standardized through the Object Management Group[45] (OMG) founded in 1989. The OMG is an industry standards consortium that produces and maintains specifications for interoperable, portable, and reusable enterprise applications in distributed, heterogeneous environments.

DDS v1.0 was published December 2004. DDS v1.4 was published March 2015. Companion specifications relating to security, remote procedure call (RPC), and other topics are continually updated. There are several proprietary and open source implementations of DDS. OpenDDS[46] is a popular open source implementation.

The primary design goal is summarized as the efficient and robust delivery of the right information to the right place at the right time. To accomplish this, a data-centric publish-subscribe (DCPS) approach was taken. The target applications expect the DCPS framework to be high-performance, efficient, and predictable. To accomplish these goals, DDS (a) allows middleware to preallocate resources to minimize dynamic resource allocations, (b) avoids properties that require the use of unbounded or hard-to-predict resources, and (c) minimizes the need to make copies of the data. DDS is a strongly typed system, meaning the programmer directly manipulates constructs that represent data. Interfaces are safer due to rigorous type checking, and execution code is more efficient because type checking enforcement is done at compile time.

---

[44]www.omg.org/spec/category/data-distribution-service/
[45]www.omg.org
[46]http://opendds.org

DDS consists of four main entities:

- **Domains** (Figure 2-28): Define a global context
  in which data, data readers, and data writers have
  ubiquitous access. The domain defines the naming
  scope for identifiers. Cross-domain interactions may
  require disambiguation using a domain identity.

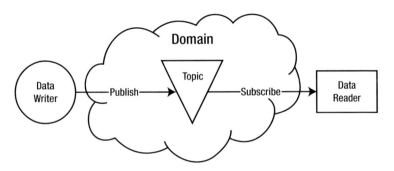

Figure 2-28. *DDS publish-subscribe data model*

- **Topics** (Figure 2-28): Are objects that conceptually fit
  between data writers and data readers. They define
  the context in which publish-subscribe interactions
  may take place. Topic names are unambiguous within
  the domain and contain a type and QoS component
  (Figure 2-29). Type and QoS attributes apply to the
  data referenced via the topic context. QoS attributes
  are themselves DDS Topics. Topics allow expression of
  both functional and nonfunctional information.

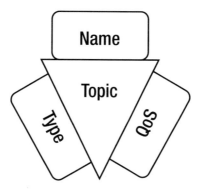

Figure 2-29. *DDS Topics have QoS integration*

- **Data Writers**: Correspond to publishers of a publish-subscribe interaction pattern and must create a Publisher instance object in order to accept subscribers or to prepare and publish data. Data writers communicate data to its publisher to initiate a publication.

- **Data Readers**: Correspond to the subscribers of a publish-subscribe interaction pattern and must create a Subscriber instance object in order to register to receive publications. Data readers communicate interest in a topic to initiate subscription registration.

Quality of Service (QoS) is a fundamental design consideration that is intimately integrated into the DDS object model. Each topic may consist of multiple data values distinguished by a key value. Different data values with the same key value represent successive values for the same data instance (e.g., a temperature sensor may maintain a short history of temperature values sensed over an interval). Different data values with different key values represent different data instances (e.g., multiple temperature sensors). QoS and type attributes apply to data instances. QoS interactions follow a *requested-offered* pattern where a data reader requests a particular QoS policy and the data writer tries to accommodate the request.

The overall flow of a DDS interaction begins with domain participants (readers and writers) joining a domain (Figure 2-30). Publishers produce data to a data partition object, while subscribers retrieve data from the data partition object. Data writers offer a QoS promise on published data based on the data reader's requested QoS level.

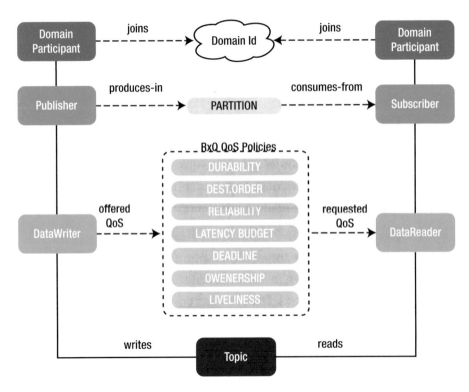

Figure 2-30. *DDS data interaction flow*

The DDS standard defines the set of possible QoS policies. These include the following QoS types:

- USER_DATA: Allows the application to attach additional information to the data object so that remote entities can obtain additional context that relates to application-specific purposes. This aids in refining discovery queries and allows selection of appropriate security credentials or enforcement of application-specific security policies.

- TOPIC_DATA: Allows the application to attach additional information to the topic object to facilitate discovery for application-specific purposes.

- GROUP_DATA: Allows the application to attach additional information to the Publisher or Subscriber entity so that application-specific policies may regulate the way data reader listeners and data writer listeners behave.

- DURABILITY: Allows data to be read or written even when there are no current subscribers or publishers. Multiple degrees of data volatility can be defined.

- DURABILITY_SERVICE: Allows configuration of a service that implements durability attributes.

- PRESENTATION: Controls the scope of access given various data interdependencies. Coherent_access controls whether the service will preserve groupings of changes made by a publisher. Ordered_access controls whether the service will preserve the order of changes. Access_scope controls the scope of access in terms of data instance, topic, or group.

- DEADLINE: Controls the interval in which a topic is expected to be updated. Publishers must supply updates within the deadline interval, and subscribers can set a timer to check for most recent updates based on the interval.

- LATENCY_BUDGET: Allows applications to specify the urgency of the message by specifying a latency duration.

- OWNERSHIP: Controls how data writer objects interact with published data. *Shared* access means multiple writers can update the data item. *Exclusive* access means only one writer can update it. SHARED-EXCLUSIVE means multiple updaters coordinate their updates.

- LIVELINESS: Controls mechanisms for determining if network entities are still "alive."

- TIME_BASED_FILTER: Allows data readers to see at most one change to a topic at a minimum periodicity.

- PARTITION: Allows a logical partition inside a "physical" partition. Physical partitioning may have safety and security benefits, while logical partitions may have performance benefits.

- RELIABILITY: Allows reliability to be defined in terms of levels, BEST_EFFORT being the lowest and RELIABLE being the highest.

- TRANSPORT_PRIORITY: Allows alignment with transport layer QoS capabilities.

- LIFESPAN: Allows specification of when a data value becomes stale.

- DESTINATION_ORDER: Controls how each subscriber resolves the final value of the data instance when written by multiple writers.

- HISTORY: Controls when data instance changes before it is communicated to data readers. KEEP_LAST means the server keeps the most recent update. KEEP_ALL means the server will attempt to deliver all instances of changed data.

- RESOURCE_LIMITS: Controls how many resources can be applied to achieve quality of service objectives.

- ENTITY_FACTORY: Controls the flexibility of nodes in their ability to replicate or produce additional entity instances.

- DATA_LIFECYCLE: Controls how persistent or temporal data are relative to the availability of either the data writer or data reader.

DDS QoS design is one of its features that most distinguishes it from other IoT and IIoT frameworks. QoS mechanisms have both safety and security implications in that they improve data integrity – goals common to both disciplines. QoS mechanisms must be implemented in ways that ensure the integrity of the QoS system. Otherwise, the expected quality of service is suspect. Hence, trustworthy implementation of the DDS framework is essential to realizing the QoS richness anticipated by its designers.

DDS Framework Architecture

The DDS framework layering (Figure 2-31) consists of several layers beginning with an IP network layer. TCP and UDP transports make up the next layer followed by the DDS Wire Protocol for Real-Time Publish-Subscribe (DDSI-RTPS) layer. The DDS layer defines the data model abstractions described earlier. The DDS framework defines several vertically integrated technologies for security, remote procedure call (RPC), and extensions to its data typing system.

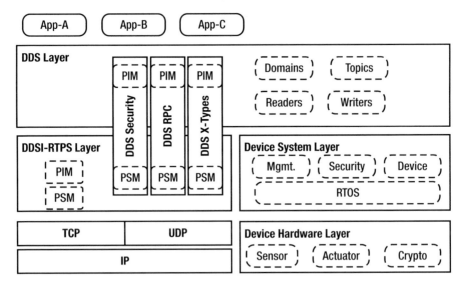

Figure 2-31. *DDS framework layering*

Implied by the DDS layering architecture is a Device System layer that implements the IoT device capabilities including native security and manageability capabilities. These capabilities depend on a Device Hardware layer that must have ties to the actual sensor, actuator, security, or other hardware features. The Device System layer exposes native device capabilities to the DDS framework through available interfaces. Different DDS framework implementations may make different implementation choices regarding how to best integrate the framework with a specific device.

The DDS specification helps isolate platform-specific elements of DDS from platform-independent elements by specifying a platform-independent model (PIM) and a platform-specific model (PSM) of DDS structures. The PSM definition ensures porting efforts result in minimal impact to the semantics and operation of the PIM while still allowing quality integration with the native platform.

The PIMs and DDS layer ensure DDS applications can expect a consistent environment for sharing information that is strongly typed and syntactically interoperable. A summary of DDS application properties is as follows:

- Applications can autonomously and asynchronously read and write data that is decoupled spatially and temporally.

- DDS data is loosely coupled due to virtualized data spaces that are designed for scalability, fault tolerance, and heterogeneity.

- As with all distributed systems, the data model must consider a data consistency model. DDS defines *data spaces* that tolerate inconsistent data but *eventually* becomes consistent. Data readers will eventually see a write but may not observe it at the same time.

- DDS discovery model isolates discovery from network topology and connectivity details so that applications may focus on data objects that are most relevant to application objectives.

- The DDS data model allows location transparency since topics, data readers, and data writers are conceptually separated from the underlying physical devices and network nodes. Integration across Cloud, enterprise, plant and mission control, shop floor, or device networks doesn't require redefinition of data syntax and semantics.

- DDS data spaces (aka domains) are decentralized. A DDS system may host multiple data spaces that involve readers and writers from any data space. There is no central point of failure.

125

- Connectivity among DDS entities is adaptive, meaning connections can be established and torn down dynamically. The underlying communications infrastructure can optimize for the most efficient data sharing approach.

DDS domains have global data space (Figure 2-32), meaning topics are visible to all data writers and readers that are members of the same domain. Data writers and readers may be members of multiple domains simultaneously to allow interaction with topics from different domains. It is even possible to construct a domain broker that gives the illusion of the same topic appearing in separate domains.

DDS domain interactions can become rather complex. This complexity may be especially appreciated when an access control policy is needed that places restrictions on various data writer and data reader interactions that span multiple domains.

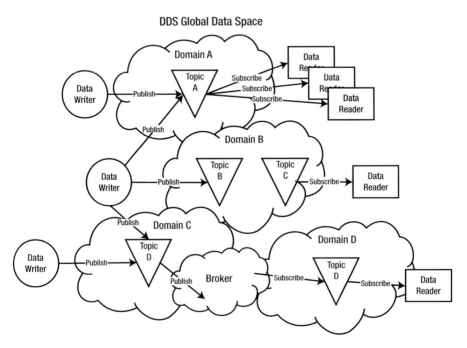

Figure 2-32. *DDS Global Data Space example*

DDS Security

DDS security consists of three main elements (Figure 2-33): (1) RTPS messages with security enveloping structures, (2) token-based security context, and (3) pluggable security modules.

Security Enveloping

Security is closely integrated into the DDS data model. Cleartext DDS data messages are encapsulated within DDS enveloping structures that support encryption, integrity, authorization, and authentication. The RTPS system uses the security enveloping structures as its main messaging structure so that the real-time publish-subscribe optimizations are preserved even when security is applied.

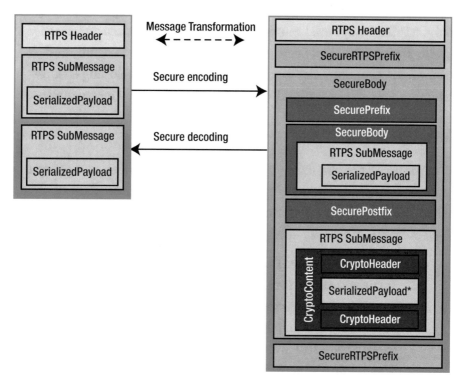

Figure 2-33. *RTPS message encoding/decoding with secure encapsulation*

A cleartext RTPS message consists of an RTPS header and one or more RTPS submessages each containing a serialized payload. To prepare a cleartext message for delivery over an unsecure channel, the cleartext message must be transformed into a secure RTPS message. Figure 2-32 illustrates the transformation. Integrity-protected RTPS submessages are wrapped by a secure body and have a secure prefix and secure postfix component. The prefix defines the integrity protection mechanism, security context, and algorithms. The secure postfix contains a hash or signature of the secure body. If the RTPS submessage requires confidentiality protection, the serialized payload of the submessage is encrypted, forming a CryptoContent element consisting of a CryptoHeader and CryptoFooter. The CryptoHeader defines the encryption method, security context, and algorithms. The CryptoFooter contains the ciphertext version of the serialized payload. All the RTPS submessages belonging to the RTPS message are bound together using another layer of security enveloping consisting of SecureRTPSPrefix, SecureRTPSPostFix, and SecureBody elements. The second layer of security enveloping ensures submessages can't be omitted, appended, or substituted by an attacker.

Security Tokens

All of the privileges obtainable by DDS entities are described using a *security token* data structure. There are tokens that facilitate secure discovery, participant permissions, and secure message exchange. Security tokens allow exchange of security information using the DDS messaging capability.

- **Discovery tokens**: Facilitate establishment of security contexts for subsequent secure interactions. The *IdentityToken* contains summary information of a domain participant in a manner that can be externalized and propagated using DDS discovery. The *IdentityStatusToken* contains authentication information of a domain participant in a manner that can be externalized and propagated securely. The *PermissionsToken* contains summary information on the permissions for a domain participant in a manner that can be externalized and propagated over DDS discovery.

- **Permissions tokens**: The PermissionsCredentialToken encodes the permissions and access information for a domain participant in a manner that can be externalized and sent over a network. It is used by the access control plugin which manages domain access and specific reader-writer interactions.

- **Message tokens**: The *CryptoToken* contains all the information necessary to construct a set of keys to be used to encrypt and/or sign plain text transforming it into ciphertext or to reverse those operations. The *MessageToken* is a superclass of several message tokens used to maintain security context when multiple message exchanges are required such as authentication and key exchange protocols.

Security Plugin Modules

The DDS framework takes a modular approach to security so that platform-specific capabilities can be exposed to and utilized by DDS entities. There are five pluggable security modules (Figure 2-34): (1) authentication, (2) access control, (3) cryptography, (4) logging, and (5) data tagging.

- **Authentication plugin**: The principal joining a DDS domain must authenticate to a domain controller, and peer DDS participants may be required to perform mutual authentication and establish shared secrets.

- **Access control plugin**: Decides whether a principal is allowed to perform a protected operation.

- **Cryptography plugin**: Generates keys and performs key exchange, encryption, and decryption operations. Computes digests and verifies message authentication codes. Signs and verifies signatures on messages.

- **Logging plugin**: Logs all security relevant events.

- **Data tagging plugin**: Adds data tags for each data sample.

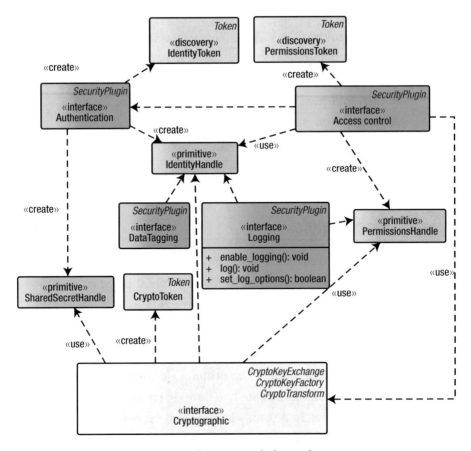

Figure 2-34. *DDS security plugin module architecture*

DDS security offers a comprehensive well-integrated security solution that aligns well with DDS design philosophy focusing on data and publisher-subscriber interactions. Security is modular, enabling platform-specific services and hardware to be effectively utilized and incorporated.

DDS quality of service parameters though originally designed to meet industrial safety requirements may also help achieve security objectives. The OWNERSHIP and PARTITION QoS parameters capture expected data sharing and partitioning semantics. Security mechanisms used for data isolation and protection may be useful toward meeting these quality expectations. LIFESPAN and HISTORY properties describe data persistence characteristics that inform regarding object reuse requirements and which data may require stronger confidentiality and integrity protection.

However, DDS goals toward heterogeneous operation make assumptions regarding the quality and condition of security plugins. An attacker might easily compromise the plugin or spoof the plugin interface allowing an attack plugin to take control. Peer nodes are not easily able to detect such attacks. For example, DDS doesn't appear to support attestation protocols that would query a peer principal's security subsystem to provide proof of device provenance and integrity of the system firmware, software, plugins, and DDS framework layers.

Framework Gateways

This chapter has focused almost exclusively on open standard IoT framework solutions, some of which have been omitted here for brevity. There are tens if not hundreds of *brownfield* frameworks with varying degrees of openness and standardization, but many are specific to an industry vertical. Cloud-connected IoT is another category of IoT framework integration mostly ignored here as well. Although many of the open standard frameworks claim interoperability with cloud environments, the IoT cloud ecosystem largely takes a *walled-garden* approach.[47] Most have a proprietary IoT framework or support both a proprietary and open framework solutions with integration to their proprietary cloud back end. Some of these include Amazon Web Services (AWS) IoT, Apple Homekit,[48] Bosch IoT Suite, Cisco IoT Cloud Connect, General Electric Predix, Google Cloud, IBM Watson Cloud, Microsoft Azure, Oracle IoT Cloud, Salesforce IoT, Samsung ARTIK Cloud Services,[49] and SAP IoT Platform. Dell's EdgeX Foundry[50] takes a slightly different approach enabling services at the *edge*, where edge refers to both the edge of the IoT network and the edge of the cloud hosting environments. The ecosystem that traditionally supplies the *pipe* between IoT device and Cloud is interested in *moving up* the IoT stack to add more value. IoT framework technologies help enable that mobility.

The IoT framework standards organizations seem to understand that a multitude of "standard" IoT frameworks hinders one of the main motivations for IoT frameworks – interoperability! Industry efforts to consolidate frameworks have taken place already. The AllSeen Alliance and UPnP Forum have merged with the Open Connectivity Foundation. The OpenFog Consortium joined forces with the IIC and the IPSO Alliance was acquired by the Open Mobile Alliance (OMA) to form OMA SpecWorks.[51] Collaborations between framework standards organizations also help resolve interoperability challenges. For example, the OCF is thought to be working on an OCF[52] to OneM2M bridge[53] (aka framework gateway).

---

[47] www.electronicdesign.com/embedded-revolution/iot-frameworks-ties-bind

[48] https://developer.apple.com/homekit/

[49] https://artik.cloud

[50] www.edgexfoundry.org

[51] www.businesswire.com/news/home/20180327005208/en/
IPSO-Alliance-Merges-Open-Mobile-Alliance-Form

[52] https://wiki.iotivity.org/bridging_project

[53] https://openconnectivity.org/draftspecs/Cleveland/CR2595_Cleveland_
Bridging_Security_20181004.pdf

But these efforts are solutions to an interoperability problem created by the industry's eager response to an IoT interoperability problem. Ironically, the "success" of IoT seems to have created a more complex environment for IoT interoperability as both standard and proprietary "connectivity" frameworks and toolkits proliferate. Framework gateways naturally come to the rescue, but at what cost to usability, manageability, and security?

Framework Gateway Architecture

This section outlines several approaches for gatewaying (aka bridging) IoT frameworks, considers security implications of each, and suggests an idealized architecture for secure IoT framework gateways.

Type I Framework Gateway

A type I framework gateway (Figure 2-35) combines unmodified framework gateways using a common framework gateway application. The application performs all necessary object model translations and data structure mappings to achieve interoperability. The application (i.e., developer) must have intimate understanding of data object syntax and semantics for both (all?) sides of the translation. Some objects in a first IoT network may not have a suitable corresponding counterpart (sensor, actuator, controller) in the other IoT network for the applications to simply "wire" them together. Instead, it must create an abstraction that approximates an object that is recognizable and considered to be a safe alternative interaction. For example, a dimmable light bulb in Network A may support 10 levels of brightness, while a dimmer control in Network B supports 100 levels of control. The gateway application provides the mapping function that divides by 10 in one direction and multiplies by 10 in the other direction. In some cases, there may not be a reasonable mapping, and the gateway application developer may take some other approach such as exposing the devices to a console interface so that a user can resolve any mapping conflicts or ambiguities. Polyglot[54] is an example technology that aids in the development of type I IoT framework gateway applications.

Type II Framework Gateway

A type II framework gateway (Figure 2-35) expects the network Connectivity, Node Interaction, and Data Object layers are dissimilar, but there is a Data Object layer mapping object that relates Framework A objects with Framework B objects. A gateway application supplies administrative control such as installing, updating, and monitoring an object translation component that exists within the Data Object layer. Typically, designers of each interoperating framework must collaborate to identify semantically similar but syntactically dissimilar elements and their mapping functions. The design collaboration may reveal disconnected design semantics as well that may be clarified in related gateway-specific specifications or may result in specification revisions that clarify ambiguities. For example, one framework might expect all objects to be discoverable through its hosting endpoint device, while another framework might expect discovery is handled using a dedicated discovery service. The object translation layer defines the framework-specific discovery conventions so that endpoint devices can function unmodified. This might involve having the gateway device advertising itself as a discovery service operating on behalf of devices represented in a foreign network. The OCF-AllJoyn bridging specification[55] is an example type II framework gateway that supports bidirectional bridging and device

---

[54]https://github.com/UniversalDevicesInc/polyglot-v2
[55]https://openconnectivity.org/specs/OCF_Bridging_Specification_v1.3.0.pdf

interactions within a common operational domain. See the"Security Considerations for Framework Gateways" section for more insight on interdomain bridging considerations.

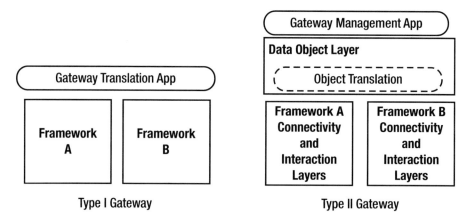

Figure 2-35. *Layering architecture for type I and type II framework gateways*

Type III Framework Gateway

A type III framework gateway (Figure 2-36) anticipates a common data object layer is in place. However, because the lower layers are dissimilar, not all data objects will be common. Therefore a data object translation capability is also required. The Connectivity and Node Interaction layers are dissimilar, but there is a message translation model that relates the interface definition model for Framework A to the interface definition model for Framework B. An example message translation operation might relate publish-subscribe messages defined by Message Queuing Telemetry Transport (MQTT)[56] to the publish-subscribe model defined by eXtensible Messaging and Presence

---

[56]MQTT Version 3.1.1. Edited by Andrew Banks and Rahul Gupta. 29 September 2014. OASIS Standard. Latest version: http://docs.oasis-open.org/mqtt/mqtt/v3.1.1/mqtt-v3.1.1.html

Protocol (XMPP).[57] Another example mapping technology is the Internet Engineering Task Force (IETF) OSCORE[58] specification that maps HTTP message security to CoAP messages and vice versa.

A traditional framework may not be regarded as a type III gateway depending on the set of protocols and message types the framework supports. If a framework includes support for both HTTP and CoAP, for example, then mapping between may be a normal IoT framework function. However, given Framework A support for only HTTP and Framework B support for only CoAP, the type III gateway translation comes into play.

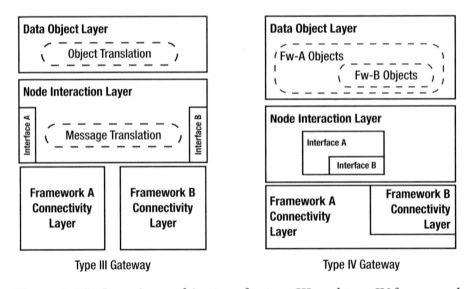

Figure 2-36. *Layering architecture for type III and type IV framework gateways*

---

[57]Internet Engineering Task Force (IETF) RFC 6120, March 2011. `https://xmpp.org/rfcs/rfc6120.html`

[58]Internet Engineering Task Force (IETF) "draft-ietf-core-object-security-15," Expires March 4, 2019. `https://datatracker.ietf.org/doc/draft-ietf-core-object-security/`

Type IV Framework Gateway

The fourth framework gateway class, type IV, considers the case where Framework A is a superset of Framework B. The superset and subset frameworks remain unmodified, but applications may interact with devices from either framework seamlessly. The gateway function exists when Framework A objects are exposed to Framework B and when Framework A peers are different from Framework B peers. Though subtle, this is a system boundary crossing that requires security controls. An example of this scenario is OneM2M where LWM2M supplies the device management capabilities for a OneM2M framework. Nevertheless, LWM2M also may stand alone as an independent IoT framework. The type IV framework gateway has an object model where the Framework A object model is flexible enough to encompass the Framework B object model. Likewise, the interface definitions in the Node Interaction layer have a superset-subset relationship, and the connectivity layers are similarly encompassing. The gateway function may be provided as an application of the framework or may have embedded mapping operations. The OCF framework resource naming specification allows resources to be identified using a Uniform Resource Identifier (URI)[59] of arbitrary nesting depth. A LWM2M object identifier is a URI that is constrained to two layers of nesting, and object names are numeric. The LWM2M namespace fits within the OCF namespace; hence an OCF to LWM2M gateway function could be implemented.

---

[59]Internet Engineering Task Force (IETF), RFC 3986, January 2005. `https://tools.ietf.org/html/rfc3986`

Security Considerations for Framework Gateways

Framework gateways may facilitate interdomain interactions in addition to facilitating interoperability between dissimilar IoT frameworks. Security at the framework gateway should address at least two important security questions: (1) Does the gateway bridge network domains and to what extent is the gateway trusted to perform these duties? (2) Where in the framework layering do authentication, authorization, integrity, and confidentiality protections begin and end for a given message transiting the gateway?

The Industrial IoT Consortium (IIC) describes brownfield-greenfield security integration in terms of security gateways (Figure 2-37). In this model, the gateway occupies both an interoperability and a security function. Legacy IoT endpoints may enjoy intra-brownfield interactions (often without native security), but when protocol directs interaction with the Secure Endpoints, the Security Gateway must augment legacy messages with message protections. This entails encrypting or signing messages before the Secure Gateway forwards Legacy Endpoint messages to Secure Endpoints. It may also require authenticating Secure Endpoints before allowing them to access Legacy Endpoints.

The Security Gateway function ensures crossing a network domain doesn't weaken security. Security gateways may be expected to perform the following security operations:

- Authenticate endpoints to the gateway and gateway to the endpoints.

- Authenticate endpoints from a foreign domain to endpoints in the local domain. This may require creation of a virtual endpoint on the gateway device if interior endpoints can't support the needed security capabilities.

- Integrity and confidentiality protect messages passing through the gateway. The gateway may need to decrypt then re-encrypt using native domain's recognized security associations, security algorithms, and protocols. On rare occasion domains have all these security elements in common.

- Authorize access to objects in a local domain by endpoints from a peer domain.

- Inspect and log activity between the domains.

- Establish endpoint credentials in the peer network environment. Different domains may have dissimilar security services for authentication, authorization, and key management. The gateway may be required to host security services on behalf of a local domain so that a peer domain can utilize its chosen set of security services.

- Perform data structure translation and protocol mapping functions previously described. Modification to data objects and protocol message that are integrity and confidentiality protected necessarily implies the gateway is authorized and trusted to perform these transformations.

In general, the gateway is expected to be one of the most trusted nodes in the network. Since it connects multiple domains, it likely needs to be the most trustworthy node across all the connected domains.

To achieve the preceding security goals, a Security Object layer (Figure 2-40) is needed in addition to the framework's Data Object layer. The Security Object layer must be common to all domains that connect through the framework gateway; otherwise, there is little confidence that security for the domains is correct.

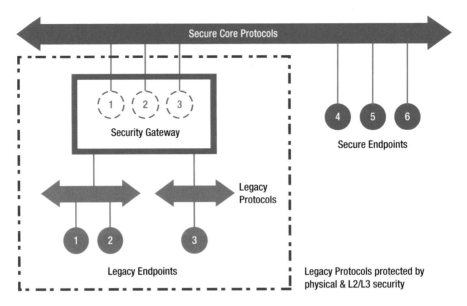

Figure 2-37. *Framework gateway as a secure endpoint/proxy to unsecure legacy endpoints*

Security Endpoints Within the Gateway

When a message enters a framework gateway, it arrives with security protections specific to its native network. Those protections terminate somewhere within the framework gateway where it is assumed the gateway will preserve the security properties throughout until the message emerges on another network where the destination network's native protections are applied. The framework gateway must satisfy authentication, authorization, integrity, and confidentiality protections in a manner that is consistent with both source and destination networks as the message transits through the gateway. The place where the network's native protection mechanism ends or begins is referred to as a *security endpoint.* The place where confidentiality protection (i.e., encryption) ends (or begins) is the confidentiality endpoint. The place where network native authorization protection ends is the *authorization endpoint* and

140

so forth. The various framework gateway types have different semantics and make different assumptions about security endpoint termination and origination. This section highlights some of these differences.

Security Endpoints in Type I Gateways

The security endpoints in a type I gateway (denoted by up arrow and down arrow in Figure 2-38) could in theory terminate at or near the application interface since the gateway translation and mapping functions are applied at the application level. Given a scenario where security protections are applied directly to framework objects rather than to protocols or interfaces, the data confidentiality and integrity protections may persist until the last possible moment before the framework hands off the data to the application.

Most IoT frameworks require security endpoint termination within the framework layers or in protocol layers beneath so that the framework data objects can be manipulated. This implies the data will be unprotected through some portion of framework layering before handing off to the Gateway Translation Application and again in the reverse flow. The security expectation for type I gateways is the framework architecture must strictly isolate resources belonging to Framework A from resources belonging to Framework B. Attacks originating from Framework A should be ineffective at compromising Framework B resources without first compromising the gateway or the Framework Translation Application. This simplifying assumption can be quite powerful because there are few if any exceptional cases. Exceptional cases have a tendency to expose security weaknesses that lead to exploits.

Note that within each framework context, native network operations may require *authentication endpoints* for network packet delivery that terminate within the framework. This differs from security endpoints associated with application layer message confidentiality and integrity protection.

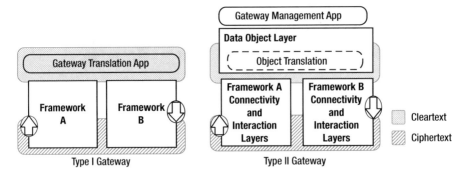

Figure 2-38. *Security considerations of type I and type II gateways*

Security Endpoints in Type II Gateways

A type II gateway requires translation at the Data Object layer implying security endpoints must exist at the base of the Data Object layer or below. The gateway application largely doesn't participate except to provide administrative oversight; hence there isn't an expectation the Gateway App should be privy to object data.

Framework A resources at the Interaction and Connectivity layers are strictly isolated from Framework B. However, because the object translation logic is shared across Network A and Network B, the Data Object layer, compromise of this layer implies access to both A and B networks. The authors feel the Data Object layer should be a third isolation environment where access to Framework A or Framework B isolation environment doesn't imply, automatically, access to the Data Object layer isolation environment. Rather, the respective isolation environments should have well-understood interfaces and semantics for crossing environment boundaries. Object translation steps necessarily invoke environment boundary-crossing primitives.

Note that in cases where framework design choices result in a security endpoint terminating in the connectivity or interaction layer, for example, if Transport Layer Security (TLS) is used for confidentiality. The isolation environment must preserve confidentiality of data as it passes between the various isolation environment boundaries.

Security Endpoints in Type III Gateways

A type III gateway (Figure 2-39) requires message protocol translation at the Node Interaction layer and may require object translation at the Data Object layer. Managing security endpoints that terminate at different layers can be tricky. If confidentiality endpoint occurs within the Data Object layer, then message translation can proceed in the Node Interaction layer since message payloads are opaque at this layer. Nevertheless, an authentication or authorization endpoint is required at this layer that authorizes a boundary crossing, for example, from Framework A to Framework B.

However, if A and B disagree on data object format, then the payload transits to the Data Object layer for object translation before it is repackaged into a Framework B message body. The Data Object layer must correctly apply confidentiality endpoint processing, possibly resulting in application of a Framework B–specific confidentiality endpoint before transitioning back to the Node Interaction layer. All of this security context must be preserved and must resist confused deputy attacks.

Isolation of respective connectivity layer environments from Node Interaction and Data Object environments seems reasonable from a security isolation perspective but appears concerning from a performance optimization perspective.

Security Endpoints in Type IV Gateways

A type IV gateway (Figure 2-39) expects data objects, interfaces, message formats, and network connectivity are a subset of the first framework. Therefore, data object, interface, and message translation might not even be needed. If it is needed, it occurs on the context of the superset framework, meaning the security endpoints that are valid for the subset framework are also valid for the superset framework. This is a nice simplifying assumption that allows for flexible isolation strategies. The point where the security endpoint begins can largely be configurable.

One important consideration is whether or not interaction with Framework B allows access of superset data objects not normally part of subset objects by Framework B. Given this scenario, the boundary crossing occurs at the line where superset and subset objects intersect. Gateway isolation mechanisms should allow separation of resources along these lines. Success or failure at applying the isolation mechanism falls largely along two vectors: (a) the degree of modularity found in the implementation of the frameworks and (b) the level of granularity with which the isolation mechanism is able to conscribe resources.

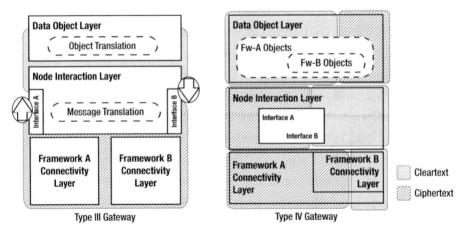

Figure 2-39. *Security considerations of type III and type IV gateways*

Security Framework Gateway Architecture

This section describes an idealized security framework gateway architecture (Figure 2-40) that more easily would support the security, isolation, performance, and flexibility requirements needed to facilitate framework gateway challenges. The meaning of an *idealized* architecture is it attempts to describe IoT framework architecture where security is central to the design and integrated from the start. It may serve as a guidepost from which to better evaluate security hardware and software solutions presented in subsequent chapters.

A prominent feature in our idealized framework architecture is the addition of the Security Object layer containing commonly understood and specified security objects and data model representations. In our experience, many IoT framework architectures cite industry standards such as X.509, TLS, and COSE in response to questions of security interoperability. However, they do not capture the semantics of what it means to be secure. There have been attempts at defining security policy languages such as XACML and SAML, but these, or something similar, have not yet been integrated into IoT frameworks.

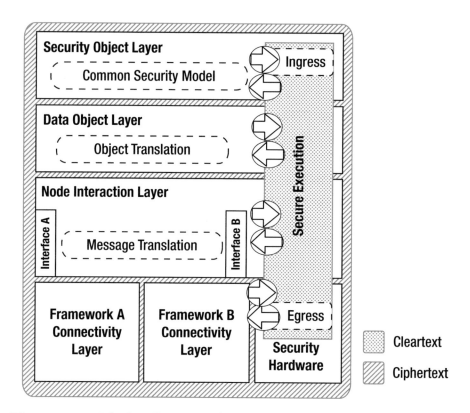

Figure 2-40. *Idealized security framework gateway*

Secure execution is another component to our idealized architecture. Secure execution is a hardware-supported mode of execution enterable when a security endpoint in the framework is required to perform security-related functions and exits upon completion. Since a security endpoint could exist at any framework layer, secure execution can be entered at any framework layer. Framework data are in cleartext while in the secure environment and ideally, confidentiality and integrity protected while outside the environment.

Framework context is maintained across ingress and egress transitions so that layer crossings can be recognized as these may correspond to network boundary crossings in a gatewaying usage context. The Security Object layer use of the Secure Execution resource preserves its isolation properties with respect to the other layers. Data passing between framework layers, which have layer isolation requirements, relies on the Secure Execution environment technology to enforce isolation requirements, these include decryption upon ingress, tenant-specific resource isolation while in the SE environment and encryption upon egress.

Although the authors are not aware of a secure execution technology that fully implements the idealized framework architecture, there are a few technologies that come close. For example, Intel Software Guard Extensions (SGX), ARM TrustZone, and virtualization have compelling potential. Chapter 3 explains in greater detail various Intel hardware security features and how they apply to IoT.

Summary

IoT frameworks occupy an important position in IoT system design as an effective strategy for empowering IoT application developers to more easily construct rich distributed IoT applications. Many of the connectivity challenges resulting from fragmented brownfield systems are hidden behind IoT frameworks. IoT applications simply expect the dissimilarities in machine control networks, process control systems, manufacturing execution systems, and cloud integration are conveniently "simplified" for all intents and purposes.

Nevertheless, the IoT ecosystem hasn't settled on a single IoT framework technology that satisfies every industry and meets every need. Neither is there consensus over standardization of open IoT frameworks as there are multiple framework standards efforts. New and existing proprietary approaches also seem to have gained ground as the size of IoT grows. The recent proliferation of IoT frameworks, toolkits, and middleware combined with existing brownfield IoT suggests greater challenges to come for interoperable applications in a heterogeneous distributed world of IoT.

IoT framework standards organizations seem to recognize these challenges and have responded by merging organizations and standards. They have developed gatewaying and bridging technologies that let framework application interoperate through dissimilar frameworks. Noted mergers include OCF, AllJoyn, UPnP, IPSO, OMA, IIC, and OCF. There is continued interest in framework gateway interoperability among remaining frameworks, but it isn't clear that the industry needs to converge to a single or even a small number of frameworks as security, safety, reliability, and other factors may in fact motivate keeping some parts of IoT systems separated.

Framework gateways are positioned on the edges of IoT networks addressing interoperability needs but also should be considered the most trusted security control points since crossing organizational domains often coincides with translating from one IoT network protocol to another.

This section highlighted several IoT frameworks showing how various IoT system integration and interoperation requirements may be addressed. We considered challenges facing framework application interoperation in an environment of multiple frameworks. The industry's eager embrace of IoT frameworks has led to the need for framework gateways that reassert the desire for interoperability, but also for security. We further consider ways to secure framework gateways looking at various approaches and trade-offs.

In summary, frameworks appear to offer significant value for enabling interoperable IoT applications by hiding much of the complexity of multiple connectivity technologies, messaging solutions that incorporate multiple hundreds or thousands of nodes, and data schemas that present consistent, declarative, and vendor-neutral expressions of IoT objects. We've shown that frameworks are great tools to manage IoT device complexity, but the security robustness or hardening can only be achieved by leveraging the underlying HW security capabilities dealt with in detail in Chapter 3 and are exposed via API and different framework and protocol layers by the SW as detailed in Chapter 4. The external interactions that an IoT device experiences during the lifecycle depend upon the stimulus from myriad connectivity interfaces, and this is dealt with in detail in Chapter 5.

CHAPTER 3

Base Platform Security Hardware Building Blocks

Every distraction is a possibility, Every downfall is an opportunity.

—Ria Cheruvu

Historically, the attacks on platforms have been transitioning from application-level software (SW) to user mode SW to kernel mode SW to firmware (FW) and now hardware (HW). The frequency of HW- and FW-level vulnerabilities increased substantially from 2003 to 2019 and therefore reinforces a concrete need for HW-based security to harden the platform. This is evident from the data cataloged in the National Vulnerability Database (NVD) organized as CVEs; more information about NVD can be found at `https://nvd.nist.gov/`. The Common Vulnerabilities and Exposures (CVE) is a list of entries with the information that identifies a unique vulnerability or an exposure and is used in many cybersecurity products and services including the NVD; more information about CVE can be found at `https://cve.mitre.org/`. The NVD has been mined to derive the statistics and visualizations with pertinent search terms such

© The Author(s) 2020
S. Cheruvu et al., *Demystifying Internet of Things Security*,
https://doi.org/10.1007/978-1-4842-2896-8_3

as **Firmware** and **Hardware**. It is evident from Figure 3-1 (a) that the firmware-related CVEs have increased significantly and 2017–2018 saw the biggest jump when the hacker community started attacking the FW on the platforms. Similarly Figure 3-1 (b) shows that during the same time period, the HW-related CVEs also hit a peak. Please note that all these CVEs need to be investigated carefully for the impacted areas within a platform. But the trends are clearly pointing toward the HW as the last line of defense.

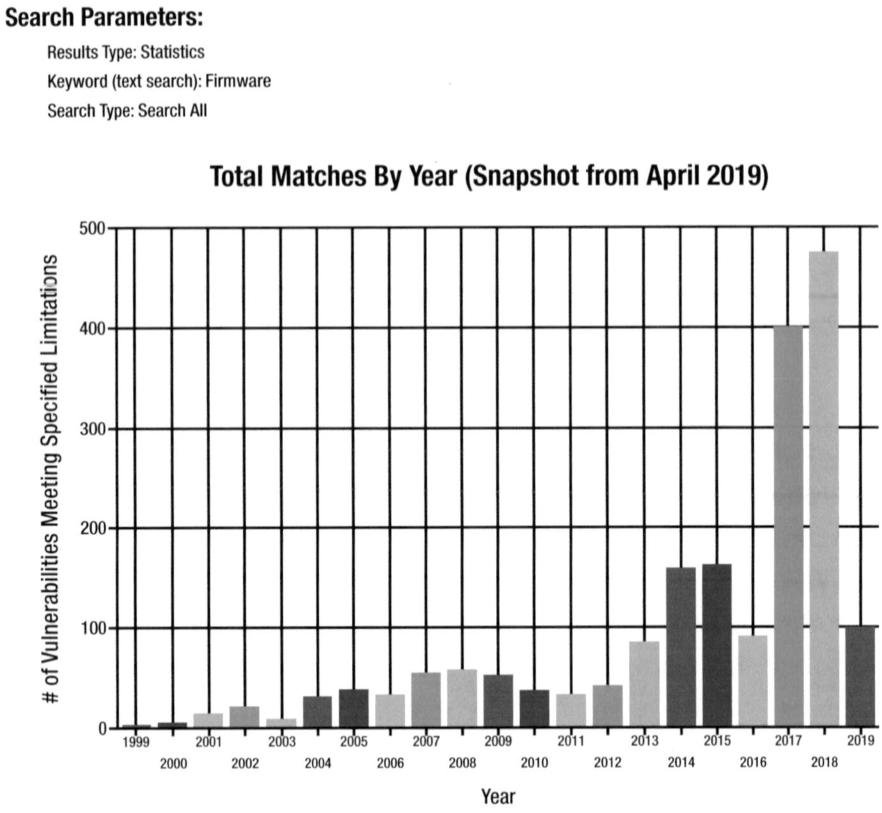

Search Parameters:

Results Type: Statistics
Keyword (text search): Firmware
Search Type: Search All

Figure 3-1. (a) Firmware vulnerability trend chart[1]

---

[1]https://nvd.nist.gov/vuln/search/statistics?form_type=Advanced& results_type=statistics&query=Firmware&search_type=all

Search Parameters:

Results Type: Statistics
Keyword (text search): Hardware
Search Type: Search All

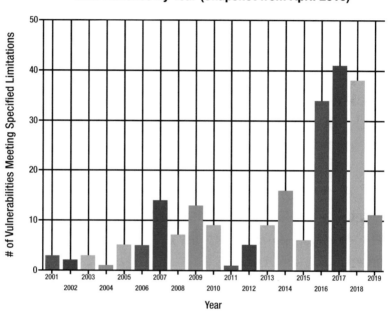

Figure 3-1. *(b) Hardware vulnerability trend chart²*

This chapter describes the technologies involved in securing an IoT device anchored to a Hardware Root of Trust (HWRoT) and ultimately booting into a Trusted Execution Environment (TEE). Security in an IoT environment generally involves four areas of focus:

- Protecting the device

- Protecting user identity

---

²https://nvd.nist.gov/vuln/search/statistics?form_type=Advanced&
results_type=statistics&query=Hardware&search_type=all

- Protecting the data

- Managing the security at runtime

Each of these areas are worthy of detailed explanation in itself. This chapter delves into the rich set of security and privacy technologies Intel has available in their product lines and how they may be used to implement secure IoT systems. Intel's discrete CPU-PCH or System-on-Chip (SoC) products have two classes of security features; one class of features are implemented in the CPU as New Instructions (NI) with some examples being AES-NI, SHA-NI, and so on. The second class of security features are implemented in the isolated security engines with examples including Converged Security and Manageability Engine (CSME).

Note   Please note that by the time this book is published, some new security features may be released by Intel, and therefore please refer to Intel web site or contact the relevant OEM/ODMs for latest information.

Background and Terminology

Before the actual security capabilities can be described, it is important to understand the terminology, the threat pyramid, the relevance of end-to-end security, and Intel Security Essentials for leveraging built-in HW security technologies.

Assets, Threats, and Threat Pyramid

Security design begins with the process of identifying a set of assets that are to be protected and classifying these assets according to the different levels of protection based on strategic or other pertinent value vectors. A real-life scenario of protecting assets in our home would be to protect our house keys (hang on wall), wallets (place in an enclosed cabinet), passports, and jewelry (in a safe in the master bedroom). For IoT deployments, security is also determined by the return on investment (ROI). Figure 3-2 depicts the relationship between them.

- Assets (A): Anything valuable to us that is worth protecting. What assets are we protecting? It is pertinent to classify the assets and prioritize. Example asset profile = {physical devices, internal fuses, keys, content, data at rest/in transit, etc.}

- Threats (T): What are we protecting against? Become aware of threat surfaces, the areas of exposure to threats.

- Vulnerabilities (V): What are the known weaknesses in the system that can be exploited?

- Mitigation: How are we going to protect?

- Robustness rules: Specific to assets/threats. Documented conditions/criteria for protecting specific assets against specific threats.

- Threat modeling: A process to evaluate the threat scenarios considering the vulnerabilities for specific assets. This process is iterative and is expected to be done whenever the bill of materials (BOM) list in a platform changes.

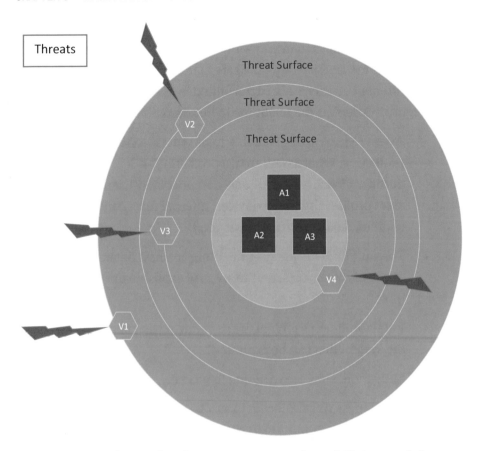

Figure 3-2. *Relationship between assets, vulnerabilities, and threats*

Inverted Threat Pyramid

The threat pyramid shown in Figure 3-3 depicts the surfaces/layers vulnerable to cyberattacks (both physical and remote) in an IoT device. The volume of attacks is high at the top and requires fewer resources, whereas the volume of attacks at the bottom is lower and requires a high amount of resources. In other words, the attack surfaces have varying degree of exposure and mandate a defense in depth approach at the platform levels.

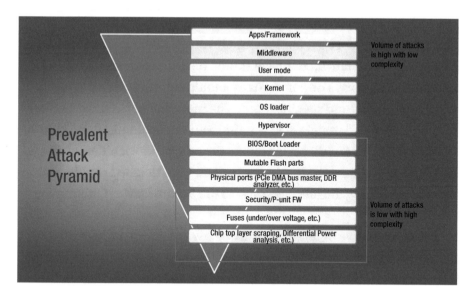

Figure 3-3. *Attack pyramid*

The rectangle outlines the IA value additions where the related security IP capabilities exemplify the assets that can be used to protect customer's assets. The effort to create exploits at the top of the inverted pyramid is low, and the ROI on the compromised assets is also low. Due to this low effort, the number of exploits is also significantly higher. As we traverse down the inverted pyramid, the effort it takes to create exploits increases significantly along with the cost, and thereby the number of exploits is typically lower and targeted in nature. The bottom six layers could be qualified as HW, and side-channel attacks plus physical attacks are relevant. The discussion of such side-channel and physical attacks is outside the scope of this book.

Sample IoT Device Lifecycle

The IoT device lifecycle pertaining to security is complicated with security involved in every phase of an IoT device lifecycle (Figure 3-4). During the build phase, the security SDK/API is critical for simplifying the device build. The provisioning/configuring phases would require tools that scale across different CPU families and involve assigning a persona to the IoT device. The deployment phase should be flexible for seamless and potential anonymity. The connectivity should comply with the relevant security standards and specifications. The management of these devices must be secure and seamless. The retirement or decommissioning phase is equally critical for an IoT device due to the integration of different assets/secrets from multiple vendors in the system. For a detailed supply chain interactions during the lifecycle, refer to the Secure Device Onboarding technology.[3]

IoT devices have different security needs as they go through their lifecycle (on average it is many years significantly more than traditional PCs). Security is pivotal to enable IoT devices and sustain those on the market. Each stage of the device lifecycle has its specific requirements, starting from providing what is needed for onboarding a device during the start of its life to security management functions that secure runtime operations. Intel has a critical role with enabling design-in the best practice HW security model with solutions and ecosystem relationships. Intel targets to enable security capabilities and solutions for each phase working with the ecosystem. Security is not one-off, it evolves along the lifecycle with each stage having unique needs. Best practices are required to secure the entire lifecycle.

---

[3]www.intel.com/content/www/us/en/internet-of-things/secure-device-onboard.html

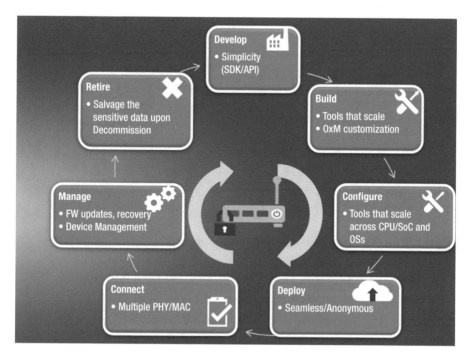

Figure 3-4. *IoT device lifecycle*

End-to-End (E2E) Security

While security pertaining to an IoT device is important, a practical IoT deployment warrants scaling security across an E2E spectrum starting with edge/Things connected to Network and then fog or Cloud. The typical E2E security involves edge/Things ➤ Gateway/Network ➤ Fog ➤ Cloud. Refer to Figure 3-5.

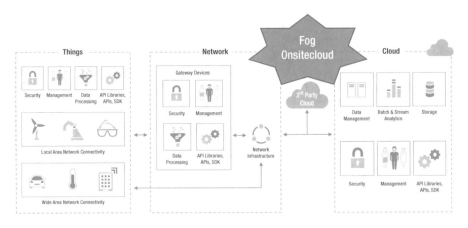

Figure 3-5. *Typical E2E security components*

Assets exist at different stages and often cross trust boundaries.

A typical flow (for a sensing application) is explained with confidentiality (encryption/decryption) and integrity (sign/verify) attributes:

1. The device securely identifies with the Gateway/ Cloud (could be one time or periodic depending upon the policy enforcement).

2. The device has/interfaces to sensors (smart/dumb) and actuators, collects the data, and controls the sensors and drives the actuators.

3. Device may run some local analytics and optionally store the data encrypted.

4. Device encrypts or signs (or both) (depending on the policy) the data and sends it to Gateway.

5. Gateway decrypts/authenticates the data.

6. Gateway may run some local analytics.

7. Gateway encrypts/signs and sends the data to fog/ Cloud.

8. The instances on fog/Cloud decrypt/authenticate the data.

9. Cloud applications run analytics.

10. Cloud applications encrypt/sign and store the data in databases.

Security Essentials

Security Essentials is an Intel brand initiative that defines a set of foundational security capabilities that Intel processors and Systems on Chips (SoCs) will support in order to establish a secure baseline upon which the ecosystem can build rich, secure usage models (see Figure 3-6). Security Essentials establishes a set of capabilities along with technology options for implementing each of the targeted capabilities. This allows us to project a common security posture across all supported platforms, establish a baseline for security that the industry can rely upon, and promote reuse and consistency in Intel-based security solutions. Intel provides training, collateral, technology summits, and Technology Alignment Programs with customers and ecosystem partners. In some cases, Intel partners with Independent BIOS Vendors (IBVs) and Independent boot loader vendors to enable the ecosystem with fast, secure, and functionally safe boot loader solutions.

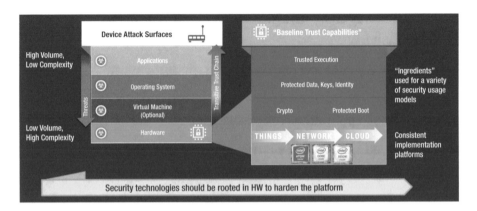

Figure 3-6. *Trusted secure foundation*

Security Essentials focuses on four buckets of capabilities: Device Identity, Protected Boot, Protected Storage, and trusted execution environment. These are later explained briefly.

Device Identity

A hardware identity refers to an immutable, unique identity for a platform. The identity has to be somehow inseparable from the platform. A hardware embedded cryptographic key, also referred to as a *Hardware Root of Trust*, can be an effective device identifier. The Trusted Computing Group (TCG) defines hardware-roots-of-trust as part of the Trusted Platform Module (TPM) specification. All TPM vendors are required to implement a hardware root of trust for storage. Intel® Platform Trust Technology (PTT) implements TPM functionality using a security engine integrated in many of its SoC products.

The IEEE community defines a device identity specification, IEEE 802.1AR, that has been adopted by the TCG. This means TPM-based device identity complies with interoperable and industry-accepted approach for secure device identity.

A software (SW) identity refers to a cryptographic fingerprint (SWFP) that describes important software that may execute on a platform. The SWFP can be reliably verified given a *whitelist* of SWFP values known to be legitimate. SWFP is an important aspect of securely booting a platform where the goal of secure boot is to detect malicious changes to software images before they are loaded into memory.

The TCG defines methods for securely booting a platform where the SWFP of each software image loaded into memory is *measured* (aka cryptographically hashed) into a Platform Configuration Register (PCR), which is securely stored by a TPM. PCR measurements are available for comparison with whitelist values during the boot process and are available for *attestation* after the platform boots. Attestation is a protocol for proving to a peer platform that it booted a particular way. The attestation verifier might also use the whitelist to verify a peer platform node booted satisfactorily.

An IoT system that enforces a common and attested secure boot policy is a way to establish trust in a distributed set of IoT nodes. Distributed trust is an important component to establishing a secure IoT network.

Protected Boot

This capability defends against sophisticated bootkits and rootkits which have been demonstrated that reside in very early boot code and are able to launch a variety of attacks on the system. These attacks materialize without the knowledge of OS and thereby are invincible to be detected by the anti-malware entities. The TCG defines an architectural requirement for secure platform boot by defining a root-of-trust-for-measurement (RTM) where the platform must provide a secure platform reset and initial boot executive that is implemented in hardware, but TCG stopped short of defining a particular implementation.

The Unified Extensible Firmware Interface (UEFI) forum defines an interface where the UEFI BIOS boot image can be integrity verified by the RTM before it can execute, thereby ensuring the remainder of the BIOS boot process can be performed according to TCG defined secure boot principles.

Intel® TXT (Trusted Execution Technology) anticipates scenarios where a hard power reset, as a way to return to a trusted environment, is infeasible. Instead, Intel® TXT transitions the CPU to a secure operational mode using an IA instruction, then proceeds to boot a hypervisor or OS without invoking BIOS.

Intel Boot Guard is the hardware-based root of trust for system boot process. It provides an architectural enforcement of OEM boot policies and a protected initial measurement & verification of first OEM component. OEM boot policy is provided in FPF programmed by the OEM.

Protected Storage

The Storage Networking Industry Association (SNIA) defines storage security as

> *Technical controls, which may include integrity, confidentiality and availability controls that protect storage resources and data from unauthorized users and uses.*

Protected storage is a fundamental security capability required to support many other security capabilities. The Trusted Platform Module (TPM) implements secure storage primitives for several types of security objects including cryptographic keys, configuration registers, and whitelist values. Protected storage encompasses the following properties:

- Data confidentiality: Unauthorized entities cannot read the data.

- Data integrity: Unauthorized entities cannot modify the data or unauthorized data modification can be detected.

- Anti-replay protection: Unauthorized entities cannot replay/reuse stale data to storage.

Intel® Platform Trust Technology (PTT) is an implementation of the TCG Trusted Platform Module specification in a SoC that relies on hardware isolation of flash and other memory to prevent access outside of the TCG defined interfaces. Intel® QuickAssist Technology (QAT) is a hardware data encryption accelerator that also implements key storage protections. A common approach for building secure storage for data that exceeds the capacity of hardened secure storage resources calls for bulk data encryptions that allow ciphertexts to be stored on traditional storage media, but where encryption keys are stored in hardware. It is common to build a hierarchy of data encryption keys so that different access and lifecycle controls can be applied to different data. In some cases the key hierarchy itself is too large to fit into hardware-protected storage; therefore intermediate keys may be used to encrypt data encryption keys and so on until the top most keys of the hierarchy can be stored in hardware.

Trusted Execution Environment (TEE)

In general, a Trusted Execution Environment (TEE) refers to an execution environment that is isolated from the normal general-purpose execution environment. For example, the core CPU is a general-purpose execution environment, and a security coprocessor is an isolated environment. Trusted execution environments may include HW/SW/FW that establishes an isolated environment. By carefully controlling the infrastructure that produces the HW/FW/SW that implements it, the TEE can have strong guarantees regarding safe and reliable execution of TEE workloads. Typically workloads that involve the use of cryptographic keys to ensure confidentiality and integrity protection of data as it is transformed to and from ciphertext are performed using a TEE.

There are several TEE technologies available across a variety of architectures. ARM® TrustZone creates an isolated execution environment within the ARM core. Intel® Software Guard Extensions (SGX) takes a similar approach and allows multiple instances of trusted execution environments for different applications and tenants. Intel® Converged Security and Manageability Engine (CSME) is a security coprocessor that is integrated into Intel chipsets. The CSME can be used to offload security-sensitive operations to shield them from possible attacks from the normal CPU environment. Intel® TXT allows trusted execution using CPU cache lines as RAM to minimize dependencies on external resources. It can be used for general-purpose TEE operations when cache coherency isn't needed. Intel® Virtualization Technology (VT) suite offers another form of TEE where a trusted hypervisor creates execution environments with distinct thread, memory, interrupt, and IO contexts. Virtualization allows full OS and application images to run which may be counterproductive to security due to increased attack surface of a large OS and application framework. Therefore, it may yet be appropriate to employ some other TEE capability in concert with virtualization.

Built-In Security

Built-in security features are essential to protect, detect, and correct the security issues in a platform. These features depicted in Figure 3-7 enable to protect the identity and data assets on the platforms from attacks, detect when attacks are launched, and then aid in deploying the corrective measures to make the platforms resilient.

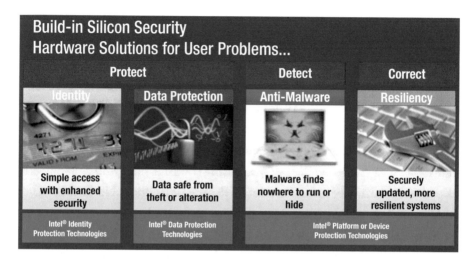

Figure 3-7. HW solution pillars for user problems

The identity is based on HW and possesses immutable properties and simplified access. The data asset protection includes data at rest and in transit. The detection mechanisms constitute anti-malware FW/SW components to find the malware and then pipeline into deploying the corrective measures via FW and/or SW over the air updates. Intel's value proposition includes three layers of ingredients as shown in Figure 3-8.

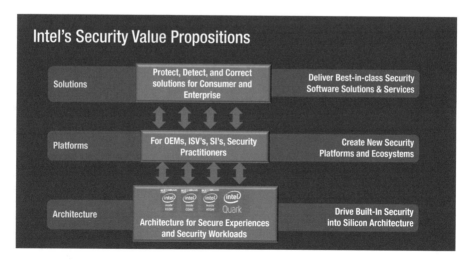

Figure 3-8. Security value propositions

At the bottom layer, the Intel Architecture allows leveraging built-in security features to build the platforms at the middle layer and, at the top layer, create ecosystems enriched with deployment of best-in-class security software solutions. These solutions at the top layer enable the protection, detection, and corrections in both consumer and enterprise class solutions. Intel security assets and solutions enable building and deploying an end-to-end system of systems as depicted later. The end-to-end system starts with edge devices or things on the left possessing minimal compute capacity and less robust security features; these edge devices are connected to Gateways/Network, to fog, and then connected to the cloud back ends.

The scalable strategy as shown in Figure 3-9 is to provide a minimally viable set of security capabilities that scale from low compute MCUs to atom class to Core and to Xeon server, microserver class products. Across the product lines, the four groups of security technologies are available in different capacities for implementing security features. The device identity based on HW is key for an IoT device, and protected boot ensures that only well-known FW/SW is being executed and protected storage ensures the storage of secrets and/or data securely. The trusted execution environment allows execution of code at runtime in an isolated and protected environment immune from SW and HW attacks.

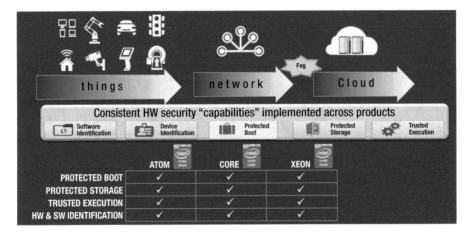

Figure 3-9. *Consistent HW security capabilities*

Base Platform Security Features Overview

Let's review the security features present in the base platform profiles of IA CPU/SOC at a very high level. As alluded to in previous sections, the security features are implemented in CPU and on dedicated security engines as shown in Figure 3-10.

Figure 3-10. *CPU and dedicated security engines*

Intel CPUs come standard with a suite of cryptographic operations that can be performed on the main CPU. Secure, protected encryption starts with a random number seed, typically provided by a pseudorandom number generator within the client. Intel® Secure Key provides a clean source of random numbers through generation in hardware, out of sight of malware. Intel® SGX provides TEE with smallest TCB within the CPU boundaries for application to utilize.

CPU Hosted Crypto Implementations

These features include CPU new instructions for encryption/decryption, sign/verify, and random number generation: AES-NI, SHA-NI, SHA1 and SHA256, RDRAND, RDSEED, ECC. This section describes the Security features/primitives New Instructions (NI) as supported in the Intel CPUs (as opposed to in an isolated security engine IP block). CPU crypto capabilities are supported by the CPU and the fabric. In the following sections, we will learn how the hardware-enhanced security strengthens Anti-Malware Defenses via the OS Guard (SMAP, SMEP), performing encryption/decryption, sign/verify, and random number generation. CPU security features and accelerators are available to trusted execution environments implemented by the CPU as well including Intel® SGX, Intel® VT, and Intel® TXT.

Malware Protection (OS Guard)

Intel CPU/SoCs expose HW features for OS to defend the platform against malware attacks. The particular and effective features include CPU new instructions to enable Supervisor Mode Execution Prevention (SMEP) and Supervisor Mode Access Prevention (SMAP). The SMEP feature prevents the code executing in privileged mode (ring 0) from executing code in application mode (ring 3). SMAP is a CPU-based mechanism for user-mode address-space protection and prevents supervisor accesses to data on user pages.

OS Guard (SMEP)

SMEP when enabled prevents a specific (important) privilege escalation attack vector which is supervisor mode execution from user pages. The OS can set CR4.SMEP to enable this feature, and no changes are required to applications or other OS software. However, there might be some compatibility issues with third-party ring 0 software. The changes in VMM are limited to supporting/virtualizing CR4.SMEP bit and corresponding CPUID bit. It is important to note the non-objectives so that platform-level protections can be deployed appropriately. SMEP doesn't prevent "all" privilege escalation attack vectors, nor does it prevent a specific class of vulnerability (e.g., buffer overflow).

OS Guard (SMAP)

SMAP extends the protection that previously was provided by SMEP and was developed with the Linux community, supported on kernel 3.12+ and KVM version 3.15+. The support depends on OS or VMM being used, and the CR4.SMAP has to be set to enable the feature. SMAP is analogous to SMEP (supervisor mode execution prevention) for data. There are legitimate instances where the OS needs to access user pages, and SMAP does provide support for those situations. Code executing in ring 0 (supervisor mode) is prevented from accessing the data in ring 3 (user mode). When/if CR4.SMAP = 1, CPU generates Page Fault (#PF) for the following accesses: accesses to data (not instruction fetch), data is on user-accessible page (U/S bit is 1 in all relevant paging structure entries), access is made with supervisor privilege which normally means CPU Privilege Level (CPL) < 3, applies also to supervisor accesses made with CPL = 3 (e.g., loads from GDT on segment loads). The resulting #PF establishes error code in the normal way.

Encryption/Decryption Using AES-NI

AES is a symmetric encryption standard that's widely used in the following use cases: full disk encryption, data in transit encryption, and enterprise application–specific security. All the modern compilers support the AES HW accelerators, and developers can also use via C/C++ intrinsics. Intel® Advanced Encryption Standard New Instructions (Intel® AES-NI) is a set of seven new instructions in the Intel® processor series. Four instructions accelerate encryption and decryption. Two instructions improve key generation and matrix manipulation. The seventh aids in carry-less multiplication. By implementing some complex and costly substeps of the AES algorithm in hardware, Intel AES-NI and PCLMULQDQ accelerate execution of the AES-based encryption. The result is faster, more secure encryption, which makes the use of encryption feasible in new use-cases. Some of the properties are outlined here:

- Improve the compute efficiency of cryptographic algorithms.

- Vector AES is a promotion of AES-NI to vector form, enables two (256-bit) or four (512-bit) lanes, and increases AES throughput of cores.

- FIPS197 compliant.

- Compilers, libraries, and emulator platforms are all available now.

- AESENC, AESENCLAST, AESDEC, AESDECLAST.

- AES Encrypt Round, AES Encrypt Last Round, AES Decrypt Round, AES Decrypt Last Round.

- Instructions have both register-register and register-memory variants.

- AESIMC and AESKEYGENASSIST: Assist with AES Key Expansion, AES Inverse Mix Columns, and AES Key Generation Assist.

The platform support for AES can be determined by inspecting *cpuinfo* output and *openssl* commands as shown in the following:

```
$ grep -o aes /proc/cpuinfo
```

To verify the proper cipher order, use the following command:

```
"openssl ciphers -v"
```

See the following list that shows AES at the top of the list:

```
Openssl speed aes-256-cbc
Openssl speed -engine aesni -evp aes-256-cbc
```

    http://ask.xmodulo.com/check-aes-ni-enabled-openssl.html

```
openssl  speed -elapsed aes-128-cbc
openssl  speed -elapsed -evp aes-128-cbc
```

    https://software.intel.com/en-us/articles/improving-openssl-performance

Sign/Verify Using Intel® SHA Extensions

The Intel® SHA Extensions are a family of seven Streaming SIMD Extensions (SSE)–based instructions that are used together to accelerate the performance of processing SHA-1 and SHA-256 on Intel® Architecture processors (Figure 3-11). Given the growing importance of SHA in our everyday computing devices, the new instructions are designed to provide a needed boost of performance to hashing a single buffer of data. Using the SHA Extensions, the Intel® SHA Extensions can be implemented using direct assembly or through C/C++ intrinsics. The 16-byte aligned 128-bit memory location form of the second source operand for each instruction is defined to make the decoding of the instructions easier. The memory form is not really intended to be used in the implementation of SHA using the extensions since unnecessary overhead may be incurred. Availability of the Intel® SHA Extensions on a particular processor can be determined by checking the SHA CPUID bit in CPUID (EAX=07H, ECX=0):EBX.SHA [bit 29].

- New instructions in CPU to encrypt/decrypt data.

- The Intel® SHA Extensions are comprised of four SHA-1 and three SHA-256 instructions.

- There are two message schedule helper instructions each, a rounds instruction each, and an extra rounds-related helper for SHA-1.

- FIPS Pub 180-2 compliant.

Instruction	Op 1	Op 2	Op 3	Opcode
		SHA1 New Instructions		
SHA1RNDS4	xmm (rw)	xmm/m128 (r)	imm8	0F 3A CC /r ib
SHA1NEXTE	xmm (rw)	xmm/m128 (r)	NA	0F 38 C8 /r
SHA1MSG1	xmm (rw)	xmm/m128 (r)	NA	0F 38 C9 /r
SHA1MSG2	xmm (rw)	xmm/m128 (r)	NA	0F 38 CA /r
		SHA256 New Instructions		
SHA256RNDS2	xmm (rw)	xmm/m128 (r)	<xmm0> (implicit)	0F 38 CB /r
SHA256MSG1	xmm (rw)	xmm/m128 (r)	NA	0F 38 CC /r
SHA256MSG2	xmm (rw)	xmm/m128 (r)	NA	0F 38 CD /r

Figure 3-11. *SHA instruction family*

The availability of the SHA Extensions in a platform can be detected using the code in Listing 3-1. It is always a good idea to check the available HW crypto capabilities before leveraging them.

Listing 3-1. Detecting the SHA Extensions

```
int CheckForIntelShaExtensions() {

    int a, b, c, d;
    // Look for CPUID.7.0.EBX[29]
    // EAX = 7, ECX = 0
    a = 7;
    c = 0;
```

```
asm volatile ("cpuid"
Intel® SHA Extensions: New Instructions Supporting the
Secure Hash Algorithm on Intel® Architecture Processors
14
:"=a"(a), "=b"(b), "=c"(c), "=d"(d)
:"a"(a), "c"(c)
);
// Intel® SHA Extensions feature bit is EBX[29]
return ((b >> 29) & 1);

}
```

Intel® Data Protection Technology with Secure Key (DRNG)

This section explains about the usage of Digital Random Number Generator (DRNG) with the new instructions supported in IA CPUs. For any IoT device, the ability to generate high-quality cryptographic keys is crucial. Two such instructions RDRAND and RDSEED are explained along with the method to determine the support and the associated programming usage. Intel® Secure Key constitutes the Intel® 64 and IA-32 Architectures instructions RDRAND and RDSEED and the underlying Digital Random Number Generator (DRNG) hardware implementation. High-quality keys for cryptographic protocols can be generated using the RDRAND instruction, and the RDSEED instruction is provided for seeding software-based pseudorandom number generators (PRNGs). RDRAND retrieves a hardware-generated random value from the NIST SP800-90A compliant Digital Random Bit Generator (DRGB) and stores it in the destination register given as an argument to the instruction. The size of the random value (16-, 32-, or 64-bits) is determined by the size of the register given. The carry flag (CF) must be checked to determine whether a random value was available at the time of instruction execution.

RDRAND is available to both OS modes: system (ring 0) or application (ring 3) software running on the platform. There are no hardware ring requirements that restrict access based on process privilege level. As such, RDRAND may be invoked as part of an operating system or hypervisor system library, a shared software library, or directly by an application. Before using the RDRAND or RDSEED instructions, an application or library should first determine whether the underlying platform supports the instruction and hence includes the underlying DRNG feature. This can be done using the CPUID instruction. In general, CPUID is used to return processor identification and feature information stored in the EAX, EBX, ECX, and EDX registers. For detailed information on CPUID, refer to References CPUID A and B. To be specific, support for RDRAND can be determined by examining bit 30 of the ECX register returned by CPUID, and support for RDSEED can be determined by examining bit 31 of the EBX register. A bit value of 1 indicates processor support for the instruction, while a value of 0 indicates no processor support. The Intel Digital Random Number Generator (DRNG) is a high-quality, high-performance, HW-based random number generator.

- It supports NIST SP 800-90 A, B, and C compliant functionality and is FIPS 140-2 Level 2 certifiable.

- It generates random numbers at a rate of 1 byte per clock.

- It is available early in the system boot/OS load process.

Both RDRAND and RDSEED return random numbers that are compliant to the US National Institute of Standards and Technology (NIST) standards on random number generators (Figure 3-12).

Instruction	Source	NIST Compliance
RDRAND	Cryptographically secure pseudorandom number generator	SP 800-90A
RDSEED	Non-deterministic random bit generator	SP 800-90B & C (drafts)

Figure 3-12. *NIST compliance for RDRAND and RDSEED*

As depicted in Figure 3-13, the RDRAND instruction is handled by microcode on each core. This includes an RNG microcode module that handles interactions with the DRNG hardware module on the processor chip. The entropy source (ES) produces random bits from a nondeterministic hardware process. HW AES in CBC-MAC mode distills the entropy into high-quality nondeterministic random numbers. The deterministic random bit generator (DRBG) is seeded from the conditioner.

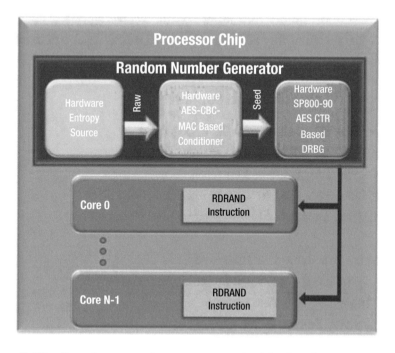

Figure 3-13. *Random number generator inside the chip*

The availability of RDRAND and RDSEED can be detected using the following register bit decoding (Table 3-1).

More information can be found at: https://software.intel.com/en-us/articles/intel-digital-random-number-generator-drng-software-implementation-guide

Table 3-1. *Feature Information Returned in the ECX Register*

Leaf	Register	Bit	Mnemonic	Description
1	ECX	30	RDRAND	A value of 1 indicates that processor supports the RDRAND instruction
7	EBX	18	RDSEED	A value of 1 indicates that processor supports the RDSEED instruction

With the information from Table 3-1 and by leveraging the code in Listing 3-2, the availability of RDRAND and RDSEED can be detected in a platform.

Listing 3-2. Detecting DRNG Support

```
/* These are bits that are OR'd together */
#define DRNG_NO_SUPPORT 0x0 /* For clarity */
#define DRNG_HAS_RDRAND 0x1
#define DRNG_HAS_RDSEED 0x2
int get_drng_support ()
{
    static int drng_features= -1;
    /* So we don't call cpuid multiple times for
     * the same information */
    if ( drng_features == -1 ) {
        drng_features= DRNG_NO_SUPPORT;
```

```
    if ( _is_intel_cpu() ) {
        cpuid_t info;
        cpuid(&info, 1, 0);
        if ( (info.ecx & 0x40000000) == 0x40000000 ) {
            drng_features|= DRNG_HAS_RDRAND;
        }
        cpuid(&info, 7, 0);
        if ( (info.ebx & 0x40000) == 0x40000 ) {
            drng_features|= DRNG_HAS_RDSEED;
        }
    }
}
    return drng_features;
}
```

One of the advantages of security hardening and acceleration capabilities applied to the core architecture is that performance enhancements derived from core silicon manufacturing process improvements also apply to security features. In many cases, this approach ensures security features' manufacturing costs scale with the other core features.

Converged Security and Manageability Engine (CSME)

This describes the Converged Security Engine capabilities including the silicon, FW, and SW ingredients. This is similar to a security coprocessor which has its own ROM, RAM, instruction set, and an isolated execution environment. Refer to a simplified architecture diagram in Figure 3-14. An excellent deep dive can be found in the book *Platform Embedded Security Technology Revealed* (www.apress.com/9781430265719).

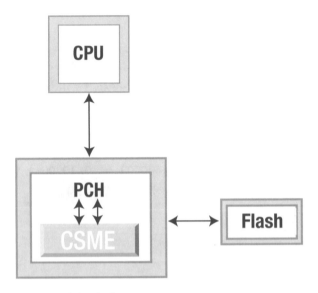

Figure 3-14. *CSME block diagram*

Features are implemented in the isolated security execution engine or equivalent to a security coprocessor. CSME is an embedded subsystem in Platform Controller Hub (PCH). It is a mini SoC within the PCH and contains a small processor, SRAM, crypto blocks, and I/O's. CSME serves three main platform roles: chipset (secure initialization/survivability), security (boot/runtime protection and enable trusted execution of platform applications), and manageability (optional extensions for out-of-band network management).

CSME supports the following:

- Crypto operations, boot, DAL, manageability (AMT, in above atom).

- The CSME supports crypto operations, HW Root of Trust–based secure boot (verified and measured), Active Manageability Technology, and other features.

- Content Protection: PAVP, Digital Rights Management (DRM)-Widevine, PlayReady, and Adobe Access. The CSME supports multiple DRMs for protecting the premium audio/video content by encrypting and/or digital watermarking.

- Secure Debug: DFX, JTAG lock. The CSME supports secure debug and manages access to DFX register space by allowing locking and unlocking of JTAG interface through which ICE emulators could be plugged in for debugging during pre/postproduction and to debug the field return parts.

- Identity Protection Technology: The CSME also supports protecting user's identity via multifactor authentication, biometrics, iris, and others.

Secure/Verified, Measured Boot and Boot Guard

Protecting the boot flow is critical to ensure that the device is not running compromised code whether it is the FW on the flash components or SW running from the mass storage device. Secure/verified boot is a process where a device authenticates the different FW/SW ingredients in the boot chain and establishes a chain of trust. Measured boot is a process where the device authenticates to a network for admission. To implement measured boot, the device stores the hash values of the boot chain ingredients, and SW entities collect these values and transmit them to a server for attestation.

Trusted Execution Technology (TXT)

The TXT is prominent in the server and microserver domain where a comprehensive security strategy is employed including a Measured Launch Environment (MLE) and instrumented OS. More about this will be discussed in the "Runtime Protection – Ever Vigilant" section.

Platform Trust Technology (PTT)

PTT is a FW implementation of the Trusted Computing Group (TCG) Trusted Platform Module (TPM) and complies with the TPM 2.0 specification. This FW is executed on the CSME or CSE on atom platforms. This feature is the most important for an IoT device which has board-level constraints imposed by BOM cost and real estate. PTT is essential for measured boot and attestation mechanisms.

Enhanced Privacy ID (EPID)

The EPID allows a device to possess an immutable "privacy preserving platform identifier" – in many use cases, it isn't required that the particular instance of the CPU be known, only that the platform is of a particular class or origin. In these situations, trust can be established without sacrificing privacy. Through this immutable identity, more secrets can be provisioned in the field during the course of the IoT device lifecycle including anonymous identification for provisioning of secrets, premium content, DRMs, and operation.

Memory Encryption Technologies

In future processors, Intel plans to introduce two new in-memory data protection capabilities including Total Memory Encryption (TME) and Multi-Key TME, or MKTME. TME technology encrypts the platform's entire memory with a single key.

TME

When enabled via BIOS configuration, this will help ensure that all memory accessed from the Intel CPU is encrypted, including customer credentials, encryption keys, and other IP or personal information on the external memory bus.

MKTME

The second new technology extends TME to support multiple encryption keys (Multi-Key TME, or MKTME) and provides the ability to specify the use of a specific key for a page of memory. This architecture allows either CPU-generated keys or tenant-provided keys, giving full flexibility to customers. This means virtual machines (VMs) and containers can be cryptographically isolated from each other in memory with separate encryption keys, a big plus in multitenant cloud environments. VMs and containers can also be pooled to share an individual key, further extending scale and flexibility. This includes support for both standard DRAM and NVRAM. Refer to the following for more information.[4, 5]

Dynamic Application Loader (DAL)

DAL technology allows building, deploying, and managing the lifecycle of a small trusted applet (Java-based applets) using the DAL SDK and Runtime environment.

---

[4]https://software.intel.com/en-us/blogs/2017/12/22/intel-releases-new-technology-specification-for-memory-encryption

[5]https://software.intel.com/sites/default/files/managed/a5/16/Multi-Key-Total-Memory-Encryption-Spec.pdf

Software Guard Extensions (SGX) – IA CPU Instructions

SGX constitutes a new set of CPU instructions, kernel/user mode drivers and Runtime environment, and API/SDK. This framework allows developers to build the trusted parts of the application code into enclaves. The inherent assumption is that the partition of the application into trusted and untrusted domains is already done prior to implementing SGX. SGX can be used to seal legitimate software inside an enclave to protect from attacks by the malware, irrespective of the privilege levels whether it is ring 0 or ring 3.

Identity Crisis

With the projected 50 billion IoT devices on the network, wouldn't it be ultracritical to ensure that a device is talking to the right device at the other end? A masqueraded device can do lot of damage. A method to prevent this is to implement a device identity that's immutable and use this identity to attest and provision initial secrets and additional secrets in the field during the course of the device's life. The same phenomenon applies to human identity as well. It is vital to realize that a masqueraded device is substantially hard to detect and quarantine. Intel Identity Protection Technology (IPT) uses Dynamic Application Loader (DAL) to implement mechanisms to protect the user identity via multifactor authentication and others.

The device identity (ID) decision tree can be used to select the right ID for a particular implementation. As shown in Figure 3-15, a security architect/engineer can decide the right identity based on the platform requirements and use cases. If an identity is required but mutable (changeable), a SW identity may suffice, but immutable identity requires identity to be in HW. If this identity now has to be anonymous, select EPID, else the identity as supported in PTT/TPM may be adequate. The EPID's cryptographic properties are briefly explained in the following section.

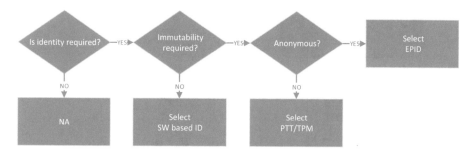

Figure 3-15. *Device identity decision tree*

Enhanced Privacy Identifier (EPID)

The EPID is a novel technology that addresses all aspects of the active anonymity problem: *authentication, anonymity, and revocation.* Intel® Enhanced Privacy ID (Intel® EPID) provides an immutable hardware root of trust, enabling IoT networks to confidently identify devices and to secure their communications.

Anonymity

Intel EPID also offers sophisticated privacy capabilities that enable anonymous communication to safeguard networks and customers' data. EPID is an anonymous digital signature scheme with the following attributes (Figure 3-16): a private key for signing and a single group public key for verifying signature of multiple keys. EPID is an open standard: ISO/IEC 20008/20009 and TCG Mature Technology, shipping since 2008, 2.4B keys since 2008.

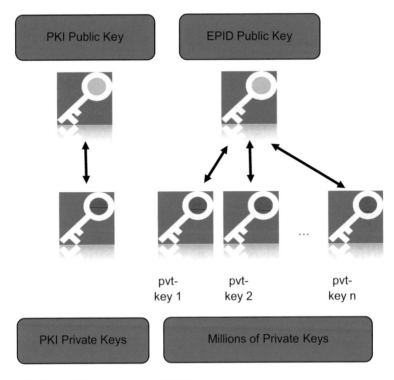

Figure 3-16. *PKI system vs. EPID*

As depicted in the figure, the PKI is a system with a public-private key pair, whereas the EPID is a system with one public key associated with many private keys formed into a group. In both cases, the private keys are provisioned into the devices, and the public keys are available to the back-end servers for authentication/admission.

PTT/TPM

The Endorsement Key (EK) supported in the Intel® PTT or discrete Trusted Platform Module (TPM) serves as a direct identity for IoT devices. An Endorsement Key is a special purpose TPM-resident RSA key that is never visible outside of the TPM. An EK certificate is used to bind an identity, in terms of specific security attributes, to a TPM. The primary use of an EK certificate is to authenticate device identity during Attestation Identity Key (AIK) certificate issuance.

Device Boot Integrity – Trust But Verify

Imagine the IoT device booting an image that's not the original from boot storage. In this circumstance, any protections that you deploy at higher layers wouldn't be adequate to protect the device. Once the immutable identity is ensured as explained in the previous section, it becomes vital to follow through by booting securely. The boot loaders such as BIOS, UEFI, coreboot, and FSP can be classified into pre-OS boot loaders and will be referred as such. Let's unravel the *boot chaos with many terms employed in the industry today:

- Trusted Boot: Definition varies according to industry. Used to characterize a trusted system with a chain of trust.

- Secure Boot: HWRoT based. Authenticates starting with the first instruction executed on host (Core/Xeon/Atom).

- UEFI Secure Boot: UEFI Boot manager ensures device boots only signed FW and OS loaders. UEFI Driver signing and protocol extensions. This is also known as BIOS as Root of Trust.

- Windows Secure Boot: Leverages UEFI Secure Boot to continue into Windows OS, a Windows certification requirement.

- Direct Boot: An OS image such as Linux bzImage is loaded from stage 2 of the pre-OS boot loader.

- Verified Boot: Cryptographically verifies the Initial Boot Block of the pre-OS boot loader or UEFI or BIOS using boot policy key. A verified boot using Intel Boot Guard is shown in Figure 3-17.

- Immutable Root-of-Trust exists in the hardware.

- Root-of-Trust protects the initial boot process.

- It uses cryptographic keys to authenticate and validate the integrity of the Initial Boot Block (IBB).

- IBB maintains a secure boot chain by passing control to the next stage boot image after authentication and integrity verification.

- The final stage boot image passes control to the OS after authentication.

- Measured Boot: Measures the Initial Boot Block (IBB) and subsequent stages into platform storage such as Trusted Platform Module (TPM) or firmware-based TPM or secure storage.

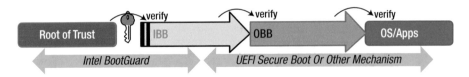

Figure 3-17. *Verified boot flow with Boot Guard*

The following terms will be useful to understand the following sequence that describes the process of Measured Boot using Boot Guard as shown in Figure 3-18:

- Hashing algorithms typically employed include Hash_alg = SHA1, SHA256, SHA384, SM3.

- Extending: It is a process of updating a PCR with a hash.

- PCR: Platform Configuration Register hosted inside PTT/TPM. The PCR 0–7 are used for pre-OS environment, and PCR 8–15 are used for OS and beyond. Refer to the TCG TPM specification for recommended PCR allocations.

- The new PCR value can be computed with PCR_new = Hash_alg(PCR_old || Hash_alg(data_new)).

- Logging: Keeps a log of all measurements in an ACPI table.

- ACM: Intel Authenticated Code Module, integrated in the BIOS/UEFI/boot loader for authenticating and measuring the IBB.

1. Upon power ON, CSME starts by computing the hash of ACM, and the hash of the ACM is stored in PCR 0.

2. The ACM computes the hash of IBB and extends it into PCR 0.

3. The IBB computes the hash of OEM Boot Block (OBB) aka the second stage pre-OS boot loader and extends the hash into PCR 0 and stores the hash of Platform Config Data into PCR 1.

4. The OBB computes the hash of OS loader and stores the corresponding hash into PCR 4. It stores the hash of Firmware Boot Policy in PCR 7.

5. The OS loader computes the hash of OS kernel and stores the hash into PCR 8.

6. The OS kernel can compute the hash of the user mode drivers/libraries and applications and extend the respective hashes into PCR 8–15 to meet the platform chain of trust requirements.

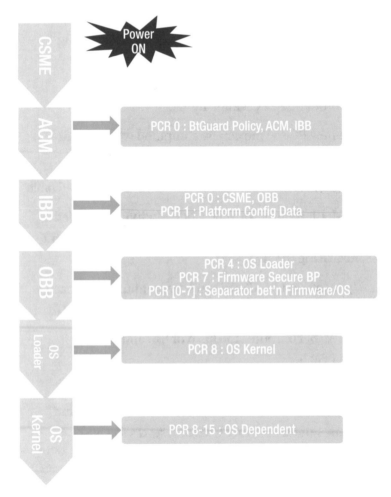

Figure 3-18. *Measured Boot sequence*

Secure Boot Mechanisms

The stack below describes the lowest layer to be the HW layer, and above that is the firmware layer which includes the modules required to handle the HW IP blocks and Digital Rights Management. Above that is the boot loader/UEFI used to initialize the CPU and chipset. The optional hypervisor supports the Virtual Machine Manager (VMM) functionality. The upper layers include the OS ingredients for kernel and User mode.

Above that layer are the middleware/frameworks and applications. This diagram (Figure 3-19) also illustrates the security goal that trust begins at the lowest layers and must be extended into the layers above – and that doing so requires conscious techniques to get it right. If/when those techniques fail, the stack recovers by falling back to lower layers.

The stack includes booting into application TEEs and the need to distinguish security-sensitive function and workloads that should be separated from "traditional" function and workloads. We can refer to the TEE and lower layers as the trusted computing base upon which the rest of the stack depends. The stack also supports networking and the idea that lower layers implementing the TCB can be linked (in an IoT use case) so that a Distributed TCB (DTCB) can be formed that supports distributed trusted workloads such as key management/migration, device management, SW/FW update of an IoT fog/network, and so on.

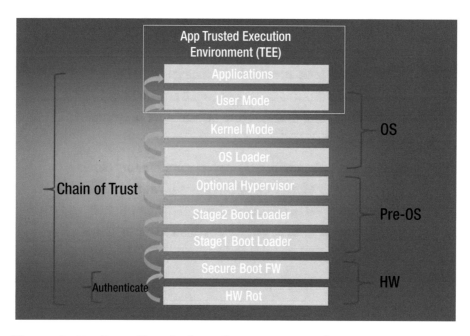

Figure 3-19. *Describes the boot flow on a core along with the chain of trust and signing implications*

Secure Boot Terminology Overview

Secure Boot Types: With the Field Programmable Fuse (One Time Programmable) profile options within the SoC, you can configure the device in an unsecured boot where the boot ingredients in stages are assumed to be trusted and no authentication is performed, referred to in Figure 3-20.

- Verified Boot: Boot policies are enforced during the boot process. Starting with the Root of Trust for verification, the currently executing module verifies the next module against a policy. The boot process is stopped if secure boot guarantee is violated. It is important to note that this only provides assurance that the boot policy was enforced.

- Measured Boot: Integrity measurement is placed into the TPM. Starting with the Root of Trust for measurement, the currently executing module places the integrity measurement of the next module into the TPM. Computer is *not* stopped if secure boot guarantee is violated and provable to remote systems via attestation.

- Secure Boot: A boot process which implements either Verified Boot, Measured Boot, or both. Verified Boot is often referred to as Secure Boot; Measured Boot is often referred to as Trusted Boot (also refers to TBoot sometimes).

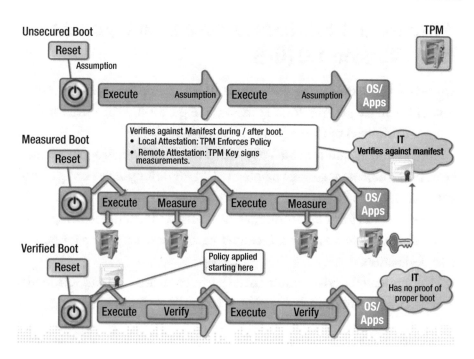

Figure 3-20. *Types of boot*

IOT devices are inherently vulnerable to physical attacks primarily due to their ability to connect to billions of devices. A first step in building a robust device is to ensure that the very first component of the boot loader is authenticated. This is implemented by a method known as secure boot which is based on a hardware root of trust in a platform. The immutable code running on on-die ROM in an isolated environment on a security engine forms an anchor. This ROM code loads the stage 1 of the boot loader into security engine's SRAM and cryptographically authenticates the image before executing it on the host CPU. The secure boot method on Intel Architecture is explained in detail including the HW and cryptographic blocks. Refer to Figure 3-21.

Overview of BIOS/UEFI Secure Boot Using Boot Guard Version 1.0 (BtG)

The verified boot flow using FSP+coreboot leveraging the Intel Boot Guard version 1.0 on Skylake platform is shown in Figure 3-21. The terms are explained followed by the sequence.

IPF: Infield Programmable Fuses also known as Field Programmable Fuses (FPF) represent storage inside the CPU/SoC for policy configuration and are One Time Programmable (OTP). The provisioning tools are provided by Intel for programming these fuses in the manufacturing flow.

Platform Power Sequence: Includes starting boot sequence for power rail stabilization.

Authenticated Code Module (ACM): Intel provided FW module loaded from flash, authenticated and executed in CPU's cache as RAM (CAR).

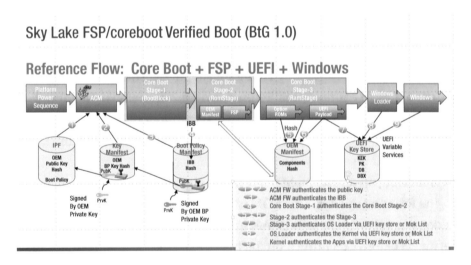

Figure 3-21. *FSP/coreboot-based verified boot on Skylake using Boot Guard 1.0*

The sequence is outlined here:

- ACM authenticates Core Boot Stage-1.

- Core Boot Stage-1: Authenticates Core Boot Stage-2 using the BPM.

- Core Boot Stage-2: Authenticates Core Boot Stage-3 using the OEM Manifest.

- Core Boot Stage-3: Authenticates OS Loader (Windows or Grub/ELILO or others).

- OS Loader (Linux or Windows or RTOS): Authenticates kernel image.

- Kernel: Authenticates the user mode and applications.

Refer to this link for starting with coreboot: `www.coreboot.org/Lesson1`

Firmware Support Package (FSP) is provided by Intel for initializing Intel silicon, designed for integration into a boot loader of the developer's choice. FSP source code can be leveraged for ideas and references for implementing verified and measured boot using Intel Boot Guard and PTT/TPM; more information can be found at: `https://firmware.intel.com/learn/fsp/about-intel-fsp`

Data Protection – Securing Keys, Data at Rest and in Transit

At rest: Storing data/secrets/content securely on the storage and whole disk encryption is the most popular example. This also is a very important problem. If a malware or even a legitimate application can access the secrets that it's not authorized, it causes an unstable device. Certain regulations such as General Data Protection Regulation (GDPR) mandate protecting the privacy of the data both at rest and in transit. For more information on encryption-related protection of data, refer to

`https://ec.europa.eu/commission/sites/beta-political/files/`
`data-protection-factsheet-sme-obligations_en.pdf`. Section (83) calls
for encryption for confidentiality in: `https://eur-lex.europa.eu/legal-`
`content/EN/TXT/PDF/?uri=CELEX:32016R0679&from=EN`

Article 6, 4 (e) also calls for encryption or pseudonymization
of personal data which ensures reidentifying only with additional
information. This is in contrast to anonymity where the anonymized data
can no longer be reidentified.

Runtime protection problem: How do we protect the data and the
code from each other in the system during Runtime? TEEs are an excellent
method for this. Examples include SGX.

It is useful to think about theft threats and the idea that attackers
are able to perform brute force crypto hacking as they have access to all
the encrypted data and wrapped keys and so on. Encrypting using AES
before storing the data on a disk makes it harder for attackers to reverse
engineer and steal the secrets. An example use case for this is the Windows
BitLocker technology which implements the whole disk encryption with
strong passwords. There are increased threats due to persistent memory
technologies supported by Optane and 3D Xpoint. These are persistent
storage technologies making them subject to theft threats. Memory
encryption is a mitigation where any/all data that goes out of the CPU/SOC
on bus is encrypted whether it's destined for DRAM or SSD. The encryption
technologies such as AES XTS 265 and secure boot existing in Optane + 3D
Xpoint can be utilized to protect assets concerning flash-based memory.

Intel Platform Trust Technology (PTT)

Intel® PTT is a implementation of the Trusted Platform Module (TPM)
2.0 specification in firmware. CSME/TXE Engine is used as cryptographic
processor for TPM implementation. SPI flash (TXE/CSME filesystem) is
used as secure storage. PTT currently implements only mandatory and
recommended TPM 2.0 commands mentioned in MSFT "signal and profile
document."

As shown in Figure 3-22, the PTT includes random number generator, encryption/decryption, sign/verify, secure key generation, secure key/data storage, device identity both unique and anonymous, and device attestation.

Figure 3-22. *PTT components*

Windows PTT Architecture

On Windows as shown in Figure 3-23, the host SW components include the Trusted Base Services (TBS), the TPM.sys kernel mode driver, and ACPI which interact with PTT FW through Memory Mapped IO (MMIO)–based

PTT interface. The PTT interface in turn calls into the TXE or CSME. The SPI storage is used as the secure storage where the keys and other secrets are stored encrypted and signed to ensure confidentiality and integrity. The CSME contains internal crypto engines and SRAM and uses SPI flash to store the keys in an encrypted format.

Pre-OS environment (BIOS/UEFI/coreboot) implements the following:

- Selects between available PTT/TPMs

- Enables/disables PTT/TPM

- Issues TPM clear (PPI)

- Logs measurements in TPM and ACPI for OS

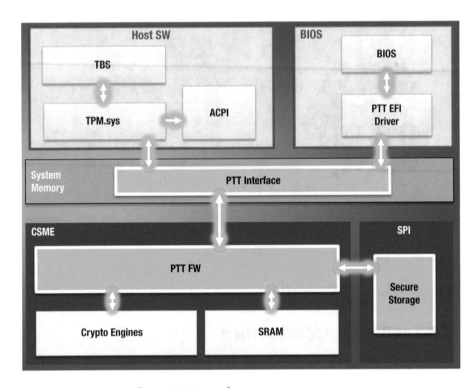

Figure 3-23. *Windows PTT stack*

Linux PTT Software Stack

As shown in Figure 3-24, in Linux OS stack, a PTT-based application has multiple mechanisms to interact with PTT including PKCS #11 and Feature API, and an expert application developer can directly interact with System API.

- TPM Device Driver (TDD) handles physical data transmission in ring 0/kernel mode.

- TPM Command Transmission Interface (TCTI) handles marshalling and unmarshalling of full TPM commands.

- System API (SAPI) enables creation and handling of TPM objects, sessions, and policies.

- Enhanced SAPI (ESAPI) enables management of the created objects, sessions, and policies.

- Feature API (FAPI) designed to capture 80% of common use cases combining operations with profile definitions.

- TAB controls access to the TPM in multiple application scenarios.

- RM manages the limited TPM resident memory.

- PKCS #11 – WIP on TPM 2.0.

TPM through SAPI specifications and implementations are mature, while ESAPI and FAPI implementations are still developing.

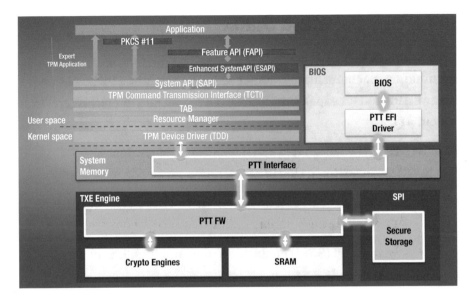

Figure 3-24. *Linux PTT stack*

Runtime Protection – Ever Vigilant

Most of the IoT devices spend their life in this phase where the device is functional and performing its intended persona. This phase is critical for devices that are "always on." The assets to be protected include data, code, and identity. Once the chain of trust is stable (secure booted), to maintain the stable chain of trust, every bit and byte must be authenticated before admitting into the system on every supported interface (USB, serial, BT/ Wi-Fi). This objective can be achieved with high robustness level using a Trusted Execution Environment (TEE). The technologies available for implementing Runtime protections include Intel VT, SGX, CSME, and TXT.

Intel Virtualization Technology (Intel VT)

Virtualization abstracts hardware that allows multiple workloads to share a common set of resources. On shared virtualized hardware, a variety of workloads can colocate while maintaining full isolation from each other, freely migrate across infrastructures, and scale as needed.

198

CPU virtualization features enable abstraction of the full prowess of Intel® CPU to a virtual machine (VM). All software in the VM can run without any performance or compatibility hit, as if it was running natively on a dedicated CPU. Live migration from one Intel® CPU generation to another, as well as nested virtualization, is possible.

Memory virtualization features allow abstraction, isolation, and monitoring of memory on a per virtual machine (VM) basis. These features may also make live migration of VMs possible, add to fault tolerance, and enhance security. Example features include direct memory access (DMA) remapping and extended page tables (EPT), including their extensions: accessed and dirty bits and fast switching of EPT contexts.

I/O virtualization features facilitate offloading of multicore packet processing to network adapters as well as direct assignment of virtual machines to virtual functions, including disk I/O. Examples include Virtual Machine Device Queues (VMDQ), Single Root I/O Virtualization (SR-IOV, also a PCI-SIG standard), and Intel® Data Direct I/O Technology enhancements (Intel® DDIO).

Graphics Virtualization Technology (Intel® GVT) allows VMs to have full and/or shared assignment of the graphics processing units (GPU) as well as the video transcode accelerator engines integrated in Intel System-on-Chip products. It enables usages such as workstation remoting, desktop-as-a-service, media streaming, and online gaming.

Virtualization of security and network functions enables transformation of traditional network and security workloads into compute. Virtual functions can be deployed on standard high-volume servers anywhere in the data center, network nodes, or Cloud and smartly colocated with business workloads. Examples of Intel® technologies making it happen include Data Plane Development Kit (DPDK), Intel® QuickAssist Technology, and Hyperscan.

Intel® Virtualization Technology for Connectivity (Intel® VT-c) is a key feature of many Intel® Ethernet Controllers. With I/O virtualization and Quality of Service (QoS) features designed directly into the controller's silicon, Intel VT-c enables I/O virtualization that transitions the traditional physical network models used in data centers to more efficient virtualized models by providing port partitioning, multiple Rx/Tx queues, and on-controller QoS functionality that can be used in both virtual and nonvirtual server deployments.

As shown in Figure 3-25, the isolation capability enabled by VT technology is being utilized to create an architecture with a Trusted Execution Environment (TEE). The TEE is implemented as a secure VM with privileged execution and access to resources; examples include Microsoft VSM and Trusty (`https://source.android.com/security/trusty/`).

Virtualization and VM Isolation components include Intel® VTx (CPU), Intel® VTd (I/O), VmFunc (Hypervisor).

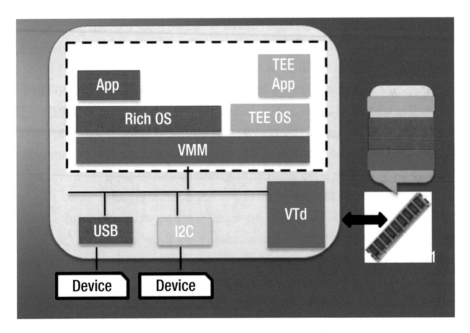

Figure 3-25. *TEE using virtualization environment*

TEE OS: Thin OS running alongside rich OS. Examples are Microsoft VSM, Android Trusty, and so on.

Rich OS: Regular OS that executes non-security-sensitive workloads. Examples are Microsoft Windows, Linux, Android, and so on.

Trusted computing base (TCB): VMM + TEE OS + TEE App.

Isolated execution: VMs are isolated from each other by the VMM.

Trusted Input/Output: Can be implemented by assigning I/O Controllers to different VMs.

Software Guard Extensions (SGX)

This section explains the usage of Software Guard Extensions (SGX) for implementing a Trusted Execution Environment (TEE) with the new instructions supported in IA CPUs. For any IoT device, the ability to execute code that handles secrets/assets in a protected environment is crucial. SGX leverages the partitioning of code into trusted and untrusted domains which interact with each other via well-defined SGX instructions.

How does SGX work as shown in Figure 3-26? The following model describes the interactions between the application and the SGX enclave.

1. Application is built with trusted and untrusted parts.

2. Application runs and creates enclave which is placed in trusted memory.

3. Trusted function is called; code running inside enclave sees data in clear; external access to data is denied.

4. Trusted function returns; enclave data remains in trusted memory.

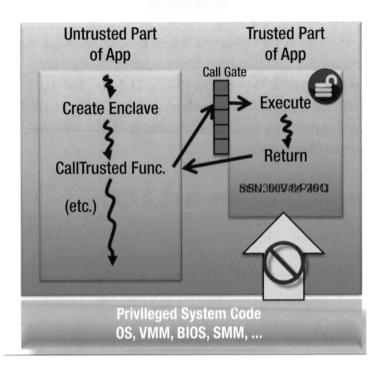

Figure 3-26. *SGX in action*

It is important to understand the software development model for the benefit of the developers (Figure 3-27):

- Sensitive code and data are partitioned into an "enclave" module which is a shared object (.so).

- Define the enclave interface and use tools to generate stubs/proxies.

- SGX Libraries provide APIs (C/C++) to encapsulate heavy-lifting implementation.

- Use a familiar toolchain to build and debug.

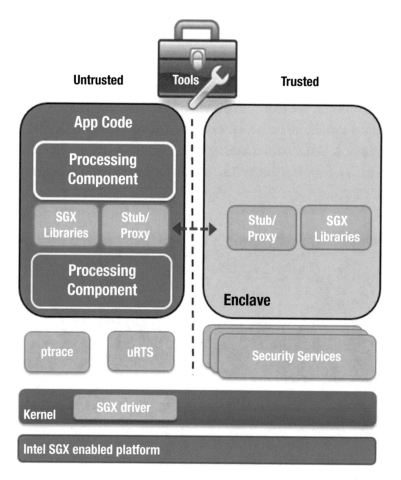

Figure 3-27. *SGX SW development model*

For further details, please refer to SGX web portal at: `https://software.intel.com/en-us/sgx`

Intel CSE/CSME – DAL

Intel Converged Security Engine in CSE/CSME is a dedicated engine for security and provides a HW root of trust for the platform. Dynamic Application Loader (DAL) exposes a general-purpose execution environment and is in production use since 2011 (Sandy Bridge) and exists in almost every Intel-based platform. It extends the CSE FW by dynamically loading signed CSE applications at Runtime. It allows faster deployment of FW applications by decoupling the application development from the platform development lifecycle. The FW applications are stored on host filesystem, thus avoiding flash size considerations. DAL enables binary-level portability for applications and is based on a virtual machine; DAL applications are written in the Java programming language. Refer to Figure 3-28.

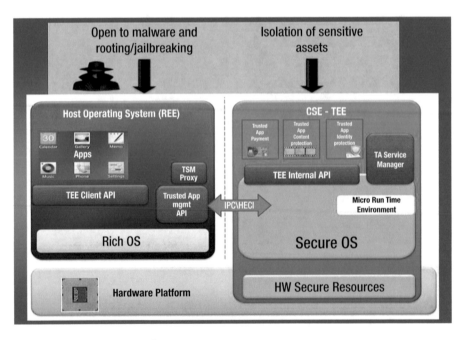

Figure 3-28. *DAL architecture*

Isolation from Rich Execution Environment

All the trusted applications (TAs) run in an isolated environment as supported by DAL and with the following attributes:

- TAs run in separate Java-like VM environment.
- TA-to-TA snooping is prevented using sandboxing.
- DAL prevents TA direct access to resources of other TAs.

Authenticity and Security

The DAL applications or TAs are subjected to the following robustness rules:

- DAL allows installation of signed and encrypted DAL TA in the CSE (security coprocessor).
- The TA can use the secure services, that is, secure storage to access SPI flash.
- Intel or OEM signed TAs can be installed.

Portability

The TAs have the binary-level portability subjected to the following scope:

- DAL is based on a virtual machine; DAL applications are written in Java.
- DAL enables binary-level portability for FW applications across the OS and HW platform.

Following are sample applications where DAL is deployed:

- Intel® Identity Protection Technology (Intel® IPT).

    - Identity protection and e-payment: OTP (one-time password), PTD (protected trusted display), PKI (public key infrastructure), NFC (near field communication).

    - Intel® PKI (PEAT) for IT market: Symantec Managed PKI, Intel IT.

    - McAfee (Intel Security): MFAb (Multifactor Authentication for Business), True Key – using IPT.

- Intel® Security Assist (ISA): A self-updater service which recommends security products to end users.

- China UnionPay (CUP): Implementing a Tap and Pay e-Commerce solution.

- Intel® Software Guard Extensions (Intel® SGX): The "Secure Enclaves" technology consumes CSME platform services using DAL.

- IOT Retail SmartPOS (Point Of Sale): Based on Atom platforms with Android.

Intel Trusted Execution Technology (TXT)

Intel® Trusted Execution Technology (Intel® TXT) provides hardware-based security technologies to help build a solid foundation for security. Built into Intel's silicon, these technologies address the increasing and evolving security threats across physical and virtual infrastructures by complementing Runtime protections such as antivirus software. Intel TXT also can play a role in meeting government and industry regulations and data protection standards by providing a hardware-based method of verification useful in compliance efforts.

As shown in Figure 3-29, Intel® TXT capable processors and chipsets allow establishing of the "root of trust" and "Measured Launch Environment" (MLE) to support trust decisions; within the computing platform, a MLE is needed. A "root-of-trust" is also needed which should be established first at the silicon level and then extended to the entire solution stack. The technology draws upon a rich set of security/virtualization features embedded into the IA processors and also integrated into the BIOS as well as other platform ingredients.

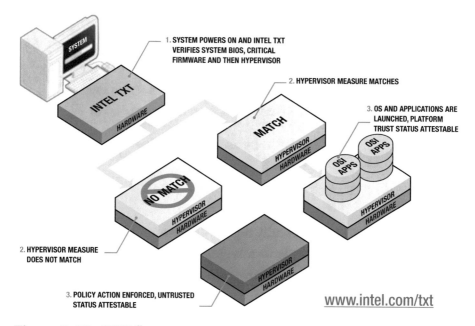

Figure 3-29. *TXT flow*

Figure 3-30 depicts the critical enabling requirements for the technology in server implementations. Intel TXT is specifically designed to harden platforms from the emerging threats of hypervisor attacks, BIOS, or other firmware attacks, malicious rootkit installations, or other software-based attacks. It increases protection by allowing greater control of the launch stack through a Measured Launch Environment (MLE) and

207

enabling isolation in the boot process. More specifically, it extends the Virtual Machine Extensions (VMX) environment of Intel® Virtualization Technology (Intel® VT), permitting a verifiably secure installation, launch, and use of a hypervisor or operating system (OS).

A chain-of-trust built on top of Intel® TXT

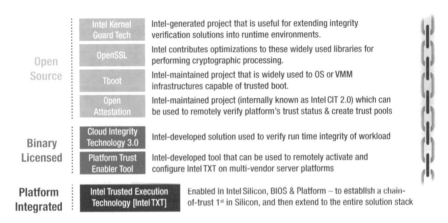

Figure 3-30.   TXT chain of trust

Intel TXT gives IT and security organizations important enhancements to help ensure more secure platforms; greater application, data, or virtual machine (VM) isolation; and improved security or compliance audit capabilities. Not only can it help reduce support and remediation costs, but it can also provide a foundation for more advanced solutions as security needs change to support increasingly virtualized or "multitenant" shared data center resources.

Threats Mitigated

Intel assets as described earlier can be leveraged to improve the robustness and to defend against both zero-day and other attacks. Refer to Figure 3-31.

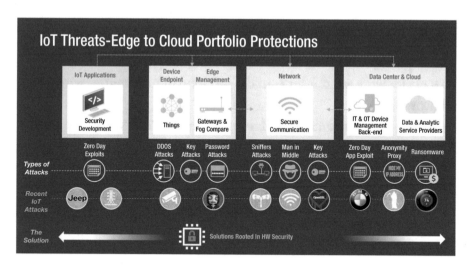

Figure 3-31. *Mitigation of IoT threats*

Zero-Day Attacks

Attacks that are designed to exploit a previously unknown vulnerability are referred to as zero-day attacks.[6] These attacks are harder to detect in time to minimize the damaging impact.

IoT applications: The impact of a compromise due to zero-day attacks can be minimized by handling all the high-value assets/secrets in a protected Runtime environment such as a TEE. DAL, SGX, and Trusty provide such defenses. Examples include remote car control in the jeep scenario and Ukraine power grid.

- Mitigation: Intel® Security Essentials, Intel Stratix® FPGA, protected boot, and attested software measurements can be implemented to mitigate the risks resulting from the preceding zero-day attacks. These solutions also enable a simplified TEE-based IP protection for ecosystem.

---

[6]https://csrc.nist.gov/glossary/term/zero-day-attack

Other Attacks

Other high impacting attacks include the distributed denial of service (DDOS), network attacks, and attacks on cloud infrastructures which hold rich troves of data.

Device Endpoint and Edge Management: The DDOS/key/password examples include CCTV Hijack and Mirai botnet.

- Mitigation: Intel® Secure Device Onboard can be deployed to mitigate the risks resulting from the preceding attacks. This is accomplished by not shipping devices with default credentials and instead use EPID identity designed-in for privacy preserving provisioning model to eliminate human misconfiguration with automated onboarding.

Network: Sniffers and man-in-the-middle examples include Tornado Siren Hijack, WPA CRACK, and Heart Bleed.

- Mitigation: Intel® Security Essentials API, Intel® Platform Trust Technology, Intel® Software Guard Extensions. Simplified HW secured key management and provisioning APIs. HW secured SSL transport APIs. PTT or TEE protected data and key storage.

Data Center and Cloud: Anonymity Proxy and ransomware examples include Infotainment VIN Online service app, Reaper, Thermostats, and WannaCry.

- Mitigation: Wind River Helix Device Cloud. Automated Over-the-Air (OTA) updates for firmware and software, provisioning, credential management, suspend, decommission, and firewall policy update to isolate/quarantine.

Conclusion

Security is not a blanket and requires pragmatic approach. It needs understanding of the assets to be protected against a set of threats in a system consisting of a set of vulnerabilities. Intel has a lot of HW security assets which can be leveraged to boot an IoT device securely and continue building on the chain of trust tethered to a HWRoT. Intel has security features residing in the CPU and PCH. The device identity, boot integrity, data protection, and Runtime protection are the four fundamental buckets of capabilities for securely booting into a TEE with a relevant TCB and later into a distributed TCB.

References

- https://software.intel.com/en-us/articles/
  intel-sha-extensions

- https://software.intel.com/en-us/articles/
  intel-advanced-encryption-standard-
  instructions-aes-ni

- www.intel.com/content/dam/doc/white-paper/
  enterprise-security-aes-ni-white-paper.pdf

- https://software.intel.com/sites/default/
  files/m/d/4/1/d/8/10TB24_Breakthrough_AES_
  Performance_with_Intel_AES_New_Instructions.
  final.secure.pdf

Security Hacks

- `http://spectrum.ieee.org/cars-that-think/`
  `transportation/self-driving/hackers-take-`
  `control-of-a-moving-jeep`

- `http://spectrum.ieee.org/automaton/robotics/`
  `robotics-hardware/video-friday-bacteria-`
  `driving-robot-drone-with-gun-freaky-snakebot`

- CPUID A: Intel® 64 and IA-32 Architectures Software
  Developer's Manual, Volume 2: Instruction Set
  Reference, A-Z. [Online] `http://www.intel.com/`
  `content/www/us/en/processors/architectures-`
  `software-developermanuals.html.`

- CPUID B: Intel® Processor Identification and the CPUID
  Instruction. [Online] April 2012. `http://www.intel.`
  `com/content/www/us/en/processors/processor-`
  `identification-cpuidinstruction-note.html.`

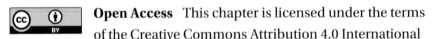

CHAPTER 4

IoT Software Security Building Blocks

Oleg Selajev from Oracle Labs is famous on Twitter for saying, "The '*S*' in the IoT stands for security."[1] Oleg does not spell poorly; instead, he was bemoaning the sad state of affairs in IoT security. Despite the truth in Oleg's statement, security does not have to be absent in IoT.

Chapter 3 took a comprehensive look at the hardware security offerings in the Intel Architecture. Putting these hardware features to use in an IoT platform requires software. This chapter looks at the software components used to secure IoT systems and how those software components make use of the underlying hardware security features described in Chapter 3.

In this chapter we define a software stack, building on top of the hardware all the way up to the IoT applications, and describe how to put the "*S*" back into IoT. As a way to guide our exploration of software security in IoT, the opening section introduces a generic architectural model that graphically depicts software components of a secure IoT device or gateway. A more detailed section is then dedicated to each component in our model, and we will define the necessary security

---

[1] www.cnet.com/news/iot-attacks-hacker-kaspersky-are-getting-worse-and-no-one-is-listening/

© The Author(s) 2020
S. Cheruvu et al., *Demystifying Internet of Things Security*,
https://doi.org/10.1007/978-1-4842-2896-8_4

features as well as how those features contribute to the overall IoT device security. Our architectural model is a generalization of IoT devices, and no generalization is ever perfect; as Alexandre Dumas once said, "All generalizations are dangerous, even this one."[2] Therefore, in Chapter 6, we look at some actual Intel and open source software products and compare them with our generic model.

Due to the breadth of the software topic, this chapter is the longest in the book. For this reason, we have organized the sections so that they do not need to be consumed in a linear fashion, although they do build on one another. Figure 4-1 provides a map of the sections, and the topics covered in each one, including the security concerns discussed. The reader is encouraged to review the figure to find topics that are most relevant or interesting to them. Throughout the chapter, we provide forward and backward references to other sections that may contain additional relevant information, making navigation to the most interesting information a bit easier.

---

[2]Alexandre Dumas, quote, `www.brainyquote.com/quotes/alexandre_dumas_136868`

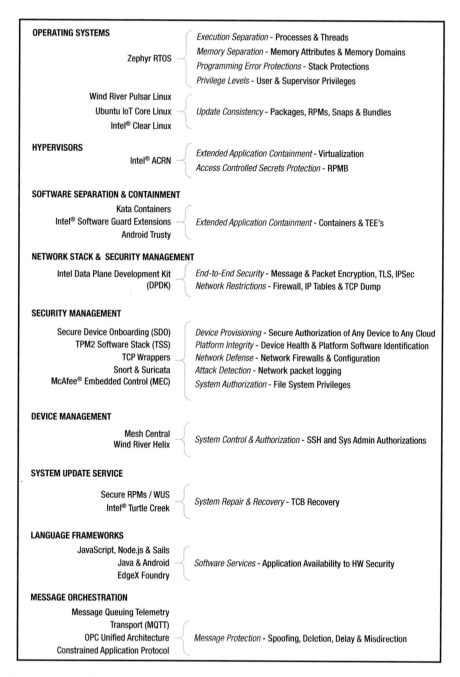

Figure 4-1. *Section outline and security topics*

Understanding the Fundamentals of Our Architectural Model

Before we explore the details of IoT software security building blocks, let us take a quick tour through our architectural model to establish a context for each of the building block components and how they fit together to create an IoT device. Our architectural model is shown in Figure 4-2 and is divided in four quadrants, where each quadrant contains software for a different purpose. Vertically, the figure is divided into platform software, which is the software that creates the *platform environment*, and application software, which is the software that creates the *platform behaviors* of the system. Horizontally, the figure is divided between the management plane, which handles management of the system, and the application/data plane, which is everything else not management related.

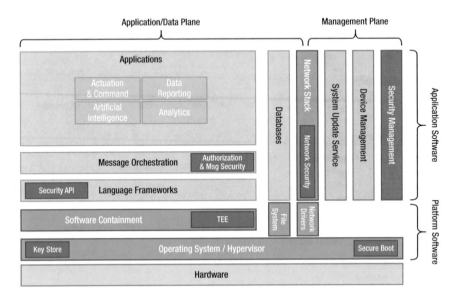

Figure 4-2. *Generic IoT stack diagram*

Beginning at the bottom is the *hardware* covered in Chapter 3. All hardware is implied by this element, including the processor, memory subsystems, flash and other storage, security coprocessors, wired and wireless communication hardware, or anything else physically connected to the processing unit and its motherboard. This chapter does not cover any of these elements, but refers back to the content in Chapter 3 where appropriate.

Directly above the *hardware* is the *operating system/hypervisor* element which is the system software in direct control of the hardware and may be a commercial or open source operating system, or it may be an hypervisor that creates one or more virtual hardware devices for the rest of the software to operate within.

The *software containment* element is optional, but if provided on the system includes technologies like containers and Trusted Execution Environments (TEE). This level of additional containment improves security by reducing privileges and controlling unintended interactions between applications. Both containers and virtualization with hypervisors provide containment. We devote a bit of time to discuss the differences and benefits of each.

Figure 4-2 also shows two components that are not covered individually, but will be interspersed among the other platform software components: the filesystem and the network drivers. These are shown in the diagram to aid in understanding the connection between the application part of the stack and the platform software.

Moving up from the *platform* software to the *application software*, we look at the *management plane*. The *management plane* software is made up of *security management*, *device management*, and the *system update service*. It also includes the *network stack*.

The *network stack* is most often included in the system software or part of the operating system. However, for our purposes, including it in the operating system obscures it and diminishes its importance to IoT systems. The network stack deserves its own separate treatment because it actually enables a system to communicate with other devices, turning that system into an Internet of Things device. Additionally, the network stack is the entry point for the majority of attacks on IoT systems. It straddles both the application/data plane and the management plane, because it is used extensively by both. It includes communication protocols and network interfaces. The network stack subsection covers software elements needed to secure the network stack, like firewalls and intrusion detection systems (IDS). Chapter 6 is dedicated to covering the network protocols themselves.

Security management is the management software that performs security relevant management operations and used when exercising security management procedures and controls. The functionality in security management includes device identity and attestation, key distribution and certificate management, access control policy, logging rules, configuring and querying the system update service, and policy for network security, firewalls, virus scanners, and host intrusion detection software. Oftentimes these features are included as part of the actual software that performs device management. In our treatment, security management is separate from other management features to highlight adherence to the least privilege principle.[3] Security management features should require a higher level of privilege and additional authentication for an administrator to activate.

The *device management* element includes all the management features that are not part of security management. This includes querying and managing the state of the device, rebooting/restarting the platform, examining and downloading log files (but not deleting log files or stopping logs from being generated, as this is a security management function), starting and stopping and restarting applications, configuring applications, managing databases, and configuring message queues and software orchestration settings.

---

[3]Saltzer and Schroeder. *The Protection of Information in Computer Systems.* 1975. This paper defines several foundational security design principles which are referred to throughout this chapter.

The *system update service* is the last component of the management plane. While this element is controlled by the security management element (or the device management element in some platforms), it is typically composed of platform and operating system–specific elements in order to update more than just the application software and execution containers on the system. Updates to system and device firmware, boot loaders, and BIOS normally require special software and services to properly coordinate the version dependencies and be able to set the platform into the state where such components can be updated. The system privilege to update firmware and trusted software on the device must be strictly separated from everyday management functions.

The *application/data plane* contains the software that creates the actual behavior of the IoT device. This includes language frameworks, message orchestration, databases, and the applications themselves. Our discussion of these elements is limited, because we focus only on the parts of these elements that leverage hardware security features.

The *language frameworks* contain libraries and services used by application software. Examples of these include the Android framework in Java, Node.js libraries, and the Sails framework in JavaScript.

Message orchestration enables applications on the same platform to communicate, but more importantly enables machine-to-machine (M2M) communications over the network. Protocols like MQTT, message queue, and publisher-subscriber frameworks (pub-sub) like Kafka fall into the message orchestration bucket.

Databases are an important part of IoT systems, as they allow the data that is generated, manipulated, and consumed by IoT systems to be stored, collated, and massaged. There are multiple different types of database systems, including SQL and NoSQL. The types of operations possible on data and the security and privacy of that data are dependent on the database chosen.

The last element of Figure 4-2 is the *applications* themselves. This chapter is not able to cover all types of applications due to the broad diversity of IoT. However, in Chapter 6, several IoT use cases are explored, including a more detailed discussion of the security interactions and trade-offs between the platform and the software that is required to compose a working IoT system.

The next sections will look at each of these IoT software components in varying detail, and in each primary component section, we will introduce security topics relevant to that component.

Operating Systems

When considering software security in any platform, the first consideration should be the operating system. The operating system traditionally is the lowest, most base level of software on any system. It controls what hardware is activated and limits what other software can do. The operating system provides the baseline feature set for all the other software on the platform. If the operating system does not provide some basic feature, or does not allow other software to control or access some aspect of the system (hardware or software), then no other part of the platform can make up for that gap. If a particular security feature is missing from the operating system, then the rest of the software on the platform is likely exposed to significantly more threats. In this section, we take a look at some basic features of operating systems and discuss what security capabilities the operating system should be contributing to the security of the platform. The following is a basic list of security services that an operating system should provide:

- **Execution Separation:** Provides structures and mechanisms to separate different execution units of programs, so that their execution does not interfere with other executing programs; this separation includes processes, threads, interrupt service routines (ISRs), and critical sections.

- **Memory Separation:** Provides mechanisms to separate the different types of memory used by executing programs; this type of separation normally includes process memory, thread-only stacks, shared memory, and memory mapped I/O.

- **Privilege Levels:** Provide structures to separate executing programs into different privilege levels; this separation includes task identifiers for executing programs, user and group identities to own executing programs, and administrator vs. user privilege levels.

- **System authorization:** Provides structures and mechanisms to assign rights to objects and verify the privilege level of execution units against those rights; this includes setting the default privilege level assigned to programs and then enforcing those privileges when programs access system resources, by either permitting or restricting certain operations. This system authorization mechanism allows the implementation of the least privilege principle.[3] In systems with human users, this extends to authentication of users and assignment of privileges to programs under the user's control.

- **Programming Error Protections:** Provide structures and mechanisms to stop errors in executing programs from enabling attackers to manipulate those errors and take over the platform; these typically include stack overflow protection, detection and prevention of heap corruption, and restriction on control flow redirection. All these mistakes result in software attacks that allow a hacker to inject arbitrary code and take over a platform. Control flow protections include protection

221

from *Return-Oriented Programming* (ROP) and *Jump-Oriented Programming* (JOP) (see sidebar for detailed explanation[4, 5]).

- **Access-Controlled Secrets storage**: Provides mechanisms to store program secrets and prevent those secrets from being accessed by unauthorized users or programs, including the administrator; the system normally provides this through a hardware-backed secure storage.

WHAT IS ROP/JOP?

Return-Oriented Programming (ROP) and Jump-Oriented Programming (JOP) are two techniques used by attackers to create exploit code without having to download large binaries to the target platform. Buffer overruns have been used since the Morris Internet Worm to inject code onto a platform and cause that code to execute.

However, various countermeasures, including DEP (Data Execution Prevention) and ASLR (Address Space Layout Randomization), as well as network defenses that detect and prevent downloads of large binary data, have made such attacks more difficult. Instead of downloading new code, attackers use ROP and JOP techniques to reuse code already on the target platform, allowing attackers to construct their attack code on the fly. Since most software today includes shared libraries, the attacker leverages this to find *gadgets* in software and libraries already existing on the platform and strings the gadgets together into attack code.

---

[4]Jonathan Pincus and Brandon Baker. Beyond stack smashing: Recent advances in exploiting buffer overruns. Security & Privacy, IEEE, 2(4):20–27, 2004.

[5]N. Carlini and D. Wagner. ROP is still dangerous: Breaking modern defenses. In USENIX Security Symposium, 2014.

Gadgets are very small segments of code in existing libraries that perform meaningful subfunctions, like moving data into a register or setting up for a system call. Gadgets either end in a *return* statement or a *jump* statement, allowing the attacker to string multiple gadgets together to craft a new control flow, that, overall with many gadgets, accomplishes their evil task. ROP uses return statements, while JOP uses jump statements. Both are effectively the same attack.

Choosing an operating system for an IoT platform *is* primarily about choosing the one with the best services that also executes reliably on the chosen platform hardware. The capabilities provided by the underlying hardware often affect what the operating system is capable of providing. Some operating systems are designed for servers, or even specifically for cloud deployments, while others are designed to be used in the smallest IoT devices. Small devices typically do not have the computing power or hardware features necessary for an advance operating system to execute. Operating systems designed for low-power processors typically do not have a rich set of services, because the power and performance budget available on the processor just will not support it. CPUs in constrained devices might not have a full memory management unit (MMU) with advanced features like total memory encryption (TME) or memory integrity technology. These types of features are common in server CPUs. Without these hardware capabilities, the operating system is left to provide best-effort security services. In coming to a final decision on what operating system to use for an IoT system, it is also important to evaluate the threats to the operating system and what countermeasures the operating system provides to neutralize those threats. You can then determine if the hardware chosen for your device is powerful enough to resist the attacks the device is likely to encounter.

Threats to Operating Systems

Operating systems run at the highest privilege level, with access to nearly everything on a platform. A successful attack on an operating system can garner the attacker complete control of the platform, often with privileged access to other platforms on the same network. Table 4-1 shows the products (not just operating systems) with the most number of distinct reported vulnerabilities, with data accumulated from 1999 through 2018. As this table shows, there are a large number of different attacks on operating systems. In fact, operating systems make up more than half of the top 50 products with the most vulnerabilities. Although there are numerous types of attacks, it is possible to organize operating system threats into threat classes, all of which execute in similar patterns.

Table 4-1. Products with Highest Reported Number of Vulnerabilities over a 20-Year Period

	Product Name	Vendor Name	Product Type	Number of Vulnerabilities
1	Linux Kernel	Linux	OS	2124
2	Mac Os X	Apple	OS	2084
3	Android	Google	OS	1925
4	Firefox	Mozilla	Application	1741
5	Debian Linux	Debian	OS	1670
6	Chrome	Google	Application	1546
7	Iphone Os	Apple	OS	1495
8	Ubuntu Linux	Canonical	OS	1123
9	Windows Server 2008	Microsoft	OS	1110
10	Flash Player	Adobe	Application	1060

---

[6]www.cvedetails.com/top-50-products.php. Retrieved 9 September 2018.

Attacks typically follow a common pattern, called a cyber kill chain®, shown in Figure 4-3, where an attacker executes a series of steps to compromise a target. The attacker begins by observing the target (Step 1), and then deciding how to attack the system, by fashioning some type of weaponized code (Step 2).

The weaponized software might be a program that runs from a web server or a crafted response packet in a protocol. The attacker delivers the attack in Step 3, which might entail a spear-fishing email, or hijacking a network connection, or injecting spoofed packets for a protocol. The actual attack occurs in Steps 4 and 5, and those steps can be iterative, where the attacker pivots from one compromised application or piece of software and uses that as a base to attack another piece of software or system service. Each pivot intends to increase the attacker's control of the platform or penetrate deeper into the network in order to gain complete control of the platform and the entire system.

With the background of the cyber kill chain in mind, we will review different classes of attacks on an operating system and describe how these attacks demonstrate an attacker pivoting progressively deeper into a system, as one attack builds on another. The following five items represent the common attack pattern used in Step 4, exploitation:

- **Fault Injection**: A fault injection creates or forces an execution fault in a process or thread; part of the responsibility for this threat rests on the applications themselves, but because fault injection is the first step to overcoming the operating system itself, the OS must take some responsibility to protect against the vulnerabilities that create this threat. The operating system uses containment to prevent these types of threats from growing into greater threats to the platform, but usually allows the fault to stop the execution of the attacked process or thread. From our

basic list of security services, the operating system uses
programming error protections, including control
flow protections and stack smashing protections, to
mitigate this threat.

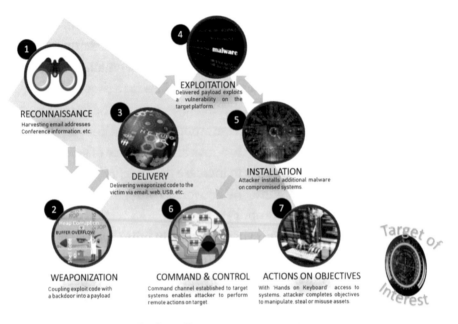

Figure 4-3. *Cyber kill chain[7]*

- **Arbitrary Code Execution**: Arbitrary code execution
  is the injection of an attacker's code into a process
  or thread on the platform, causing the injected code
  to run in place of the existing process or thread,
  effectively taking on that process or thread's identity

---

[7]Cyber Kill Chain Diagram, www.lockheedmartin.com/en-us/capabilities/
cyber/cyber-kill-chain.html

and authorizations. Arbitrary code execution clearly violates **execution separation** by allowing unauthorized code to corrupt an execution unit, but also violates the **memory separation** guarantee of an operating system, by allowing what should be data to corrupt the code executed by the platform. If fault injection succeeds, either because the application mitigations were not effective or the operating system did not provide any protections against fault injection, then the typical escalation of a fault injection is arbitrary code execution. An attacker places code into the data used to trigger the fault and constructs the fault injection to force execution of, or redirection to, the injected code as part of the fault. Buffer overflows and heap corruption are common mechanisms used by attackers to create arbitrary code execution exploits.

- **Breech of Containment**: Breech of containment is code in one execution unit observing or interfering with the code or data in another execution unit. Once an attacker has achieved arbitrary code execution, the next step is to leverage that power to extract data or further corrupt other execution flows within the platform. Side-channel attacks are a common mechanism used by attackers to extract data and observe program execution. Side channels are so dangerous because they allow a lower-privileged execution unit to observe a higher-privileged execution unit, potentially extracting secrets like passwords and cryptographic keys from those other execution units. These attacks violate **memory**

separation by allowing one program to view or infer data from another program; oftentimes, the way a program breeches the memory separation is through attacks on the **execution separation**. A common example of this execution separation breech is speculative branch prediction, although there are other examples as well.

- **Escalation of Privilege**: Escalation of privilege is overcoming the operating system's authorization mechanisms or code that is able to assume a level of privilege in the operating system that should not have been allowed. After breeching containment and extracting secrets from other execution units, an attacker can leverage those secrets to assume a higher privilege level. In some cases, it is possible for the attacker to inject a fault into the operating system itself and force it to grant a privilege that should not have been given to the attacker's code unit. In both cases, the attacker has escalated the privileges that the operating system grants to the attacker's process. This escalation violates the expected behavior of the **system authorization** mechanisms.

- **Rootkit**: A rootkit is malware that penetrates into the operating system itself and subsumes some of its operations. Following arbitrary code injection, an attacker can chain subsequent arbitrary code injections, containment breeches, and/or escalation of privilege attacks to eventually inject the attacker's code into the operating system itself. In some cases, the attack is a simple one-two chain; in other cases, it may be a series of more complex actions. If the attacker can then modify the operating system code on disk or in flash, the attacker can remain permanently on the system. Once an attacker has achieved this level of penetration into the system, it is often extremely difficult to remove the attacker from the system without a complete rebuild of both the software and firmware on the device. With rootkit access, an adversary can normally overcome even the **access-controlled secrets protections** provided by the platform, making all secrets and execution units on the device manipulable by the attacker. A rootkit can actually change the behavior of the operating system, by modifying access control decisions, hiding execution units, and reducing or removing memory protections between different execution units through changes to page table allocations.

As this list illustrates, one of the most basic threats to a computing system is *code and data corruption*. The cyber kill chain outlines the attacker's steps to take over a system, which usually involve a chain of attacks escalating an attacker's position from injecting code into a single application, to interfering with another running application, to eventually changing the entire operating system's behavior. The importance of code and data corruption protections cannot be overstated. Extrapolating from Turing's theory of computation, given enough time, modifications to code can result in serious consequences, as has been demonstrated by various academic papers on ROP and JOP.[8]

---

[8]Minh Tran, Mark Etheridge, Tyler Bletsch, Xuxian Jiang, Vincent Freeh, and Peng Ning. On the expressiveness of return-into-libc attacks. In Recent Advances in Intrusion Detection, pages 121–141. Springer, 2011.

In the following sections, we examine several operating systems used in IoT systems and discuss the security features available in those products. Rather than repetitively inspect the same features on several operating systems, we select different security topics on each operating system to inspect in depth. However, for each operating system, we provide a summary to review their protections, the mitigations they have chosen, and their shortcomings.

Zephyr: Real-Time Operating System for Devices

The Zephyr operating system is an open source OS designed for constrained devices running on microcontroller units (MCUs) or in other minimalistic environments. Zephyr runs on many different chips and architectures, including Intel® x86, ARM® Cortex-M, Tensilica® Xtensa, and others. Many IoT devices at the edge utilize these small processors with limited memory. The Zephyr documentation can be found at `http://docs.zephyrproject.org/`.

In this section, we want to focus on the basic operating system responsibilities of containment and privilege. Since an RTOS is severely limited in what it can provide, these most basic features comprise almost all of what an RTOS can offer. Since Zephyr may not be familiar to most readers, it is an interesting OS to explore, and Zephyr's simplicity makes it easy to highlight the limits of these protections and where usages can go wrong.

Zephyr, like most real-time operating systems (RTOS), is built as a single monolithic binary image; this means that both the operating system and the applications are compiled into one binary that is run on the platform. But unlike most other RTOS systems that were designed purely for size and performance requirements, Zephyr's documentation states that during design, careful thought was put into the security of the operating system. Figure 4-4 shows the Zephyr operating system decomposed into application code, OS services, and the kernel. The next few subsections will review how Zephyr operates and compare the security architecture[9] against the security properties that an operating system should exhibit. Zephyr version 1.12.0, which is the most current version as of this writing, is used for this review.

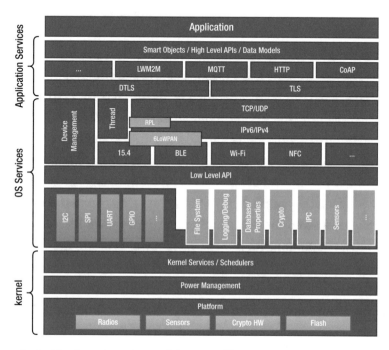

Figure 4-4. *Zephyr system architecture[10]*

Zephyr Execution Separation

Even though the Zephyr OS and the applications are built into a single binary, the OS still provides **execution separation**. In Zephyr, the primary execution unit is a thread. An application is composed of multiple threads that run forever in an endless loop. The application is defined and built

---

[9]http://docs.zephyrproject.org/security/security-overview.html

[10]Zephyr System Architecture Diagram, http://docs.zephyrproject.org/security/security-overview.html

at compile time using CMake and make; the system's threads are defined at compile time or can be created dynamically at Runtime. Each thread is separated from other threads in time and space.

The Zephyr OS separates threads in time through scheduling, and the OS saves and restores thread state automatically when threads are put to sleep. Scheduling of threads is organized through a hierarchy of priorities, allowing more important threads to preempt lower-priority threads, ensuring that the most important jobs are completed without interruption. Each thread is scheduled by the OS according to its priority. The highest-priority threads are *cooperative threads* whose priority is set to a negative number. Cooperative threads run until completion or until they voluntarily yield the processor using k_yield(). *Preemptive threads* have a positive priority value and are given a certain amount of time to run or are preempted when they perform an action that makes them not ready to run, like waiting on a semaphore or reading from a device or file. Cooperative threads must cooperate with the system and yield back to the OS so other things can run; if they misbehave, they can starve a system and force even higher-priority threads (threads with a numerically lower priority value) from running. Cooperative threads should only be used for high-priority tasks that cannot be interrupted. If a cooperative thread has a long operation to execute, it should break up the long operation into smaller pieces with a call to k_yield() at a convenient point. k_yield() returns back to the operating system, and the cooperative thread gets rescheduled if there is a higher-priority thread with something more important to do. If there is no higher-priority thread waiting, k_yield() just returns back to the thread and the long operation can continue.

Zephyr provides other refinements to the scheduling policy, including

- k_sched_lock() and k_sched_unlock() to define critical sections in preemptive threads, temporarily preventing them from being preempted.

- `k_busy_wait ()` which prevents a cooperative thread from being preempted when it performs some type of wait action that would make it unready and would normally cause it to be preempted.

- `CONFIG_METAIRQ_PRIORITIES` which is a configuration setting to define the numerically lowest cooperative thread priorities, making them act like IRQs and actually preempt other cooperative threads.

- Threads can change their thread priority, or another thread's priority, to a higher priority level (lower number numerically), even changing it from a preemptive thread to a cooperative or Meta-IRQ thread, if they are executing with privileges.

In addition to thread execution priorities used to enforce time separation of threads, Zephyr assigns a thread privilege to each thread. There are only two privileges, supervisory and user. By default, threads are assigned the supervisory privilege. This gives threads the ability to see all devices and access all of memory. A thread can drop its supervisory privilege and become a user-privileged thread by calling `k_thread_user_mode_enter()`, but once becoming a user-privileged thread, it cannot regain its supervisory privileges. Threads can temporarily perform an operation at the user privilege by spawning a new thread to perform the task and setting that new thread's privilege to the user privilege level.

Operating all or many threads at the supervisory privilege level is dangerous, since all of memory is exposed to those threads, even sensitive memory used by the kernel. User-privilege threads should be used as often as possible because Zephyr provides memory separation for user-privilege threads. Memory separation for user-privileged threads is discussed in the next section.

Since all of Zephyr's applications and libraries are enumerated at compile time, and there is no dynamic loading of applications or dynamic linking of libraries or other code, Zephyr reduces the attack surface created by interfering applications and library code conflicts.

Why does all this matter for security? Creating threads at the right privilege level is important for a system to remain stable in the face of an attack. If all threads are running at the supervisory privilege level, an attacker only has to find a single thread that it can attack via a buffer overflow and then gain control of the whole system. An attacker with control over a supervisory thread can see all memory, halt other threads, or modify stack values to create gadgets for ROP and JOP attacks, allowing the attacker to create their own programs with new, potentially destructive, functionality.

But even if user-privileged threads are enabled, if the right segmentation of memory partitions is not performed, user threads will be able to corrupt each other's memory partitions.

If user threads are enabled and restrictive memory partitioning is used, this will severely limit the types of attacks a remote adversary can perform. This is especially true if the threads that access the network and perform the bulk of the work on the system are user threads. But even if an attacker cannot gain access to an administrative thread, if they can take over a high enough privileged user thread, then by using k_sched_lock(), the attacker can starve out other threads. This situation can be mitigated by using the system's watchdog timer or even creating your own watchdog thread at the Meta-IRQ level to monitor and correct misbehaving threads. A detailed discussion of this is found later in the "Security Management" section.

Zephyr Memory Separation

In Zephyr, all threads have their own stack region, and their state is swapped out when they are removed from the running state. This provides basic (space) separation between threads. However, this protection does nothing to stop a misbehaving supervisory thread which has access to all of memory; and recall that by default all threads are given supervisory privileges. This means that thoughtful, security-aware design is required to build a secure system with Zephyr.

Zephyr provides user threads to address this problem of too much privilege. Zephyr allows threads to be created as user-privilege threads, or allows threads to drop their supervisory privilege and become user threads. Memory access afforded to user-privilege threads is restricted. User-privilege threads are granted access to a specific set of memory locations by assigning a thread to a *memory domain*. A memory domain contains one or more *memory partitions*. A memory partition is a contiguous segment of memory with defined access rights (i.e., read, write, execute). Thus, a memory partition can be defined as read-only, and another memory partition can be defined as read-write. Both these memory partitions can be added to the same memory domain, and one or more user threads can be assigned to the memory domain. All threads assigned to a memory domain have the same access to that memory. A thread can belong to more than one memory domain. Memory domains can be created at compile time or created dynamically at Runtime.

For x86, the definitions for memory domain rights are found in the Zephyr source tree at `arch/x86/include/mmustructs.h`. x86 allows partitions to be defined as read-only, read-write, read-execute, and even the dangerous read-write-execute. And partitions can be defined to restrict access to user threads, but if a permission is granted to a user thread for a particular memory partition, then privileged threads also have the same access to that memory partition. It is important, then, to structure your applications with as few supervisory threads as possible. This follows the least privilege principle.

Zephyr Privilege Levels and System Authorization

As we already discussed, Zephyr defines two privilege levels: user and supervisor. The previous section discussed the impact privilege levels have on memory access. This section reviews how the privilege levels affect access to logical structures, devices, and files.

Zephyr allows for the construction of various logical structures, including FIFOs, LIFOs, mailboxes, and message queues. These logical structures allow different threads to communicate and share data. All these structures are mapped to memory addresses. This means that access to these structures can be restricted to only certain user threads, but any supervisory thread can access these structures as long as they know the address.

Physical devices, such as USB ports, SPI controllers, I2C interfaces, Ethernet ports, and GPIOs, are controlled by device drivers. Device drivers are accessible via APIs and are not restricted. Any thread merely links to the appropriate header file (i.e., `i2c.h`) and then can access the device. Zephyr does not implement any restrictions or authorization for device access.

Zephyr supports several different filesystems, including Newtron Flash File System (NFFS), FATFS support, and FCB (Flash Circular Buffer). The FATFS is an open source implementation of the well-known *File Allocation Table* (FAT) filesystem from the old PC DOS. The implementation supports creation of a filesystem in RAM, on MMC flash, or through a USB drive. No file permissions are supported on FAT, but read-only, hidden, and system file attributes are supported.

The Newtron Flash File System (NFFS) is a minimal filesystem for flash devices and provides no protections or attributes for files. The source code for Newtron can be found at `http://github.com/apache/mynewt-nffs`.

Since Zephyr does not implement any user or persistent thread identity, no authorization mechanisms are found in the logical structures, device drivers, or for the filesystem. This can represent a security problem if a thread is taken over by an attacker and manipulated to perform malicious actions, since the thread can be modified via arbitrary code injection to access resources it normally would not access, and the operating system enforces few limitations.

Zephyr Programming Error Protections

Zephyr does implement several safeguards to protect threads from being taken over by remote attackers. These safeguards include stack protections and memory protections. The previous sections have discussed the memory protections; this section reviews the stack protections.

Programming errors can create vulnerabilities in software that allow untrusted input to overrun or underrun buffers, writing this untrusted data into memory. Specially crafted inputs can result in buffer overruns or underruns that rewrite elements on the stack, or rewrite code pages in RAM, allowing an attacker to change a thread's flow or the code that it executes. Zephyr implements stack protection to detect overruns on the stack, and then halt a thread to prevent it from executing from a modified stack.

Other protections, like Intel's® Control-Flow Enforcement Technology that protects against ROP and JOP, are not yet implemented in Zephyr, but may be added in the future.

Zephyr's Other Security Features

While Zephyr does not directly provide secure storage, it does provide a few other security additions, including a cryptographic library and API for security modules and TEEs.

Zephyr includes an embedded cryptographic library written by Intel, called TinyCrypt. This can be found in the Zephyr source tree at ext/lib/crypto. TinyCrypt includes basic cryptographic functions including

- AES symmetric encryption using CBC, CTR, CMAC, and CCM modes[11]

- Elliptic curve asymmetric cryptography using Diffie-Hellman (DH) or the Digital Signature Standard (DSA)

- HMAC and direct use of the hash function, SHA2-256

Zephyr also includes the latest mbedTLS from ARM, which includes TLS v1.2 (Transport Layer Security) and many more cryptographic functions. Details on mbedTLS can be found on the web site http://tls.mbed.org.

Zephyr also includes an API to access a hardware random number generator, based on the processor on the particular board that is being used. This allows access to true hardware entropy if the hardware supports it. If there is no hardware entropy source, an interface to a pseudo entropy function is provided (see /ext/lib/crypto/mbedtls/library/entropy_poll.c).

Currently, the APIs for hardware crypto, Trusted Platform Modules (TPMs) and Trusted Execution Environments (TEEs), are very limited. Future versions of Zephyr are planning to implement APIs for these devices.

---

[11]CBC = Cipher Block Chaining, CTR = Counter mode, see https://csrc.nist.gov/publications/detail/sp/800-38a/final

CMAC = Cipher-based Message Authentication Code, see https://csrc.nist.gov/publications/detail/sp/800-38b/final

CCM = Counter with CBC for Message authentication, see https://nvlpubs.nist.gov/nistpubs/legacy/sp/nistspecialpublication800-38c.pdf

Zephyr Summary

Table 4-2 includes a summary of Zephyr compared with our operating system security requirements.

Table 4-2. *Zephyr RTOS Security Summary*

Operating System Security Principles	Grade	Comments
Execution Separation	A	Zephyr provides all the standard separation capabilities of a standard operating system, with flexible application of those structures to address real-time concerns.
Memory Separation	C	Although some memory separation is provided, the ability of supervisory threads to see all of memory is a major weakness. Memory domains provide reasonable protections especially for the class of processors used by Zephyr.
Levels of Privilege	B	Two levels of privilege are common in systems today and even in popular operating systems, like Microsoft Windows, which has access to multiple different rings, but makes use of only two ring levels. There are however examples of extra protections – special supervisory modes and TEEs – that are currently lacking in Zephyr and thus warrant a slightly lower grade.
System authorization	D	Without any real system authorization, Zephyr leaves a significant gap for attacked threads to misbehave. While this is normal in MCUs, improvement is required.

(continued)

Table 4-2. (*continued*)

Operating System Security Principles	Grade	Comments
Protection from programming errors	C	Basic stack protection is the new normal. Control flow protection is the bar set by the industry today, which is lacking in Zephyr.
Access-Controlled Secrets storage	F	With the combination of no filesystem authorizations and no special secrets storage, Zephyr leaves a system vulnerable to any attacked thread. Systems with secrets should use a Secure Element or TPM to protect secrets, but this requires custom additions to Zephyr's device support.

While Zephyr provides some basic security features, like memory regions, and separate threads with stack protections, and user and privilege modes, Zephyr is limited in the services and protections that are available due to its focus as a minimalistic RTOS. But, even in other more powerful operating systems, similar process and thread structures are used, leading to similar attacks and pitfalls, so Zephyr is instructive to analyze. Our security lessons from Zephyr are applicable to all platforms and operating systems. Threads can be attacked and therefore should run at the lowest privilege possible. Privileges can be abused, maliciously or unintentionally, and therefore guards should be in place to check proper behavior of the system. Memory subsystems and filesystems can be exploited to leak or corrupt data; therefore, cryptographic protections such as encryption and integrity protection should be used. As we explore other software on our generalized IoT system, we will highlight how a defense in depth approach can work to minimize risk and reduce the impact of successful attacks.

Linux Operating Systems

Linux is a common operating system used for both cloud and IoT instances. It is feature rich and comes in many different distributions (distros) that enhance or embellish one capability or another. The security properties of Linux are well known, and there are complete tomes that do an excellent job of covering this topic,[12] so this section will not repeat that material here. Instead, this section looks at the concept of enhanced containment, but we do so from the perspective of an interesting IoT problem – updating the operating system and application software on a platform. The Linux distros covered here include Wind River Pulsar, Ubuntu IoT Core, and Clear Linux.

It is important to understand the update problem before progressing into the details of the distros. The update problem encountered in operating systems is one of both synchronization and access. Synchronization between different software elements of a system, and between the software and hardware of the platform, is required. An update to a system can destroy this synchronization. Access relates to the permissions and capability to update all parts of the system, including the operating system kernel, the boot software, and all types of firmware on the device.

A bad software update creates an incompatibility between two different software components on your device or an incompatibility between the software and the hardware of your device. An update problem is observed when two or more software components interfere with one another. The result of any of these conflicts can be a slowdown in operation, the failure of one or more services, a computer shutdown during operation (i.e., a crash), or even a failure to boot the device. It is not uncommon for some Linux updates to cause a failure to boot after a kernel update, which then requires a rebuild of the boot device in order to remedy the situation. A good software update requires synchronization between the hardware and all the software on the platform.

---

[12]Multiple Linux topic books by Apress, `www.apress.com/us/open-source/linux`

The word *all* introduces the other part of the update problem: *Access.* We defer the access issue until the section on secure updates, but it is important to understand the complexity of the update problem here and realize that the distributions we discuss now do not solve the whole problem. The access problem is caused by some updatable software on a device that resides in one or more difficult to reach hardware storage areas, normally referred to as firmware. The operating system itself may not be able to reach all these firmware locations. The device may need to be placed into a special operating mode, or an update must be submitted at a particular time during the boot process for the firmware update to be successful. This special access required to update firmware may be difficult or impossible to do without human intervention. If some part of the device's regular software is updated, and it depends on a newer version of firmware that is not present on the device, the instability of a bad software update may be the result.

If an operating system update causes an IoT platform to fail to reboot, or to crash so often that a new update cannot be pushed to the device, this requires a human being to go out to the device and repair or replace it. This physical maintenance drives up the cost for IoT deployments, resulting in an erosion or destruction[13] of the return on investment (ROI) for the IoT system. Driving operational costs down to preserve ROI requires the elimination of such physical interactions.

All three of the distributions covered in this section attempt to address the software update problem for IoT but do so in different ways. As we review these different solutions, we find the commonality is all about containment and finding ways to isolate the inconsistent dependencies.

---

[13]Destruction of the ROI can occur when many devices are impacted by a bad system update, either simultaneously or repeatedly over time. The cost of "rolling a truck" to repair devices can drive operational costs to completely consume any profit or efficiency gained by the IoT system.

Pulsar: Wind River Linux

Wind River provides various different operating systems for embedded sectors, including IoT. VxWorks[14] is a family of products representing their RTOS offerings. Pulsar[15] is Wind River's small, high-performance Linux distribution designed for manageability and IoT.

Pulsar is a binary distribution of Linux based on the Yocto Project. A primary focus of Pulsar is to provide a regular cadence of updates for the packages that are included in Pulsar, including the kernel. As shown in Figure 4-5, Pulsar is a container-based Linux, allowing the download of different features and functionality as containers. However, within the containers, updates are managed in a traditional manner using software packages.

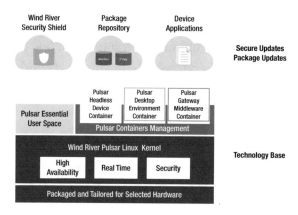

Figure 4-5. *Pulsar Linux architecture and service updates[16]*

---

[14]Wind River VxWorks, www.windriver.com/products/vxworks/

[15]Wind River Pulsar, www.windriver.com/products/operating-systems/pulsar/

[16]From www.windriver.com/products/product-overviews/ Pulsar-Linux-Product-Overview/

Using containers as a separation capability reduces destructive interactions between applications and makes the whole platform more stable. Additionally, by using containers, there is greater security in the platform as a whole, since the containers have a reduced privilege on the platform, making an attack on an application in a container less likely to leak out and affect the whole device. Pulsar can update whole applications on the device seamlessly by just replacing a container.

Wind River addresses the issue of stable updates by providing an update service over a secure channel, where the updates themselves are comprised of RPMs (Red Hat Package Manager), a common Linux update mechanism. All RPMs are signed with a Wind River RSA[17] private key, ensuring the RPMs are genuine and not modified from what Wind River intended. All updates on Wind River's package repository have gone through extensive testing to ensure they are stable on the Pulsar-supported platforms. Constant reviews of the published Common Vulnerabilities and Exposures (CVE) databases, and the open source mailing lists, ensure the latest defects and issues are addressed in the quarterly updates.

Wind River Linux includes the following features, discussed elsewhere in the chapter:

- Wind River Helix Device management system

- Mosquitto MQTT

- OCF and IoTivity (See Chapter 2 Consumer IoT Framework Standards)

- UEFI or MOK Secure Boot (See Chapter 3, Device Boot Integrity - Trust But Verify)

- Support for Trusted Platform Module (TPM) (See Chapter 3, PTT/TPM)

---

[17]RSA (Rivest-Shamir-Adleman) is an asymmetric cryptographic algorithm that uses a private key to digitally sign data and a separate public key that anyone can use to verify the signature.

Pulsar includes the following other technologies that improve the security on the device:

- Virtual private network (VPN) provided by the open source StrongSwan IPSec/L2TP/PPTP project.

- STIG scripts: System lockdown scripts are included in Pulsar to configure the system for secure deployment, using the US government's Security Technical Implementation Guide (STIG)[18] scripts.

CONTAINERS

Containers are a type of software separation technology that allows one or more applications, and their dependent libraries, packages, and services, to run in an operating system created *namespace*.

In an operating system, certain resources are organized into namespaces. For example, all the users are in a namespace; this means you can have only one user named *root* and one user named *dave* (users are actually based on numeric identifiers, but the concept still holds). If there are two users both named *dave*, they would be the same user. Likewise, the same namespace concept exists with devices, file paths, and certain logical resources, like network ports and process identifiers.

Inside a container, the operating system gives the container its own namespace for certain types of resources. So one container can open port 443 for a web server to listen to incoming traffic, and a different container can also open port 443, and there would be no conflict. Outside the container, some type of mapping must be done to disambiguate the two network traffic flows (see the "Containers" section for details). In our example with the user identities, two containers can both have the user *dave*, and they would not

---

[18]STIG Home, https://iase.disa.mil/stigs/Pages/index.aspx

be associated to the same user; thus there would be no conflict between the containers and no privilege leakages or access overlap between the applications in the containers.

Containers also use another kernel feature called cgroups. Cgroups create a kernel structure that limits the amount of memory and CPU processing that is available to processes within a cgroup. This can be used to ensure the processes in a cgroup do not starve out other groups. This ensures that all containers get a fair amount of processing time, and one container cannot hog the CPU and prevent applications in other containers from executing.

Different containerization engines package these features in different ways to allow an environment to be created and managed that provides usable software separation for applications. These are all referred to generally as containers, but different containerization engines may have slightly different properties and controls.

Ubuntu IoT Core

Ubuntu is a popular Debian Linux distribution that includes desktop, server, and cloud versions. Ubuntu IoT Core is a new distribution that is headless, meaning that it does not include the elements an operating system normally provides for a screen, keyboard, and mouse – there is no user interface. Ubuntu IoT Core is intended to be used on devices that do not have buttons; they are intended to be turned on, and the device just does its thing, whatever that is.

Ubuntu IoT Core runs differently from the normal Ubuntu distributions. It uses a construct called a *snap*. Everything in Ubuntu Core is a snap, even the kernel. Developers create snaps that contain all the dependencies for their application or service. Users download snaps from the snap store and can add in (snap in) any snap they want to their system. Each snap is separated from the others in Ubuntu IoT Core, using similar separation constructs as containers! One difference however is that snaps are transactional and can be rolled back easily if there is a problem. Thus, trying out a snap leaves no artifacts on the system, and a snap can be completely removed at any time. (reference for diagram in Figure 4-6. `https://computingforgeeks.com/install-snapd-and-snap-applications-on-fedora/`).

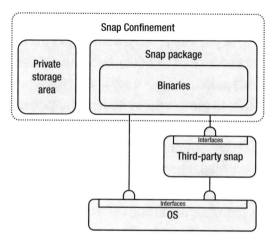

Figure 4-6. *Ubuntu IoT Core snap architecture*

A snap is actually a filesystem (the SquashFS filesystem) along with a YAML file that contains the snap's metadata. A snap is completely relocatable and does not depend on having specific libraries or configurations in a particular directory, like the /etc directory. The snap must carry all its dependent libraries with it in the SquashFS, kind of like a TAR or ZIP file with everything it needs packaged up inside it. The code for the snap in SquashFS filesystem is read-only, but once the snap is installed, a writeable section of the filesystem is created. When a snap is installed, it can be granted permissions to access things outside its filesystem, like the network or devices. If the system does not grant those permissions, then the install fails. In this way, a snap is similar to an app in the Android operating system.

Ubuntu IoT Core is claimed to be more reliable and more secure. Snaps are signed with cryptographic keys, just like Pulsar's RPMs, but snaps manage their own dependencies and are separated from other applications. Ubuntu IoT Core creates isolation between applications (snaps) using AppArmor and Seccomp.

AppArmor[19] is a security model built into the Linux kernel as part of the Linux Security Modules (LSM) framework. Other models supported by LSM include SELinux, Smack, TOMOYO Linux, and Yama. AppArmor allows the definition of security profiles that restrict the behavior of applications, and access to files (inodes), based upon a set of mandatory access control (MAC) policies. AppArmor comes installed with various preconfigured profiles to protect the system and applications, but these are modifiable by an administrator. Applications that do not have a policy defined execute in an unconfined manner (no special MAC restrictions). Policies reside in `/etc/apparmor/` and user-specific profiles are defined in `${HOME}/.apparmor/`.

Seccomp[20] is a Linux kernel mode used to limit the kernel system calls available to a process. Seccomp is short for secure computing and reduces the attack surface that the Linux kernel exposes through system calls. Seccomp was originally designed to expose only a certain set of kernel APIs available, but Seccomp 2 added filtering, allowing more flexible definitions of what kernel APIs are allowed to be used by a process. Seccomp is effective in restricting the actions an attacker can perform through injected code attacks, because a call to a restricted system call sends the SIGKILL to the process, terminating the offending program.

The combination of AppArmor and Seccomp allows Ubuntu to restrict the allowable actions of installed snaps. The inherent restrictions of a snap simplify the policy for these security tools, which

---

[19]https://gitlab.com/apparmor/apparmor/wikis/home/
[20]www.kernel.org/doc/Documentation/prctl/seccomp_filter.txt

can be complex. Additionally, the filters that restrict the snap's actions actually document how the snap is supposed to behave, and what the app can and cannot do, which acts as a type of disclosure to the system administrator. In conclusion, the containerization of snaps includes a separate filesystem, special permissions with AppArmor and Seccomp, and documented interfaces to connect to other applications and services on the platform through the snapd service.[21] Using these strong security protections, and the ability to rollback misbehaving snaps, Ubuntu IoT Core provides a secure and stable operating system for IoT deployments.

Intel® Clear Linux

Clear Linux[22] addresses the operating system update problem by allowing frequent updates to the operating system, reducing the time a platform lacks the most recent updates, and preventing incompatible updates from being downloaded and installed on a system. Clear Linux is designed for a Linux distribution maintainer and provides tools allowing the maintainer to directly consume upstream projects, add them to their distribution, and maintain the distribution on an update server that keeps all the connected systems updated. It is easy to see the value of Clear Linux to an IoT deployment that is using a customized Linux kernel.

---

[21]https://tutorials.ubuntu.com/tutorial/advanced-snap-usage#1
[22]Clear Linux, https://clearlinux.org/

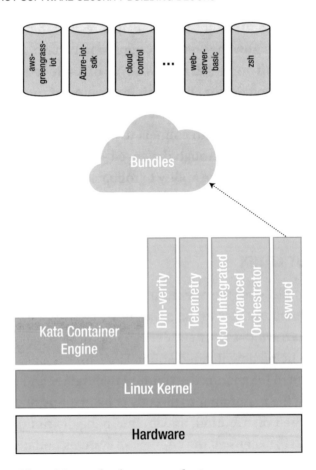

Figure 4-7. *Clear Linux deployment chain*

Clear Linux manages all the applications and software on the system using *bundles* instead of packages. Packages are hard to manage because of all the dependencies, and oftentimes different packages have dependencies on different versions of other packages. When two different packages are installed, and each requires different versions of another dependent package, installing both of those packages creates contention. Either one package will be able to use the newer (or older) version of the dependent package, or the application will break. Pulsar addresses this contention by putting applications and services into containers, which separates the dependencies from each other; Ubuntu uses a similar approach with snaps. Clear Linux removes the contention with bundles, which is just a different containment mechanism. A bundle removes the outside dependencies and includes all the software needed for an application.

In Clear Linux, the operating system is completely made up of bundles. When one bundle is updated, it creates a completely new version of the OS. This new OS version is built and tested as a whole – there is no extra package to be added later. For the distributor, this makes updating simpler and guarantees that the OS update will work and will not brick the system. It is also the reason that updates need to be easier and happen more frequently.

Just making updates come faster is not really a solution. Updating an entire operating system every week could kill a system, not to mention bog down the network. Clear Linux solves this problem by including tools to allow updates to be smaller. Rather than an update requiring a full reinstall, the update can be a binary diff between versions. This is critical for IoT deployments, because sending down a new kernel that is multiple megabytes in size is just not practical over certain network connections.

Linux Summary

Linux supports strong security capabilities in both the kernel and the application space. Although we did not cover all of Linux's security features, Table 4-3 provides a summary of the operating system security features of Linux for comparison with Zephyr in our previous section.

Table 4-3. *Linux Security Summary*

Operating System Security Principles	Grade	Comments
Execution Separation	A	All Linux distributions discussed here support the standard separation capabilities (process, threads, ISRs) of operating systems.
Memory Separation	A	Linux utilizes the hardware memory management unit (MMU) to provide paged memory separation for all processes, with read-write-execute permissions. Unlike Zephyr, even a process running as root is restricted.
Levels of Privilege	A	Linux, like Microsoft Windows, has access to multiple privilege rings, but makes use of only two ring levels. Linux also supports other special supervisory modes and TEEs; for details see the section on containment.
System authorization	A	Linux provides authorization for structures using a common user-group-other identity structure with read-write-execute privilege bits. Extensions for other security models through the Linux Security Modules (LSM) and other frameworks, like AppArmor and Seccomp covered in the Ubuntu section, are readily available and integrated into the Linux kernel.

(continued)

Table 4-3. (*continued*)

Operating System Security Principles	Grade	Comments
Programming Error Protections	B	Basic stack protection is provided in the Linux kernel since version 3.14[23] and is turned on automatically in version 4.16[24] – strong stack protections are also an option. Control flow protection is not yet fully upstreamed in the kernel, but patches exist for 64-bit user applications.[25]
Access-Controlled Secrets Protection	C	Linux does not directly provide standard features for secrets storage, but support for the Trusted Platform Module (TPM), Secure Elements, and hardware security modules (HSM) are prevalent.

In this section, our discussion focused on the update features provided in different Linux distributions and how the distros are solving the problem of interfering applications and overly complex dependencies. These solutions used different forms of containment to solve the update problem. Clear Linux solves the problem by creating a new package format for updates called a bundle and then uses a series of tools to ensure the different bundles create a stable system. If an instability is found, a new update is easy to create by correcting a bundle. System updates are made less burdensome by incorporating special binary diff updates that take less time to download.

---

[23]https://lwn.net/Articles/584225/

[24]www.thomas-krenn.com/en/wiki/Linux_Kernel_Versions

[25]https://lwn.net/Articles/758245/

Pulsar and Ubuntu take a different approach and use advanced features of Linux to construct special containment for applications and even parts of the operating system itself (in the case of Ubuntu, anyway). These containment features are used to create Linux containers, which we look at in a bit more detail in a future section.

We also noted that even with these features, the problem of access required to update firmware on the platform is not solved by this approach, and additional capabilities are needed. We look at solutions to the access problem in the section on secure software updates.

Hypervisors and Virtualization

Virtualization is a generic term applied to several techniques that increase resource sharing and hardware utilization in a computer system. Modern operating systems like Linux provide *virtualized* memory, where more memory appears to be available than is actually physically present. Parts of memory used by idle processes are stored on disk, freeing more physical memory for the currently running process; short delays are incurred when the idle process becomes active and the operating system reloads physical memory with the contents from disk. Although some delays are incurred, they are outweighed by the benefit of having more physical memory available to the running process.

Platform virtualization works in much the same way, allowing multiple operating systems to run simultaneously on a single computer. Memory is virtualized, as well as the processor, storage, graphics, and other I/O devices on the platform. A small control program, called a hypervisor or Virtual Machine Manager (VMM), manages the virtualized hardware and mediates between the different virtual machines (VMs). Figure 4-8 shows a generic virtualized system. Each VM runs a guest operating system and application software that are logically separated from each other by hardware and software controls managed by the hypervisor.

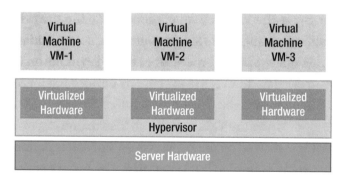

Figure 4-8. *Generic virtualization architecture*

There are actually two different types of hypervisors. Figure 4-8 depicts a Type 1 hypervisor or native hypervisor that runs directly on the hardware. Type 1 hypervisors are typically more performant and can utilize the hardware better, because they have complete control of the hardware. VMWare, Xen (for Linux), and Hyper-V (Microsoft) are examples of Type 1 hypervisors.

There are also Type 2 hypervisors, which run on top of an existing operating system. This allows a *regular* OS to run virtual machines too. VirtualBox by Oracle is a Type 2 hypervisor that runs on Linux. KVM is a Red Hat hypervisor that runs as part of the Linux kernel; some regard it is Type 2 hypervisor since other things can run on the Linux OS, but Red Hat claims it is a Type 1 hypervisor since it has direct control of the hardware through the kernel. Either way, it is a pretty good hypervisor. There is a question that frequently comes up relating hypervisors to containers. The question is: Which is better, containerization or virtualization? We discuss this later in the *"Software Separation and Containment"* section. For now, we focus on virtualization.

How does virtualization work? In Intel Architecture, virtualization is supported by the Virtual Machine Extensions (VMX) mode. This mode defines two privilege levels, one for the hypervisor, called *VMX root operations*, and one for the VMs, called *VMX non-root operations*.

As one might guess, the VMX root operations mode is more privileged. The hypervisor, operating in VMX root operations mode, initializes certain control registers in the processor to establish limits on the VMs. The hypervisor releases the VMs to execute by performing a *VM*-Enter instruction. The VMs are then executing in the restricted VMX non-root operations mode. When the VMs execute an instruction or perform an operation that is restricted by the hypervisor, a *VM exit* is performed by the processor, returning control to the hypervisor. The hypervisor can either perform the operation on behalf of the VM in a safe manner, or it can reject the operation and return some type of exception to the VM; in extreme cases, the hypervisor can even terminate the offending VM entirely.

The exact details of virtualized processor state are beyond the scope of this book. However, the curious may elect to read the *Intel 64 and IA-32 Architectures Software Developer's Manual Volume 3*. Chapters 23 through 33 cover VMX mode. These chapters discuss the virtual machine control structure (VMCS) that contains the state used by the processor to implement virtualization and discusses all the elements of the controlled state, including

- Virtual processor state, including control registers, debug registers, base registers, and segments

- Bit flags controlling what events cause a VM exit, for example, interrupts, use of IO ports, and so on

- Bit flags indicating how a VM's state is saved when a VM exit is performed

- Bit flags indicating how a VM's state is restored on VM entry

- Indicators for VMX aborts (the reason a VM abnormally exited into the hypervisor)

- Indicators for VMX exits (the reason for a normal return to the hypervisor)

There is also another distinction among hypervisors. In the discussion earlier, we described virtualization as though the operating systems in the virtual machines were no different than an operating system on a platform that is not virtualized. When the operating systems in the VMs are not aware they are being virtualized, this is called *full virtualization*. In some systems, or with some applications, it is very difficult to fully virtualize the system. This may be because there are complex devices that need to be shared between the virtual machines, or it may be that an application has very stringent performance requirements. In these cases, it is counterproductive to perform full virtualization – the cost to do so would outweigh the benefits. In these cases, the hypervisor implements a *para-virtualized* strategy, where the operating system, device drivers, and perhaps even the applications themselves are aware that they are being virtualized and are modified in order to behave better in the virtualized environment. Para-virtualization is accomplished by configuring VMX in a way that allows the VMs themselves to perform certain operations, for example, the ability to directly interface with certain IO ports. The VMCS allows the hypervisor to give some VMs more control than other VMs. However, the VMs must cooperate with the hypervisor and are trusted to cooperate in a trustworthy fashion. Intel's ACRN hypervisor is an example of a para-virtualized hypervisor, which we will discuss in more detail after we review the security threats to virtualization and hypervisors.

Threats to Hypervisors

Just like operating systems, the threats to hypervisors are numerous and dangerous. A successful attack on a hypervisor can lead to an attacker acquiring complete control over the platform and every virtual machine running on it. NIST-SP-800-125A Revision 1[26] outlines the baseline set of

---

[26]https://nvlpubs.nist.gov/nistpubs/SpecialPublications/NIST.SP.800-125Ar1.pdf

security functions a hypervisor should perform. These hypervisor security functions have similarities to the security services that we defined for operating systems. But because this specification limits itself to virtualization of servers, and specifically does not address embedded systems, we use the NIST set of functions as a baseline. In our list that follows, the first five items are from NIST and are roughly equivalent to the security services we defined for operating system; protection from programming errors is a sixth security service we add to NIST's list. We then add three additional security services that are unique to IoT instances and not considered by NIST's analysis. The set of security services for IoT hypervisors are

- **VM Process Isolation (i.e., Execution Separation and Memory Separation)**: Each VM's execution should be separated from all other VMs' execution using multiple logical processor structures; a fault in one VM should not affect other VMs.

- **Device Mediation and Access Control (i.e., Levels of Privilege and Access-Controlled Secrets Storage)**: Hypervisors provide methods for VMs to share access to devices through various methods, including giving VMs direct access to hardware, para-virtualization of the device, or device emulation within the hypervisor. Access to the devices must be controlled to prevent effects from one VM leaking over to other VMs. This includes controlling direct memory access (DMA) devices to protect both memory read and write. If the platform offers secrets storage, the hypervisor should provide access to such storage in a manner that prevents other VMs from interfering with each other's usage, or from viewing, modifying, or using the secrets in that secure storage location (see Chapter 3, section on "*Intel Virtualization Technology (Intel VT)*").

- **Prevent Abuses by Guest VMs through their Direct Execution of Commands (i.e., System Authorization)**: As we stated earlier, para-virtualized systems allow VMs to cooperate with the hypervisor; the hypervisors in these systems execute commands sent from the VMs. The hypervisor's execution of commands from one VM should not affect another VM and should not compromise the security of the hypervisor or its data structures.

- **VM Lifecycle Management**: VM management includes creating, starting, stopping, and pausing VMs, as well as checkpointing (snapshotting) their state. This includes monitoring the state of VMs and various tools for migrating data or VM snapshots between physical machines. The management of VMs is typically performed through add-ons to the hypervisor or through a special management VM. These management services must not allow leakage of data or control across VMs.

- **Management of Hypervisor Platform**: The configuration of the hypervisor and the platform itself must be managed, including configuring devices, virtual networking, storage, and any VM policies. This management must include proper authentication of management requests and restriction of management actions to only authorized entities.

- **Protection from Programming Errors**: This is the leftover security service from our operating system list, but has a little different perspective when viewed from the virtualization perspective. The hypervisor must set appropriate VM aborts when a VM violates restrictions on memory separation or corruption of VM control structures; stack smashing and heap smashing that occur from programming errors in one VM should not compromise the hypervisor or other VMs. These protections become much more difficult with a para-virtualized hypervisor because certain structures and interfaces on the hypervisor are accessible to the VMs.

- **Real-Time Guarantees**: In embedded systems and IoT, control loops require real-time guarantees and many devices operate with real-time restrictions on read/write operations that if violated result in data being lost. In a virtualized system, the hypervisor itself must provide these real-time guarantees in coordination with the VMs and their operating systems.

- **Deep Power Management**: In embedded systems and IoT, power usage is a critical parameter. Whether the power envelope is restricted due to battery life and energy harvesting limitations or the power/heat trade-off in an industrial environment limits equipment's power budget, management of energy usage is essential. Due to real-time guarantees and the management of physical devices or equipment, the management of power goes far beyond what is normally provided in a data center or server cloud instance. Power management cannot be left to the individual guest operating systems or VMs, because they do not have the platform view. The hypervisor, in conjunction with the VMs and guest OSes, must manage the platform constraints appropriately to prevent power spikes or violations of the equipment's defined heat envelope.

- **Protection from External Devices**: In embedded systems and IoT, virtualized systems are inevitably connected to other devices and sensors, usually in a very direct way. Because these devices can be attacked and PWNED[27] by an adversary, protection of the virtualized system from compromised devices is critical to protecting a virtualized IoT system. It should be noted that this goes beyond the normal protections a cloud server is required to enforce to protect REST APIs and network connections, which the IoT virtualized system must also do. The external IoT devices are normally connected to a low-level driver, an emulated or virtual bus implementation, or some other higher-privileged software component that must implement some type of intrusion and attack detection-prevention mechanism.

When examining the preceding list of necessary protections and the general operation of hypervisors described earlier, several threat vectors immediately come to the surface that are likely vulnerabilities in hypervisors:

- **Size and complexity of the hypervisor code**: The more complex and larger code size of a hypervisor, the more likely the hypervisor includes critical vulnerabilities, because adverse code interactions and defects are harder to find in larger code bases.

---

[27]PWNED is the Internet slang for "owning" a device or computer system; it comes from "mistyping" the "o" in the word "own" with a letter "p," ostensibly because hackers are bad typists perhaps. Its meaning goes beyond attacking and implies complete ownership of the attacked device such that the device is absconded to do whatever the attacker wishes – the device becomes part of the attacker's zombie or botnet army.

- **Attack surface of the guest VMs**: Since the VMs represent the manipulable interface to attackers, they represent the primary point of attack to virtualized systems. The more network services exposed by a VM, the more third-party code that is not written with a security mindset, and the larger the number of unprotected IoT devices connected to virtualized system, the higher the risk of vulnerabilities that can expose the hypervisor to attack.

- **Hypervisor add-ons that have vulnerabilities**: Some hypervisors have minimal services but allow add-ons or plugin modules that provide additional services, like management and configuration. These add-ons can include additional vulnerabilities.

- **Device driver virtualizations that have vulnerabilities**: Device drivers require special versions that provide virtualization features, which may react differently with different hypervisors or may operate differently on different hardware. These differences may create vulnerabilities an attacker can leverage.

Like operating systems, hypervisors are susceptible to similar classes of attacks. A recent survey paper[28] looked at reported common vulnerabilities from a reputable CVE database for the top four hypervisors. Figure 4-9 shows the types of vulnerabilities and the number of such vulnerabilities by product. The purpose of this table here is to highlight the most common attacks on hypervisors and to highlight that all hypervisors have been successfully attacked. The data should not be interpreted numerically

---

[28]Litchfield, Alan., Shahzad, Abid. *A systematic Review of Vulnerabilities in Hypervisors and Their Detection.* 23rd Americas Conference on Information Systems. Boston. 2017.

to identify which hypervisor is more secure due to a lower number of attacks. The paper notes that although VMWare had the highest number of vulnerabilities over the study period (from 1999 to 2015), it was also the only established hypervisor product in the market for the first 8 years of the study period, making such rankings of hypervisor security inappropriate. The following list briefly reviews the most prevalent classes of attacks listed in Figure 4-9, describing the security principles violated:

- **Denial of Service**: A DoS attack causes a VM to halt or create such a serious VM abort that the hypervisor refuses to allow the VM to continue to operate. A more serious DoS could affect a device on the platform, preventing all VMs from accessing the device until the platform is rebooted, violating **Device Mediation**. A DoS attack on a virtualized hardware device represents a violation of **execution separation**. Another type of DoS attack consumes resources, like network socket handles, resulting in other VMs not being able to acquire the resource necessary to execute a function.

	VMWare	Xen	KVM	Hyper-V	Total
DoS	66	131	30	5	232
Code Execution	48	12	2	3	65
Stack overflow	30	28	4	1	63
Memory Corruption	8	10	2	1	21
Cross-Site Scripting	13				13
Directory Traversal	11				11
HTTP response splitting	1				1
Bypass something	5		3	1	9
Gain information	17	16	2		35
Gain privileges	54	24	7		85
Cross Site Request Forgery	3				3
Total	256	221	50	11	

Figure 4-9. *Most common attacks on hypervisors – 16-year period*

- **Stack Overflow and Arbitrary Code Execution**: Stack smashing, heap smashing, and use-after-free vulnerabilities allow an attacker to execute their own code on the platform. This type of attack can allow escalation of code's rights, allowing it to become a privileged user. In para-virtualized environments, this can cause the VM to misbehave and violate the trust the hypervisor places in the VM, causing an execution or memory separation violation (**Prevent Abuses from Direct Execution of Commands from Guest VMs**).

- **Gain Information**: An out-of-bounds read vulnerability allows a VM to access memory outside of its logical memory space. These vulnerabilities are common with virtualized drivers and VM tools. A gain information vulnerability represents a violation of **memory separation**.

- **Gain Privileges**: Gain privilege attacks are usually executed through add-ons, like tools and plugins. An example is the CVE-2017-4943 that allowed a *showlog* plugin to gain root-level privilege of the platform management VM that controls network settings, system updates, health monitoring, and device management. Becoming root on a para-virtualized system is tantamount to a compromise of the hypervisor itself, since root on a para-virtualized VM allows the attacker to easily violate the implicit para-virtualized cooperation agreement (**Management of Hypervisor Platform**).

Many of the attacks outlined are serious, but do not directly violate a fully virtualized system; the hypervisor can properly trap and stop attacks that directly violate the virtual machine's configuration. However, when the hypervisor and VMs are operating in a para-virtualized manner, privilege escalations in the VM and process and memory violations even within the VM's logical memory space can escalate to a violation of the para-virtualization agreements. An attacker, operating as root within a para-virtualized VM, can disrupt device drivers and other critical parts of the VM's operating system that have direct access to the platform hardware as part of the para-virtualization contract. In the next section, we look at ACRN, a para-virtualized hypervisor, and explore some of the strengths and weaknesses of this approach.

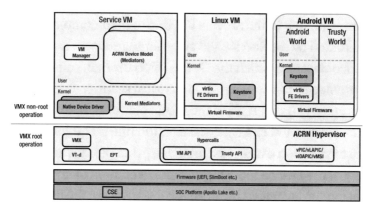

Figure 4-10. *ACRN architecture diagram*

Intel® ACRN

ACRN is a BSD open source hypervisor reference platform, built by Intel for the automotive industry, available at https://projectacrn.github.io. It is specifically designed to be a flexible and lightweight hypervisor and designed for real-time and safety-critical IoT deployments.

As shown in Figure 4-10, ACRN is a para-virtualized architecture where the guest operating systems must know they are being virtualized and cooperate with the hypervisor. A para-virtualized solution is required in the automotive world due to the nature of some devices in the system. This model enables a more performant implementation and cleaner virtualization of these devices using virtio drivers. Notice the Service Virtual Machine (VM) in the top left of Figure 4-10. The Service VM performs some critical virtualization services for the hypervisor to avoid the performance penalty of full virtualization. However, support for device interrupts is provided directly in the hypervisor by virtualizing the PIC and APIC for each VM. The critical element of the Service VM is the set of ACRN Device Model (DM) applications that mediate between VMs and devices for certain operations. For example, USB and IOC (I/O Controller) devices are emulated in the Service VM due to their complexity, and the GPU is mediated by the Service VM since emulation will not provide the performance boost for which the GPU is often used. Because of these elevated privileges, the Service VM is a critical security element in the trusted computing base (TCB) of the ACRN platform. If not carefully limited, the Service VM can easily take on too much and become a security threat due to violation of the least privilege principle. As the number and complexity of the Device Models grow, the likelihood of implementation errors that can be leveraged by an attacker grows (see the list of common attack patterns discussed in the "Threats to Operating Systems" section). If an attacker is able to successfully attack a DM, the attacker is likely to inject other code inside the Service VM, having access to many other privileges than just the compromised DM. This is an architectural trade-off between necessary performance and security risk. The risk can be managed by ensuring every DM or other software component added to the Service VM is carefully verified and undergoes penetration testing to ensure there are no security weaknesses in those modules.

For security features, ACRN supports secure boot, a Trusted Execution Environment (TEE), and secure storage in a Replay Protected Memory Block (RPMB) in flash. Figure 4-11 shows the secure boot flow for ACRN when using the Slim Bootloader (SBL). The TEE and RPMB are shown in Figures 4-13 and 4-14, respectively.

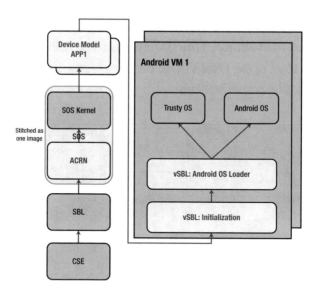

Figure 4-11. *ACRN secure boot flow*

Secure boot on Intel devices starts in the Converged Security Engine (CSE), which is the common root of trust for verification for Intel platforms (see Chapter 3, section "Intel CSE/CSME – DAL"). The CSE verifies a digital signature on the SBL; the digital signature is usually produced using the RSA algorithm and is commonly 2048-bits or 3072-bits in length. The public key is part of the SBL image, but this key is verified by the CSE using a hash of that public key kept in fuses. The fuses prevent the key from being modified in the image itself.

The SBL verifies the next stage of the platform, which includes the ACRN hypervisor and Service Operating System (SOS) kernel, which are included as a single image. The SOS kernel runs in the Service VM as VM's operating system. The SOS Kernel loads and verifies a Device Model application for each User VM that is loaded; this includes verifying a virtual Slim Bootloader (vSBL) for each User VM. The SOS uses dm-verity[29] to check the validity of the DM App and the vSBL. The vSBL then is responsible to boot the User VM; in the case of Android, this uses the Android verified boot mechanism.

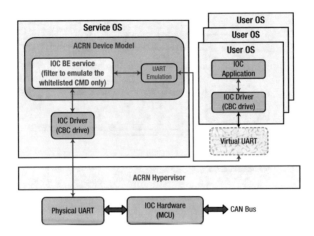

Figure 4-12. *ACRN connectivity to automotive CAN bus*

One of the key features in ACRN is support for real-time and automotive use cases. This creates extremely stringent requirements on the hypervisor and the VMs for real-time operations and connectivity. Because all VMs might require access to the CAN[30] bus, an I/O Controller is emulated in the Service OS that serializes data onto a physical serial

---

[29]DM-Verity, or Device Mapper Verity, was designed for Chrome OS and also used by Android. DM-Verity is built into the Linux kernel and uses the kernel cryptographic APIs to provide transparent integrity verification for block devices. See the Git Repository for more details at `https://git.kernel.org/pub/scm/linux/kernel/git/torvalds/linux.git/tree/Documentation/device-mapper/verity.txt`

[30]CAN bus, Controller Area Network, is a type of local bus system developed by Bosch for automotive systems to connect controllers and subsystems together. `www.canbus.us/`

bus connected to the vehicle CAN bus (Figure 4-12). In order to protect
the vehicle, the Service OS implements a firewall in each VM's Device
Model application. This filter restricts the type and content of messages
that a particular VM can place on the vehicle's CAN bus. For example, the
Android OS that implements the vehicle infotainment features is restricted
from sending messages to critical ECU components for vehicle braking
or engine control. Likewise, other VMs that render cockpit controls are
restricted from receiving messages from USB ports in the cabin.

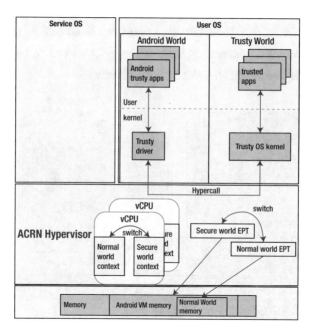

Figure 4-13. *ACRN trusted execution environment*

ACRN supports the ARM TrustZone TEE implemented in Trusty in the
Android OS. As shown in Figure 4-13, the ACRN hypervisor implements
the separation of unsecure memory (in the normal world or regular
operating system) from the secure world purely in software through
encrypted page tables (EPTs). The CPUs are also virtualized and maintain
the NS (not-secure) bit used in ARM to switch between two different
contexts in the vCPU. It should be noted that the secure world can see all

of memory, but the normal world is restricted to see only a subset. Just like we discussed in the Zephyr OS, the ability of privileged users to see all of memory makes processes and threads in the secure world potentially more dangerous. It should also be noted that the Service OS also acts like a privileged secure process with access to additional parts of memory in order to support the virtualized devices.

The last security feature in ACRN that we examine is the Replay Protected Memory Block (RPMB). RPMB is a feature of some flash devices that allows an encryption key to be used to protect data, using both confidentiality and integrity, in a reserved flash block. The data is also replay protected preventing rollback attacks where an old piece of encrypted data overwrites a newer piece of data.

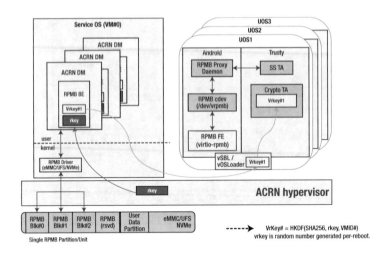

Figure 4-14. *ACRN secure storage support through RPMB*

The encryption key for the RPMB is held by a trusted entity in the platform. In Intel platforms, this trusted entity is the CSE, and the CSE shares this key with a single device driver on the platform and then locks access to the key so no other program can gain access to the key. If the key is overshared, then security of the platform diminishes. During the boot process, the Slim Bootloader (SBL) reads the platform seed (pSEED) from the CSE and passes the pSEED on to the ACRN hypervisor. Since ACRN must support multiple virtual machines, and all these VMs must not be allowed to see the other VMs' data or be able to spoof another VM's data reads or writes, ACRN cannot directly share the pSEED with the VMs. ACRN uses a NIST-approved key derivation function (HKDF-256) to derive new secrets from the pSEED, called vSEEDs for virtual seeds, and passes a unique vSEED to each VM. Each VM then chooses which device driver or process will take ownership of the vSEED. For example, in Android, the vSEED is given to Trusty since it is the TEE for that VM. Figure 4-14 shows how the seeds are then used to implement RPMB. ACRN provides the real RPMB key to the DM applications in the Service OS. The derived keys are used by each of the User VMs to protect their RPMB data; the transactions for each of the User VMs do not go to the RPMB flash or the ACRN hypervisor, but instead are routed to the Service OS. The DM App in the SOS for the particular VM verifies and decrypts the data it received from its corresponding VM and then re-encrypts the data with actual RPMB key. Each VM has access to a small part of the RPMB and can only write to its own section. This separation is enforced by the RPMB driver in the SOS and the ACRN hypervisor.

It is clear from Figure 4-14 and the preceding description that the Service OS must be trusted, since it is possible for the DM Application to forge data or delete RPMB data as if they were the User VM. Careful review of the applications in the Service OS is required to ensure no security vulnerabilities are present, and only trusted applications are allowed to run in the SOS.

Real-Time and Power Management Guarantees in ACRN

In its current rendition, ACRN provides basic real-time and power management controls. ACRN maps a physical core into the guest OS for both real-time and power management. This means that the guest OS has direct control of the core and can reflect any of the operating system's real-time characteristics to the applications in its VM. A real-time Linux kernel, for example, would run just as effectively in ACRN as on its own hardware. Since the physical cores are mapped into the VM, the hypervisor also allows the guest operating system in the VM control over that core's C-state, optimizing the core's power consumption during idle modes. The P-state, controlling the package voltage-frequency setting, is coordinated with the VM. ACRN manages the S-state, which is reflected from the User OS VMs, to the Service OS, and finally the hypervisor, in an ordered fashion. Future versions of ACRN are planning for further power and real-time management controls covering devices and real-time quality of service.

ACRN Summary

ACRN supports some strong security services, with RPMB secure storage and TrustZone TEE being two of the most significant. Many of the design and security trade-offs made in ACRN are a result of the performance requirements for automotive and IoT deployments and the need to interface with complex devices, such as the I/O Controller emulation in the Service OS for connection with the vehicle bus. Table 4-4 provides a summary of the hypervisor system security features for comparison with other systems.

Table 4-4. *ACRN Hypervisor Security Summary*

Operating System Security Principles	Grade	Comments
VM Process Isolation (Execution Separation)	B	Because ACRN is a para-virtualized hypervisor, and both the Service OS and parts of the hypervisor are accessible to guest VMs, the execution separation is not complete. This cannot be improved, however, due to the need for emulated busses and para-virtualization of certain devices.
VM Process Isolation (Memory Separation)	B	User OSs have access to both the Service OS and the ACRN hypervisor through some limited APIs. This necessarily means that some memory buffers and locations are shared, with some firewalling in place. Errors or defects in this sharing, especially if the uses of additional add-ons are integrated, can compromise the system.
Device Mediation (Levels of Privilege)	B	Device Mediation is done in the Service OS, per VM, using the Device Model application.

(*continued*)

Table 4-4. (*continued*)

Operating System Security Principles	Grade	Comments
Execution of Commands from Guest VMs	C	ACRN provides separation of commands, mostly through the Service OS and the Device Model. However, certain hypercalls go through the hypervisor itself as shown in Figures 4-10 and 4-13. Similar hypercalls are used for USB virtualization. This creates a disparity in where access controls need to be reviewed, and makes it harder to ensure all guest commands are properly mediated in every case; this represents a violation of the least common mechanism security design principle.[3]
VM Lifecycle **Management of Hypervisor Lifecycle**	C	ACRN provides a VM manager (Figure 4-10) in the Service OS; however the implementation is very slim. This is appropriate for the automotive space, but for generalized IoT, and especially for industrial usages which require sophisticated orchestration, the management features require significant add-ons. Because this is performed in the same VM as the mediation of the guest VMs, the likelihood of disastrous compromise is increased.

(*continued*)

Table 4-4. (*continued*)

Operating System Security Principles	Grade	Comments
Protection from programming errors	-	No specific controls; however the Linux OS and Android OS, for which the hypervisor was designed, provide these advanced controls. ACRN depends on these services in the guest OS.
Real-Time Guarantees and Deep Power Management	A	ACRN's entire design focuses on meeting real-time requirements for automotive, including providing optimized device drivers and virtualized access to power management controls using a virtualized PIC and APIC.
Protections from External Devices	A	ACRN provides a Service VM that mediates all external access points and utilizes VM-specific filters in the Device Model to individualize protection filters per VM instance.
Access-Controlled Secrets Storage	B	ACRN provides both a TEE and RPMB secure storage. The lower grading is a result of the implementations being primarily in software, not hardware.

In this section, our discussion focused on the unique features and architecture of para-virtualized hypervisors. We introduced the use of secure storage through the RPMB and additional containment through the use of a TEE. TEEs are discussed in more detail in the section "*Software Separation and Containment*." The design trade-offs for the hypervisor and

TEE led to potential vulnerability in the TEE due to lack of full memory separation – a similar problem was found in the Zephyr OS. These and other design trade-offs lead to some weaknesses in the system, but overall, the combination of hardware security features for VM separation and secure storage provides superior protection for the targeted IoT vertical.

Software Separation and Containment

Containment is a critical concept in security. Whether it is keeping the "bad guys" out, or protecting secrets, or just segregating high privilege operations from low privilege ones, separation and containment are paramount to safe operations. Even with the process and thread separation provided by the operating system, and the hardware-assisted virtual machine isolation, additional separation capabilities always seem to be useful to applications and IoT systems. In this section, we look at two different types of **extended application containment** capabilities: containers and Trusted Execution Environments (TEEs). We have touched on both of these topics already, but in this section, we unpack them to a deeper level.

Containment Security Principles

The principles that apply to **extended application containment** are the same principles we talked about for operating systems, which includes

- Execution Separation
- Memory Separation

The difference between applying these principles here and applying them to operating systems is the particular mechanisms used to provide the separation. The preference is for hardware separation as it is more secure. Containment through hardware separation might be provided using a completely different processor (see the "Trusty TEE Security Summary" section), or a different mode of the current processor (see the section on Virtualization or SGX later). Memory separation might include a completely different cache of memory (as in SGX and Trusty), or merely using some extra virtualization controls (the approach used in hypervisors or containers). In both cases, there are trade-offs to be made, based on the threats that are being addressed.

Threats to Extended Application Containment

The threats to extended application containment typically come from privileged attackers. These attacks can come from a privileged user or might be from an unprivileged user that performs a privilege escalation attack to acquire higher privileges. In both cases, the application containment intends to remove the possibility, or reduce the efficacy, of attacks by privileged users (e.g., root or admin user accounts).

- **Memory Disclosure from Privileged User**: A privileged user leverages their access to all memory pages in order to read data from any application.

- **Memory Tampering from Privileged User**: A privileged user leverages their access to all memory pages in order to write, overwrite, or corrupt data for any application; they may also include making memory pages unavailable to an application.

- **Data Leakage through Side Channels**: A privileged user leverages their access to data caches to perform timing attacks allowing them to determine contents of application memory.

- **Execution Interference from Privileged User**: A privileged user leverages their ability to schedule tasks or run tasks that have higher priority and starve or interrupt other applications during a critical operation.

- **Execution Leakage through Side Channels**: A privileged user leverages their ability to schedule tasks and uses speculative execution or timing operations to determine code branches executed during operation.[31]

Application containment techniques provide defenses against these attacks to varying degrees. Full separation[32] is the only complete solution, but this increases costs and adds complexity to management and control of sensitive applications. The use of different containment techniques is a trade-off between absolute security and ease of use and utility of the solution. In each containment example discussed later, we highlight the different levels of hardware usage that improve the solution's security level.

Containers

Containers are a software mechanism to increase the separation between applications. In the "Linux Section", we discuss how Wind River Pulsar uses container to improve the stability of their operating system updates; because services and components execute within containers with enhanced separation between applications, the applications are less

---

[31]For a discussion of the L1 Terminal Fault (L1TF) speculative execution attack and its specific effect on ACRN, see `https://projectacrn.github.io/latest/developer-guides/l1tf.html`

[32]Full separation means using a completely different processor with completely different memory and devices for sensitive operations.

likely to interfere with each other, increasing system stability. Ubuntu IoT Core uses a similar construct to containers, which they call snaps. Containers and snaps utilize software techniques in the operating system for separation. The long-standing debate is which approach is better – containerization or virtualization?

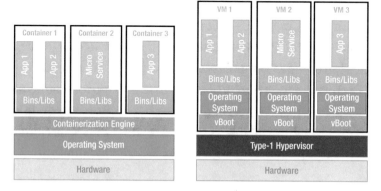

Figure 4-15. *Containers and hypervisor comparison*

In Figure 4-15, we show the relationship between a container software stack and a virtual machine (VM) software stack. What is evident from the diagram is the VM stack contains more layers of software due to the operating system in each VM.

The strength of a VM solution is the hardware separation between the different VMs; however, setting up the VMs and getting the operating systems booted in each VM takes more time. The strength of the container solution is faster startup time for each container and lower overhead of execution; the weakness in containerization is the reliance on software separation in the container engine and the underlying operating system. A best-in-class solution would be a hybrid that provides the hardware security of virtual machines with the speed of deployment and startup for containers. Kata Containers provides such a solution.

Kata Containers

Kata Containers is an open source project managed by the OpenStack Foundation, which includes technology from an Intel open source project called Clear Containers. Clear Containers is related to the Intel Clear Linux project discussed earlier in the chapter. In actuality, Kata Containers are *really* lightweight virtual machines designed to be managed like containers. The benefit of Kata Containers over regular containers is the increased security from the hardware-enforced separation provided by the hypervisor. This discussion of Kata Containers is based on the 1.2.0 release.[33]

Kata Containers uses the KVM hypervisor and works seamlessly with Kubernetes, Docker, and OpenStack. Other hypervisor support is being built and may even be available as you are reading this. Kata Containers is comprised of six different components, as shown in Figure 4-16.

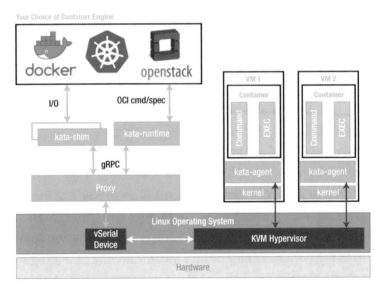

Figure 4-16. *Kata Containers architecture*

---

[33]Kata Containers, https://katacontainers.io and https://github.com/
kata-containers/documentation

- The **Runtime**, called the kata-runtime, handles
  all the Open Container Initiative (OCI) commands
  used to create and configure a container. It also starts
  the Shim instances. The kata-runtime utilizes the
  virtcontainers[34] project to perform the heavy lifting in
  a platform agnostic way. Whenever an OCI command
  is run on a container, the Runtime creates a new Shim
  to connect the container engine to the container.

- The **Shim**, called the kata-shim, is an interface
  between the container engine (like Docker, Kubernetes,
  or OpenStack) and the created container inside the
  virtual machine. The container engine has a process
  (called the Reaper) that monitors the container,
  manages the container, and *reaps* the container when
  it dies or must be killed. Because Kata Containers are
  inside a virtual machine, the Reaper cannot actually
  access the container, due to the hardware separation
  in place by the VM. The Shim pretends to be the
  container, so the container engine can connect to it for
  management, and the Shim communicates with the
  actual container using an agent. The Shim links the
  standard input and output flows and any Linux signals
  from the container back to the container engine, so the
  container engine can receive them and process them
  appropriately.

- The **Agent** (kata-agent) is part of the minimal Clear
  Linux OS image and runs inside the VM; it provides
  communication outside the VM to the kata-runtime
  and kata-shim. The Agent creates a container sandbox

---

[34]https://github.com/containers/virtcontainers

based on a set of namespaces for a container to run inside. The namespaces include UTC, IPC, network, and PID[35] namespaces. The Agent can support multiple containers running inside a VM (called a *pod*); however using Docker, only one container per pod is supported.

- The **Hypervisor** provides virtualization and is a combination of KVM with QEMU. As shown in Figure 4-17, QEMU is the Virtual Machine Manager (VMM) and creates the virtual machine for the container to run in, populates it with the virtualized kernel, and emulates virtualized devices for the VM. KVM is used to control the VM, and all VM exits return directly back to KVM. The hypervisor provides a virtual socket (VSOCK) or a serial port to communicate with the Shim or Runtime. The serial port is the default, but for Linux kernels beyond v4.8, VSOCK is available. If a serial port is used, gRPC runs over Yamux on the serial port.

---

[35]See `http://man7.org/linux/man-pages/man7/namespaces.7.html`, IPC = interprocess communication and message queues namespace, PID = process identifier namespace, UTS = hostname and Network Information Service (NIS) domain name service.

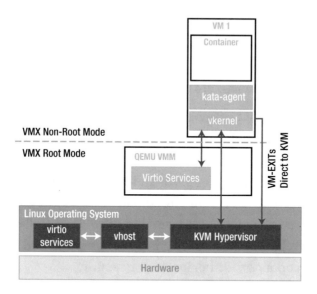

Figure 4-17. *Kata Containers hypervisor architecture*[36]

- The **Proxy** is a multiplexer for the hypervisor if a
  serial port is used to connect between the Runtime
  or Shim and the hypervisor. Multiple connections are
  required because the kata-agent can communicate
  with multiple different kata-runtime instances and
  kata-shims; each instance opens its own remote
  procedure call to the Agent using gRPC, and the Agent
  connects these to the appropriate container process
  in the VM. The Proxy is not needed if a VSOCK is used
  to connect between the Runtime and the hypervisor,
  since gRPC can run directly over a virtual socket and
  then gRPC directly handles the multiple different

---

[36]https://github.com/kata-containers/documentation/blob/master/
architecture.md

communication streams. In this case, the gRPC connections from the kata-runtime feed directly to the hypervisor over a VSOCK, and the Proxy disappears from the architecture diagram in Figure 4-16.

- The **kernel** is the operating system that runs the container inside the virtual machine. The kernel is a highly optimized kernel from Clear Linux with a minimal memory footprint and includes only the services needed to run the container workload. QEMU virtualizes or emulates everything else. The smaller Linux kernel reduces the attack surface presented to the container, further increasing security.

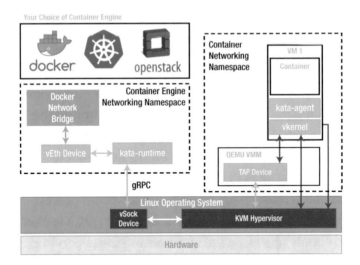

Figure 4-18. *Networking with Kata Containers*

WHAT IS QEMU?

Software Engineering can solve any problem using another layer of abstraction…except for the problem of having too many abstraction layers. QEMU is a special abstraction layer that solves several difficulties with virtualization.

Recall that KVM is a Type 2 hypervisor and part of the Linux kernel. But, KVM uses all the hardware features of VMX, so it is as fast and secure as a Type 1 hypervisor. Kata Containers combines QEMU with KVM for further speed improvements.

QEMU is a virtual machine monitor (VMM) that runs on top of an operating system host, like Linux. QEMU is also an emulator that does binary translation and can even run programs compiled for different CPUs or OSs on that host. So, QEMU is really good at emulation.

In Kata Containers, QEMU quickly boots virtual machines (VMs) for KVM by using emulation. A special version of QEMU provides highly optimized emulators to speed boot time and reduce interpretation of ACPI interfaces. Other emulators provide the root filesystem as a persistent memory device. QEMU also provides *hot-plugging* devices, during the launch process, allowing devices and virtual CPUs to be added to the VM only when needed.

All this speeds the construction of VMs and makes Kata Containers execute really fast.

Connecting containers to a network is accomplished with a virtual network created by the container engine on the host. The container engine connects this virtual network to the real network, using appropriate filters, including a network address filter (NAT). Docker connects the containers to this network using a virtual Ethernet (veth) device. However, virtual machines normally use a TAP[37] device. The problem in Kata Containers is that all devices are emulated through QEMU, and QEMU does not support veth interfaces. The solution implemented in Kata Containers requires the kata-runtime to bridge between the TAP device in QEMU and the host virtual network created by the container engine. Figure 4-18 shows this configuration graphically, with the traffic from the Docker virtual network running through the TAP device emulated by QEMU and then into the container in the VM.

Figure 4-19 shows the series of interactions between the Kata Containers components to create a container in a virtual machine. The virtcontainers library as part of the kata-runtime essentially does all the work to create the VM, start the Proxy, create the container sandbox that the container will run in, and then create the container, and finally start the kata-shim to communicate with the container.

Once the container is created, it can be started and used with the *start* message. In Kata Containers, the *start* message does not create the container as it does with most container engines. The container was already created with the *create* command, as shown in Figure 4-19. Instead, *start* just forwards the *start* message to the kata-agent, and the kata-agent starts the container's primary process.

---

[37]A TAP device copies all traffic from the network into the device, just like a "tap" on a phone line.

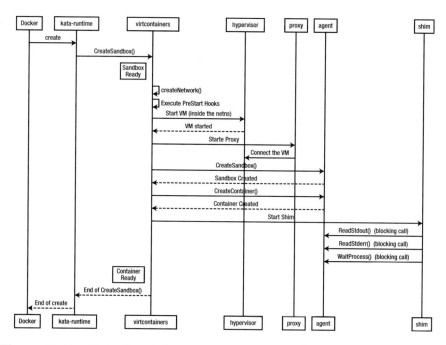

Figure 4-19. *Kata Containers create command*

Kata Containers Summary

With Kata Containers, you can have security and performance. Virtual machines utilize hardware separation to provide increased containment between containers while creatively using different software abstractions to maintain the same software APIs to start up and control the containers themselves. As we saw with ACRN, there are areas of attack that could breech the system, including the QEMU virtualized drivers, and the Kata Shim and Runtime. Table 4-5 outlines the analysis of the Kata Containers against our containment security requirements.

Table 4-5. *Kata Containers Security Summary*

Operating System Security Principles	Grade	Comments
Memory Disclosure by Privileged User	B	Most privileged attackers are restricted from viewing or tampering the VM memory. QEMU and the KVM, including their virtualized devices, remain as potential privileged attackers on the VM memory. Platforms with multi-key total memory encryption (MKTME) can provide protection but should include integrity as well as encryption. See the following article for attacks on encrypted memory: `https://arxiv.org/ftp/arxiv/papers/1712/1712.05090.pdf`
Memory Tampering by Privileged User	B	
Execution Interference by Privileged User	C	Most privileged attackers are restricted from viewing or tampering with workloads in the VM. QEMU and the KVM, including their virtualized devices, remain as potential privileged attackers on the VM execution, though this is expected and cannot be avoided. However, the Kata Shim and Runtime provide targets for privileged attackers to subvert workloads running in the VMs, and these processes are not protected.

(continued)

Table 4-5. (*continued*)

Operating System Security Principles	Grade	Comments
Data Leakage via Side Channels	C	Side channels are most concerning for VMs and container systems, as there may be applications of different trust levels running inside different containers or VMs. Updates to the Linux kernel and microcode patches for the serious side-channel CVEs are available. There continue to be security patches for KVM and QEMU, as late as October 30, 2018. For additional information, see `www.qemu.org/2018/01/04/spectre/` and `www.redhat.com/archives/rhsa-announce/2018-October/thread.html` for Red Hat kvm-qemu patches.
Execution Information Leakage via Side Channels	C	Execution leakage is similar to memory leakage and requires multi-key total memory encryption (MKTME) for protection but must also include integrity protection as well as encryption. Inference of execution is still possible under MKTME if page loads and misses are observable by the attacker. Just as we see in SGX, the operating system kernel remains as a potential attacker here.

(*continued*)

Table 4-5. (*continued*)

Operating System Security Principles	Grade	Comments
Trusted I/O	-	Trusted I/O is not supported in Kata Containers.
Application Flexibility	A	Any application can build into Kata Containers, and the support of many devices through virtual device drivers improves the level of support and flexibility of the Kata Containers solution.

Trusted Execution Environments

Even with the protections afforded to applications by containers and virtual machines, some applications are so sensitive that they require even greater separation protections. Examples of such applications include payment applications that deal with credit card transactions or authentication applications that deal with fingerprints or other biometrics. Trusted Execution Environments (TEEs) are application execution containers that are separate from the operating system and other applications on the platform and provide enhanced memory and execution separation characteristics. TEEs provide containment guarantees that prevent even the administrator or root from interfering with or peeking at the secrets of an application. This section looks at two such TEEs, Intel's Software Guard Extensions (SGX) and Android Trusty.

Software Guard Extensions

Software Guard Extensions (SGX) is a ring 3 TEE, meaning that SGX is directly accessible to applications, and applications running in SGX have the same type of privileges (ring 3) as other applications on the platform. SGX creates a TEE from a special memory cache and a secure mode of the CPU, removing the entire operating system from the trusted computing base (TCB); this means that unlike other TEEs, SGX does not even depend on secure boot to instantiate a trusted environment. For applications to use SGX however, the operating system must support access to the SGX instructions and the SGX memory cache. Support for SGX is available for Microsoft Windows and many Linux distributions, including Ubuntu Desktop. SGX has not been ported to Ubuntu IoT Core.

An application running SGX is called an *enclave*, and an SGX enclave is actually part of an application. An enclave is built like a dynamically loadable library (DLL) or shared object library (SO), to use Linux terminology. The enclave is loaded by an application and, from the operating system perspective, the enclave is an extension of the process space of the application that loaded it. There are three primary differences between a regular application and an enclave:

- The way the enclave memory is treated

- The way the enclave memory is loaded

- The way the enclave is executed

Memory for an enclave comes from a special pool of memory called the Enclave Page Cache (EPC). EPC memory is encrypted by the processor and is only accessible in SGX mode. Regular applications, or even the operating system, that try to access EPC memory see only encrypted junk. Only when an enclave is executing can the CPU provide the decryption key so the memory page contents can be viewed. Likewise writes to the EPC pages are also restricted. These guarantees are part of what makes SGX mode a TEE. Platforms must allocate memory into the EPC, thus making that memory unavailable for regular applications; a new feature of SGX is the dynamic allocation of pages to the EPC, but this is not supported on all processors yet.

The second thing that makes SGX mode a TEE is the special way that code and data are loaded into an enclave. When a regular application asks the operating system for an enclave to be created, it provides the DLL (or SO) that contains the enclave's code. That code must be signed. We will discuss how the code is signed and with what key in a moment. SGX includes a special loader that verifies the signature on the enclave as it is loading its code and data into EPC memory. If the signature indicates the enclave code is authentic, then the loader activates the enclave and the application can use the enclave functions. If the signature indicates the enclave has been tampered with or is not signed with an authorized key, then the load of the enclave fails. All code and initial data pages loaded into an enclave are verified as authentic, which indicates that the authorized party that signed that code also trusts that code. This makes the code running inside SGX trustworthy and another attribute of SGX as a TEE.

The final thing that makes SGX mode a TEE is the fact that it is a special mode of the CPU, and this creates execution separation between regular applications and enclaves. The execution of enclave code within SGX is separate from execution inside the operating system and the execution in applications. There have been side-channel attacks on SGX, just as there have been on other execution modes. This is a result of some shared micro-architectural state and shared cache state; there is also a dependency from SGX on the operating system to load and manage memory pages which creates another type of side channel. Changes to the CPU microcode have addressed the attacks that are known, and further changes are being made to hyperthreading mode to address additional issues. We talk more about this in the section on threats later.

Creating code that can be run as an enclave requires a special key. This is because the enclave code must be verified by the SGX launcher when the enclave is loaded. The SGX launcher uses a key set by the BIOS during boot to verify enclave programs. If an enclave is signed using a key which itself is signed by the SGX launcher key in BIOS, then the enclave is trusted. By default, the BIOS includes an Intel key. Intel will sign an enclave developer's key after they submit a formal request and fill out some paperwork. This means that any developer with such a key could run enclave code on any platform with an Intel processor. Intel realizes this should be a bit more controlled, so they allow the owner of the platform to change the key in the BIOS to a key of their own. This means that the platform owner can change the behavior of the SGX launcher to approve only enclaves that they themselves trust; this is done by changing that BIOS key.

SGX is a powerful mode on Intel processors that provides a trusted execution environment to applications. This gives applications the ability to put their most sensitive code inside a trusted execution container and keep the operation of that code, and any secrets that the code uses, away from other applications and even the operating system.

SGX Security Summary

Table 4-6 provides a summary of the SGX system security features for comparison with other systems.

Table 4-6. *SGX TEE Security Summary*

TEE Security Principles	Grade	Comments
Memory Disclosure by Privileged User	A	SGX uses a separate memory cache that is encrypted by the CPU and is separated from the operating system and other applications.
Memory Tampering by Privileged User	A	SGX mode prevents access to memory pages in the EPC unless an SGX application is executing, which locks out other applications and the operating system from tampering with the memory. Page attributes are set and locked at page set up time when the enclave is loaded.
Execution Interference by Privileged User	B	The operating system still controls the page tables, including allocation of pages and page eviction; a misbehaving OS can perform a DOS on an enclave and perform some side-channel attacks using the enclave's usage of pages. Protection of secrets within an SGX enclave still requires the use of constant-time programming constructs and careful use of pages and cache to avoid such side-channel attacks.

(continued)

Table 4-6. (*continued*)

TEE Security Principles	Grade	Comments
Data Leakage via Side Channels	C	Research on SGX side channels, including L1 Terminal Fault, have been reported.
Execution Information Leakage via Side Channels	B	These are a result of microarchitectural side channels in the CPU itself. CPU patches are effective in mitigating most of these attacks, other than hyperthreading-based attacks.[38] Other options including forcing CPU core scheduling are potential solutions. (`https://www.usenix.org/system/files/conference/atc18/atc18-oleksenko.pdf`)
Trusted I/O	-	Trusted I/O is not supported in SGX.
Application Flexibility	A	Any application can contain enclave code which can be loaded into SGX. Commercial development of enclaves requires a key from Intel, or the platform must be set up with a special SGX launcher key.

Android Trusty

The Trusty TEE[39] is an offering from Google that includes an operating system, a set of drivers for Android to communicate with Trusty, and APIs for applications to use applications running in Trusty. Trusty is an interesting TEE that has some very different properties as compared with Intel SGX.

---

[38]`https://software.intel.com/security-software-guidance/api-app/sites/default/files/336996-Speculative-Execution-Side-Channel-Mitigations.pdf`

[39]Google. "Trusty TEE." `https://source.android.com/security/trusty`

The first primary difference is Trusty is designed to operate on a completely separate processor from the main processor running the untrusted operating system. Trusty uses its own memory management unit (MMU) and provides virtualized memory for all the trusted apps running in Trusty. All the applications must be single threaded, though multithreaded applications may be provided in a future update.

The next significant difference with Trusty is that it can have access to devices, platform keys, and other resources and give access to those resources to Trusty applications. Since SGX runs in ring 3, it does not have privileged access to devices and does not currently have a trusted I/O mechanism.

The last difference in Trusty is that trusted applications are compiled into Trusty and run as an event-driven server. Applications cannot be added dynamically into Trusty – they must be designed and built into the Trusty kernel. And each trusted application running in Trusty is accessible to any application in the untrusted operating system; Trusty applications are not bound to a particular process in the untrusted processor.

Trusty TEE Security Summary

Trusty is an interesting TEE that provides significant trust for platform developers, but it does not expose the capability for end users to create their own trusted applications.

Table 4-7 provides a summary of the Trusty TEE security features for comparison with other systems.

Table 4-7. *Trusty TEE Security Summary*

TEE Security Principles	Grade	Comments
Memory Disclosure by Privileged User	A	Because Trusty uses a physically separate memory from the untrusted operating system and its own MMU, disclosure and tampering are avoided. The drawback is the additional HW cost for this separation.
Memory Tampering by Privileged User	A	
Data Leakage via Side Channels	A	
Execution Interference by Privileged User	A	Because Trusty uses a physically separate processor (or physical core) from the untrusted operating system and its own MMU, disclosure and tampering are avoided. The drawback is the additional HW cost for this separation.
Execution Information Leakage via Side Channels	A	
Trusted I/O	B	Trusted devices are built into the system and allocated when Trusty software is compiled.
Application Flexibility	D	Only the applications built into the Trusty software are available – no dynamic loading of software applications or services is possible.

Containment Summary

In this section, we reviewed different types of application containment, ranging from software-only containment using containers, hardware-assisted containment with virtual machines, hardware TEE with encrypted memory and special processor state with SGX, and full hardware separation TEE with Trusty. The more hardware used in the containment solution, the greater the level of security provided by the solution. However, there is a balance to be had, as we saw with Trusty, because software is more flexible than hardware. A full hardware solution, while more secure, creates limitations to what can be accomplished and what usage models applications can execute.

Network Stack and Security Management

This section signals the shift in our chapter from platform software to the management plane. Networking and connectivity are vital to an IoT system, and therefore the entirety of Chapter 5 is devoted to this subject. We leave the discussion of the network technologies and protocol stacks, including the threats, to that future chapter. However, before we leave the networking topic completely, we want to cover an important software library for network packet processing, the DPDK, as well as a few software packages that make security management easier.

Intel Data Plane Development Kit

The Data Plane Development Kit (DPDK) is a set of software libraries and device drivers that make constructing software networking stacks with advanced features very easy and very performant. We talk about the DPDK because it is a useful component to speed the development of **end-to-end security** features and in the implementation of network security policies to enforce **network restrictions**. This library exposes the features and capabilities of network cards into ring 3, enabling better performance when processing packets at high speed. This is important for edge devices implementing industrial control loops, because the DPDK allows software to reliably receive and send packets within a minimum number of CPU cycles. The Linux Foundation[40] provides a downloadable version of the DPDK, and Intel contributes specialized features and drivers that directly leverage Intel silicon performance. The DPDK boosts packet processing throughput and provides multicore support, facilitates processing of packets in user space (ring 3) to avoid costly transitions between user and kernel space, and enables direct access to devices for high-speed IO.

The latest DPDK version is 18.05 and supports the following features:

- Support for multiple NIC cards, including virtualized drivers

- Support for cryptographic operations in cryptodev library

- Support for event handling in the eventdev library

- Baseband wireless in the bbdev library

- Data compression support in the compressdev library (new in DPDK 18.05)

Figure 4-20 shows the architecture of the DPDK library.

---

[40]https://www.dpdk.org/ and documentation is available online at http://fast.dpdk.org/doc/pdf-guides/

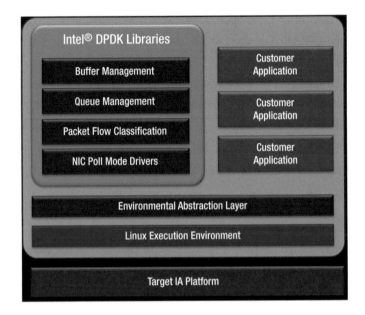

Figure 4-20. *The Intel DPDK library structure*

The DPDK is very comprehensive and supports multiple hardware capabilities across Intel, AMD, ARM, NXP, and other hardware manufacturers. In keeping with our theme in this chapter, let us review the security capabilities and the Intel-specific hardware features that are supported through the DPDK.

The DPDK supports standard modes for the Advanced Encryption Algorithm (AES), including Cipher Block Chaining (CBC) mode, Electronic Code Book (ECB) mode, Counter (CTR) mode,[11] and a special mode used primarily for block storage devices, XTS[41] mode. All modes are supported

---

[41]XTS is actually considered a tweak cipher, a modification of the underlying cipher using parameters. XTS stands for XEX-based tweaked-codebook mode with ciphertext stealing. XEX is a tweak cipher mode, which stands for XOR-Encrypt-XOR, which was designed by Phillip Rogaway, 2004, "Efficient Instantiations of Tweakable Blockciphers and Refinements to Modes OCB and PMAC," http://web.cs.ucdavis.edu/~rogaway/papers/offsets.pdf

with the standard key sizes, 128-bits, 192-bits, and 256-bits. DPDK also supported DOCSIS encryption and DES and 3DES.[42]

In addition to encryption, the DPDK supports hashing algorithms using the SHA2[43] algorithms, SHA2-256, SHA2-384, and SHA2-512. The older SHA1 algorithm is also supported, but should only be used for interoperability reasons; the use of SHA2-256 should be the minimum requirement for IoT systems.

The DPDK supports the Intel SHA-NI and AES-NI instructions (see Chapter 3, section *"CPU hosted Crypto implementations"),* providing access to hardware acceleration of these algorithms. In addition, AES-GCM, the Galois Counter Mode of AES, is further enhanced by combining the AES-NI instruction with carryless multiplication instructions to speed performance of the Galois integrity tag calculation.[44]

The DPDK provides compatibility with other software and hardware implementations of cryptography, even providing a full software implementation using the OpenSSL open source cryptographic library. Using these different plugins for the DPDK cryptodev library, a fully portable application can be built that makes use of the best hardware features the platform has to offer. The use of the DPDK allows applications

---

[42]DES, Data Encryption Standard, and 3DES, Triple Data Encryption Standard, are older modes included only for interoperability. It is strongly recommended to avoid use of these modes unless they are required for interoperability. In IoT systems, there is no good reason to use such modes.

[43]SHA, Secure Hash Algorithm, are algorithms defined in the NIST Secure Hash Standard (SHS) for cryptographic hash algorithms. The older version SHA1 is deprecated for most uses today. The SHA2 family of algorithms, https://nvlpubs.nist.gov/nistpubs/FIPS/NIST.FIPS.180-4.pdf, covers multiple hash digest bit lengths.

[44]https://software.intel.com/en-us/articles/intel-carry-less-multiplication-instruction-and-its-usage-for-computing-the-gcm-mode and https://software.intel.com/en-us/articles/aes-gcm-encryption-performance-on-intel-xeon-e5-v3-processors

direct access to the best cryptographic acceleration hardware of the Intel platform, and compatibility to other platform's cryptographic accelerators as well.

Security Management

Security management is the combination of active processes and executed procedures during installation, configuration, operation, and decommissioning of systems that preserves the confidentiality, integrity, and availability of those system and network resources for the approved mission(s) of the organization. This chapter focuses on software, not processes and procedures. However, there are software tools and agents that directly aid the security management process. We look at a few of those here, just for completeness in our discussion.

Secure Device Onboarding

The very first issue requiring a solution in an IoT system is **device provisioning** or how to provision devices so they can connect to the correct back-end cloud system or device management system. A common solution is to preprovision devices during manufacturing to connect to a specific cloud agent. Microsoft Azure Sphere uses this approach. While it works, that solution locks the device into a specific cloud, and the approach can have impacts on high-speed manufacturing. A better approach is to provide flexible and secure onboarding for any device to any cloud system. Intel's Secure Device Onboard (SDO[45]) provides this security capability using an EPID[46] device identity key. Figure 4-21 shows the provisioning lifecycle of a device, from manufacturing to installation. This can be any device from a gateway or server down to a smart sensor.

---

[45]https://software.intel.com/en-us/secure-device-onboard
[46]See the discussion of Intel's Enhanced Privacy ID (EPID) in Chapter 3.

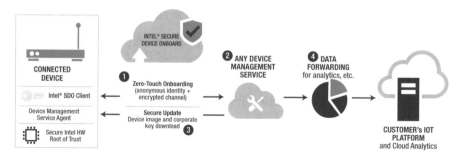

Figure 4-21. *Intel's Secure Device Onboard preserves device privacy and provisions "Any Device to Any Cloud"*

SDO utilizes a few hardware security features to construct this high-level service, including

- The platform's root of trust containing an identity key; an EPID group signature key is the preferred identity key, since it provides privacy for the device installation, but an RSA or ECDSA key may also be used.

- The Intel SDO Client firmware executing inside a TEE; SDO currently uses the CSME discussed in Chapter 3 for its TEE, but SGX or Trusty are alternative TEEs for SDO.

- Secure storage on the device to hold the manufacturer's public key, a GUID, and an ownership credential.

During manufacturing, a digital record of the device is created, which is referred to as the ownership credential. The ownership credential includes the device's unique identifier (GUID) and the owner's public key; the owner credential is signed by a private key belonging to the manufacturer and includes an integrity checksum to prevent modification or forgery of the ownership credential. The manufacturer endorses the ownership credential by digitally signing it with the manufacturer's private key when the device is sold. This endorsement can be repeated in the supply chain, allowing a deferred binding between the credentials stored in the device and those of the device management service (e.g., running within a particular AWS account) who will control the device in operation.

When the device is installed (Step 1 in Figure 4-21), the device contacts Intel's Secure Device Onboard Rendezvous server and is connected with the device management service which was specified by the device's owner. As a precursor to the device install step, the preferred device management server must have been registered with the SDO Rendezvous service by the device owner using the ownership credentials. The SDO protocol between the device and Rendezvous server validates the ownership credential, as well as the authenticity of the device and the Rendezvous server to each other. At the end of the SDO protocol, the device is forwarded to the proper device management service to complete provisioning (Step 2 in Figure 4-21), allowing the device management service to install a management agent on the device. SDO prevents unauthorized entities from taking control of the device and gives the end customer flexibility to provision the device to any management service or cloud back end. The device management service can then update the device with new software and link the device to the preferred back-end cloud system (Steps 3 and 4 in Figure 4-21). Intel SDO can also be reactivated by the device owner at any time, allowing the device to be reprovisioned or for device resale.

Intel Secure Device Onboarding solves the first problem an IoT device encounters – how to securely connect to the right back-end service for management and operations. Using hardware security elements inherent in the platform, SDO provides a low-cost and flexible solution with high security.

Platform Integrity

Once a device is provisioned, maintaining the integrity of the platform software is vital to keeping an IoT system operating. **Platform integrity** means ensuring that a device has booted the platform software intended by the system and that the platform firmware, boot loader, and operating system have not been corrupted. Device management software can query the platform's integrity state and determine if something needs to be updated or remediated. But, some software element must reside on the device to calculate the platform integrity and then communicate it up to the device management software in a meaningful way.

In Chapter 3, we discuss protected boot technologies included in Intel platforms, including PTT[47] and TPMs. These hardware elements use software in the operating system, boot loader, and BIOS to measure the platform during boot. These measurements are stored in hardware-protected storage in PTT or the TPM. The software to access these measurements is included in the trusted services stack (TSS) that was written according to the Trusted Computing Group's (TCG) specification for TPM2. As shown in Figure 4-22, this software stack is comprehensive and, besides platform integrity measurement, includes features for other TPM operations including encryption, key generation, secure storage, and attestation. The application-level APIs are all provided in the System API (SAPI)[48] or the Enhanced SAPI (ESAPI)[49] and are defined by the TCG; the FAPI is still under development. The Feature API (FAPI) would be the easiest to use and abstracts many details of the TPM from the application, while the SAPI provides near-transparent use of the TPM commands and responses.

---

[47]Platform Trust Technology (PTT) and Trusted Platform Module (TPM)

[48]https://trustedcomputinggroup.org/wp-content/uploads/TSS_SAPI_Version-1.1_Revision-22_review_030918.pdf

[49]https://trustedcomputinggroup.org/wp-content/uploads/TSS_TSS-2.0-Enhanced-System-API_V0.9_R03_Public-Review-1.pdf

TCG TPM2 SOFTWARE STACK: DESIGN

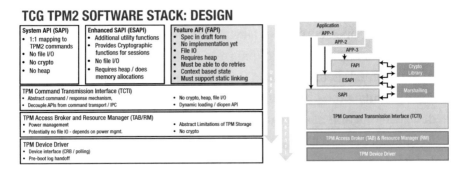

Figure 4-22. *Intel TPM2 software stack (TSS)*[50]

Network Defense

IoT systems are all about communication, and without some type of defensive measures, these IoT devices would be easy targets for network attackers. Common network defense capabilities including firewalls and intrusion defense software are important to add to any IoT device. Some devices are so small and so resource constrained that no attempt is even made to add any network protections. However, there are tools that can provide some reasonable protections and should be considered.

The first step of **network defense**, of course, is to limit the applications and services that open ports to listen for connections. In fact, if your IoT device is so resource constrained that you are considering putting no network defenses on the device, then there should be no listening services either – only outgoing connections. But because firewalling is the most basic defense, a program that intercepts the incoming network traffic to check for anomalies is important and should be considered.

On Linux distributions, the recommended program for network defense is TCP Wrappers. This program can be called from inetd or configured into the hosts.allow and hosts.deny configurations. TCP Wrappers allows the system to be configured to allow or deny connections based on the network

---

[50]https://software.intel.com/en-us/blogs/2018/08/29/tpm2-software-stack-open-source

address and protocol. Additionally, other commands can be executed when rules in the TCP Wrappers configuration are triggered, such as sending an alert email or adding an entry to the syslog. Configuration of the TCP Wrappers file can provide extensive filtering and can be set up so that normal traffic and operations easily get through without any overhead. Other options for firewalling include directly using the kernel netfilter or configuring the netfilter through ipchains. Significant material is available both on the Web and in Linux books, so that information will not be repeated here.

Finally, good logging for what is happening on the network and on a device is vital to reconstructing an attack or understanding an attempted intrusion. There are numerous programs for **attack detection** that operate on both Linux and Windows and can be compiled for other operating systems as well. TCPdump and snort[51] are common programs for detecting network intrusions or malformed packets on a device. Snort can be turned into a full-scale network intrusion detection system where devices capture traffic and send dangerous looking packets to a central server for deeper analysis. Suricata is a similar robust open source solution for intrusion detection. These types of intrusion detection system are very useful for IoT system for early detection of attacks and fast response to prevent such attacks from bringing down the IoT system.

Platform Monitoring

Security management includes monitoring a device and its workload for anomalies, in the event that a network attacker is able to circumvent the network defenses in place on the device. The monitoring functions are tied into the device management agent on the platform, allowing problems to be reported back to the management servers.

In the section on Zephyr, we discussed watchdog timers used to monitor for long running privileged threads. Remember the problem in Zephyr was a privileged thread that does not yield back to the operating

---

[51]https://www.snort.org/

system which can then starve out the execution of other processes on the system. The operating system can prevent this by using a hardware timer started before releasing control to the high-privileged thread; if the thread does not yield back in a certain amount of time, the hardware timer causes a non-maskable interrupt (NMI) that stops execution of everything else and returns control back to an interrupt service routine (ISR) in the operating system. When the operating system regains control, it can terminate the offending thread and report the situation back to the management service. Sometimes this doesn't work. It often fails because the attacked thread had enough privileges on the system, allowing the attacker to disable or continually reset the timer, effectively disabling the watchdog.

There are other unique options for performing platform monitoring that can identify side-channel attacks or threads that have potentially been corrupted by network attackers. Several techniques are published[52, 53] that utilize hardware performance counters in the CPU microarchitecture to characterize and monitor software and detect when attacks are likely present. This information can be used to shut down the attacking threads or reboot the system into a known good state.

McAfee Embedded Control

There is one last software capability that deserves mention in security management that provides some unique **system authorization** capabilities. McAfee Embedded Control (MEC)[54] is a software program

---

[52]A Survey of Cyber Security Countermeasures Using Hardware Performance Counters, https://arxiv.org/pdf/1807.10868.pdf

[53]Cache-Based Side-Channel Attacks Detection through Intel Cache Monitoring Technology and Hardware Performance Counters, https://hal.inria.fr/hal-01762803/document

[54]https://www.mcafee.com/enterprise/en-us/products/embedded-control.html

that provides extended access control and integrity to IoT platforms. MEC protects both executable as well as data files on a platform, ensuring that those files are not accidentally or maliciously modified, even by a user with administrative rights. MEC creates a new privileged user on the platform that is only accessible through the MEC admin interface and manages a database of integrity checksums over directories and files specified by the MEC admin. MEC includes an augmented launcher that is integrated with the Windows or Linux operating system, allowing MEC to check the integrity of executable files before launch. The access control database allows MEC to also specify what services and devices an executable can access, providing even stricter control on running applications. This means that even if a program were maliciously corrupted at Runtime, the attacker would not be able to use unauthorized system resources, and ROP or JOP attacks would only be able to modify the use of authorized system resources, not fundamentally change the resources to which the program has access.

MEC creates a very powerful protection for IoT devices, and this system works extremely well when the platform's software and configuration does not change regularly. MEC can be integrated easily in McAfee ePO device management suite as well (see the discussion in the *"Device Management"* section). In some versions of MEC, dynamic protection of memory is also provided, limiting the effect of buffer overflows. A limited version of MEC is included in Intel's IoT Gateway Software Suite,[55] and McAfee continues to add improvements and support for other operating systems in MEC. Upgrading to the fully featured McAfee Embedded Control Pro from the basic MEC version included in Intel's IoT Gateway is a smooth transition, fully supported by the MEC admin interface.

---

[55]https://shopiotmarketplace.com/iot/index.html#/details?pix=58

Network Stack and Security Summary

In this section we looked at various software components that can provide effective **network defense** and **attack detection**, and even be used to build comprehensive **end-to-end security** using the cryptographic library in the DPDK. Common IoT problems like **platform integrity**, **device provisioning,** and **system authorization** can be solved using specialized packages like the TSS, Intel SDO, and McAfee Embedded Control. While these problems cannot be solved for free, the cost in additional compute resources and Runtime RAM may likely provide the difference between a platform that is regularly being attacked and draining the maintenance and remediation budget and a platform with adequate tools and packages that is resilient to attack.

Device Management

IoT systems are composed of thousands of devices, and with so many devices, manual management is prohibitive. In other cases, IoT devices are physically located in remote or difficult-to-reach locations, increasing the cost of sending out a repair person in a "truck roll." Autonomous device management using a cloud-based management solution is essential to preserving an IoT system's return on investment (ROI).

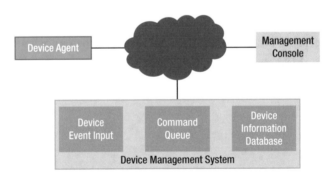

Figure 4-23. *Notional cloud-based device management system*

Cloud-based device management systems include a few common elements, as shown in Figure 4-23. On the device, a management agent performs the actions requested by the management system and also provides data to the management system on the device's health. How such an agent is installed on a device can sometimes be an issue; however **device provisioning** solutions like SDO covered in a prior section provide convenient solutions to this issue. A management console, normally implemented as a browser-based web application, retrieves data from the device management system and presents usable information to system administrators, allowing admins to schedule maintenance, perform actions on groups of devices, or even dive into details of a specific device to troubleshoot problems or investigate trouble tickets. The actual device management system in the Cloud is what separates different systems. Generally, each management system must have three elements:

- A Device Event Input queue allowing devices to provide status and report problems

- A Command Queue allowing administrators to push out commands to devices

- A Device Information Database containing information on each device in the system

The security services that device management system must provide include

- **Authentication**: Ensures that both devices and administrators on the device management system are who they claim to be. Cryptographic credentials issued to these parties are essential to maintaining proof of identity for all entities on the system.

- **Authorization**: Commands to devices can be disruptive to the services provided by the IoT system, or even potentially destructive to the device itself. A reboot command to several devices might cause a temporary denial of service, but a forced operating system update with corrupt software could bring down a system for days or even months.

- **Confidentiality and Integrity**: Although data sent via device management systems do not typically include personally identifiable information (PII), the commands and device health data can contain sensitive information. Integrity of this data is vital to prevent tampering or accidental corruption of the data in transit, but confidentiality may also be warranted depending on the information contained in commands and data updates from devices.

- **Nonrepudiation**: Guaranteed proof of source attached to health data or even the collection of other environmental data around devices could be crucial to the IoT system. Guaranteeing data originated from a particular device is part of data provenance.

- **Defense in Depth**: Is a layering of defenses to protect system elements from hacking. This includes attacks on the devices, gateways, and on the cloud systems and management consoles. Because the device management system represents the most significant network attack surface, and many of the software elements attached to the device management agents require elevated privileges to perform their operations, the device management system itself must be constructed to prevent attackers from gaining control over the IoT systems. Careful attention to the construction of both the device agent and the interfaces and APIs presented by the cloud system is necessary to prevent successful attacks.

This section reviews two different device management systems, one designed for small to medium deployments (Mesh Central) and one designed for large deployments (Helix Device Cloud).

Mesh Central

Mesh Central is a device management solution appropriate for small- to medium-sized IoT deployments. Mesh is an agent technology, which means that each managed device must be running the Mesh Agent software component. Mesh allows a Mesh Administrator to gain remote access and control of their devices through a variety of means, including direct shell access, dashboards, and connection via custom web applets. Mesh also provides peer-to-peer (i.e., Machine-to-Machine [M2M]) interactions, allowing devices to communicate directly to each other, without a human administrator being involved; this enables the IoT M2M type actions for true IoT automation.

Mesh Central is an Intel open source project and has a wide array of services targeted for remote monitoring and management of computers and devices. Users can manage all their devices from a single web site, no matter the device location or the device position behind routers and proxies, and this is all possible without needing to know the device's IP addresses. Mesh works by having each device generate a new unique RSA key pair, and the hash of the public key becomes the device's identity. Mesh devices register to the Mesh Central Cloud by communicating to devices around them and finding a path to the Mesh servers. This information is found in a signed policy file that is shared among the devices; however, this requires that devices be preprovisioned with a Mesh client and a policy file, otherwise, and IP address and a path to the device are needed for solutions like SDO to work properly.

The following is a partial list of the actions a Mesh Administrator can do to their connected devices:

- Opening a shell to run commands directly on the device

- Opening the device's graphical desktop, displaying the device's GUI, and providing mouse control on the device

- Installing, removing, and updating software on the device

- Activating a particular piece of software on the device or sending commands to that software (as if on a terminal on the device)

- Viewing files or logs on the device

The following is a brief list of Mesh Central architectural elements:

- Each device is referred to as a node and is identified by a secure, provable identifier based on a self-generated (device-generated) RSA public key.

- Nodes are organized into an overlay network, meaning routing of Mesh messages occur from the Mesh server to the device, but potentially hopping from one device in the Mesh to another device in the Mesh in order to reach the actual destination device; this path may traverse different communication networks connecting each device.

- Agent and Server APIs are available for generic, secure messaging for Admin-to-Device and Device-to-Device messaging.

- Agent Software Update is provided over-the-air (network) using signed and verified updates.

- Direct Connection from an admin web browser (via web sockets) directly to devices for custom applications in the browser to interact with, query, or control devices.

- A Mesh Developer API to add custom actions into the Mesh Agent running on devices.

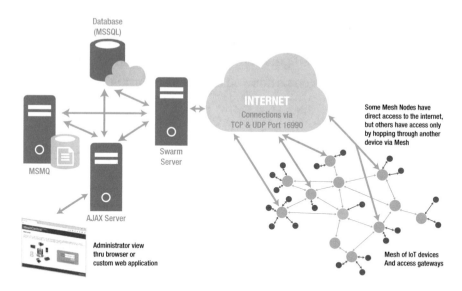

Figure 4-24. *Mesh Central device management system architecture*

As shown in Figure 4-24, Mesh Central is actually composed of four different servers:

- The AJAX Server: Provides the primary interface for Mesh administrators

- The Swarm Server: Provides the primary interface for devices into Mesh

- The Database: Usually Microsoft SQL Server, stores data about devices

- The MSMQ: Provides message delivery among servers

Mesh operates by having a bit of software, called the Mesh Agent Software, on every device. This agent runs under a privileged account on the device so that it is able to perform management on the device (e.g., run software, install applications and services, activate hardware, etc.). The Mesh Agent also has a configuration file, called the Mesh Agent Policy File, that controls what the agent is allowed to do and information about the Mesh control server.

Table 4-8. *Mesh Central Device Management Analysis*

Device Management Security Principles	Grade	Comments
Authentication	C	Mesh requires devices to generate their own identity keys in software and then registers devices to the Mesh Swarm server without any device attestation or proof from a hardware root of trust. This forces device administrators to know the hostnames of devices that should be registering and ignore or boot off devices they do not trust.

(continued)

Table 4-8. (*continued*)

Device Management Security Principles	Grade	Comments
Authorization	C	Authorization of commands requires an additional key be shared from the Mesh Administrator, because commands are not protected end to end, only hop to hop. Without this additional layering of authorization (not natively provided by Mesh), commands could be forged by a rogue Mesh node.
Confidentiality and Integrity	A	All messages traversing the Mesh are protected with strong integrity and confidentiality, and session keys are regenerated frequently. Protections are only provided hop to hop, however, not end to end.
Repudiation	D	Mesh does not leverage a hardware root of trust, so all keys are software generated. While all the right actions (e.g., encrypted messages, RSA identity keys, verification by clients) are performed, there is no protection of credentials on the device if an attacker were able to compromise software on one of the systems.
Defense in Depth	D	Mesh runs the Mesh Agent as root by default; significant rework of the client software is required to segment high privilege tasks to protected software agents.

Wind River Helix Device Cloud

Helix Device Cloud (HDC) is an IoT device management solution by Wind River. HDC is able to connect to IoT devices and gateways, manage device-generated data, automatically respond to device events, and perform remote (OTA) software updates. HDC includes a significant back-end system using Kafka that enables intelligent autonomous management of devices and provides easy and secure device onboarding and provisioning through Intel Secure Device Onboard (SDO). HDC adds an agent protocol called DXL (Data Exchange Layer) to each edge device that enables intelligent processing of data and secure end-to-end communication.

With Helix Device Cloud, administrators can

- Maintain secure two-way connectivity to gateways and devices

- Perform flexible data collection to the Cloud and even distribute that data across multiple edge nodes using DXL's powerful edge capabilities

- Receive immediate notification of device issues and use HDC Agent tools for remote diagnosis and repair

- Securely onboard new devices using SDO and upgrade new devices when first activated in the field

- Push new updates out to connected devices

- Collect and import data from IoT devices directly to enterprise systems

HDC focuses on the device management and edge aggregation services; HDC does not address applications and data analytics, but provides mechanisms for these services to reach devices through HDC using McAfee ePO plugins and call-outs to external services. For a more complete overview of HDC, see the HDC Overview whitepaper.[56]

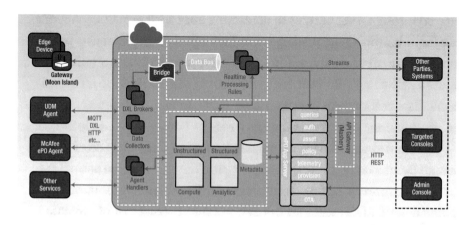

Figure 4-25. *Wind River Helix Device Cloud device management architecture*

Figure 4-25 shows the architecture of HDC. Devices connect to HDC Cloud using HTTP, DXL, or MQTT[57] protocols, and enterprise services leverage the data in HDC through a set of REST APIs exposed by HDC on the back end. Within HDC, there are three primary components: the device connection protocols, the data bus that organizes and routes messages and events, and the database that holds structured and unstructured data, analytics, metadata, and compute workloads. A fourth

---

[56]https://software.intel.com/en-us/iot/cloud-analytics/cloud-helix
[57]MQTT – Message Queuing Telemetry Transport is an ISO standard protocol based on the publish-subscribe design pattern. MQTT is described in more detail in "Message Orchestration" section.

part of HDC provides an extension interface to add features to HDC using the same extension interface as McAfee ePO,[58] allowing them to leverage each other's extensions.

One of the most interesting elements of HDC is the data bus and real-time processing rules. HDC utilizes an open source topic organization server called Kafka. With Kafka, incoming messages from devices are filtered through a set of rules to determine appropriate actions. Actions can include storing the message data into a part of the database, passing the message off to an ePO plugin, generating an alert to an administrator, or even activating some compute element in the database to create an immediate response to the reporting device. In fact, with the Kafka rules, multiple actions can be executed as a result of receiving a single message.

HDC is a secure device management system due to its use of Intel Secure Device Onboard (SDO) to provision devices and the use of DXL for secure communication. As discussed in the section on security management, SDO leverages the device's root of trust to authenticate the device during onboarding, ensuring the device is not being spoofed by an attacker. During onboarding, HDC leverages the secure channel authenticated with the device's root-of-trust key to install a new device identity key. DXL uses this new key for authentication back to HDC during TLS session establishment, making all messages passed over TLS authenticated back to the device. SDO also installs a trust anchor key for the HDC server; a trust anchor key is a key that is inherently trusted for a particular purpose. The DXL client stores the HDC trust anchor key so that it can authenticate the HDC server over TLS. On platforms that support the SGX TEE (see the section on software containment), the DXL client uses SGX to protect its identity key and the trust anchor key from attack by any malware that is able to infiltrate the device.

---

[58]McAfee ePO is an enterprise Policy Orchestration product that provides a unified and centralized management console for security management.

Table 4-9. *Helix Device Cloud Device Management Analysis*

Device Management Security Principles	Grade	Comments
Authentication	A	The device and HDC server are authenticated with RSA key pairs that were established over a secure channel through SDO using a hardware root-of-trust key.
Authorization	A	All commands down to the device are verified as authentic through DXL using a trust anchor key established during device provisioning through SDO.
Confidentiality and Integrity	A	All data and commands are protected over TLS.
Repudiation	A	The strong identity keys established using SDO validate the true device identity and link that to the RSA identity keys. Any actions or data are tied to this identity key and cannot be repudiated.
Defense in Depth	A	DXL uses the SGX TEE to ensure its operations and key material are not compromised, even if the platform is infected with malware.

Device Management Summary

Managing the devices of an IoT system is critical to security. Since all the management services occur over the network, attacks such as device spoofing, message forgery, and data disclosure are all possible. Although basic security protections over messages are possible, in

IoT system, attacks on the devices themselves can compromise key material and lead to questions regarding the provenance of data collected in the Cloud. The use of hardware security capabilities, like hardware root-of-trust keys and Trusted Execution Environments (TEEs), drastically improves the security of device management systems and, due to the lower risk of attacks, reduces the total cost of ownership of IoT systems.

System Firmware and Root-of-Trust Update Service

At the beginning of the chapter, in the "Operating Systems" section, we discussed the update problem. The Linux distributions reviewed in that section had different strategies for solving consistency among the packages and services being updated. However, the section identified a remaining problem regarding firmware updates which is how to gain the required access to firmware on the platform with the ability to perform updates.

Firmware is notoriously difficult to update. It typically resides in flash or other nonvolatile storage that is locked or inaccessible even to the operating system itself. The reason for this inaccessibility is security. Firmware is part of the most trusted parts of a system. The BIOS is the first part of the system that executes during power-on and represents the root of trust of the entire system. Other firmware may implement root-of-trust functions, such as system measurements, secure storage, or attestation reporting. Firmware in the security engines control cryptographic algorithms and keys. Firmware in network controllers (Ethernet, Wi-Fi, Bluetooth, Zigbee, LoRa) have access to all traffic entering and exiting the device and may even have access to cryptographic keys for encrypted traffic.

On personal computer-like systems using BIOS, the standard way
to perform secure firmware updates is through the *Capsule Update.*[59] A
Capsule Update is a function in the BIOS that is activated by the operating
system. The Capsule Update function is provided the addresses of capsules
in memory containing updates for certain firmware, and then the system
performs a soft reset. When BIOS takes control of the platform, it verifies
the capsules in memory, and if they are authentic and appropriate for the
platform, the capsules are used to update the appropriate firmware. For
Capsule Update to work properly, the operating system must be capable of
engaging the update service.

Not all devices support the BIOS Capsule Update. And of course for
systems without BIOS, or for IoT systems that do not use standard BIOS,
some other solution is required. In these cases, some type of custom
update procedure is required; as an example, see the update procedure
required for the Infineon TPM, a standard device on many PC platforms
(`https://www.infineon.com/cms/en/product/promopages/tpm-update/`
and `https://support.microsoft.com/en-us/help/4096377/windows-`
`10-update-security-processor-tpm-firmware`).

Threats to Firmware and RoT Update

Firmware update for IoT systems is being addressed by an Internet
Engineering Task Force (IETF) working group named SUITS (Software
Updates for Internet of Things). The SUITS working group[60] compiled
a detailed set of threats and requirements that systems implementing
updates should adhere to.

---

[59]`https://software.intel.com/en-us/blogs/2015/06/23/better-firmware-`
updates-in-linux-using-uefi-capsules and `https://software.intel.com/`
`en-us/blogs/2017/02/04/signed-uefi-firmware-updates-in-edk-ii`

[60]`https://datatracker.ietf.org/wg/suit/documents/` – At the time of this
writing, all documents in SUIT are still in the draft stage, but should be approved
as full RFCs by the time of publication.

- **Modified/Malicious Firmware Updates**: The first threat considered when updating firmware is corrupted or maliciously modified firmware. If an attacker is able to modify the firmware in transit to the platform, or even during the process of updating the firmware, then the attacker is able to inject features into the device. Accidental corruption is just as dangerous since corruption of firmware during the update process can *brick* a system (cause the system to be permanently broken).

- **Rollback to Old (Vulnerable) Firmware**: The second common threat considered for firmware is rolling back the firmware to an older version. An attacker that is able to force a system to reload an older version of firmware may be able to force an old vulnerability back into the platform, allowing them to take over the system. This is especially dangerous since the platform owner erroneously believes they are protected from that vulnerability and may not be watching for indications of compromise for that particular attack.

- **Unauthorized Update Request**: An often overlooked threat to firmware and RoT updates is the person or entity authorized to update firmware on the platform. Allowing a network attacker to force an upgrade of firmware is problematic. Obviously, an attacker successfully pushing corrupt or invalid firmware into a platform would create a problem, but even pushing a valid firmware update could create instability in the platform or a denial of service. Firmware update mechanisms should validate the entity requesting the update is authorized to do so, either because they are acting under an administrator account or their request is cryptographically proven to originate from an authorized administrator.

- **Unknown Source of Firmware**: Even if an authorized entity issues the firmware update request, the actual source of the firmware (the firmware code itself) should come from a known and approved source. Firmware that is intended to update an Infineon TPM device should not be written by Broadcom; there are potential exceptions, most notably in cases where an OEM repackages an update for their device (i.e., HP repackaging a TPM update for the devices they manufacture).

- **Application of Incorrect Firmware**: Finally, firmware must be matched to the system model and version of the hardware on which they execute. There can be many different revisions of hardware components, and firmware for one component may not operate properly on a different stepping or version.

Turtle Creek System Update and Manageability Service

Turtle Creek is the code name for an Intel product that manages application and platform updates over the air for Intel® Atom, ARM, Core, and Xeon processors. Turtle Creek allows a system administrator to remotely schedule and deploy software updates and recover malfunctioning systems to ensure business continuity and system availability. It is a cloud-based system that interfaces to many other device management systems, including Helix Device Cloud and Mesh Central which were covered in a previous section.

Turtle Creek is a microservice cloud system where each feature of the system is implemented by a microservice in a container hosted on the Cloud. This allows customized deployment of Turtle Creek features, which include the following capabilities:

- Update of the OS, application, and system firmware on supported platforms

- Recovery of platform software and firmware to known good status (factory reset)

- Control of system restart and shutdown

- Device telemetry reception for device health, data logs, and management messages

- Device diagnostics to execute pre-install and post-install checks

- Rollback recovery for any update

- Device system performance monitoring (e.g., CPU utilization, memory utilization, container performance)

- Centralized configuration manager that stores and retrieves configuration for devices used by all microservices, supporting various formats including XML, Consul database, or name-value pairs

- Comprehensive security using cryptographic signature verification for all packages using the TPM 2.0 for key and secret management and secure MQTT for messaging using TLS with end-to-end mutual authentication based on X.509 certificates.

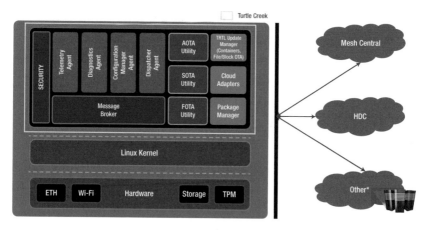

Figure 4-26. *Turtle Creek architecture*

Figure 4-26 shows the architecture of the Turtle Creek client software. Turtle Creek separates updates into three different categories based on the type of update and the repository from which the update packages are retrieved. These include Application Over-the-Air (AOTA), Software Over-the-Air (SOTA), and Firmware Over-the-Air (FOTA). AOTA supports update of application and individual software vendor's services via an update mechanism based on packages and signed RPMs using SMART and Docker container update mechanisms. SOTA supports operating system updates from an OS vendor's repository, which includes the use of the OS standard update mechanisms, like Ubuntu Update Manager and Mender[61] (for Yocto Linux). FOTA supports device or component manufacturer's ability to update custom firmware over the air and integrates firmware-specific functionality to update the device firmware components. The primary mechanism for FOTA support is BIOS Capsule Update.

---

[61]Mender is a client software embedded in Yocto that enables updates to the operating system to be installed. https://docs.mender.io/1.6/artifacts/building-mender-yocto-image

Turtle Creek's contribution to the IoT platform is twofold. First it unifies multiple disparate platform and software update mechanisms under a single management tool, making the process of managing and distributing updates easier. Second, it incorporates significant security protections on the update process, overlaying them on top of existing capabilities where necessary. Turtle Creek creates a manifest format to convey update commands and requires this update to be signed with a key in the TPM. This satisfies the security requirement for authorization of updates and ensures that the versions and source (repository) for the updates are genuine. If update packages do not include an embedded signature or source authentication, Turtle Creek's manifest can include a detached signature so the actual bits downloaded for the update can be verified that they have not been accidentally or maliciously modified. Table 4-10 outlines a more complete security analysis of Turtle Creek.

Table 4-10. *Security Analysis of Turtle Creek System Update and Management Service*

System Update Security Principles	Grade	Comments
Protect Against Modified Update Packages	A	Turtle Creek enforces RSA signatures over all update packages.
Prevent Update Rollbacks	A	Turtle Creek maintains a database of configured version numbers and packages on each device and ensures rollbacks do not occur.
Accept only Authorized Update Requests	A	Update requests are received over an authenticated MQTT channel and are contained in signed manifest file.

(*continued*)

Table 4-10. (*continued*)

System Update Security Principles	Grade	Comments
Use only Authorized Update Sources	A	Manifest file contains authorized source for download of the update mechanism.
Apply Correct Firmware/Software to the System	A	Manifest file contains attributes of the update that are checked on install to ensure invalid updates are not applied.
		In the event of a failed update or problems during update, Turtle Creek is able to restore the previous version of the software or firmware on the system reducing downtime.

System Firmware and RoT Summary

One of the most difficult problems in IoT systems is updating the base system firmware or recovering from a security vulnerability in a root-of-trust component like a TPM. Oftentimes, these firmware elements are designed to require a trusted administrator to manually watch over an update or install process. IoT devices in remote environments or hard-to-reach places cannot afford to miss such updates, but also cannot be sustained if a skilled administrator must manually install such updates. Services such as Turtle Creek which enable remote update of all software and firmware on a device are vital to both the security posture and ROI of IoT systems.

Application-Level Language Frameworks

The application-level language frameworks are the first topic in the application plane of our generic IoT architectural model from Figure 4-2. Although we are several software layers removed from the hardware of the platform, hardware-based security still plays a role in providing best-in-class software and services. As we look at different options in this space, we want to focus on how an application developer might be able to leverage hardware-based security features.

Application developers tend to choose an application framework based on the programming language they have chosen, and not vice versa. And particular programming languages tend to have certain frameworks that are popular with a majority of programmers. In this section, we will examine the common security APIs available within some of these frameworks and evaluate the ease of use for developers to utilize hardware security features.

The hardware security features focused here are partly based on the hardware features we have discussed throughout the previous sections of this chapter, as well as security features advantageous to common use cases encountered by IoT developers. These features include

- Access to **Trusted Execution Environments (TEEs)** to leverage highly secure containment features for sensitive data and operations

- Access to **Secure Storage or Protected Keystores** to protect credentials and application secrets

- Access to **message and network security features** to protect communication to other devices

- Access to **cryptographic functions in hardware**, including AES, SHA, and random number generation in order to build other security features not available from available services.

JavaScript and Node.js or Sails

JavaScript is a common language used in IoT and web services today. It is an event-driven interpreted language with a rich set of frameworks. Node.js is one common framework, designed to build network applications that handle events concurrently. Node.js is extremely flexible, so other frameworks are used to create more structure around Node.js. Sails is an example of such an extension framework.

As far as security goes, Node.js is far removed from most platform security features. However, the crypto API provided in Node.js is a wrapper around the latest OpenSSL library. This means that Node.js developers get access to the hardware implementations of AES-NI and SHA-NI through OpenSSL, as well as the hardware random number generator. Best of all, developers do not have to configure anything or worry about any platform settings – it is all handled inside OpenSSL.

One of the great advantages of Node.js is npm (node package manager). One of the great security problems with Node.js is also npm. The node package manager makes it extremely easy to add packages into your Node.js project. A simple install command issued on the command line and a *require* expression in the code add any package registered in the Node.js npm repository to your application. npm has over half a million packages and over three billion downloads every day.[62] This makes using JavaScript widgets and gadgets built by others very easy (a great benefit!). But what are you really downloading? Are you getting the latest version with the latest bug fixes? Or are you installing the latest version that was corrupted with malware? Often developers set up their Node.js applications and never audit the npm repository again. This poor discipline proliferates security vulnerabilities.

Java and Android

The Java programming language is the language used for Android devices, and because of this popularity has found its way into IoT devices as well. Google provides their Android Things operating system as a base OS and framework built on Java for small IoT devices and provides the same base

---

[62]https://nemethgergely.com/nodejs-security-overview/

security for the smallest system on a module (SoM) devices as found on larger devices, including secure boot and a secure hardware keystore. Android Things is built from the base Android system, as shown in Figure 4-27, and uses the same kernel, hardware abstraction layer, native libraries, and Java API framework as the standard Android. Android Things is intended for smallest of devices.

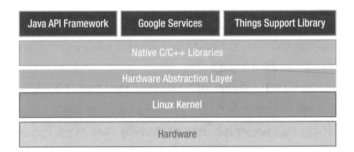

Figure 4-27. *Android Things architecture*

Android itself is popular in many larger IoT devices, including in-vehicle infotainment (IVI) systems in autonomous and smart vehicles. And the security services available through Java and the Android framework are significant.[63]

As we discussed previously, Android supports the Trusty TEE, which can be used to hold sensitive applications for the platform. One of those applications is a hardware-backed secure keystore to protection keys. This prevents keys from being used by unauthorized applications or users and can prevent keys from being exfiltrated off the device. On Intel devices, the Trusty TEE can be used to provide this service, or the keystore can be implemented in the CSME (see Chapter 3). Android also supports a verified boot mechanism where the stages of boot verify each software component is signed with a valid cryptographic key (see Chapter 3 for secure boot details).

---

[63]https://source.android.com/security/

EdgeX Foundry

EdgeX Foundry is a new Internet of Things framework for industrial edge computing sponsored by the Linux Foundation.[64] EdgeX Foundry is platform agnostic, flexible, and extensible framework providing capabilities for "intelligence at the edge" for data storage, aggregation, analysis, and action all organized into sets of microservices using Docker containers.

Figure 4-28 is the platform architecture for EdgeX Foundry, which includes four service layers and two system services. The service layers are the Export services, Supporting services, Core services, and Device services. The system services are security and device/system management.

The Export services allows data to be communicated to the Cloud and supports several protocols, including REST or message queue protocols (see the section "Message Orchestration"); Google IoT Core is also supported for sending telemetry and receiving configuration and commands. The Device services enables connections to sensors and actuators and supports multiple protocols for this purpose. Some of these protocols are wireless or wired communications protocols which are covered in more detail in Chapter 5; other protocols are message orchestration protocols, like MQTT, which is covered in the section "Message Orchestration." The Supporting services handles edge intelligence and analytics capabilities. The Core services is the linkage between *northbound* communications to the Cloud and *southbound* communications to the sensors and actuators.

---

[64]https://www.edgexfoundry.org/

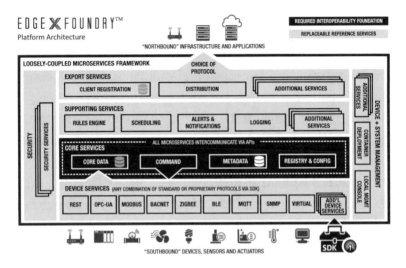

Figure 4-28. *EdgeX Foundry architecture[65]*

The Security system service includes a security store to maintain cryptographic keys and credentials and an access control service to manage REST resources and access keys using either OAuth2 or JWT tokens.

The interesting part of EdgeX is the ability to rewrite any part of the EdgeX Foundry by modifying the Docker container that supplies that service and not having to contend with changing other parts of the system. Security services for key storage can be extended to use a TPM or SGX enclave for enhanced security. Encryption routines in the Distribution container of the Export services can be upgraded to use hardware-based encryption without affecting other elements of the Supporting or Core services. This type of flexible framework makes it easy to utilize the important hardware security features that make an IoT instance more secure.

---

[65]https://docs.edgexfoundry.org/Ch-Intro.html

Application-Level Framework Summary

The application framework chosen for an IoT device can make a significant difference on the security provided to IoT applications. Frameworks like Node.js have few hardware security features built into the framework, but make it easy to add capabilities. However, access to hardware devices is rather difficult through JavaScript, limiting the options for developers.

Android takes an alternative approach and builds in many sophisticated security features into the operating system and framework itself. However, limitations, such as with the Trusty TEE which cannot dynamically add secured applications, make adding hardware-based security features difficult.

EdgeX Foundry takes a different approach, using containers to separate functionality into microservices. This framework expends effort to create the connections and APIs between components so that services can be shared. In this model, it is much easier to upgrade a service to make use of hardware security features on the platform, but allow platforms that do not have such services to use alternative implementations. Although EdgeX Foundry does not have many hardware security features built into the framework at present, the intention to encourage platform differentiation through service modifications is clearly stated.

Message Orchestration

Message orchestration performs the orderly reception and delivery of data and commands on an IoT platform. As briefly mentioned in "EdgeX Foundry" section, message orchestration protocols enable data delivery and reception off the platform to devices and the Cloud, but can also be used to move data around within an IoT platform. Message orchestration implements the publish-subscribe design pattern, often referred to as pub-sub. In this design pattern, entities with data (publishers) publish their data to a broker or message bus, and recipients subscribe to certain messages from the broker and are given only the messages for which they register. The beauty of this design pattern is that publishers do not need to know who or how many subscribers are out there, and subscribers do not have to be prepared to receive and parse messages that they are not interested in.

Several message orchestration protocols are common in IoT devices, including Message Queuing Telemetry Transport (MQTT), Constrained Application Protocol (CoAP), eXtensible Messaging and Presence Protocol (XMPP)[66], and OPC Unified Architecture (OPC UA).

Message orchestration needs to deal with several security issues in order to be secure:

- Publishers must have an identity and must be authenticated against that identity so that the source of messages are attributable to an *Authorized Publisher*.

- Subscribers must have an identity and must be authenticated against that identity so that messages are delivered only to *Authorized Subscribers*.

- Authorized Publishers may assign access control lists to messages that restrict which subscribers are allowed to receive their messages.

- Administrators may assign access control lists to message types restricting Publishers from publishing certain message types and/or restricting Subscribers from receiving certain message types.

- Authorized Subscribers may register to receive message types that do not violate an access control list.

---

[66]XMPP is not covered in this chapter due to space constraints, however details can be found in RFC 6102, https://tools.ietf.org/html/rfc6120

- The message broker will accept a message only from an Authorized Publisher, and only if the message type sent by the Authorized Publisher does not violate an access control list.

- The message broker will deliver a message to an Authorized Subscriber only if that subscriber requested messages of that type, and if that subscriber is not prohibited from receiving that message type by a valid access control list.

- Messages shall be protected from unauthorized disclosure, tampering, unauthorized deletion, reordering, and message delay.

Message Queuing Telemetry Transport

Message Queuing Telemetry Transport (MQTT) is a commonly used message orchestration protocol that enables sending data between entities on a system. The protocol is based on topic names in data packets that define a title for the data. Subscribers subscribe to topics; subscribers may use wildcards within the topic names to which they subscribe. MQTT operates over TCP/IP and supports basic operations, such as CONNECT, PUBLISH, SUBSCRIBE, UNSUBSCRIBE, and several types of acknowledgment packets.

The MQTT protocol published by OASIS[67] supports some basic security services including password-based authentication of publishers and subscribers and recommends the use of TLS for data privacy and integrity.

Several open source implementations of MQTT are in common use including Mosquitto, RabbitMQ, and HiveMQ. Table 4-11 provides a security analysis of Mosquitto MQTT.

---

[67]http://docs.oasis-open.org/mqtt/mqtt/v3.1.1/mqtt-v3.1.1.html

Table 4-11. *Security Analysis of Mosquitto MQTT*

System Update Security Principles	Grade	Comments
Authentication of Publishers and Subscribers	B	MQTT supports usernames and passwords natively. Mutually authenticated TLS is the best option for authentication over the network using public key certificates; using user ids and password is acceptable, but should be protected by TLS if the communication is over a network (broker protection of passwords should be addressed through secure storage).
		A security vulnerability in Mosquitto up until 1.4.12 allows a user with a specially formatted id to overcome the access permissions set by Mosquitto, allowing them to read or write topics they do not have permissions to access.
Access Controls on Message Topics	B	Mosquitto provides a topic configuration file that allows topics to be restricted by anonymous users, by username, or by a pattern that uses the username or client name; access control is based on "read," "write," or "readwrite" actions. This file must be manually configured, and it is a bit difficult to get correct especially when there are many topics.

(continued)

Table 4-11. (*continued*)

System Update Security Principles	Grade	Comments
Message Privacy and Integrity	D	No special protections are provided for messages, and even using TLS does not protect messages while they wait in the queue for delivery, opening the possibility for malware on the broker device to modify messages.
		Consider adding encryption and message integrity to MQTT messages at the application layer; this provides security end to end and can be used to prevent repudiation attacks as well.
Message Delivery Protections (Deletion, Delay, Reordering)	D	No special protections are afforded to the broker's queue. The broker should not be run as root, but run under a special service user id. In some installations of Mosquitto, the message queue is written to disk and susceptible to tampering. The configuration of your Mosquitto installation should be examined to ensure any files used for queuing are properly protected.

OPC Unified Architecture

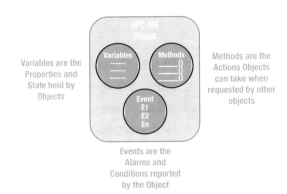

Figure 4-29. *OPC-UA notional object[68]*

OPC-UA[69, 70] is a platform-independent service-oriented architecture targeted to the industrial segment of IoT and is based on the earlier OPC Classic protocols that used the Microsoft Component Object Model (COM) and Distributed Component Object Model (DCOM). OPC-UA is therefore an object-based technology, defining objects as notionally shown in Figure 4-29 and using the TCP/IP protocol for communication between objects, which provides a much richer set of services than MQTT, but it is also much more complex with a 13-part specification of over 1200 pages.

---

[68]https://opcfoundation.org/wp-content/uploads/2016/05/OPC-UA-
Interoperability-For-Industrie4-and-IoT-EN-v5.pdf

[69]OPC officially stands for **O**bject Linking and Embedding (OLE) for **P**rocess **C**ontrol, but since OPC-UA has moved away from strict COM and DCOM protocols, the full expansion of the acronym is no longer widely used.

[70]https://opcfoundation.org/about/opc-technologies/opc-ua/

OPC-UA provides communication between components (objects) on a device and between devices using the publisher-subscriber design pattern described earlier, the observer design pattern where objects notify other objects of events, and using direct method calls between objects (even across devices using a DCOM-like mechanism). OPC-UA includes a discovery service allowing objects and devices to find each other on a network.

OPC-UA defines a comprehensive security model[71] based on security above the transport layer and uses certificate-based identities for applications and users. By default, all communication between devices is encrypted and signed, and the algorithms are negotiated at session establishment between the two parties, just like TLS. All applications are assigned a unique identity certificate, which is used to perform authentication during session establishment to other entities. The other devices/applications/servers a device is allowed to communicate with are defined in a trust list that contains those other applications' identity certificates. Access control and rights can be managed in three different ways: username and passwords, Kerberos tickets, or certificates. Table 4-12 provides a security analysis of OPC-UA.

---

[71]www.dsinteroperability.com/OPCClassicVSUA.pdf and https://
opcfoundation.org/wp-content/uploads/2014/05/OPC-UA_Security_Model_
for_Administrators_V1.00.pdf

Table 4-12. *Security Analysis of OPC-UA*

System Update Security Principles	Grade	Comments
Authentication of Publishers and Subscribers	A	OPC-UA includes multiple options for authentication, with public key certificates being included by default. Issuance of these keys can still be an issues that need to be dealt with, but from a security perspective, this is the best solution.
Access Controls on Message Topics	C	Rough access control is provided at the trust list level. OPC-UA applications have to implement their own access control in order to implement anything greater than just this device/application-level trust. Access control functions can take advantage of other information (usernames, certificates, Kerberos tokens), but this requires custom programming.
Message Privacy and Integrity	A	Message encryption and message integrity is built into OPC-UA above the transport layer and can be used to prevent repudiation attacks as well. Session security is provided end to end.
Message Delivery Protections (Deletion, Delay, Reordering)	D	For store-and-forward or pub-sub broker type message delivery, the application is responsible for creating the behavior of the application. Although patterns exist for good design, they are not provided by default for applications and require custom programming.

Constrained Application Protocol

The Constrained Application Protocol (CoAP) is a web transfer protocol specified in IETF RFC 7252[72] specifically designed for devices with limited computation and/or on a network with limited bandwidth. CoAP is a lightweight HTTP protocol and based on the same request-response REST interaction model, using commands GET, PUT, POST, and DELETE. CoAP requires DTLS (Datagram Transport Layer Security, which is TLS over the UDP protocol) for security, and much like HTTP/TLS combination, any additional access control or security on the messages themselves must be added to the applications. Table 4-13 provides a security analysis of CoAP.

Table 4-13. *Security Analysis of CoAP*

System Update Security Principles	Grade	Comments
Authentication of Publishers and Subscribers	A	Mutually authenticated DTLS is the best option for authentication over the network using public key certificates; many other authentication options are possible, but would need to be integrated into the applications (e.g., OAuth, JWT, Kerberos).
Access Controls on Message Topics	D	No special access control is provided above the rough authentication performed by DTLS. Any additional access control must be provided by the application.

(continued)

---

[72]https://tools.ietf.org/html/rfc7252

Table 4-13. (*continued*)

System Update Security Principles	Grade	Comments
Message Privacy and Integrity	D	No special protections are provided for messages beyond the network protections afforded by DTLS.
Message Delivery Protections (Deletion, Delay, Reordering)	C	Messages may be transmitted with reliability (marked as Confirmable), and for those messages, deletion recovery is handled through the acknowledgment mechanism. Every message has a unique 16-bit message id that allows detection of replay.

Message Orchestration Summary

Message orchestration solutions vary widely in their offerings from simple (CoAP) to complex (OPC-UA). The security offerings for the simpler solutions leave much to the application to implement. One of the primary benefits for MQTT is the ease with which network security can be added with TLS, and the rich set of access controls that can be configured without having to add custom code. Other solutions require applications to implement access controls, which can result in harder to diagnose defects, and duplication of the access control code in many places.

Applications

The applications are the components that give IoT devices their behaviors and consume and benefit from the security in the hardware and the software. There is much to explore in the application space, which we leave for Chapter 6, where we explore different vertical IoT applications in great detail.

Summary

Software in IoT is an enormous subject. In writing this chapter, there were many things that had to be left out or shortened in order to meet the page count and retain some semblance of a publishing deadline. If we have omitted your favorite IoT software component or feature, we assure you it is only due to the space limitations. However, we feel that the coverage we have provided of the software elements of an IoT stack is adequate to engage your design enthusiasm and get you thinking about how to expose useful security features in your IoT designs.

The goal of this chapter was to introduce how security could be provided in IoT systems, and we have shown, layer by layer, where platform security features can be exposed and built upon to add strong and effective security services to IoT devices. If the "S" for security is left out of our IoT devices, it is because we have not leveraged the software and capabilities that are available to us to make security a reality.

While it is true that the most constrained devices have less software and less hardware services, this should not be an excuse to remove security entirely. There are too many good options to solve this tough problem. When the constraints get tighter, it should mean that we focus back on the basics and jettison everything we do not need, but retain the most basic security capabilities. These basic security capabilities are the hardware features for the secure minimum viable platform enabled with the basic platform software – secure boot, secure identity, and secure storage. This is not impossible. In Chapter 6, we will show examples of exactly how to do this.

CHAPTER 5

Connectivity Technologies for IoT

Internet of Things (IoT) is a set of technologies that are enabling new use cases and delivering services across a wide variety of markets and applications. When people think of IoT, they often think of home or personal IoT. However, IoT will play a role in many commercial applications such as smart manufacturing, smart cities, autonomous cars, building automation, and healthcare. How will an IoT-enabled device communicate what it knows to the Internet? Suitable connectivity solutions range from a multitude of wired connectivity technologies such as Ethernet to wireless technologies like Wi-Fi and even 5G cellular. Many solutions need a combination of multiple communication technologies. For example, a smart car system playing video or using GPS navigation might need 4G LTE in order to communicate with the outside world and Wi-Fi and Bluetooth to communicate with devices like phones and rear seat entertainment (RSE) used by the passengers. In this chapter, we will take a look at a selected set of connectivity technologies that enable these applications.

© The Author(s) 2020
S. Cheruvu et al., *Demystifying Internet of Things Security*,
https://doi.org/10.1007/978-1-4842-2896-8_5

Ethernet Time-Sensitive Networking

Ethernet Time-Sensitive Networking (TSN) is reshaping the industrial communication landscape and laying the foundation for the convergence of Information Technology (IT) and Industrial Operations Technology (OT). TSN essentially is a set of features that have been added to standard Ethernet. By bringing industrial-grade robustness and reliability to Ethernet, TSN offers an IEEE standard communication technology that can be used to enable deterministic communications for industrial applications. Being an IEEE standard, it enables interoperability between standard compliant industrial devices from different suppliers. TSN removes the need for physical separation of critical and noncritical communication networks, reducing the cost of the infrastructure needed to allow open data exchange between operations technology network and enterprise/information technology network – a concept that is at the heart of the Industrial Internet of Things (IIoT). At the network system level, TSN supports deterministic communication based on network schedules that are distributed to devices via standard configuration interfaces.

TSN standards address a wide range of functions, and their implementation can be similarly broad, encompassing various hardware elements such as endpoints and switches, embedded software, standard interfaces, routing algorithms, and configuration tools. To ensure the highest levels of TSN performance, a system-level solution is required that takes each element into account and provides a seamless interface between them. Seamless fault-tolerant communication and enhanced cybersecurity with robust network planning, configuration, and monitoring will be a necessity in the networks of the future.

Legacy Ethernet-Based Connectivity in Industrial Applications

Today, there are multiple variants of Industrial Ethernet protocols available on the market. In most cases, the Industrial Ethernet protocol selected for use in industrial devices differs from vendor to vendor or from Industry Alliance to Industry Alliance, which means that devices are only compatible with other equipment from the same vendor or an Industry Alliance using the same protocol. This is known as manufacturer lock-in. It forces customers to either buy all industrial equipment from one vendor or a limited set of vendors who are part of the same Alliance. This approach may not be the most cost- and performance-optimized way to implement the required solution. If a customer chooses not to do this, there is considerable challenge of integrating equipment from multiple vendors into a single network system or there needs to be a set of protocol conversion gateways implemented between the various Industrial Ethernet protocols. Both options will lead to unnecessary expense and limit innovation on the factory floor over many years. Thus industrial automation architectures become hierarchical, purpose-built, and inflexible.

This approach is currently undergoing a dramatic change with the advent of the IIoT and Industry 4.0, which demands for full automation and greater insights in manufacturing. These demands are pushing industrial automation architectures to become more flexible and seamless to interoperate. In these types of increasingly converged architectures, real-time connectivity is essential for controlling critical processes, as well as for collecting and analyzing data from machines, in a timely manner. TSN offers the real-time connectivity capabilities that match and sometimes exceed what current Industrial Ethernet protocols can provide, with the added flexibility of being based on IEEE standards. Similar to what is the norm in the enterprise world, TSN Ethernet can therefore be the common communication protocol that connects industrial equipment from different vendors, simultaneously delivering the very challenging functional requirements demanded by mission-critical embedded and industrial applications.

Key Benefits of TSN

The primary strength of TSN is its status as an open standard–based technology, unaffiliated to any Industry Alliance or company. For an industrial automation market that has struggled for many years with multiple incompatible proprietary communication protocols, TSN brings several key benefits.

TSN guarantees compatibility at the network level between devices from multiple suppliers. This gives customers much greater choice of devices for building their system, avoiding manufacturer lock-in and enabling seamless connectivity across various subsystems and systems.

As TSN is part of the Ethernet standard family, it naturally scales with Ethernet, which means that the technology will not be limited in terms of bandwidth/speeds, thus allowing more and more sensors and actuators that are needed for implementing complex automation applications to be connected to a network system.

TSN supports standards-based network configuration capabilities. This means that new nodes can be added to the network and discovered without the need for costly downtimes and manual configuration. New data streams can be added to the network without the risk of disturbing existing traffic and without the need to reconfigure the entire network.

TSN can be used for communication between machines as well as from machines to enterprise systems. Communication between mission-critical TSN-based systems and existing noncritical Ethernet-based systems can be achieved over the same infrastructure. In other words, non-TSN Ethernet nodes can work over a TSN network, without modification.

Overall system costs are significantly reduced when we adopt standards-based technology. Consumer choice and competition will result in lower device prices. Research, development, and maintenance costs are all driven down when solution providers and customers can focus on one standard technology rather than a number of different proprietary protocols and solutions.

Breaking down communication barriers between critical and noncritical systems is a foundational concept of the IIoT and Industry 4.0. TSN enables the convergence of networks and systems that were previously kept separate for reasons of operational integrity, real-time performance, safety, and security.

TSN allows time-critical messages to be sent over the same communication line as all other Ethernet traffic, without disturbance or increase in delay and with controlled delay variation. Different traffic classes can coexist on the network with no impact on higher criticality level traffic from traffic with lower priority.

End-to-end latency is guaranteed even under heavy traffic load, and standard mechanisms can be used to accelerate message transport for high-priority communications. Thus, the most challenging motion control and safety-critical applications can be converged with other Ethernet traffic on Ethernet networks using TSN.

Convergence makes accessing data from industrial systems easier. With more systems on the same network, the task of gathering data from a wide variety of sources is simplified. Data from industrial systems can be sent to enterprise systems over standard Ethernet without the need for protocol conversion gateways. Overall system costs are significantly reduced by the convergence of different traffic classes on a single network infrastructure. Hardware and maintenance costs are lower because we need fewer devices and cables to build the network infrastructure.

Higher layer protocols can be combined with TSN, as the technology is implemented primarily at the data link layer (OSI model layer 2).[1] One example is the Open Platform Communications-Unified Architecture (OPC-UA) protocol.[2]

---

[1]ISO/IEC 7498-1:1994 - Information technology - Open Systems Interconnection - Basic Reference Model: The Basic Model.

[2]More details on OPC-UA can be found at https://opcfoundation.org/about/opc-technologies/opc-ua/

TSN Standards

Table 5-1 lists the TSN set of features that have been added to standard Ethernet. The features are defined and published in a number of IEEE 802.1 standards that address topics such as timing, synchronization, forwarding, queuing, seamless redundancy, and stream reservation. These individual features extend the functionality and Quality of Service (QoS) of Ethernet to enable guaranteed message transmission through switched networks, providing the fundamental capabilities such as robustness, reliability, and determinism required for an industrial communication technology.

Table 5-1. *List of Published IEEE Standards for TSN (March 2019)*

Function	Standard
Time Synchronization	• IEEE Std. 802.1AS™-2011: generalized Precision Time Protocol (gPTP)
Bounded Low Latency	• IEEE Std. 802.1Qav™-2009: Credit-based shaper • IEEE Std. 802.1Qbv™-2015: Transmission gate scheduling • IEEE Std. 802.1Qbu™-2016 & IEEE Std. 802.3br™-2016 : Frame Preemption • IEEE Std. 802.1Qch™-2017 : Cyclic Queuing and Forwarding
Reliability	• IEEE Std. 802.1Qca™-2015 : Path Control and Reservation • IEEE Std. 802.1CB™-2017 : Frame Replication & Elimination • IEEE Std. 802.1Qci™-2017 : Per-stream Filtering & Policing
Resource Management	• IEEE Std. 802.1Qat™-2010 : Stream Reservation Protocol • IEEE Std. 802.1Qcc™-2018 : SRP Enhancements and Performance Improvements • IEEE Std. 802.1Qcp™-2018 : YANG model

To address new use cases and make performance improvements, many more IEEE standards are being defined, as listed in Table 5-2.

Table 5-2. *List of Upcoming IEEE Standards for TSN (March 2019)*

Time Synchronization	• P802.1AS-Rev (Draft v8.0): Time Synchronization improvement
Bounded Low Latency	• P802.1Qcr (Draft v0.5): Asynchronous Traffic Shaping • P802.1Qcz (PAR approved): Congestion Isolation
Reliability	• P802.1Qcx (Draft v1.0): YANG Data Model for Connectivity Fault Management
Resource Management	• P802.1CS (Draft v2.1): Link-local Registration Protocol • P802.1Qcj (Draft v0.4): Automatic Attachment to Provider Backbone Bridging (PBB) services • P802.1Qcw (Draft v0.2): YANG Data Models for Qbv, Qbu, and Qci • P802.1Qdd (PAR approved): Resource Allocation Protocol • P802.1ABcu (Draft v0.6): LLDP YANG Data Model • P802.1CBcv (PAR approved): Frame Replication & Elimination YANG Model and MIB Module • P802.1CBdb (PAR approved): FRER Extended Stream Identification Functions

For latest Update, check `https://1.ieee802.org/tsn/`

The key TSN features that provide guaranteed message delivery timing are time synchronization and traffic scheduling. They are addressed by the 802.1AS and 802.1Qbv standards, respectively. All devices participating in the TSN network are synchronized to a global time and are aware of a network schedule that dictates when prioritized messages will be forwarded from each switch. TSN makes use of multiple queues per port at the egress of the switch, where messages are held until a gate opens (at a time slot specified by the schedule) to release queued messages for transmission. The timed release of messages ensures that delays in the network can be deterministically predicted and managed. This allows for the convergence of critical traffic and noncritical traffic on the same network.

The preemption feature defined in the TSN 802.1Qbu standard can be used to increase the efficiency of bandwidth use for noncritical messages. In highly converged networks, it could be the case that large low-priority frames are delayed by higher-priority traffic on the network and dropped. Preemption enables the transmission of large frames to be interrupted, sent in smaller fragments and reassembled at the next link. This maximizes bandwidth utilization for all traffic types on the TSN network. Another important benefit of message preemption is the reduction of transmission latency for so-called Express traffic, which can preempt regular (lower-priority) Ethernet packets. Especially on lower-speed networks (e.g., 10 or 100 megabits per second (Mbps)) carrying large regular Ethernet packets up to 1,500 bytes and more, the latency reduction for Express traffic can be useful for building converged networks.

TSN provides a standard method for achieving seamless redundancy for industrial communication over Ethernet. The feature allows for the simultaneous transmission of duplicate message copies across different paths in the network. The first message copy to be received in time without error is processed, while the other copies are discarded. This adds another layer of determinism to the delivery of critical messages in converged networks.

A crucial feature of TSN is the support for open, vendor-independent network configuration. This is achieved through the standardization in IEEE of YANG models for various TSN standards. These can be configured over the NETCONF protocol using encoding formats such as XML or JSON. YANG models for bridging, traffic scheduling, frame preemption, seamless redundancy, and policing ensure that configuration of key TSN features is done according to standard methods. This allows TSN networks to be composed of any standard compliant device from any vendor and can be configured by any standard compliant network configuration software.

TSN Profiles

TSN is essentially a toolbox of features that address various needs such as reliability, bounded low latency, time synchronization, and resource management. These capabilities are realized through various TSN specifications (e.g., IEEE 802.1AS-Rev, IEEE 802.1Qbv, etc.), and customers can choose the relevant standards to implement based on their specific application needs. Profile standards are being specified for some of them to describe which TSN standards to use and how. A TSN profile selects features, options, configurations, and protocols to build a bridged network for the given TSN application. Table 5-3 shows a list of select TSN profiles that are currently being defined.

Table 5-3. *List of TSN Profiles (March 2019)*

Industry	TSN Profile
Industrial Automation	• IEC/IEEE 60802 (Draft v0.3):TSN Profile for Industrial Automation
Automotive In-Vehicle Networks	• IEEE Std. 802.1BA™ -2011 : Audio Video Bridging system [AVB Profile] • IEEE Std. 1722™ -2016: Transport Protocol for Time-Sensitive Applications [+AVTP Control format message types: FlexRay, LIN, CAN, MOST, Sensor, etc] • IEEE Std. 1722.1™ -2013: Audio Video Discovery, Enumeration, Connection management and Control (AVDECC) • P802.1DG (PAR approved): TSN Profile for Automotive In-Vehicle Ethernet Communications
Service Provider Networks	• P802.1DF (PAR approved): TSN Profile for Service Provider Networks

(continued)

Table 5-3. (*continued*)

Industry	TSN Profile
Mobile Fronthaul	• IEEE Std. 802.1CM™ -2018: TSN for Fronthaul [Mobile Fronthaul Profile] • P802.1CMde (PAR approved): Enhancements to Fronthaul Profiles to Support New Fronthaul Interface, Synchronization, and Syntonization Standards

The following sections provide an overview of the major TSN standards.

802.1AS/AS-Rev

Enhanced Generic Precise Timing Protocol: Timing and synchronization are vital mechanisms for achieving deterministic communication. 802.1AS is a profile of the IEEE 1588 PTP (Precision Time Protocol) synchronization protocol that enables synchronization compatibility between different TSN devices (Figure 5-1). This lays the foundation for the scheduling of traffic through each participating network device. 802.1AS-Rev is being defined to add support for fault tolerance and multiple active synchronization masters (Figure 5-2). Multiple clock-masters for redundancy enable high availability of TSN networks – in cases when a grandmaster becomes faulty, system elements such as end nodes and bridges are still able to remain synchronized by obtaining the timing information from the redundant grandmasters. 802.1AS-Rev is also a profile of the IEEE 1588 PTP synchronization protocol.

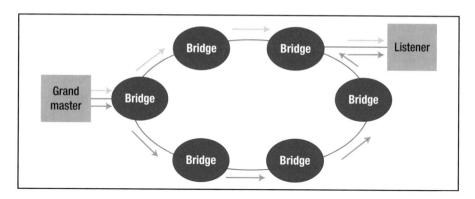

Figure 5-1. *802.1AS operation*[3]

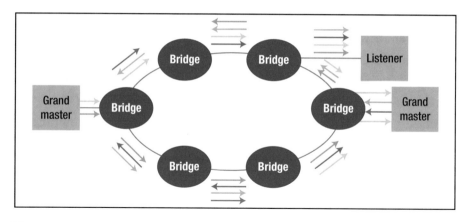

Figure 5-2. *802.1AS-Rev operation*[4]

[3]Figure 5a: Single grand master transmitting 2 copies using separate paths.
`https://www.synopsys.com/designware-ip/technical-bulletin/ether-time-sens-net-for-auto-adas-socs-2018q2.html`

[4]Figure 5b: Multiple grand masters transmitting 2 copies using separate paths.
`https://www.synopsys.com/designware-ip/technical-bulletin/ether-time-sens-net-for-auto-adas-socs-2018q2.html`

802.1Qbv

Time-Aware Shaper: Scheduling of traffic is a core concept in TSN. Based on the shared global time provided by 802.1AS, a schedule is created and distributed between participating network devices. 802.1Qbv defines the mechanisms for controlling the flow of queued traffic through gates at the egress of a TSN switch (Figure 5-3). Frames are assigned to queues based on Quality of Service (QoS) priority. The transmission of messages from these queues is executed during scheduled time windows. Other queues will typically be blocked from transmission during these time windows, therefore removing the chance of scheduled traffic being impeded by nonscheduled traffic. In other words, there is a gate in front of each queue which opens at a specific point of time which is reserved for that queue. This means that the delay through each switch is deterministic and that message latency through a network of TSN-enabled components can be guaranteed. The IEEE 802.1Qbv standard defines up to eight queues per port for forwarding traffic. The scheduler is designed to separate the communication on the Ethernet network into fixed length, repeating time cycles.

Figure 5-3 shows an example with four queues, with a cycle time of td and guard band of tg. At time t0, the time-critical data queue, Queue 3 is open. Once that frame is transmitted, the best effort Queues 0, 1, and 2 are opened. Before the end of the cycle, at time t0-tg, all the non-time-critical data is blocked, so that the port is free to transmit the time-critical data at the start of the next cycle. This is essentially a time-division multiple access (TDMA) scheme.

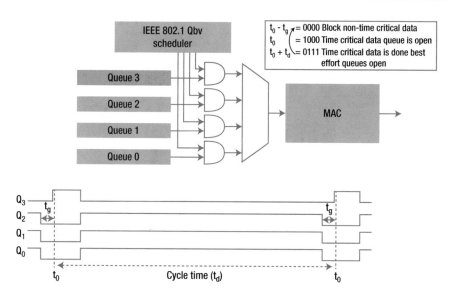

Figure 5-3. *802.1Qbv operation*[5]

802.1Qbu

Frame Preemption: While the 802.1Qbv mechanisms protect critical messages against interference from other network traffic, it does not necessarily result in optimal bandwidth usage or minimal communication latency. Where these factors are important, the preemption mechanism defined in 802.1Qbu can be used (Figure 5-4). 802.1Qbu allows the transmission of standard Ethernet or jumbo frames to be interrupted in order to allow the transmission of high-priority frames, and then resumed afterward without discarding the previously transmitted piece of the interrupted message. Frame preemption always operates on a link-by-link basis. A frame is only fragmented from one Ethernet switch to the next Ethernet switch, where it is reassembled.

---

[5]Time-aware shaper allows scheduling. https://www.synopsys.com/designware-ip/technical-bulletin/ether-time-sens-net-for-auto-adas-socs-2018q2.html

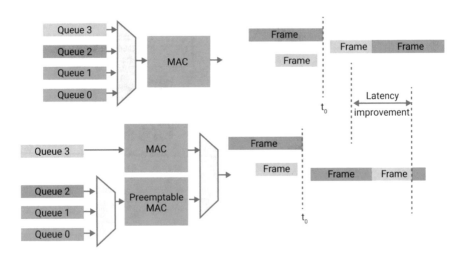

Figure 5-4. *802.1Qbu frame preemption*[6]

In Figure 5-4, without preemption as shown in the top, if a high-priority frame in Queue 3 arrives after a low-priority frame, the high-priority frame is delayed until the transmission of the low-priority frame is finished. In the case of an Ethernet port with preemption enabled, as shown in the bottom, the low-priority traffic passes through a preemptable MAC. The transmission of the low-priority frame is stopped, once a high-priority frame arrives and the high-priority frame from Queue 3 is allowed to go out. Once the transmission of the high-priority frame is completed, the rest of the low-priority frame is transmitted. Each partial frame is completed by a CRC32 for error detection. In contrast to the regular Ethernet CRC32, the last 16 bits are inverted to make a partial frame distinguishable from a standard Ethernet frame. Also the start frame delimiter (SFD) is changed.

---

[6]Preemption reduces latency of time-critical data streams. https://www.synopsys.com/designware-ip/technical-bulletin/ether-time-sens-net-for-auto-adas-socs-2018q2.html

802.1CB

Frame Replication and Elimination: Redundancy management implemented in 802.1CB follows similar approaches known from High-Availability Seamless Redundancy (HSR) (IEC 62439-3 Clause 5) and Parallel Redundancy Protocol (PRP) (IEC 62439-3 Clause 4). It supports zero switch over time when a link fails or frames are dropped. To increase availability, redundant copies of the same messages are communicated in parallel over disjoint paths through the network as shown in Figure 5-5. Time-critical frames are expanded to include a sequence number, and then they are replicated where each identical copy follows a separate path in the network. The redundancy management mechanism then combines these redundant messages to generate a single stream of information to the receiver(s). At any point in the network where the separate paths join again, duplicate frames can be eliminated from the stream as shown in Figure 5-5. The 802.1Qca standard for Path Control and Reservation defines how such paths can be set up. The standard also allows for auto configuration.

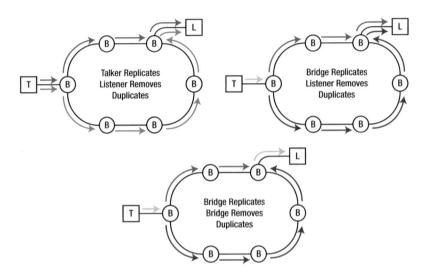

Figure 5-5. *802.1CB frame replication and elimination*[7]

802.1Qcc

Enhanced Stream Reservation Protocol: The enhancements to Stream
Reservation Protocol (802.1Qat) include support for more streams,
configurable stream reservation classes and streams, better description of
stream characteristics, support for layer 3 streaming, deterministic stream
reservation convergence, and User Network Interface (UNI) for routing
and reservations. 802.1Qcc supports offline and/or online configuration
of TSN network scheduling to provide network management for control
plane. It supports a "Central Controller" or predefined "Engineered
Configuration" of the network.

[7]Frame Replication & Elimination Page 16. https://bcourses.berkeley.edu/
files/66071146/download?download_frd=1

The fully centralized configuration model is depicted in Figure 5-6. It is composed of Centralized User Configuration (CUC) entity and a Centralized Network Configuration (CNC). Computing the configuration setting and enforcing it (e.g., setting up gate schedules, reserving resources, etc.) in bridges are done by CNC. Thus CNC will be in charge of configuring TSN features such as credit-based shaper, frame preemption, scheduled traffic, per-stream filtering and policing, and frame replication and elimination for reliability. The CUC is responsible for building up the applications' requirements.

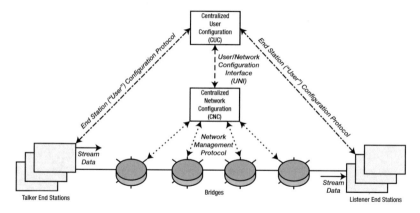

Figure 5-6. *802.1Qcc centralized network configuration*[8]

802.1Qci

Per-Stream Filtering and Policing: This protects against faulty and/or malicious endpoints and switches and isolates faults to specific regions in the network. It works at the ingress of the switch (forwarding engine) in order to protect the outgoing queues from being flooded with frames. In this process,

---

[8]Figure 3: Centralized Network Configuration. https://www.odva.org/
Portals/0/Library/Conference/2017-ODVA-Conference_Zuponcic_Hantel_
Klecka_Didier_TSN_Influences_on_ODVA_Technologies_FINAL.pdf

the data packets are checked to ensure that they fit to a reserved data stream at the network input. If this is not the case, the packet will be filtered out and rejected and won't be forwarded further. This can be leveraged to prevent attacks on level 2 of the OSI layer model. It utilizes well-known flow identifiers and policers used in the industry. Per-Stream Filtering and Policing (PSFP) allows filtering and policing decisions to be made on a per-stream basis. The various stages of data flow for one stream are depicted in Figure 5-7.

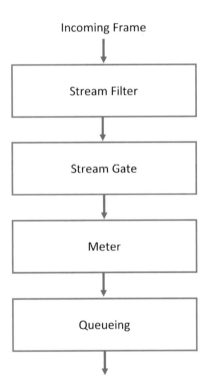

Figure 5-7. *802.1Qci per-stream filtering and policing*

802.1Qch

Cyclic Queuing and Forwarding: This defines cycles for forwarding traffic that is queued using 802.1Qci to assign buffers and 802.1Qbv to shape traffic. This cyclic enqueuing and queue draining procedure gives a defined (but not optimal) upper boundary for latency. Basically this is a simplified way to use TSN if controlled timing is desired, but reducing latency to absolute minimum is not highly important. The synchronized operations effectively allow bridges to synchronize their frame transmissions in a cyclic manner, achieving zero congestion loss and bounded latency, independently of the network topology.

In this scheme, time-sensitive streams are scheduled (enqueued and dequeued) at each time interval resulting in a worst-case deterministic delay of two times the cycle time between the sender (talker) and the next (intermediate) receiver (listener). As shown in Figure 5-8, each high-priority traffic frame scheduled on a cycle is scheduled to be received at the next bridge in the next cycle. A guard band before the start of the cycle prevents any interfering low-priority traffic from affecting the high-priority traffic. 802.1Qch can be combined with frame preemption, to reduce the cycle time from the transmission time of a full size frame to the transmission time of a minimum size frame fragment. Thus, preemption can improve the performance for high-priority traffic. For this to work correctly, all frames must be kept to their allotted cycles, that is, all transmitted frames must be received during the expected cycle at the receiving bridge.

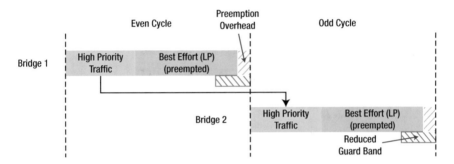

Figure 5-8. *802.1Qch operation with preemption (802.1Qbu)*[9]

To summarize, the network transit latency of a frame is completely characterized by the cycle time and the number of hops. Therefore, the frame latency is completely independent of the topology parameters and non-TSN traffic.

802.1Qcr

Asynchronous Traffic Shaping: This provides bounded latency and jitter (relatively lower performance levels) without the need for time synchronization. It aims to smoothen traffic patterns by reshaping streams per hop, implementing per flow queues and prioritizing urgent traffic over lower-priority traffic. Previously described TSN standards such as Time-Aware Shaper (802.1Qbv) and Cyclic Queuing and Forwarding (802.1Qch) depend on network-wide coordinated time and packet transmission at enforced periodic cycles, resulting in suboptimal utilization of available network bandwidth. 802.1Qcr operates asynchronously, without the need

---

[9]Illustration of CQF with preemption for a linear network. https://arxiv.org/pdf/1803.07673.pdf

for bridges and endpoints to synchronize in time. Therefore, it is expected that this technique can utilize available network bandwidth efficiently under heavy link utilization with mixed criticality traffic.

TSN and Security

Since TSN is Ethernet based, the security mechanisms that are state of the art today can be employed to secure the TSN network. Traditional security solutions such as firewalls will be the key to this. Since firewalls need to inspect packets, the resulting computational overhead in firewalls can create an additional transmission delay. This delay should be taken into account while configuring the TSN network schedules. If security mechanisms introduce longer delays than that are tolerable by the TSN application, they can be implemented at the border or periphery of the TSN network, such as an Industrial Demilitarized Zone that connects the TSN industrial control network to the rest of the IT system.

OPC-UA Over TSN

Of the many higher layer industrial communication protocols that could be combined with TSN, one of the prominent ones is OPC-UA. Much like TSN, OPC-UA is an open, standard technology that is vendor independent and useful for a wide range of industrial applications. The combination of OPC-UA and TSN therefore provides a complete open, standard, and interoperable solution that fulfills a plurality of industrial communication requirements.

By representing data in a uniform way, OPC-UA enables interoperability between devices that could not previously share data and gives you new insight into a wealth of information. For this reason, it has been adopted and integrated into products by all of the major industrial automation vendors. OPC-UA was originally limited to a client or server architecture; however the recently released publish/subscribe (PubSub) extension now enables multicast communication. In combination with TSN, OPC-UA

PubSub allows data to be sent with precise timing and thus be used for real-time industrial applications as illustrated in Figure 5-9. In the horizontal direction, OPC-UA-based controller-to-controller communication can be done over TSN. In the vertical direction, OPC-UA-based controller-to-cloud communication can be done directly, via a gateway or broker. This enables IT (Information Technology) systems having less stringent timing requirements to interwork with OT (Operations Technology) systems that need guaranteed data delivery with precise timing.

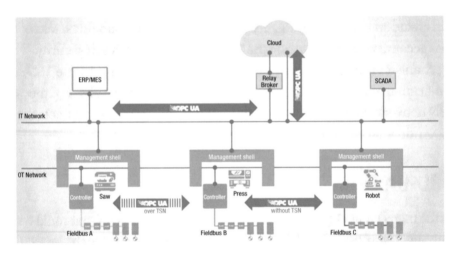

Figure 5-9. *Factory automation network with OPC-UA over TSN*

OPC-UA also enables a standard method for configuring TSN networks online and in a dynamic way. This does not require you to input any system parameters for the scheduler as these are all taken from the OPC-UA application parameters within each device. A broker mechanism as defined by the OPC Foundation provides an interface between OPC-UA applications and TSN scheduling software.

Overview of Wireless Connectivity Technologies

The IoT will require several wireless technologies if it's to meet its potential. For example, Bluetooth Low Energy and IEEE 802.15.4 are good choices for battery-powered sensors, but for devices that are constantly moving, or are not near a LAN (local area network), such relatively short-range wireless technologies are not suitable for connecting to the Internet.

Even if a LAN is present, manufacturers might prefer longer-range wireless technology for its convenience and autonomy. For example, a white goods manufacturer could select cellular technology over Wi-Fi because it enables a refrigerator or washing machine to connect to the Cloud automatically, eliminating the need for a consumer to enter a password to add the appliance to a home's LAN. In these situations, low-power wide area networks (LPWAN) or Narrowband IoT technologies could come to the rescue.

Considerations for Choosing Wireless Technologies for IoT

There are many wireless networking technologies that are deployed in IoT today, each with a different set of capabilities. Here are some of the key considerations when choosing these different solutions.

Spectrum

Wireless spectrum can be characterized as either licensed or unlicensed. Access to licensed spectrum is typically purchased from local government to provide an organization exclusive access to a particular channel in a particular location. Operation in that channel should be largely free of interference from competing radios. The drawback is that the spectrum of interest may be extremely scarce or expensive to access. In some other cases, radio connectivity bands allowed in one country may not be available in other geographical area for same usage. For instance, mobile networks in India use the 900 MHz and 1800 MHz frequency bands, while GSM (Global System for Mobile communications) carriers in the United States operate in 850 MHz and 1900 MHz frequency bands. To deploy an IoT device globally, then it may have to support multiple radio bands making the device costly as well as time-consuming to develop. Even when more easily accessible, it can take months to gain the approval to operate, so licensed bands are not well suited to rapid deployments. Unlicensed spectrum is generally open and available to anybody to use with no exclusive rights granted to any particular organization or individual. The downside is that competing systems may occupy the same channel at different power levels leading to interference. Manufacturers of radio systems operating in unlicensed bands include capabilities in these radios to adapt their operation for this potential interference. These techniques include adaptive modulation, automatic transmit power control and out-of-band filtering, and so on.

Range and Capacity

Several factors impact the amount of data capacity that can be delivered at a particular distance. Those factors include spectrum, channel bandwidth, transmitter power, terrain, noise immunity, and antenna size. In general, the longer the distance to be covered, the lower the data capacity. The longest propagation distance can be achieved by using a low-frequency narrowband channel with a high-gain antenna, while higher capacities could be achieved by selecting wider channels, with limited range. For optimal performance for each application, we need to choose the best combination of channel size, antenna, and radio power and modulation schemes to achieve the desired capacity.

A radio link can be described as being line of sight when there is a direct optical path between the two radios making up the link. A link is called non-line of sight when there is some obstruction between the two radios. Near line of sight is simply a partial obstruction rather than a complete obstruction. In general, lower-frequency solutions have better propagation characteristics than higher frequencies. Higher-frequency solutions that operate in multi-gigahertz range are typically line-of-sight or near line-of-sight systems. From 1 GHz to 6 GHz range, the propagation characteristics capabilities will vary depending on other factors, and typically below 1 GHz the propagation becomes much better, making those frequencies suitable for longer range. Figure 5-10 shows a landscape of data rates and ranges of common wireless technologies.

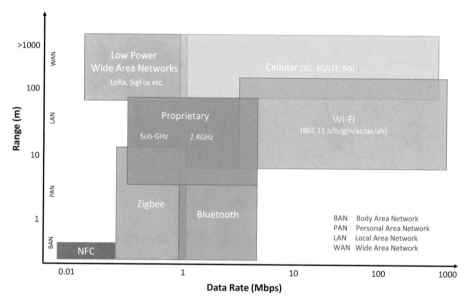

Figure 5-10. *Range and data rate for various wireless technologies*

Network Topology

Network topology is the arrangement of the elements in a network, including its nodes and connections between them. Common network topologies used for wireless connectivity are depicted in Figure 5-11.

371

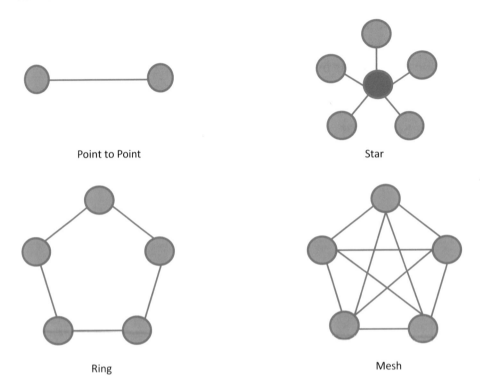

Point to Point

Star

Ring

Mesh

Figure 5-11. *Common network topologies*

Point-to-point topologies are best suited for delivering lots of capacity over long distances. Point-to-point connections cover longer distances that are less susceptible to interference as the antenna patterns are narrower so the energy can be focused in the direction of the desired transmission. PTP links are also used for short-range connections to the wireline backbone. Resiliency in a PTP link can be provided by deploying in 1+1 or other redundant configurations with parallel sets of radios.

Ring topologies are excellent for resilient operations of high-capacity links covering a large area. This configuration is typically used in the backhaul network.

Mesh networks can be built using multiple point-to-point links or with specialized meshing protocols to enable multiple paths from point A to point B. Mesh networks have the downside of each packet traversing multiple hops and so can lead to lower capacity and increased latency for a given infrastructure.

Point-to-multipoint (or star) networks provide scale and capacity over a geographic area. Point-to-multipoint networks are typically deployed to cover sectors or cells. The key differentiating capability to look for in point-to-point networks is their ability to scale in the number of nodes per cell but also the ability to place cells next to each other without interference.

Quality of Service

System builders and operators need to make the most efficient use of available spectrum by deploying multiple services on the same network and also making sure that mission-critical information is transmitted with highest priority. A network should support multiple Quality of Service (QoS) levels and the ability to sort traffic based on both layer 2 and layer 3 standard traffic classifiers. In this way, the transmitter of the data packet can mark the class of service or priority, and the end-to-end network will ensure that the packet is delivered with the desired level of low latency and availability.

Network Management

The capability to manage a network has a direct impact on the total cost of ownership of the IoT system. Networking systems that allow centralized management of configuration, fault detection, performance tuning and continuous monitoring, and security validation minimize the cost and effort. They also reduce unplanned outages and increase system availability and reliability.

Security

The security of wireless communications is growing in importance. Primary techniques to look for here is the ability to encrypt the over-the-air link, using a network, mesh, or link key. Besides this we need to secure management interfaces with HTTPS and SNMP. Systems should also provide the ability to create multiple user accounts with password complexity rules. Previously, many traditional automation and control solutions have not been exposed to security issues faced by the IT systems, but recently have become hacking targets as their solutions get connected to the Internet. Major security breaches could slow down the adoption of IoT.

As can be seen from Figure 5-12, several local area network (LAN) and wide area network (WAN) technologies with different levels of security and network management requirements need to work seamlessly to realize an end-to-end IoT system.

Figure 5-12. *End-to-end IoT systems need various connectivity technologies to work together*

Wi-Fi

Wi-Fi is a wireless connectivity technology based on the IEEE 802.11 standards. Initially created for wireless local area network (WLAN) applications, Wi-Fi is also increasingly used for peer-to-peer and wireless personal area network connections (WPAN). It provides secure, reliable, and fast wireless connectivity. A Wi-Fi network can be used to connect electronic devices to each other, to the Internet, and to wired networks that use Ethernet technology. It can provide real-world performance similar to that of basic wired networks. Wi-Fi networks operate in the 2.4 GHz and 5 GHz radio bands, with some products that contain both bands (dual-band). Wi-Fi is also pushing into a third band – the 60 GHz band – using ultra-wideband channels and the baseband solution originally developed by WiGig. The Wi-Fi Alliance is a wireless industry organization that promotes wireless technologies that are based on IEEE 802.11 and their interoperability. The Alliance also certifies products that comply with its specifications for Wi-Fi interoperability, security, and application-specific protocols.

Wi-Fi offers low power consumption and low cost relative to cellular. Unlike cellular, Wi-Fi operates in unlicensed spectrum, resulting also in lower data transmission costs. Range is limited by proximity to a wireless router or relays, and the quality of connection can be diminished by network congestion. There are several different Wi-Fi standards optimized for IoT applications. Next, we will take a brief look at them.

Wi-Fi Direct enables two or more devices to connect directly in the absence of a traditional Wi-Fi hotspot.

With the broad availability of the 802.11ac Wi-Fi standard, Wi-Fi operates in the 5 GHz band with wider channels (Note: 802.11n could also operate in 5 GHz but in smaller channels), thus enabling more capacity. Theoretical throughput of 11ac can exceed 1 Gbps.

Also known as Low-Power Wi-Fi, 802.11ah operates in the sub-1 GHz band. It is viewed as central to IoT, given support for extended range Wi-Fi and efficient power profile. 11ah extends Wi-Fi beyond 2.4 and 5 GHz, enabling coverage in challenging environments such as in building, basements, and so on. It also supports low-cost sensors without a power amplifier, and minimum data rates result in short-term data bursts.

802.11p is an approved standard for vehicle-to-vehicle communications. It uses dedicated short-range communications (DSRC) for applications such as toll collection, interaction between cars, and safety and roadside communications.

With the increased adoption of Wi-Fi networks for IoT applications arose the need for providing wireless network in places where connecting an access point (AP) to wired network infrastructure (e.g., a wired Ethernet switch) was not possible. A typical example would be the case of positioning an AP in the middle of a large warehouse, since the length of an Ethernet cable is limited to 100 meters. Some other use cases are the extension of an indoor wireless network to a parking lot or a campus, providing Wi-Fi coverage to outdoor industrial areas such as an oil refinery and others. Such a network can service applications like wireless security cameras, utility meters, flow and pressure sensors, vehicle tracking systems, and so on.

802.11s defines Wi-Fi mesh networking. As shown in Figure 5-13, mesh networks allow rapid deployment with lower-cost backhaul, and they make providing coverage in hard-to-wire areas easier. Inherently, mesh networks are self-healing, resilient, and extensible. Under the right conditions, they increase the range of the network due to multihop forwarding and provide higher bandwidth and better battery life due to the lower power transmissions caused by shorter hops between neighboring nodes.

Classic 802.11 WLAN

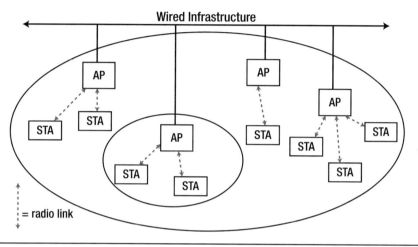

WLAN with Mesh

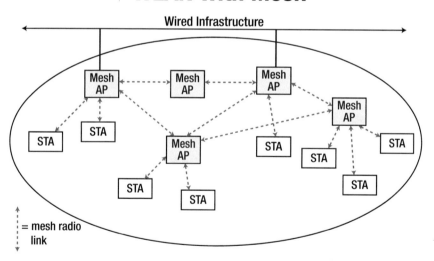

Figure 5-13. *Comparison of classic and mesh wireless local area network topologies*

Wi-Fi uses TCP/IP stack for Internet connectivity. Wi-Fi technology is hugely popular for consumer electronics and enterprise applications due to its ubiquitous presence in laptops, tablets, smartphones, and home entertainment devices. Wi-Fi access points are deployed today in many public spaces such as stadiums, airports, bus and railway stations, coffee shops, and schools. They are also present in most homes and offices. The increasing demand for cost-effective and easy Internet access along with the interoperability and ecosystem programs run by Wi-Fi Alliance has contributed to the wide adoption of this technology across the world. This worldwide availability makes Wi-Fi a natural choice for IoT connectivity, for applications that can leverage existing infrastructure without the need for custom protocol translators or gateways.

Today, most Wi-Fi networks operate in the 2.4 GHz and 5 GHz ISM (industrial, scientific, and medical) band. With more channels being available in the 5 GHz spectrum, higher data rates are possible. Wi-Fi networks have a start topology, with the access point acting as an Internet gateway. The transmit power permitted by Wi-Fi standards are high enough to enable in-home coverage in many cases. In large buildings, multiple access points and range extenders are often deployed at different locations to ensure adequate coverage and to avoid dead zones. Some Wi-Fi products support multiple antennae and transmitter and receiver chains for diversity. This helps in overcoming dead zones as well as increases data throughput.

Wi-Fi and TCP/IP software stacks are fairly complex and big in size. In traditional applications like laptops, smartphones, and tablets with adequate processing power and memory footprint, this was not a major issue. IoT devices – or things – often come with very low processing power and memory size and are typically battery powered. Till recently, adding Wi-Fi connectivity to those devices was neither practical nor cost-effective. Today, many wireless modules with embedded microcontrollers that run the TCP/IP stack and Wi-Fi software are available, thus offloading the task of networking from the main microprocessor unit. Wi-Fi devices targeted for low data rate IoT applications apply advanced sleep protocols and support fast on/off times to reduce the average power consumption dramatically. Since many IoT applications do not need the maximum data rates that Wi-Fi offers, intelligent power management techniques can efficiently draw bursts of current from the battery for very short intervals and keep products connected to the Internet for multiple years without battery replacement.

Wi-Fi modules for IoT applications typically integrate the RF frontend, thus eliminating the need for extensive radio design experience for the embedded system designer. They often come pre-certified for regulatory compliance such as FCC (Federal Communications Commission) in the United States, thus making the system certification process less time-consuming. Wi-Fi is the most ubiquitous wireless Internet connectivity technology today. Its high power and complexity has been a major barrier for IoT developers, but new silicon devices and modules reduce many of these barriers and enable Wi-Fi integration into emerging IoT applications and battery-operated devices. On the other hand, latest Wi-Fi standards offer very high bandwidth and capacity where needed, such as in video surveillance, retail, and sports arena applications. Thus Wi-Fi can support a wide variety of applications. Table 5-4 summarizes the Wi-Fi technologies currently available in the 2.4 GHz and 5 GHz spectrum.

Table 5-4. *Wi-Fi Protocol Summary*

Protocol	Frequency	Channel Width	MIMO	Maximum data rate(theoretical)
802.11ac wave2	5 GHz	80, 80+80, 160 MHz	Multi User (MU-MIMO)	1.73 Gbps[1]
802.11ac wave1	5 GHz	80 MHz	Single User (SU-MIMO)	866.7 Mbps[1]

(*continued*)

Table 5-4. (*continued*)

Protocol	Frequency	Channel Width	MIMO	Maximum data rate(theoretical)
802.11n	2.4 or 5 GHz	20, 40MHz	Single User (SU-MIMO)	450 Mbps[2]
802.11g	2.4 GHz	20 MHz	N/A	54 Mbps
802.11a	5 GHz	20 MHz	N/A	54 Mbps
802.11b	2.4 GHz	20 MHz	N/A	11 Mbps
Legacy 802.11	2.4 GHz	20 MHz	N/A	2 Mbps

[1] *2 Spatial streams with 256-QAM modulation.*
[2] *3 Spatial streams with 64-QAM modulation.*

To increase the relatively short range of Wi-Fi – specifically for IoT sensors that don't require high data rates – 802.11ah was introduced. It operates in the 900 MHz and uses target wake time to reduce the amount of energy a device needs to stay connected to the network. Devices wake up for very short times at defined intervals to accept messages. It penetrates through walls and obstructions better than high-frequency networks. It is well suited for smart building applications, like smart lighting, smart HVAC, and smart security systems. It would also work for smart city applications, like parking garages and parking meters. Since there is no global 900 MHz standard, the adoption rate of 802.11ah is currently very low. Table 5-5 summarizes the key characteristics of 802.11ah.

Table 5-5. *802.11ah Overview*

Name of Standard	IEEE P802.11ah (low power WiFi)
Frequency Band	License-exempt bands below 1 GHz, excluding the TV White Spaces
Channel Width	1/2/4/8/16 MHz
Range	Up to 1Km (outdoor)
End Node Transmit Power	Dependent on Regional Regulations (from 1mW to 1 W)
Packet Size	Up to 7,991 Bytes (w/o Aggregation), Up to 65,535 Bytes (with Aggregation)
Uplink Data Rate	150 Kbps ~ 346.666 Mbps
Downlink Data Rate	150 Kbps ~ 346.666 Mbps
Devices per Access Point	8191
Topology	Star, Tree
End node roaming allowed	Allowed by other IEEE 802.11 amendments (e.g., IEEE 802.11r)
Governing Body	IEEE 802.11 working group
Status	Targeting 2016 release

802.11ax represents the next phase of Wi-Fi. The Wi-Fi Alliance coined the term "Wi-Fi 6" when referring to the IEEE 802.11ax standard, indicating the sixth generation of Wi-Fi. Continued growth in the number of Wi-Fi-enabled devices, increased per-user traffic demand, greater number of users per access point (AP), higher-density Wi-Fi deployments, growing use of outdoor Wi-Fi, heterogeneous device and traffic types, and a desire for more power and spectral efficiency are all major driving forces behind 802.11ax. There are many 802.11ax enhancements in the 2.4 GHz band that will help increase the viability of Wi-Fi for Internet of Things

(IoT) applications. These include target wake time (TWT), orthogonal frequency-division multiple access (OFDMA), 2 MHz clients, and coexistence improvements with other IoT wireless technologies. With sub-1 GHz Wi-Fi HaLow (802.11ah) having gained very little traction to date, there is still considerable potential for 2.4 GHz Wi-Fi in the IoT. If certain 2.4 GHz 802.11ax implementations can offer comparable battery life to 802.11n, or other short-range wireless IoT connectivity solutions, it may open new opportunities for Wi-Fi across several IoT vertical applications. The standard builds on the strengths of 802.11ac while adding efficiency, flexibility, and scalability. Table 5-6 shows the major technical differences between 802.11ac and 802.11ax standards.

Table 5-6. *802.11ac and 802.11ax Comparison*

	802.11ac	802.11ax
Bands	5 GHz	2.4 GHz and 5 GHz
Channel Bandwith	20 MHz, 40 MHz, 80 MHz, 80+80 MHz, & 160 MHz	20 MHz, 40 MHz, 80 MHz, 80+80 MHz, &160 MHz
FFT Sizes	64, 128, 256, 512	256, 512, 1024, 2048
Subcarrier Spacing	312.5 kHz	78.125 kHz
OFDM Symbol Duration	3.2 us + 0.8/0.4 us CP	12.8 us + 0.8/1.6/3.2 us CP
Highest Modulation	256-QAM	1024-QAM
Data Rate: 1 Spatial Stream	433 Mbps (80 MHz, 1 SS)	600.4 Mbps (80 MHz, 1 SS)
Data Rate: 8 Spatial Streams	6933 Mbps (160 MHz, 8 SS)	9607.8 Mbps (160 MHz, 8 SS)

For Wi-Fi connectivity technology, security has two aspects. First is controlling who can connect to and configure the network and equipment. Second aspect deals with securing the data travelling wirelessly across your Wi-Fi network from unauthorized access by using encryption. For the overall network to be secure, one should also consider measures to protect the gateways and the connections across the Internet using virtual private network (VPN), firewalls, and so on.

Bluetooth

Bluetooth operates in the unlicensed industrial, scientific, and medical (ISM) band at 2.4 GHz using a spread spectrum, frequency hopping, and full-duplex signal at a nominal rate of 1600 hops/sec. The 2.4 GHz ISM band is available and unlicensed in most countries. Its range varies from 1 m to 100 m depending on which class of radio is used. Class 2 is the most commonly used radio. It has a range of around 10 m and uses 2.5 mW of power.

Bluetooth provides a short distance wireless connection with low power consumption, even compared to Wi-Fi. Bluetooth Low Energy (also known as Bluetooth Smart or BLE) further reduces the power consumption profile of traditional Bluetooth. For example, Bluetooth devices can sustain battery life for weeks or months, while Wi-Fi can be hours or days. Data transfer rates are somewhat limited at about 1 Mbps (though theoretical throughput is up to 24 Mbps), though the range extends up to about 100 meters (300+ feet). Similar to Wi-Fi, Bluetooth can be used for machine-to-machine connections and device pairing. Bluetooth 4.1 was introduced in December 2013, which enables devices to communicate with each other before feeding that data back to a host and interoperates with LTE.

The Bluetooth SIG controls the Bluetooth standard. Bluetooth technology was originally proposed as a standard for communications between phones and computers. The main use case that made Bluetooth initially popular was hands-free phone calls with headsets and in-vehicle infotainment systems in cars. With the advent of smartphones, high-fidelity music streaming and health and fitness accessories have also become more popular.

Bluetooth is a PAN (personal area network) technology primarily used today as a cable replacement for short-range communication. It can be used in a point-to-point or star network topology. It supports data throughputs up to 2 Mbps, with up to eight connected devices.

Original Bluetooth standard is today commonly referred to as Bluetooth Classic, to distinguish it from Bluetooth Low Energy. Bluetooth Low Energy, sometimes known as Bluetooth Smart, is an addition to the Bluetooth specification. Bluetooth SIG adopted it in the Bluetooth 4.0 standard in 2010 to enter the low-power IoT space.

Though Bluetooth Low Energy also uses the 2.4 GHz ISM band, it is not compatible with Bluetooth Classic. Bluetooth Low Energy uses 40 2 MHz-wide channels, whereas Bluetooth Classic uses 79 1 MHz-wide channels. Compared to Bluetooth Classic, Bluetooth Low Energy greatly reduces the power consumption of Bluetooth devices by supporting lower data throughput and enables lengthy lives for battery-operated devices. Bluetooth Low Energy also offers a beaconing capability and location-based services. Bluetooth Low Energy has proven to be very popular, triggering an explosion of new applications in spaces as diverse as fitness, toys, and automotive applications. It is now the main driving force behind many new Bluetooth standards.

Over the years, Bluetooth SIG has announced major revisions to the specifications to improve security, battery life, and easier interoperation with IP-based networks. For example, Bluetooth 4.2 specification added industrial strength security with elliptic curve cryptography (ECC)-based key management and Advanced Encryption Standard (AES) counter with cipher block chaining message authentication code (CCM) cryptography for message encryption.

Bluetooth 5 offers a choice of data rates and operating ranges – 2 Mbps, 1 Mbps, 500 Kbps, and 125 Kbps. The lower the data rates, the longer the ranges. The increases in range and data rate capabilities make Bluetooth Low Energy increasingly attractive in nonconsumer segments such as industrial data loggers or smart energy meters. Along with these, Bluetooth Low Energy's inherent advantage of built-in compatibility with mobile devices, it is an excellent choice for data display and retrieval, Internet connectivity, and initial provisioning and configuration of IoT devices in the field. Table 5-7 shows a comparison of Bluetooth Classic and Bluetooth Low Energy technologies.

In 2017, the Bluetooth SIG released the mesh profile and mesh model specifications. Mesh networking technology enables the use of Bluetooth Low Energy for many-to-many device communications in home automation applications such as smart lighting, low-power wireless sensor networks, and so on. It also enables extended range communication using intermediary nodes to relay the data across the network. These new mesh standards are compatible with both the Bluetooth 5 and Bluetooth 4.x standards.

Table 5-7. *Bluetooth Low Energy and Bluetooth Classic Comparison*

	Bluetooth Low Energy (LE)	**Bluetooth Classic [Basic Rate/Enhanced Data Rate (BR/EDR)]**
Optimized For…	Short burst data transmission	Continuous data streaming
Frequency Band	2.4 GHz ISM Band (2.402–2.480 GHz Utilized)	2.4GHz ISM Band (2.402–2.480 GHz Utilized)
Channels	40 channels with 2 MHz spacing (3 advertising channels/37 data channels)	79 channels with 1 MHz spacing

(*continued*)

Table 5-7. (*continued*)

	Bluetooth Low Energy (LE)	Bluetooth Classic [Basic Rate/Enhanced Data Rate (BR/EDR)]
Channel Usage	Frequency-Hopping Spread Spectrum (FHSS)	Frequency-Hopping Spread Spectrum (FHSS)
Modulation	GFSK	GFSK, $\pi/4$ DQPSK, 8DPSK
Power Consumption	~0.01x to 0.5x of reference (depending on use case)	1 (reference value)
Data Rate	LE 2M PHY: 2 Mb/s LE 1M PHY: 1 Mb/s LE Coded PHY (S=2): 500 Kb/s LE Coded PHY (S=8): 125 Kb/s	EDR PHY (8DPSK): 3 Mb/s EDR PHY ($\pi/4$ DQPSK): 2 Mb/s BR PHY (GFSK): 1 Mb/s
Max Tx Power*	Class 1: 100 mW (+20 dBm) Class 1.5: 10 mW (+10 dBm) Class 2: 2.5 mW (+4 dBm) Class 3: 1 mW (0 dBm)	Class 1: 100 mW (+20 dBm) Class 2: 2.5 mW (+4 dBm) Class 3: 1 mW (0 dBm)
Network Topologies	Point-to-point (including piconet) BroadcastMesh	Point-to-point (including piconet)

Security in Bluetooth mesh networking is concerned with the security of more than individual devices or connections between peer devices; it's concerned with the security of an entire network of devices and of various groupings of devices in the network. Consequently, security in Bluetooth mesh networking is mandatory. This is achieved by implementing the following fundamental security measures:

- Encryption and authentication: All Bluetooth mesh messages are encrypted and authenticated.

- Separation of concerns: Network security, application security, and device security are addressed independently.

- Area isolation: A Bluetooth mesh network can be divided into subnets, each cryptographically distinct and secure from the others.

- Key refresh: Security keys can be changed during the life of the Bluetooth mesh network via a key refresh procedure.

- Message obfuscation: Message obfuscation makes it difficult to track messages sent within the network and, as such, provides a privacy mechanism to make it difficult to track nodes.

- Replay attack protection: Bluetooth mesh security protects the network against replay attacks.

- Trashcan attack protection: Nodes can be removed from the network securely, in a way which prevents trashcan attacks.

- Secure device provisioning: The process by which devices are added to the Bluetooth mesh network to become nodes is a secure process.

Zigbee

Zigbee is based on the IEEE 802.15.4 link layer and typically operates in the 2.4 GHz ISM band. Its networking layer has been designed with mesh topology operations in mind from the ground up. This provides the ability to scale the network geographically through multihop operations (for applications such as smart meters), as well as increases fault tolerance and reliability as backup paths are created through the mesh between any two points.

Zigbee is designed, promoted, and maintained by the Zigbee Alliance. Zigbee 3.0, the latest specification, increases choice and flexibility for users and developers and delivers the confidence that products and services will all work together through standardization at all layers of the stack. Zigbee 3.0 is built on the Zigbee PRO, which enhances the IEEE 802.15.4 standard by adding mesh network and security layers along with an application framework and to become a full stack, low-power certifiable, interoperable Zigbee solution. Zigbee provides a complete solution that enables true device interoperability between different manufacturers. The Zigbee protocol suite incorporates the Zigbee cluster library: a standard library of device types, data models, and behaviors built by original equipment manufacturers (OEMs) operating in different vertical markets and proven in actual deployments for many years. A rigorous certification program managed by the Zigbee Alliance guarantees interoperability between Zigbee devices, verifying device type behavior and functionality from an end product perspective and ensuring that products from different manufacturers can operate together.

The Zigbee protocol suite includes standard commissioning, security, network, and device management procedures. Various device types can join and be authenticated in the network and be factory reset or decommissioned in an interoperable way, guaranteeing end-to-end device interoperability from the start of device operation and seamlessly integrating with data collectors or hubs.

Zigbee-based applications mostly target the smart home and smart building domains, with focus in lighting and home control and physical security segments. Many telecom, security, and Internet service providers have endorsed Zigbee as the protocol of choice when introducing their home automation services to consumers, and many lighting manufacturers have a series of smart bulbs supporting this protocol.

Zigbee takes full advantage of IEEE 802.15.4 physical radio standard and operation in unlicensed bands worldwide at 2.4 GHz (global), 915 MHz (Americas), and 868 MHz (Europe). Raw data throughput rates of 250 Kbps can be achieved at 2.4 GHz (16 channels), 10 Kbps at 915–921 MHz (27 channels), and 100 Kbps at 868 MHz (63 channels). Transmission distances range from 10 to 100 meters, depending on power output and environmental characteristics. Sub-1 GHz channel transmission ranges up to 1 km. Table 5-8 provides a quick overview of the Zigbee technology.

Zigbee effectively uses the allocated bandwidth to convey both application data to operate devices and network management procedures like mesh and routing management with a very small energy footprint. Zigbee's addressing scheme is capable of supporting hundreds of nodes per network (up to 64K), and multiple network coordinators can be linked together to support extremely large networks. The logical size of a Zigbee network ultimately depends on which frequency band is selected, how often each device on the network needs to communicate, and how much data loss or retransmissions can be tolerated by the application.

Table 5-8. *Overview of Zigbee Technical Specifications*

Solution	Description
Network Protocol	Zigbee PRO 2015 (or newer)
Network Topology	Self-Forming, Self-Healing MESH
Network Device Types	Coordinator (routing capable), Router, End Device, Zigbee Green Power Device
Network Size (# of nodes)	Up to 65,000
Radio Technology	IEEE 802.15.4-2011
Frequency Band/Channels	2.4 GHz (ISM band) 16 channels (2 MHz wide)

(*continued*)

Table 5-8. (*continued*)

Solution	Description
Data Rate	250 Kbits/sec
Security Models	Centralized (with Install Codes support) Distributed
Encryption Support	AES-128 at Network Layer AES-128 available at Application Layer
Communication Range (Average)	Up to 300+ meters (line of sight) Up to 75–100 meters indoor
Low Power Support	Sleeping End Devices Zigbee Green Power Devices (energy harvesting)

NFC

Near field communications (NFC) is a short-range wireless communication technology designed to build on existing high-frequency (HF) (13.56 MHz) contactless and RFID technology. Using 13.56 MHz on the ISM band and with a typical operating distance of up to 4 cm, today NFC enables an exchange rate of between 106 Kbps and 848 Kbps. NFC creates a short-range wireless connection able to operate in three different modes of operation: card emulation, read/write, and peer-to-peer. NFC technology enables a wide range of use cases from keyless access to e-wallet in smartphone and smart tags for medical applications. This is due to ease of implementation and the ability to embed tags into credit cards, smartphones, and other wearable devices.

GPS/GNSS

GPS is a satellite-based radio navigation system that provides users with location, velocity, and time information. A GPS receiver acquires each visible satellite's signal and measures the individual time delays. Applying these time delays to known radio wave propagation characteristics allows the distance to each satellite to be calculated. GPS accuracy correlates with the number of satellites successfully acquired by a GPS receiver. New systems are under development, such as Glonass, Galileo, and Compass, which, when used in conjunction with GPS, will improve global coverage, reduce time to fix location, and increase performance in challenging environments. Location data collected by onboard GPS trackers are vital to many applications in the transportation industry such as fleet management, asset tracking, and autonomous vehicles.

Cellular

Cellular technologies provide "always-on" connectivity to the backbone network – to the Cloud. Similar to mobile phones for consumer applications, cellular data for IoT can be connected over 2G, 3G, or 4G networks. Benefits include broad coverage leveraging existing base station infrastructure as well as mobility (e.g., cars). Potential drawbacks include power consumption, fees associated with data transfer over licensed spectrum owned by carriers, and potential gaps in coverage.

As demand for ubiquitous connectivity for IoT devices gets ever stronger, cellular networks can deliver reliable and secure IoT services using existing network infrastructure. Massive investments have been made in spectrum allocations and network deployments to ensure good coverage for the entire population in most countries. The same networks that are used to connect people can now be leveraged to connect things.

Traditional cellular options such as 2G, 3G, or higher category 4G modems consume a lot of power and don't fit well with applications where only a small amount of data is transmitted infrequently, such as smart meters, asset trackers, healthcare equipment, agriculture sensors, parking spaces, and street lights. Cellular IoT is designed to meet the requirements of such low-power, long-range applications. It takes existing technology that we already use every day for our smartphones and scales it back to meet the needs of low-power devices.

When it comes to analyzing cost of a communication solution, the total cost of ownership includes spectrum costs, infrastructure costs, and operational expenses. As cellular networks are already in place, very little new infrastructure needs to be installed. The base stations, cell towers, buildings, and power supply are already in place, all around the world. The technology also has the potential to cover hundreds of thousands of IoT devices per square kilometer – many more than other communication options.

No single technology or solution is ideally suited to all the different potential massive IoT applications, market situations, and spectrum availability. As a result, the mobile industry is standardizing several technologies, including Long-Term Evolution for Machines (LTE-M) and Narrowband IoT (NB-IoT). NB-IoT is ideally suited for low bandwidth, infrequent communication from a relatively stationary device, while LTE-M suits higher bandwidth or mobile and roaming applications.

A good application for NB-IoT is the use of remote environmental sensors to measure temperature, wind, pressure, and so on. These devices can send regular updates from a fixed location while optimizing battery use. Such a device could last for up to 10 years, or longer if solar powered and in the right geographical position.

Similarly, an asset tracker with condition monitoring through several sensors, which is mobile and roaming from country to country, is well served by an LTE-M solution that offers highway speed mobility, international roaming between countries and operators, and efficient firmware updates.

Advantages of cellular connectivity for IoT include

- The use of open standards based on existing infrastructure means coverage will reach virtually everywhere where people live.

- Many devices can operate simultaneously because of the advanced coexistence mechanisms in the LTE standard and licensed band operation, as is already proven today with the large number of cellphones used concurrently within a small area.

- No limiting regulatory regulations, so you can transmit up to 23 dBm and negotiate for as much airtime as you need.

- Standard TLS/DTLS security for end-to-end security is supported on top of the on-air encryption of the LTE network aided by the SIM credentials. This keeps data secure from the device to the cloud server.

- As cellular network coverage increases and technologies are available in low-complexity, low-power variants, cellular technology is a great choice for the world's IoT needs.

5G Cellular

The first-generation mobile network (1G) was all about voice and used analogy technology. 2G enabled voice and texting (short messaging service – SMS) using digital technology. 3G was about voice, texting, and data. 4G was everything in 3G but faster, and 5G will be even faster. 5G will be fast enough to download a full-length HD movie in seconds. The transition from 2G to 4G happened in a span of about 20 years as shown in Figure 5-14.

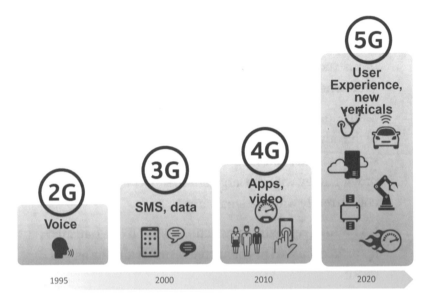

Figure 5-14. *Evolution of cellular technologies*

The real performance of a cellular network will vary by provider, their configuration of the network, the number of active connections in a given cell, the radio environment in a specific location, the capability of the device in use, plus all the other factors that affect radio performance. It is safe to assume that the throughput will be much closer to the lower bound for data throughput, and the latency will be trending toward the higher bound for packet latency for a given generation. Table 5-9 provides a summary of data rates and latency of different generations of cellular technologies.

Table 5-9. *Comparison of Data Rates and Latencies of Different Generations of Cellular Technologies*

Generation	Peak Data Rate	Practical Data Rate	Latency	Description
1G	No Data	No Data	No Data	Analog systems
2G	100s of Kbps	100–400 Kbps	300–1000 mS	First digital systems as overlays or parallel to analog systems
3G	10s of Mbps	400 Kbps– 5 Mbps	100–500 mS	Dedicated digital networks deployed in parallel to analog systems
4G	100s of Mbps	1–50 Mbps	<100 mS	Digital and packet-only networks
5G	10s of Gbps	TBD	1–20 mS	Digital and packet-only networks

5G is much more than just faster networks. It supports the unique combination of high-speed connectivity, very low latency, and ubiquitous coverage, making it natively suitable for supporting IoT use cases. 5G will enable us to control more devices remotely in applications where real-time network performance is critical, enabling new user experiences in many different verticals. For example, it can be used for remote control of heavy machinery in hazardous environments, thereby improving worker safety. With its low latency, it can improve access to healthcare by enabling remote surgery. 5G connectivity will support smart vehicles and transport infrastructure such as connected cars, where the variation in delay could mean the difference between a smooth flow of traffic and an accident. It is evident that 5G will spur innovation across many industries and prove to be an enabling platform for IoT solutions to become an integral part of our economy.

Key Standards, Regulatory, and Industry Bodies Involved in 5G

There are multiple cellular standards and release versions, and the classification of any given network as 3G, 4G, or 5G is definitely too coarse. Here is a quick survey of the key players behind the evolution of various cellular technologies:

- **ITU**: (International Telecommunications Union) Agency of the UN, coordinating telecom operations and services globally. Their ITU-R sector is charged with developing future 5G standards and coordinating harmonized spectrum use.

- **3GPP**: Collaboration between seven global telecommunications standards organizations engaged in research and development of 5G standards.

- **ETSI**: Organization in Europe producing globally applicable standards for Information and Communication Technologies.

- **OCF**: Comprised of technology suppliers for product, software, platform, and silicon dedicated to driving open standards for IoT solutions.

- **IEEE**: A technical professional organization dedicated to enabling the development of new use cases and standards to accelerate time to market of technologies developed on a consensus basis.

- **5G-ACIA**: 5G Alliance for Connected Industries and Automation ensures the best possible applicability of 5G technology and 5G networks for the manufacturing and process industries by addressing, discussing, and evaluating relevant technical, regulatory, and business aspects.

New Use Cases Enabled by 5G

5G addresses existing, emerging, and future use cases. 3GPP (3rd Generation Partnership Project) has grouped the high-level use cases of 5G into three categories, based on the functionality and performance that 5G would need to enable these use cases. The three sets of use cases, primarily based on the 5G performance attributes, are listed here and are shown in Figure 5-15:

- *Enhanced Mobile Broadband (eMBB)*: Use cases requiring high data rates across a wide coverage area, providing immersive experiences such as augmented reality and virtual reality. eMBB will initially be an extension to existing 4G services and will be among the first 5G services. The three main attributes of 5G that enable eMBB use cases are

  Higher capacity: Which makes broadband access available in densely populated areas, both indoors and outdoors, like city centers, office buildings, and public venues like stadiums or conference centers.

  Enhanced connectivity: Broadband access must be available, with adequate quality of service everywhere to provide a consistent user experience.

  Higher user mobility: Will enable mobile broadband services in moving vehicles including cars, buses, trains, and even planes.

  eMBB traffic is characterized by large payloads and by a device connection pattern that remains stable over an extended time interval. This allows the network to schedule wireless resources to the eMBB devices preventing the chance of two eMBB devices accessing the same resource simultaneously. The objective of the eMBB service is to maximize the data rate while guaranteeing a moderate reliability.

- *Massive Machine-Type Communications (mMTC)*: This addresses the need to support a very large number of devices in a small area, which may only send data sporadically. IoT use cases such as smart homes, smart cities, and weather and agricultural smart sensors are good examples. A large number of mMTC devices may be connected to a given cellular network, but at a given time only a subset of them could be active and attempt to communicate their data. The large number of potentially active mMTC devices makes it infeasible to preallocate resources to individual mMTC devices. Instead, it is necessary to provide resources that can be shared through random access. The objective in the design of mMTC is to maximize the arrival rate that can be supported in a given radio resource.

- *Ultra-Reliable Low-Latency Communications (URLLC)*: These use cases impose strict requirements on latency and reliability for mission-critical communications, such as remote surgery, autonomous vehicles, or industrial control applications. The number of potential devices supported per unit area is considered to be smaller than mMTC. Supporting URLLC transmissions requires a combination of scheduling, so as to ensure a certain amount of predictability in the available resources and thus support high reliability. Random access is also required in order to ensure that too many resources do NOT idle due to the intermittent nature of scheduled traffic. Due to the low latency requirements, a URLLC transmission should be localized in time. Diversity, which is critical to achieve high reliability, can be achieved by using multiple frequency or spatial resources. Compared to eMBB, the rate of a URLLC transmission is relatively low, and the main requirement is ensuring a high reliability level.

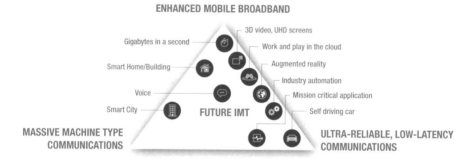

Figure 5-15. *New use cases enabled by 5G*

Key Technology Enablers for 5G

- *5G NR*: 5G New Radio is the new air interface technology being defined to support the features of 5G. The air interface specifies the radio frequency (RF) section of the connection between a mobile device and the mobile network. OFDM (orthogonal frequency-division multiplexing) family of waveforms will be used for 5G. This allows wireless network providers to more easily scale carrier bandwidth needed for each application and support diverse spectrum. 5G New Radio will use new spectrum well beyond the range of most current wireless technology, improving network availability and throughput. Massive MIMO (multiple input multiple output) technologies enable efficient use of large number of antennae and, along with 3D beamforming technologies, allow increase in capacity, coverage, and cell edge performance. The 5G NR self-contained slot structure delivers significantly lower latency than LTE thanks to support for fast uplink/downlink turnaround and scalable slot durations.

- *Network Function Virtualization (NFV)*: Today's networks are dedicated, static, and hardware resource-based and can't meet tomorrow's demands. Decoupling and shifting network functions from proprietary hardware to software-based services on open servers "virtualizes" the network. To support the many new use cases for 5G, NFV provides significant capabilities for communication service providers that will lead to more innovation, fast service deployment, and reduced operating expenses.

- *Software-Defined Networking (SDN)*: SDN is a framework for creating intelligent networks that are open, programmable, and application aware. It makes network programmable by separating the control plane (telling the network what goes where) from the data plane (sending packets to specific destinations) – centralizing and automating network engineering tasks and reducing the amount of manual intervention and coordination. This drives rapid service creation, reducing time to market for new offerings.

- *Network Slicing*: This can be employed to enable enhanced network flexibility. SDN and NFV create opportunity to "slice" networks, so that a single physical network can be partitioned into many virtual networks. Each slice is self-contained with all necessary functions and is customized to match the level of delivery complexity required by the service-level agreement, as illustrated in Figure 5-16. Delivering customized connectivity and computing power for different types of segments, devices, and services opens new ways for communication service providers to monetize their offering. For example, they can provide third parties with access to operate their slices independently, creating new Network-as-a-Service (NaaS) business model.

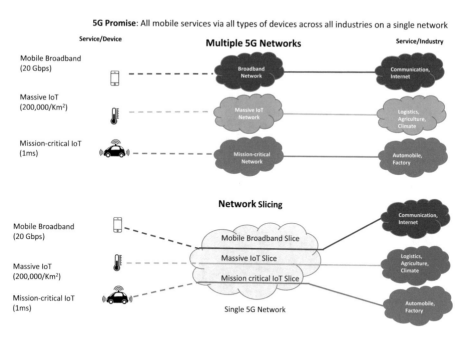

Figure 5-16. *Network slicing concept*

- *C-RAN*: Cloud or Centralized Radio Access Network
  helps to optimize network architecture by virtualizing
  base station functions; mobile base stations are
  comprised of a baseband unit (BBU), handling data
  processing, and a radio unit (RU), sending/receiving
  radio waves and managing the radio resources.
  Separating the BBU from the mobile base station radio
  unit pools data processing functions into a centralized
  server as shown in Figure 5-17. This allows multiple
  radio units to be controlled from one server reducing
  CAPEX and OPEX for communication service providers.
  This also increases the ability to address interference
  issue in high-density area and improves network
  efficiency with shared processing and load balancing.

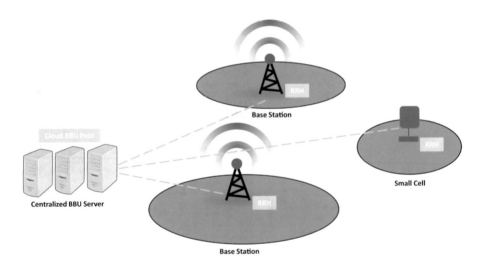

Figure 5-17. *Cloud RAN concept*

LPWAN – Low-Power Wide Area Networks

Low-power wide area network (LPWAN) technologies have low power draw and provide coverage to wide geographical areas. They provide connectivity for devices and applications that require low mobility and low speeds and infrequent data transfer, such as sensors. LPWAN technologies fill the gap between mobile cellular (3G, LTE) and short-range wireless (e.g., Bluetooth, Wi-Fi, and Zigbee) networks and are designed for machine-to-machine communications. LPWAN devices have a long battery life because they transmit only small packets of data at infrequent intervals. LPWAN solutions provide a wide area of coverage that is not limited by distance between the access points (i.e., base stations or towers) using new modulation techniques and frequency choices. They also do not typically require line-of-sight communications. They therefore require far fewer access points per unit area than traditional cellular wireless technologies.

There is no single standard for LPWAN, and there are a number of competing technologies, providing different levels of coverage and capacity. We will take a look at three of them.

LoRa

LoRa Alliance is an open, nonprofit association with over 500 members globally among telcos, system integrators, and manufacturers. LoRaWAN is an open standard with a certification program to guarantee interoperability that is governed by the LoRa Alliance. LoRaWAN network semiconductor technology is proprietary to California-based semiconductor manufacturer Semtech. See Table 5-10 for the summary of technical specifications of LoRa technology.

Table 5-10. *LoRa Overview*

Name of Standard	LoRaWAN
Frequency Band	433/868/780/915 MHz ISM
Channel Width	EU: 8x125kHz, US 64x125kHz/8x125kHz Modulation: Chirp Spread Spectrum
Range	2-5k (urban), 15k (rural)
End Node Transmit Power	EU:<+14dBm US:<+27dBm
Packet Size	Defined by User
Uplink Data Rate	EU: 300 bps to 50 kbps US:900-100kbps
Downlink Data Rate	EU: 300 bps to 50 kbps US:900-100kbps
Devices per Access Point	Uplink:>1M Downlink:<100k
Topology	Star on Star
End node roaming allowed	Yes
Governing Body	LoRa Alliance
Status	Spec released June 2015, in deployment

Sigfox

One of the most widely deployed proprietary LPWAN technologies is Sigfox, which was established in France in 2009 and deployed its first network in mid-2012. As of August 2018, there were networks in some 50 countries globally with a target of 60 by the end of the year. Table 5-11 captures the key features of Sigfox.

Table 5-11. *Sigfox Overview*

Name of Standard	SigFox
Frequency Band	868 MHz/902 MHz ISM
Channel Width	Ultra narrow band
Range	30-50km (rural), 3-10km (urban), 1000km LoS
End Node Transmit Power	-20 dBm to 20 dBm
Packet Size	12 bytes
Uplink Data Rate	100 bps to 140 messages/day
Downlink Data Rate	to 4 messages of 8 bytes/day
Devices per Access Point	1M
Topology	Star
End node roaming allowed	Yes
Governing Body	SigFox (proprietary)
Status	In deployment

Weightless

Cambridge-based Weightless SIG (Special Interest Group) was founded in 2008 to develop standards for M2M communications in white space (unused TV spectrum). Weightless originally developed three standards for different use cases which employ different technologies and provide varying levels of packet size and data rates. Today it promotes Weightless-P, which is shown in Table 5-12 – an ultra-narrowband protocol for bidirectional communications now known simply as Weightless technology.

Table 5-12. *Weightless Overview*

Name of Standard	Weightless
Frequency Band	Sub-GHZ ISM
Channel Width	12.5 kHz
Range	2km (urban)
End Node Transmit Power	17 dBm
Packet Size	10 byte min
Uplink Data Rate	200 bps to 100 kbps
Downlink Data Rate	same
Devices per Access Point	Unlimited
Topology	Star
End node roaming allowed	Yes
Governing Body	
Status	In deploymnet

Comparison of Low-Power LTE and Other LPWAN Technologies

There are several technologies upon which LPWANs can be based as seen earlier and can be classified into those based on proprietary systems and those based on open standards.

Low-power Long-Term Evolution (LTE) has taken off since the 3rd Generation Partnership Project (3GPP) introduced a specification for two forms of the technology – LTE-M and Narrowband-IoT (NB-IoT) – in Release 13 of the standard. The new specification makes it easier for manufacturers to design and develop the inexpensive, compact, and low power consumption wireless LTE modems that LPWANs demand.

LTE is an open standard, operates in a licensed portion of the RF spectrum, leverages existing infrastructure for coverage, and has coexistence mechanisms that enable scaling to high node counts per base station.

Low-power LTE operates in up to 44 different licensed frequencies across the world, ranging from 450 MHz to 2.6 GHz. By using the licensed spectrum, the owners of the spectrum allocation (the carriers) can control and prioritize data, and the bands are immune from interference from other sources of RF radiation.

Because the spectrum allocation isn't shared with other RF transmissions, the coexistence between connected devices is much easier to manage. LTE's coexistence technology is based on proven frequency- and time-domain solutions and other mechanisms such as "autonomous denials" of conflicting RF signals. Consequently, LTE can support a node density of up to 200,000 active low-power modems per base station. Finally, data carried over LTE is safe from prying eyes because the standard has incorporated advanced security from its inception. These features ensure that carriers can offer reliability and high quality of service.

In contrast, proprietary technologies limit the participation in the vendor ecosystem and innovation in technology evolution over time. As they operate in unlicensed allocations of the RF spectrum (typically sub-1 GHz), coexistence could also be a challenge. They must share RF spectrum with many other services. While basic interference avoidance techniques are employed, so many services are sharing the spectrum allocation that it is extremely to match the node density, reliability, and quality of service of LTE.

Proprietary LPWAN vendors are also faced with the major challenge of building infrastructure to support their networks. These are likely to be expensive and long-winded projects slowing adoption. In contrast, worldwide LTE infrastructure is largely in place comprising 480 networks in 157 countries. Some upgrading (mainly of software) is required to support low-power LTE, but this is relatively a less complex effort compared to building the infrastructure in the first place. Because the infrastructure is installed, support for low-power LTE is likely to be added rapidly, further encouraging its uptake.

Companies adopting low-power LTE for their IoT-connected products can leverage this infrastructure without bearing its build or maintenance costs, instead investing in their own services and business models.

A Case Study – Smart Homes

A typical smart home gateway is illustrated in Figure 5-18.

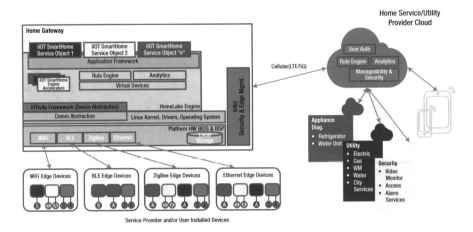

Figure 5-18. *Smart home system using multiple connectivity technologies*

In reality, many IoT endpoints and gateways will employ multiple communication technologies based on cost, improved flexibility, and interoperability. A primary example is connected thermostat which incorporates both Wi-Fi and ZigBee. Many smart meters support cellular, ZigBee, RF mesh, and Wi-Fi capabilities. A key advantage of Wi-Fi and Bluetooth is that they are already embedded in essentially all smartphones. This type of coexistence of multiple technologies in a single system is illustrated in the smart home IoT system example shown earlier. The gateway supports Wi-Fi and Ethernet for LAN connections that need higher bandwidth such as audio and video applications. PAN and mesh networks based on Bluetooth Low Energy and ZigBee are used for energy-efficient sensors and controllers for lighting, security, and so on. The gateway provides WAN connectivity to Cloud using cellular technologies like LTE and 5G. Local analytics and intelligences provided by the gateway. The cloud service providers enable cloud-based applications to deliver the various services.

Summary

There are many connectivity technologies that can be used for enabling IoT. Each one has its own benefits and shortcomings. One should choose a technology or a combination of technologies that is best suited for the application. Cost, ease of system integration, and security should also be considered along with features such as throughput, range, power consumption, network topology, and existing infrastructure.

The IEEE has already standardized dozens of use cases and applications for IoT protocols. In addition to the basic communications standards discussed earlier (layer 2 in the OSI stack), which handle the underlying communications, there is a need for standardization at higher layers of the stack as well. Working groups belonging to many industry alliances such as OPC Foundation, Industrial Internet Consortium, 5G-ACIA, and ZigBee Alliance and standardization bodies such as ETSI coordinate and establish the priorities and enabling technologies of the Industrial Internet in order to accelerate market adoption and drive down the barriers to entry.

References

1. IEEE Time-Sensitive Networking Task Group: https://1.ieee802.org/tsn/

2. P60802 – Time-Sensitive Networking Profile for Industrial Automation: https://standards.ieee.org/project/60802.html

3. Wi-Fi Alliance: www.wi-fi.org/discover-wi-fi

4. Bluetooth SIG: www.bluetooth.com/bluetooth-resources

5. Zigbee Alliance: www.zigbee.org/zigbee-for-developers/zigbee-3-0/

6. 3GPP: www.3gpp.org/

7. Industrial Internet Consortium: www.iiconsortium.org/

8. OPC Foundation: https://opcfoundation.org/

9. 5G Alliance for Connected Industries and Automation (5G-ACIA): www.5g-acia.org/

10. Time-Sensitive Networking Standards: IEEE Communications Standards Magazine (Volume: 2, Issue: 2, JUNE 2018). https://ieeexplore.ieee.org/document/8412457

11. Avnu Alliance: The Business Impact of TSN for Industrial Systems Whitepaper. https://avnu.org/business-impact-paper/

12. Time-Sensitive Networking: From Theory to Implementation in Industrial Automation. www.intel.com/content/dam/www/programmable/us/en/pdfs/literature/wp/wp-01279-time-sensitive-networking-from-theory-to-implementation-in-industrial-automation.pdf

13. Ultra-Low Latency (ULL) Networks: The IEEE TSN and IETF DetNet Standards and Related 5G ULL Research. https://arxiv.org/pdf/1803.07673.pdf

14. A Survey on 5G Networks for the Internet of Things:
     Communication Technologies and Challenges.
     `https://ieeexplore.ieee.org/document/8141874`

15. 5G Technology Overview, Intel: `www.intel.com/`
     `content/www/us/en/wireless-network/5g-`
     `technology-overview.html`

16. Intel Wireless Solutions: `www.intel.com/content/`
     `www/us/en/products/wireless.html`

17. Intel® IoT Industry Solutions for Smart
     Manufacturing: `www.intel.com/content/www/`
     `us/en/internet-of-things/infographics/`
     `iot-industry-solutions-smart-manufacturing-`
     `infographic.html`

18. Smart Homes with Intel® Internet of Things (IoT)
     Technologies: `www.intel.com/content/www/us/en/`
     `internet-of-things/smart-home.html`

CHAPTER 6

IoT Vertical Applications and Associated Security Requirements

> *It is not the critic who counts; not the man who points out how the strong man stumbles, or where the doer of deeds could have done them better. The credit belongs to the man who is actually in the arena, whose face is marred by dust and sweat and blood.*
>
> —Theodore Roosevelt[1]

Throughout the previous chapters of this book, we have presented how different parts of an IoT system could be built and what components and frameworks are important and useful. In this chapter, we present what Intel is doing in the arena of IoT as complete vertical solutions. IoT spans a broad range of different markets, and therefore solutions must be tailored to the specific purposes of those markets and the specific security threats

---

[1] www.goodreads.com/author/quotes/44567.Theodore_Roosevelt

© The Author(s) 2020
S. Cheruvu et al., *Demystifying Internet of Things Security*,
https://doi.org/10.1007/978-1-4842-2896-8_6

encountered or expected in those environments. There are similarities, to
be sure. Each industry has different security demands due to the nature
of the information handled and the mandate to conform to particular
regulatory and industry standard bodies' requirements. This chapter
will provide an overview of the different verticals, associated security
requirements, threats, and mitigations.

The IoT ecosystem is fragmented by nature with multiple verticals, but
at the end of the day, we strive to leverage a common set of hardware and
software building blocks, augmented with accelerators, to meet domain
unique requirements. Security is a horizontal capability, as we have
shown in Chapters 3 and 4. However, because of the differences within
each vertical market, frequently different verticals expand and enhance
the common set of security capabilities in order to achieve what their
particular market demands. This perspective is shown in Figure 6-1 which
articulates unique vertical security and regulatory requirements built from
a common set of security minimal viable platform features. Successfully
accomplishing this customization necessitates a system of systems
perspective, which is an understanding that no system exists in a vacuum
but must interact with other systems – human, technological, and process.
As we delve into each vertical market in this section, common themes from
the security MVP will stand out to the reader, but these will be adapted
by each domain to address security and privacy by design, security-
performance trade-offs at the system level, and integration into existing
systems and processes – the system of systems perspective.

Before diving deeply into each vertical domain, we present a
brief overview of each domain and point out the commonalities, and
differences, between them.

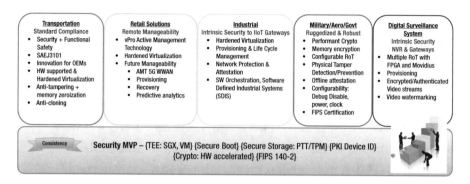

Figure 6-1. *IoT vertical framework: enhance the foundation with value-added features to enable verticals*

The **Transportation Solutions** domain is focused on safety and leverages the foundational security MVP, augmenting HW/FW/SW capabilities to meet the prevalent standards and regulations including SAE J-3101, EVITA, HIS, AutoSAR, and autonomous driving standard (levels L1–L5). Anti-tampering which is related to preventing and/or detecting an attempt to alter or modify the platform for stealing secrets is critical to achieving transportation safety. Anti-cloning is related to preventing and/or detecting an attempt to copy or clone the platform including the HW/FW/SW. Some of these capabilities may align with other verticals. The Transportation Solutions domain also has some unique requirements such as memory zeroization where the state of the memory is initialized to a known value (zero) to eliminate the secrets from DRAM and to meet safety requirements for known state of software structures and variables. Virtualization support in hardware is mandatory for the transportation domain in order to maximize hardware utilization while minimizing cost without compromising security – this usually involves VTd and VTx technologies as we saw in the ACRN hypervisor in Chapter 4.

When a capability is aligned across more than two verticals, it makes sense to move this capability into the security MVP foundation. This then implies that some verticals do not make use of every security MVP feature. However, as we have found at Intel, as features move into the security

MVP, other vertical domains begin to leverage that capability as well. An example of this is FIPS 140 Level 2 which is now a common requirement across all the verticals.

The **Retail Solution** domain's security is focused on protecting the credit card payment information and the data in financial transactions. The identity of the users at the POS terminals is also of significance, leading to unique protections to handle personally identifiable information (PII). A new retail segment known as responsive retail addresses targeted marketing for the brick-and-mortar retailer while improving the shopping experience for consumers using advertisements customized according to the age, gender (using facial and body imaging), and other characteristics of the consumer. The retail domain in general is also heavily invested in remote manageable devices (upgradable and recoverable) over wired and wireless networks (in-band and out-of-band). Provisioning devices with the proper software loads and unique credentials to facilitate transactions to financial institutions and suppliers is an important, though not unique, characteristic of retail IoT systems.

In the in-band recovery scenario, a corrupt application can be recovered with the help of the operating system, and a corrupt operating system can be recovered with the help of the BIOS/UEFI/boot loader. We discussed some of these capabilities in Chapter 4, where we introduced the difficult problem of upgrading the platform firmware, such as the BIOS/UEFI/boot loader itself. For these situations, an out-of-band capability or physical access is required to recover the platform from corrupted firmware.

The **Industrial Solutions** domain covers the convergence of IT (information technology) with OT (operational technology), along with the related issues of incorporating existing systems and infrastructure (brownfield deployments) with new systems, capabilities, and infrastructure (greenfield deployments). Traditionally OT dealt with the factory and manufacturing floor tasks, and IT infrastructure managed the office and back-end tasks. Creating a smart factory requires the convergence of IT and OT, allowing the data to flow seamlessly between IT and OT for effective decision making and factory process execution. In a brownfield scenario, industries have long been deploying the devices and equipment with legacy bus interfaces and little to no network connectivity. The greenfield scenario is where the equipment and devices can all be true IoT with maximum high (or higher) bandwidth connectivity. Bridging the gap between brownfield and greenfield requires the use of proxy gateways with network protections and network admission technologies using device attestation. Software orchestration is essential in Industrial IoT (IIOT) where standards compliant architecture such as ISA-95 and Software-Defined Industrial Systems (SDIS) are federated for service orchestration, allowing all devices to both consume and provide services. Security services center around integrity and availability, and device recovery and reprovisioning for new services or changeovers to new tasks must be done quickly and efficiently or the loss on revenue can be steep.

The **Military, Aerospace, and Government** domain has the highest and most robust security requirements, and the need for performant crypto features, including encryption/decryption, digital signature/ verification, and random number generation, has high-throughput requirements. This domain also demands a configurable Root of Trust (RoT), augmenting the Intel RoT with a particular custom hardware Root of Trust private to the domain with higher robustness requirements. The alternative roots of trust include customized RoT in an Intel SoC/PCH or an FPGA. Physical tamper prevention, detection, and recovery are key features which are also tied to the secure debug ports, protections from side-channel attacks on clock, and prevention/detection of power glitching, among a host of other hardware-specific attacks. When attesting the IoT devices in this domain, in addition to remote attestation, a local or offline attestation feature is a mandatory requirement. Many advanced security requirements appear first in the Government domain and then

417

slowly begin to appear in other domains. Side-channel resistance is a recent example; protection from covert and side channels has been a long-standing requirement in the military domain, but not until the appearance of the Spectre and Meltdown attacks the side-channel protections are included in commercial RFPs. However, since these attacks were disclosed, side-channel protections are the new baseline and part of the common security MVP.

The **Digital Surveillance System (DSS)** domain is focused on network video recorders, networked Internet Protocol (IP) cameras, and computer vision accelerators. In a DSS system of systems, there is a need for multiple roots of trust including Intel SoC, FPGA, and Movidius. Provisioning the DSS cameras and video recorders is critical to prevent the IP camera–related attacks, including the Mirai botnet attacks which used default and brute-force login credentials[2] and the Persirai botnet which took over cameras using a recent zero-day vulnerability.[3] DSS systems also require performant crypto features, since the video stream must be encrypted and watermarked at line rate speeds. Another critical requirement for the DSS segment is data provenance, authenticated and integrity-protected metadata and attributes attached to the video and photographic data to prove the data, time, location, and device used for collection.

The DSS domain encounters some unique data protection and privacy regulations such as EU's General Data Protection Regulation (GDPR) and the California data privacy regulations which impact every type of business and impose severe penalties for not complying.

---

[2]https://motherboard.vice.com/en_us/article/8q8dab/15-million-connected-cameras-ddos-botnet-brian-krebs

[3]www.darkreading.com/attacks-breaches/new-iot-botnet-discovered-120k-ip-cameras-at-risk-of-attack/d/d-id/1328839

Common Domain Requirements and the Security MVP

The IoT Base Platform MVP is defined with foundational building blocks and the realization that the security requirements are achieved, up to nearly 90% in many cases, through common silicon used across all the domains. System design is dynamic, and decision vectors usually include security, privacy, resiliency, availability, and safety. The MVP is a triad of HW, FW, and SW capabilities that enables dynamic design where the domain features from HW, FW, and SW are selected diligently to reflect the trade-offs and optimize for the relevant decision vector. The NIST Cyber-Physical Systems Framework[4] for HW and SW co-design articulates trade-offs between the cyber and physical components of the IoT system.

Matthew Rosenquist articulated in a blog post[5] that although security is valuable, it comes at a cost – the cost for new equipment, the cost for training personnel on new technology, and the cost to develop new processes to utilize the technology. But just because we do not pay the cost to build security into our systems does not mean the cost goes away. We still incur costs due to the risks we inherently adopt by rejecting certain security features and the potential (and actual costs) to clean up after a security incident. These choices leading to costs of failure determine the risk management process as shown in Figure 6-2. A potential future cost of a security incident must be weighed against the actual cost to add security and the soft cost incurred by productivity impacts due to additional security. Good security design involves teaming up with customers and end users to understand these costs and balance the overall system to achieve reasonable security, preventing or deterring the most egregious

---

[4]https://nvlpubs.nist.gov/nistpubs/SpecialPublications/NIST.SP.1500-201.pdf
[5]https://itpeernetwork.intel.com/security-is-about-balancing-tradeoffs/

and most likely threats while providing a useful and useable system. Often ignored are the external costs where unrelated third-party entities suffer the consequences of attacks, and one specific example is the DNS-administrating company Dyn. For almost an entire day, Mirai botnet took down the sites including Twitter, CNN, Guardian, Netflix, and so on whose DNS services were being administered by Dyn.[6] The optimal security is a balance of cost, user experience, and risk. Since the IoT domains are different, and the threats are ever evolving, and the user interface and experience paradigms change, this balancing act becomes a dynamic living act. The security MVP is only the start of that act. Engagement in the domain and balancing domain-specific requirements is the process. The detailed sections that follow articulate Intel's perspective and engagement in these IoT-specific domains.

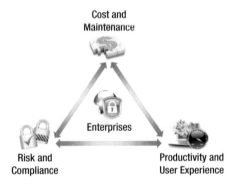

Figure 6-2. *Balancing security against cost, risk, and productivity*

One additional comment is warranted to the reader at this point. It has become a norm to employ complementary technologies such as FPGA accelerators, Movidius Computer Vision IP, and ASIC accelerators to meet the requirements from applications in various domain solutions. These complementary technologies augment the base platform for increased

---

[6]www.theguardian.com/technology/2016/oct/26/ddos-attack-dyn-mirai-botnet

performance, HSM[7] needs, functional safety, and real-time latency workloads. These technologies are outside the scope of this book, but details on these technologies can be found on the Intel web site.[8] Finally, although we provide a reasonable overview of the use cases, threats, and security objectives for the domains, the following coverage is not meant to be comprehensive, and to do so would require a much more exhaustive threat modeling exercise, with subsequent peer reviews, to refine the threat model and design for specific products.

Some Common Threats

Just as the domains share a common hardware and software security MVP, the domains have threats that are common across all vertical domains as well. These common threats are discussed in this section.

Device masquerading: A device employed or modified by a hacker is tricked to identify as a legitimate system on the IoT network. This sometimes can be extremely difficult to detect and rectify. The consequences and methods employed to launch such an attack depend upon the particular use case, and these idiosyncrasies are discussed next.

Boot integrity compromise: The pre-OS FW such as BIOS or other boot loaders can be tampered with by modifying or replacing/reprogramming the image on flash device. This can have serious consequences since all other layers in the stack are on the top of this layer in the bootstrapping sequence.

Offline storage–related attacks: Mass storage or any removable storage media can be attacked offline by copying the media or stealing the physical media device, and then sifting through the data to find secrets, or using brute force techniques on keys or passwords to reveal sensitive data.

---

[7]Hardware security module (HSM) for key storage and trusted cryptographic operations

[8]www.intel.com

Retail Solutions

The retail POS devices are becoming a part of the IoT domain, and increasingly these devices such as the POS terminals, mobile payments, and so on are connected to the Internet and accessed by cashiers and staff using tablets and other mobile devices. In this section, we'll discuss what is required to be Payment Card Industry (PCI) compliant on Intel platforms and a way to get there.

According to the PCI specification, the hackers are mainly interested in stealing the cardholder data. "By obtaining the Primary Account Number (PAN) and sensitive authentication data, a thief can impersonate the cardholder, use the card, and steal the cardholder's identity."

Sensitive cardholder data can be stolen from many places including a compromised card reader or data in a payment system database, snooping the store's wireless or wired networks. Each of these is a trust boundary, and the assets need to be protected as they traverse each boundary.

Securing the cardholder data starts where it is captured at the point of sale and as it flows into the payment system. The ideal approach is refraining from storing any cardholder data. The protection should span card readers, POS systems, networks and wireless access routers, payment card data storage and transmission, and online payment applications and shopping carts.

Not complying with PCI and the associated security objectives will result in potential liabilities including the following: customer base loses confidence and goes to other merchants resulting in decreased sales, additional cost of reissuing new payment cards, losses from fraud claims, higher incremental costs of compliance, legal costs, settlements and judgments, fines and penalties due to financial regulation violation, termination of ability to accept payment cards, lost jobs (C-suite security and other positions), and in the worst case going out of business.

The PCI Data Security Standard (DSS)[9] version 3.2.1 high-level overview is reproduced in Figure 6-3, and the Intel security assets that enable building a PCI compliant device are discussed.

PCI Data Security Standard – High Level Overview

Build and Maintain a Secure Network and Systems	1. Install and maintain a firewall configuration to protect cardholder data
	2. Do not use vendor-supplied defaults for system passwords and other security parameters
Protect Cardholder Data	3. Protect stored cardholder data
	4. Encrypt transmission of cardholder data across open, public networks
Maintain a Vulnerability Management Program	5. Protect all systems against malware and regularly update anti-virus software or programs
	6. Develop and maintain secure systems and applications
Implement Strong Access Control Measures	7. Restrict access to cardholder data by business need to know
	8. Identify and authenticate access to system components
	9. Restrict physical access to cardholder data
Regularly Monitor and Test Networks	10. Track and monitor all access to network resources and cardholder data
	11. Regularly test security systems and processes
Maintain an Information Security Policy	12. Maintain a policy that addresses information security for all personnel

Figure 6-3. *High-level overview of PCI Data Security Standard*

Security Objectives and Requirements

Assets in a retail IoT device include the following:

- Data at rest and in transit: Cardholders' data and transactional information.

- Identity of the consumer: Personally identifiable information (PII) should be stored under strict access control, preferably using encryption for data-at-rest.

- Identity of the POS device: Device's credentials are essential to mitigate the remote hacker attacks and to have a robust connection to the device cloud infrastructure.

---

[9]www.pcisecuritystandards.org/pci_security/

- The hardware components: The HW BOM list in the platform must always be protected via a transparent supply chain during production and deployment and guarded in the field as appropriate.

- The FW including pre-OS boot loader: The FW on the platform is a critical asset.

- Kernel and user mode SW components: The OS kernel and user mode SW components including applications are all important assets.

Threats

The PCI DSS standard has outlined high-level threat groups. Figure 6-4 takes those groups and extends it to include responsive retail. System compromise or theft can be realized by masquerading the retail POS device. Data at rest or data in transit can be stolen by leveraging offline data and network sniffers/monitors for traffic analysis. The provisioning step can be compromised or missed/blocked updates can be leveraged to compromise the system. Identity theft and credit card disclosure of payment information are equally important concerns. The retail advertisement terminals can be compromised to display graffiti or distorted images on digital bulletin boards. The runtime environment of a retail POS or another device can be infected with malware to do extensive persistent damage to the assets on the device and on the Cloud. The following bills from California State Legislature mandate provisioning a unique password and a device certificate for unique authentication before first use:

- California Senate Bill[10] No. 327, CHAPTER 886 TITLE 1.81.26. SECURITY OF CONNECTED DEVICES, 1798.91.04. (b) (1) and (2).

---

[10]http://leginfo.legislature.ca.gov/faces/billTextClient.
  xhtml?bill_id=201720180SB327

- California Assembly Bill[11] No. 1906, CHAPTER 860
  TITLE 1.81.26. SECURITY OF CONNECTED DEVICES,
  1798.91.04. (b) (1) and (2).

VIRUS/MALWARE

SYSTEM COMPROMISE OR THEFT

CONTENT GRAFFITI

DATA THEFT

IDENTITY THEFT

PROVISIONING/UPDATING

Figure 6-4. *Threat groups of retail segment including responsive retail*

The same threats can be mapped to a typical platform stack shown in Figure 6-5, and the mitigations using Intel technologies are also included. The HW layer includes all the relevant HW components including the System on Chip, storage, SRAM, scanner, communications modules, and so on. The stack continues upward with boot loader FW, OS Kernel to services to applications.

---

[11]https://leginfo.legislature.ca.gov/faces/billTextClient.
 xhtml?bill_id=201720180AB1906

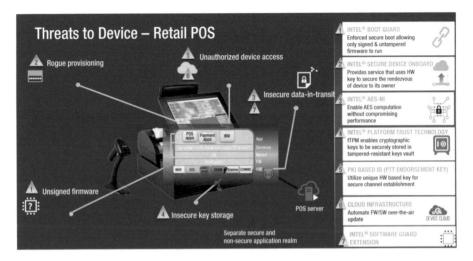

Figure 6-5. *Threats to Retail POS devices with mitigation using Intel HW security building blocks*

Threat #1: Allows hacker to easily break the integrity of the boot firmware and OS image. Hacker infiltrates the system by subverting execution flow. The mitigation is to implement Boot Guard as explained in Chapter 3 to establish a chain of trust based on a HW Root of Trust. When a FW is tampered and an attempt is made to boot with this unsigned FW, the Boot Guard will detect and will hold the device in reset to prevent further compromises of the sensitive assets.

Threat #2: Unauthorized actors could provision devices to their preferences including usernames, passwords, password reminders, and so on. The Intel Secure Device Onboarding technology could be leveraged to provision the device persona and force to change the default passwords with stricter ones and strong password reminders plus a dual factor authentication. Refer to Chapter 4 for details on SDO.

Threats #3, #7: Transaction data, logging to POS server. This is a critical threat for which an exploit could violate the P2PE requirements of PCI DSS where the cardholder's data could be obtained by hackers on the network. Intel AES technology in the CPU can be used to encrypt the cardholder's information to enforce confidentiality. To increase the robustness of this part of the solution, the encryption process can be done inside an SGX enclave to protect from ring 0 or rootkit attacks.

Threat #4: Leaves the cryptographic keys used to protect platform and owner secrets easily recovered or potentially retained in storage. This is once again a critical task to protect the keys used for encrypting the cardholders' data by storing the keys in a PTT/TPM so that these keys are never exposed to hackers.

Threats #5, #6: Weakness may grant remote hacker access to the device and in turn local network from any remote location. This is a powerful exploit, and mitigation requires strong device credentials such as the Endorsement Key in PTT/TPM to be authenticated by device cloud infrastructure without much manual intervention (to eliminate potential and expensive human errors). All the POS devices should have the firewall and intrusion detection systems implemented. The network routers both wired and wireless must have firewall and intrusion detection SW actively monitoring the network traffic for logging anomalies in real time and store the data for analytics SW. It is important to have analytics SW to mine these logs for patterns for zero-day or known vulnerabilities. A complete platform security stack built pertinent to retail Solutions with Intel security ingredients is shown in Figure 6-6.

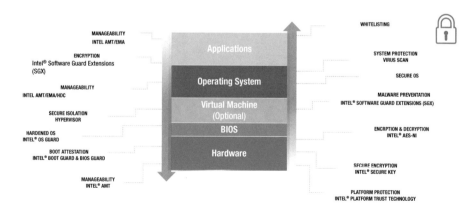

Figure 6-6. *Platform security stack built pertinent to Retail Solutions*

At the HW layer, the manageability with Intel Active Management Technology (AMT), secure boot with attestation, encryption, secure key, PTT/TPM, and platform protection are required to be implemented. UEFI/BIOS layer leverages the HW root of trust from Boot Guard and extends the chain of trust (transitive) to the upper layers in the stack. The hypervisor or VMM is optional; if present, it authenticates the VM pre-OS FW and the OS VMs while leveraging the VT HW capabilities to provide the necessary isolation between VMs. The OS is expected to be hardened by leveraging the Intel HW security features such as OS Guard for preventing ring 0 privilege escalation attacks, PTT for secure key storage, and AES and SHA New Instructions for performant crypto operations. The OS can also leverage the SGX for TEE applications and all the while enabling the in-band manageability features via Intel AMT. The application layer implements app whitelisting, virus/malware scanning, and so on.

The end-to-end data flow in a retail POS architecture is shown in Figure 6-7. The entities involved include the payment terminals, peripherals, the POS software inside an Intel-based platform, secure channels of communication, service provider data centers, bank gateway, and store servers.

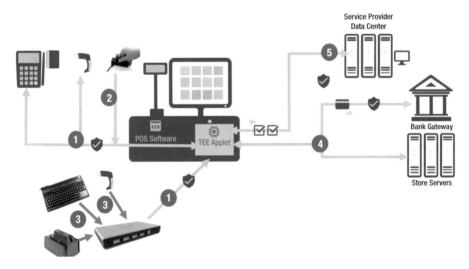

Figure 6-7. *The end-to-end data flow in a Retail POS architecture*

1. Native devices pair (cryptographically) directly with the applet for private/secure communications which involves mutual authentication via digital signatures and confidentiality through encryption/ decryption and integrity through sign/verify. Establish secure channels from peripherals and servers to process data through the TEE applet. The TEE applet could be an SGX application enclave running inside the TEE to protect the sensitive and valuable code and the data. This will prevent the exposure of credit card or other PII during processing in the memory since the memory contents are encrypted inline.

2. Legacy devices should encrypt the data to the applet using the Derived Unique Key Per Transaction (DUKPT) with AES-256. DUKPT is a method to manage the key between two endpoints; this key has properties: unique per transaction, symmetric, is a derived key from Base Derivation Key (BDK) known to both endpoints. This key is used in the AES algorithm for encryption and decryption. Currently Triple DES (TDES) is being used, but according to the guidance from NIST on Transitioning the Use of Cryptographic Algorithms and Key Lengths, two-key TDES is deprecated and three-key TDES should be used only for 2^{20} (64-bit) blocks and should not be used after 2023.[12]

---

[12]https://csrc.nist.gov/CSRC/media/Publications/sp/800-131a/rev-2/ draft/documents/sp800-131Ar2-draft.pdf

3. The Dock protects legacy insecure devices to the applet; sample devices include magnetic ink character recognition, keyboards, and barcode scanner. This Dock performs as a proxy for the legacy devices which inherently may be insecure and abstracts the devices by consuming the data in the clear and protecting it before sending to TEE applet.

4. Data can be encrypted for transmission to bank gateways or store servers. Use TEE applet to create a safe place to process transactions and enact policies.

5. Management servers manage policies and behavior of the system. Through a secure channel from a console to the applet, the provisioning of keys, credentials, and policies is performed. This helps in managing peripheral crypto keys and telemetry data remotely and enables pull requests to access transactions at the request of the retailer.

Design trade-offs: Considering the PCI standard and vectors, functional safety is not a primary factor, but security and privacy are the critical factors. As outlined in PCI DSS standard, the resiliency in terms of mitigating physical attack threats is also applicable where a card reader could be stolen and replace legitimate devices with fraudulent devices to steal the card data.

Standards – Regulatory and Industry

The PCI Digital Security Standard (PCI DSS) is one of the main standards that mandate most of the preceding security objectives. The PCI DSS also mandates FIPS 140-2 for secure storage of keys via a PTT/TPM.[13]

---

[13]www.pcisecuritystandards.org/pci_security/

Transportation Solutions[14]

The solutions in a vehicle can be grouped into Software-Defined Cockpit (SDC) as shown in Figure 6-8. Intel Silicon and solutions enable building SDC applications for the next generation of advanced automotive electronics. The SDC itself can be subdivided into rear seat entertainment, digital instrument cluster, in-vehicle infotainment, and advanced driver-assistance system (ADAS). The rear seat entertainment solutions include a DVD/Blu-ray player, virtual office, and connection to IVI front system and mobile devices with Cloud connectivity.

The digital instrument cluster unit includes display for speed, fuel level, odometer, trips, and so on. This cluster may also be able to project images on the windshield (heads-up display) with alerts for low fuel or low tire pressure via tire pressure monitoring system (TPMS).

The in-vehicle infotainment (IVI) unit includes the GPS-based navigation system, audio/video entertainment systems, and connection to mobile devices for phone communication and music with voice recognition features. This unit also includes a backup camera and cameras for parking assist. The unit may include gesture or touch inputs.

The advanced driver-assistance system (ADAS) is a complex system of systems with features including blind spot monitoring, adaptive cruise control, lane departure warning, cross traffic warning, brake assist and collision avoidance, self-parking, and driver monitoring for fatigue or undesirable distractions.

---

[14]Credit: David Zage, Platform Solutions Architect from TSD for domain expertise and the content.

In Vehicle Experience Solutions

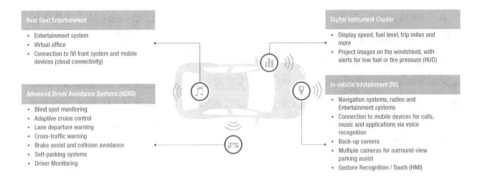

Figure 6-8. *Software-Defined Cockpit – in-vehicle experience solutions*

Connected Vehicle Infrastructure

As the vehicles start communicating with the external environment spanning more than just the Cloud, many IoT-related threats become pertinent. In Figure 6-9, the vehicle communicates with many clusters including GPS systems, Vehicle-to-vehicle (V2V) network, local repair shop or dealership network, roadside assistance network, mobile devices, Radio Data Systems, and Internet backbone via Internet service provider (ISP) through 4G/5G wireless. Some of these network clusters such as repair shops and roadside assistance may also connect to the Internet backbone.

The devices in a car communicate with different external entities in regular and autonomous driving applications:

- Vehicle to vehicle (V2V): These communications are occurring in real time between vehicles on the roads.

- Vehicle to infrastructure (V2I): These communications are occurring between the vehicle and the infrastructure such as dealership or an auto body shop or a traffic management system.

- Vehicle to device (V2D): These communications are occurring between a vehicle and a device such as smartphone over Bluetooth, remote control key, wireless diagnostics device, and so on.

- Vehicle to Cloud (V2C): These communications are occurring between a vehicle and a private or a public cloud to retrieve or upload the recent traffic/weather updates via GPS and Radio Data interfaces.

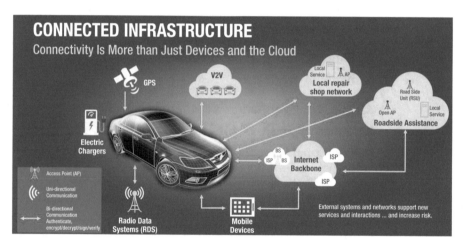

Figure 6-9. *Connected vehicle infrastructure – more than just devices and Cloud*

Security Objectives and Requirements

- Each electronic control unit (ECU) in the connected vehicle is expected to have the following security attributes:

  - A unique, hardware-based ID that's immutable and standards compliant

  - Capability for mutual authentication

  - A HW root of trust

- Protected Boot (verified and measured)

- Secure storage for key material

- Tamper detection, prevention, and policy enforcement

- A Trusted Execution Environment

- All intra-car information has the *option* of integrity (hash, HMAC), confidentiality (encryption), authentication (digital signatures), and nonrepudiation (digital signatures).

  - All data pertaining to users/occupants is encrypted to maintain privacy.

  - All inter-car information is authenticated and has integrity (hash, HMAC) and confidentiality (encryption).

  - Near real-time, secure over-the-air updates for SW and FW.

- All safety-critical operations are partitioned; other services are virtualized for both efficiency and security.

- Car network

  - Runs Anomaly Detection SW on the device and the gateway within the vehicle for detecting known and zero-day vulnerabilities. This SW could also connect to a Threat Intelligence database on the Cloud for cross-referencing the signatures for quantifying and classifying against known viruses and malware signatures/patterns.

  - Provides whitelisting for identities allowed to authenticate and send data externally

Threats

With the preceding security objectives in the context, let's discuss the attacker profiles, threat surfaces, and specific threats. Figure 6-10 depicts five attacker profiles with diverse technical knowledge, access levels, and goals. A car thief possesses varied technical knowledge with wireless and/or physical access with a goal of stealing the car which may entail disabling the alarm and jumping the wires to start the car and drive off. A car thief may employ remote attacks through Telematics Control Unit (TCU)/IVI and On-Board Diagnostics (e.g., On-Board Diagnostics (OBD-II) routinely accessed during service or tuning in the clear).

A hacker may possess medium to high technical knowledge with a remote/wireless access and may operate with goals to either get fame or steal any PII including passwords to music, credit card payment information, and so on. A hacker may employ device masquerading and launch remote attacks through Telematics Control Unit (TCU)/IVI. A hacker may also go after information disclosure of third-party algorithm/IP.

A criminal may possess medium to very high technical knowledge with wireless and/or physical access with an intent to harm the passengers and the bystanders. A criminal may employ remote attacks through Telematics Control Unit (TCU)/IVI and On-Board Diagnostics (e.g., OBD-II).

A workshop technician may possess medium to very high technical knowledge with physical access and will operate with a goal to modify the settings such as rewinding the odometer, fuel usage/statistics, and so on by leveraging the On-Board Diagnostics (e.g., OBD-II). A similar attack profile is where a persistent vehicle alteration is done by a legitimate user to modify the original design by either increasing the performance, jailbreaking, customizing the user interface, adding new regions into DVD/Blu-ray player, and so on.

A counterfeiter or a competitor may possess high to very high technical knowledge with physical access and may wish to study the design/ architecture to reverse engineer and steal Intellectual Property or clone the device. This attacker has physical access to the device in a laboratory environment with access to sophisticated tools/logic analyzers, IR/ thermal scanning, differential power analysis, and so on to monitor the vehicle networking bus traffic using On-Board Diagnostics (e.g., OBD-II) interfaces. The potential assets to be recovered could be intellectual property spanning Silicon, board-level HW, FW, and OS-level ingredients.

Attacker	Technical Knowledge	Access	Goal
Car-thief	Varied	Wireless/Physical	Steal car
Hacker	Medium - High	Wireless	Fame
Criminal	Medium - Very high	Wireless/Physical	Harm passengers
Workshop/tuner	Medium - Very high	Physical	Modify settings
Counterfeiter/ competitor	High - Very high	Physical	Study architecture

Figure 6-10. *Attacker profiles in the Transportation Solutions domain*

Automotive Threat Surfaces: Refer to Figure 6-11 for distinct hackable areas in a vehicle. These areas can be organized into three groups, physical access, in-vehicle network structure, and wireless/remote access to the vehicle.

Physical access

- On-Board Diagnostics (e.g., OBD-II routinely accessed during service or tuning in the clear)

- Entertainment media (e.g., DVD, USB, etc.)

- Access to ECUs

- External sensors (vision, acoustic, radar, LIDAR, etc.)

In-vehicle network structure

- Connections to OBD-II

- Vehicle networking bus (CAN, KLINE, MOST, Ethernet AVB, etc.) connections to various ECUs

Wireless access to vehicle

- Keyless entry

- Bluetooth and Bluetooth-connected devices

- TPMS

- Cellular, Internet, and applications (V2X)

- Radio/audio system(s)

- Remote telematics

Figure 6-11. *Distinct hackable areas in a vehicle*

Mitigations

Mitigating the preceding threats would require a defense in depth approach as shown in Figure 6-12, beginning with securing the vehicle systems and followed by securing the communications:

Securing the vehicle systems includes the following assets:

- Sensors and actuators: All the sensors and actuators must be authenticated (digital signatures) before communicating and protect the integrity (sign/verify using SHA3) and confidentiality (using AES-256) of the valuable data on the bus interfaces.

- Computer vision and AI (path planning): The machine learning or deep learning assets such as the weights, training data, test/validation data, models, and so on must be protected by encrypting the assets on the storage and decrypting into the memory in a TEE. The details for this architecture are outside the scope of this book.

- Networks and ECUs: The networks and any gateways must have firewalls and intrusion detection systems, and the ECUs must be securely booted and deploy the HW security building blocks as listed here.

Securing communications:

- Vehicle to everything (V2X): All the devices on the V2X interfaces must be mutually authenticated (using digital signatures) before communicating and protect the integrity (sign/verify using SHA3) and confidentiality (using AES-256) of the valuable data on the bus interfaces.

- Maps, code, and data to/from the Cloud: The maps database and access to online databases must be authenticated and authorized via digital signatures and login credentials. Any data exchange with the Cloud must also be subjected to the same protections.

- Infotainment, mobile devices, wearables: The infotainment devices and mobile devices including wearables/smartphones/others must be mutually authenticated (digital signatures) before communicating and protect the integrity (sign/verify using SHA3) and confidentiality (using AES-256) of the valuable data on the bus interfaces

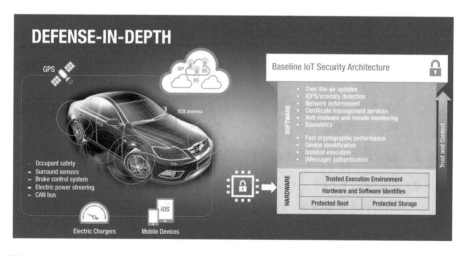

Figure 6-12. *Defense in depth architecture*

The threats explained earlier can be effectively mitigated by leveraging the Intel HW security building blocks shown in Figure 6-13. The boot integrity of the automotive systems can be secured with protected boot (verified and measured boot). The protected storage feature can be leveraged to store the keys securely and perform low bandwidth

439

encryption/decryption and sign/verify of the message data. For higher robustness and high bandwidth use cases, the authentication of data whether it is messages or others can be achieved in the TEE such as SGX by invoking SHA-NI in the CPU instruction set.

Hardware security building blocks:

1. Unique Device ID using PKI compliant keys/ certificates via PTT/TPM.

2. True RNG using the RNG instructions in the CPU. With reasonably good entropy to be used as a nonce or a seed for subsequent key generation.

3. Verified boot using Boot Guard to ensure a HW Root of Trust and a robust transient chain of trust.

4. Secure storage using PTT/TPM for both data and keys.

5. Trusted Execution Environment using SGX.

6. Cryptographic acceleration using AES and SHA new instructions.

7. Key generation using PTT/TPM for application keys.

8. Secure clock using tamper-resistant HW supplied timers for precise logging of retail transactions.

9. Monotonic counters – HW supplied and tamper-resistant counters that are guaranteed to increment only.

10. Secure debug for locking/disabling the debug ports at the factory and ability to unlock/enable to securely debug.

11. Physical tamper detection and protection against side-channel attacks.

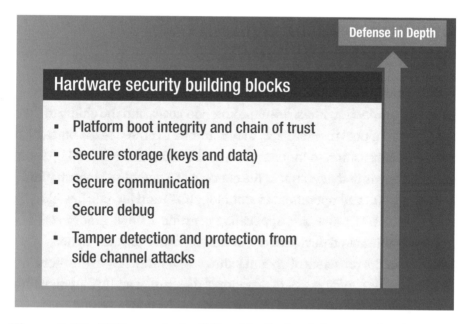

Figure 6-13. *HW security building blocks for defense in depth*

Design trade-offs: For the Transportation Solutions domain, functional safety, security, privacy, and resiliency are all pertinent. The automobiles have a long life and are safety/life critical by design; it is essential to integrate safety and security to prevent false positives and false negatives from functional safety infrastructure. There is also a need for the automobiles to detect the physical tamper and send a "kill pill" to the platform to trigger a lockdown of the security engine and vault the secrets to avoid unauthorized disclosure. This is critical so that Break Once Run Everywhere (BORE) attacks to retrieve the universal keys are mitigated.

Standards – Regulatory and Industry

The SAE J3101 is one of the main government regulations that mandate most of the preceding security objectives. FIPS 140-2 L2/3 and NHTSA are also considered vital for the US markets.

Industrial Control System (ICS) and Industrial IoT (IIoT)

As the manufacturers and producers seek to respond to greater pressures for higher production rates, lower production costs, and the ability to compete in a global marketplace, they continue to embrace the efficiencies created by a transition to Industry 4.0 and the Industrial IoT (IIoT). These are broad terms that encompass the concept of a combined information technology (IT) and operational technology (OT) and include flexible automation of OT processes, application of artificial intelligence to OT problems, automated device and process orchestration, and higher resiliency in the presence of system failures, to name a few of the more prevalent topics. In Figure 6-14, a notional diagram of an IIoT architecture is portrayed for the purpose of identifying security concerns and discussing threats and security objectives.

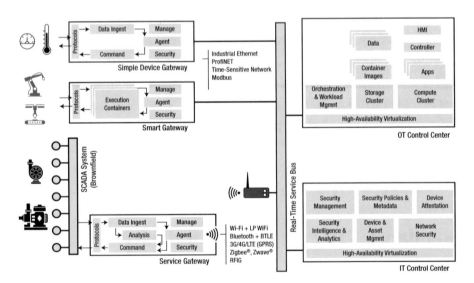

Figure 6-14. *Notional Industrial IoT architecture*

This architecture in Figure 6-14 is notional because it is not created from any actual deployment nor is it intended to portray a particular type of industrial plant. Instead it depicts different types of components in an industrial setting that are typical of the devices Intel produces or contributes components for in the IIoT. The notional diagram depicts an *Edge-to-Cloud* and a *SCADA-to-Edge-to-Cloud* architecture. On the left side of the diagram are various gateways that control devices. Simple devices such as meters, tank levels, temperature sensors, and vibration sensors can be controlled using a simple gateway. These gateways may control many such devices simultaneously. More complex devices such as industrial robots or CNC machines require more advanced smart gateways. These devices have the ability to load different types of control programs and workloads and may include real-time control loops that encompass line and human safety protocols. Finally, existing systems also need connectivity to the back-end IIoT systems and are connected through a service gateway that supports existing protocols and may translate those data elements into different forms to be carried in newer protocols and reformatted messages. All three types of gateways may be connected by various communications technologies including wired and wireless technology.

The back-end systems are still logically segmented into OT and IT concerns, though in the IIoT they may share some physical computing devices and servers. OT control is focused on orchestration and workload management and providing clear visibility of the systems and operations to OT engineers.

Security Objectives and Requirements

Assets in the IIoT gateways are included in the following security objectives, where sub-bullets are security objectives derived from top-level security objectives. These objectives are aligned with the IIC.[15]

---

[15]Industrial Internet Consortium. *Industrial Internet of Things Volume G4: Security Framework*. September 2016. www.iiconsortium.org/white-papers.htm

- **Data at rest and in transit**: All commands received by the gateway from the OT/IT control centers must be protected from modification (integrity), duplication (replay), and optionally disclosure (confidentiality).

- **Identity of the device**: All devices shall maintain at least one identity public and private key pair used to uniquely identify the device to other entities.

- **Identity of the control authority**: All commands received by the gateway from the OT/IT control centers must be verified as authentic by comparing the signing public key with authorized trust anchor keys. This security objective and the previous one imply the following derived security objective to address trust anchors and identity keys.

  - **Protection of trust anchors and identity keys**: All identity keys and trust anchors must be securely stored in the gateway to prevent use by unauthorized software processes/users. A trust anchor key is a public key of an entity (like the OT control center) that is inherently trusted by the device; an identity key is a public and private key pair that is used to prove the device's identity to other entities. Protection of identity keys should include limiting the use of the identity key to a RoT (see Chapter 3).

- **Integrity of the boot system and operating system**: Verification of boot firmware and software, with secure storage of trusted measurements collected during boot, shall be enforced at every soft and hard boot event.

- **Trusted reporting of device health**: Devices shall be capable of reporting their current health including measurements from their last boot cycle and any software or firmware updates performed since their last boot. This reporting must include a proof of origin signature that unambiguously attests to the source of the report (Root of Trust for Reporting) and all claimants producing data for the report (Root of Trust for Measurement).

- **Verification of software updates, configuration, and workloads**: All updates to the device shall come from an authorized source verified against one of the device's trust anchors; updates shall be protected from modification (integrity) and verified by the device prior to first use that the update has not been corrupted. Updates include new or updated software and firmware, configuration files, and workloads.

- **Whitelisting of applications and network endpoints**: Devices shall maintain a whitelist of authorized software and the identity and address of network endpoints that are authorized to communicate with the device, and the device shall prevent the execution of any software not on the whitelist and ignore/terminate any communication streams from network endpoints not on the whitelist.

- **Management of connected peripherals**: Devices shall maintain a whitelist and authorized configuration of all connected peripherals, whether wired or wirelessly connected to the device, and ignore or disconnect any peripherals not authorized to be connected with the device.

- **Storage integrity**: Devices shall maintain the integrity of stored elements including software, configuration files, workloads, data measurements, and processing logs; devices shall prevent unauthorized access to stored elements.

Design trade-offs: Industrial systems are designed specifically for harsh environments and for interoperability with existing systems and devices. Requirements around these constraints dominate the design decisions. Oftentimes, this means removing security protections, like encryption, because end systems cannot perform those security functions or intermediary systems are dependent on receiving this data unencrypted and do not have the capability to add this layer of protection. In addition, industrial type systems tend to require low power profiles, either because they are deployed in a remote location (oil pumping station) with limited power capabilities or crowded together in a small space where heat from power dissipation is considered a problem. In both cases, lower powered devices tend to have fewer security capabilities. The important trade-off in these cases is to support security features that address the most critical threat – identification of proper control authorities using protected trust anchors for authentication of commands, configuration, and software update.

Threats

The threats to IIoT systems are composed of both external threat actors and insiders. Both groups can mount destructive attacks on IIoT systems, though most threat analysis focuses on external attackers. Figure 6-15 identifies the primary threats and consequences.

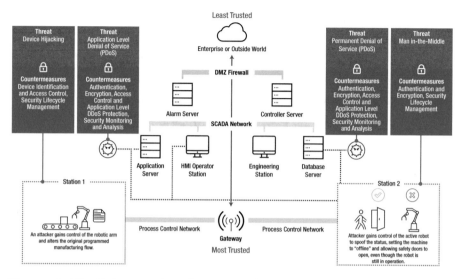

Figure 6-15. *Primary IIoT threats and consequences*[16]

Threat #1: Device hijacking – An attacker uses vulnerabilities in the device software to inject their own software or firmware on the device and corrupt data, stop executing processes, falsify health or data reporting, or disrupt the industrial operations flow.

- Mitigation: Use of advanced containment techniques to isolate software, including virtualization, containers, and TEEs. Ability to restart workloads or execute workloads as microservices limits the attack surface and time an attack can be active.

Threat #2: Device masquerading – An attacker creates a digital twin of the real device and intercepts or copies data to discover proprietary information or to deny the real device access to important information, commands, or workloads.

---

[16]Diagram from `www.rambus.com/iot/industrial-iot/`

- Mitigation: Device identity and mutual authentication for all communications flows from the OT/IT center are vital to prevent these attacks. Physical and logical protection of the device's identity credentials prevents an adversary from stealing credentials. Storage of a device's unique identity credentials within a TEE is required to prevent the use of a digital twin to masquerade as the real device.

Threat #3: Application-level data tampering and denial of service – An attacker uses metadata spoofing or replay, SQL injection attacks, or resource exhaustion attacks to trick a device into performing an improper action or creating a temporary DoS attack on the device.

- Mitigation: End-to-end authentication of all command flows and proper whitelisting of network endpoints are critical to preventing such attacks. Recognizing and responding to DoS and DDoS network attacks requires network infrastructure and the ability to reconfigure network components to isolate and quarantine misbehaving devices.

Threat #4: Permanent denial of service (PDoS) attacks – An attacker is able to inject a firmware update or critical operating system update that damages the hardware of the device or takes the device offline requiring depot-level service to repair the device.

- Mitigation: All updates and changes to the device require an authorized command from the OT that is cryptographically verified from a secured trust anchor on the device. Device management agents with privileged capabilities on the device must not also have direct network capability, in order to reduce network attacks that also give attackers elevated privileges on the device, because such elevated privileges allow an attacker to perform actions that can modify the base firmware and software on the device.

Threat #5: Tampering and information disclosure of OT data – An attacker modifies or collects data flowing between the OT center and a device, exposing proprietary data.

- Mitigation: All data between the OT/IT centers and the device should include confidentiality protection (end-to-end security), but minimally must include integrity protections.

Standards – Regulatory and Industry

There is not one standard that defines the Industrial IoT (IIoT), and within different segments of the industrial industry there are different regulatory or standards groups provide specific guidance and direction. It is not possible to cover all of these groups here. Generally, standards and industry groups attempt to create a set of interoperable frameworks and middleware, along with connectivity and data or protocol standards that enable the creation of heterogeneous system of systems to enable the IIoT. Figure 6-16 provides an overview of the major standards influencing Intel designs.

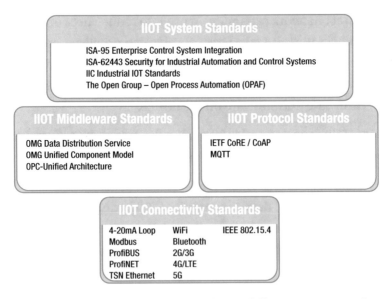

Figure 6-16. *Common IIoT standards, middleware, protocols, and connectivity standards*

Digital Surveillance System

Information security in digital surveillance systems (DSS) became a public problem in 2015 and 2016, culminating in the Mirai DDoS attacks, the largest botnet-based distributed denial of service attacks ever at that time in which two separate attacks took Akamai and Dyn (and all their customers) offline for hours. Because surveillance devices often need to be accessible over the Internet, not to mention that the industry moved only recently from analog interconnections to digital IP interconnections, information security is a new problem for the DSS segment. What can compound this problem is the industry is a physical security–driven industry (as opposed to IT driven), and the industry's expertise in cybersecurity for surveillance systems has lagged the general Internet cybersecurity awareness.

The DSS segment spans more than just traditional building surveillance and closed-circuit TV (CCTV) systems. DSS includes mobile surveillance around vehicles and human beings, including vehicular cameras and emergency response body camera systems. And extending beyond simple surveillance, DSS includes the use of camera systems in smart cities for intelligent traffic control and smart toll collection systems. As briefly discussed in the last section, the use of camera systems in retail can aid a business in understanding customer experiences in brick-and-mortar retail establishments, adding extending information to the business intelligence systems that improve customer experience, inform decisions on product placement, and aid the design of store layout. As usage of these DSS systems increase, the opportunity for a repeat of the attacks like Mirai, Persirai,[17] Devil's Ivy,[18] and Peekaboo[19] can become more of a threat. Intel®'s robust hardware-based integrated security provides a capability stack which improves system security.

---

[17]Trend Micro. May 9, 2017. Persirai: New Internet of Things (IoT) Botnet Targets IP Cameras. `https://blog.trendmicro.com/trendlabs-security-intelligence/persirai-new-internet-things-iot-botnet-targets-ip-cameras/`

[18]Senrio. July 18, 2017. Devil's Ivy: Flaw in Widely Used Third-Party Code Impacts Millions. `https://blog.senr.io/blog/devils-ivy-flaw-in-widely-used-third-party-code-impacts-millions`

[19]Threatpost. September 17, 2018. Zero-Day Bug Allows Hackers to Access CCTV Surveillance Cameras. `https://threatpost.com/zero-day-bug-allows-hackers-to-access-cctv-surveillance-cameras/137499/`

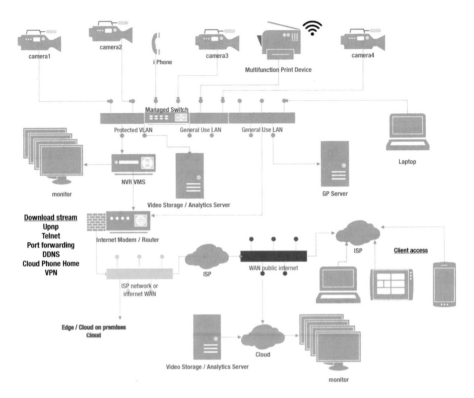

Figure 6-17. *Digital Surveillance System (DSS) typical network architecture*

In Figure 6-17, the network architecture of a typical DSS system is portrayed. Video flows from the camera to a managed switch where many devices may actually be connected, including other servers and individual laptops. The video data is typically separated from other traffic on the managed switch via a protected VLAN. This does not encrypt or otherwise protect the traffic or video streams, it merely creates a different logical segment on the network reserved only for video traffic. Depending on the type of managed switch, this may not present much difficulty for an attacker to overcome. Besides the cameras, a network video recorder (NVR) video management system (VMS) is also connected to the managed switch. This system enables the recording of multiple video streams to a storage array. There is typically a local storage array also connected to the managed switch on the VLAN, but a remote storage array in the Cloud provides long-term storage. This means that the NVR VMS and the local storage device are involved in uploading the video streams to the Cloud. Viewing of the video streams may be done locally, off the NVR VMS system, or remotely. Remote access may be enabled to the NVR VMS system, or more may be provided only from the Cloud, depending on the network security at the local installation and the security features enabled on the NVR VMS.[20]

From the network architecture in Figure 6-17, it is also seen that input to the NVR VMS may come from devices other than video cameras. Multifunction print devices are capable of capturing scanned images and using the NVR VMS to store those images for the user. Additionally, a phone can be used to pipe in multimedia including audio only, audio and video, or other encoded streams as a download service (where the phone is acting as a modem) and supply those inputs to the NVR VMS. These input streams are important to understand in the overall DSS segment, since maintaining security for devices other than IP cameras needs to be incorporated into the network security, monitoring, and patch update systems.

The Cloud segment of the DSS system includes analytics and advanced artificial intelligence (AI) algorithms used to process media files (audio, video, and still image) and collect data or file/index media according to criteria. This section does not address cloud security concerns, which must be properly accounted for in any DSS system. Cloud security is adequately addressed by other resources.

---

[20]Credit: Jody Booth, Platform Solutions Architect, DSS team, IOTG, Intel – source of DSS Network Architecture diagram

Security Objectives and Requirements

Using Figure 6-17 as the target for security analysis, the DSS segment includes the following security objectives, which focus on the primary video and audio assets in the system:

- **Data at rest and in transit**: All incoming data streams received by the NVR VMS from the managed switch must be protected from modification (integrity), duplication (replay), and disclosure (confidentiality).

- **Identity of the device**: All devices attached to the managed switch should be uniquely identified; the use of MAC addresses is not considered secure as these can be spoofed by a network adversary. Devices should maintain at least one identity public and private key pair used to uniquely identify the device to other entities and used to set up protected (integrity protected) streams to the NVR VMS.

- **Integrity of the boot system and operating system**: Verification of boot firmware and software, with secure storage of trusted measurements collected during boot, shall be enforced at every soft and hard boot event for all elements of the system, including peripherals connected to the managed switch, the NVR VMS, and the local storage array.

- **Trusted reporting of device health**: Devices shall be capable of reporting their current health including measurements from their last boot cycle and any software or firmware updates performed since their last boot. This reporting must include a proof of origin signature that unambiguously attests to the source of the report (Root of Trust for Reporting) and all claimants producing data for the report (Root of Trust for Measurement). This reporting should be collected by the NVR VMS system when devices connect to record/store their multimedia streams.

- **Verification of software updates, configuration, and workloads**: All updates to the device shall come from an authorized source verified against one of the device's trust anchors; updates shall be protected from modification (integrity) and verified by the device prior to first use that the update has not been corrupted. Updates include new or updated software, firmware, and configuration files.

- **Whitelisting of network endpoints**: Devices shall maintain a whitelist of authorized network endpoints that are authorized to communicate with the device, and the device shall ignore/terminate any communication streams from network endpoints not on the whitelist.

- **Management of connected peripherals**: The managed switch shall maintain a whitelist of all connected peripherals, whether wired or wirelessly connected to the switch, and ignore or disconnect any peripherals not authorized to be connected with the device. Authentication of connected devices should be performed via cryptographic credentials, not merely MAC or IP addresses which can be spoofed.

- **Storage integrity**: Devices shall maintain the integrity of stored elements including media streams, media metadata, software, configuration files, and processing logs; devices shall prevent unauthorized access to stored elements. Particular care must be taken to protect private keys and symmetric encryption

keys that are used for signatures, in transit data
confidentiality and integrity or storage confidentiality
and integrity. Many systems are required to
produce evidence (surveillance videos, body cams,
vehicle cams) and this evidence must provide
cryptographically assured provenance of the media
files and the media file's metadata which ensures those
data items are free from tampering. This protection
is paramount to support legally binding evidentiary
claims for authenticity and originating source.

Design trade-offs: DSS systems, especially the end collection devices
(cameras and audio recorders), are extremely cost sensitive, yet must
compete on the ability to collect data in various formats and transmit that
data over the network. Those two primary goals translate to specialized
hardware capabilities. But the end devices must also operate on very
limited power budgets, not unlike the industrial systems, and therefore
design trade-offs tend to remove the majority of the security features.
Based on the history of attacks these systems have encountered, protection
of the software running on these devices are most important. Protected
trust anchors that authenticate control authorities and authorize firmware
and software updates have the most effect on maintaining security for
these devices. Back-end infrastructure, such as the video recorders,
control systems, and storage arrays, are normally standard off-the-shelf
server class devices that can utilize the full suite of hardware and software
protections available on the commercial market.

Threats

Threats to DSS systems are primarily from outside network adversaries.
However, from some systems, privileged insiders may need to be included in
the threat analysis, especially when such DSS systems are used for building
or other surveillance, and a privileged insider can be coerced, bribed,

or forced to delete or modify evidence captured by the NVR VMS. Stolen credentials can also make a network outsider appear to be an authorized insider. The following threats should be considered in any DSS system:

Threat #1: Device hijacking – An attacker uses weak authentication credentials (Mirai attack) to take control of a peripheral device on the DSS system; or an attacker uses vulnerabilities in the peripheral device software (Devil's Ivy or Perisai attacks) to inject their own software or firmware on the device and stop media capture, falsify metadata, or misuse the device computing power to perform other actions (mine for Bitcoin, perform a DDoS attack).

- Mitigation #1: Device credentials must be changed prior to installation and fielding of devices. Intel's Secure Device Onboarding protocol provides a fast and secure mechanism to provision devices with new credentials and configuration without requiring specialized or highly skilled system installation crews. Devices must never have default credentials or default management logins. Inspection of open ports and SNMP capabilities are required to ensure no unauthenticated or easily guessable password credentials are available to an attacker.

- Mitigation #2: Although this threat is virtually the same as seen in other segments, the mitigation requirements due to power limitations and smaller compute often prevent using TEEs or software containers to prevent or limit the impact of compromised software. Frequent health checks on the device firmware are required to monitor for any potential zero-day attacks, and response to firmware corruption requires signed updates using a hardware root-of-trust (RoT) that cannot be modified by an attacker, even one that replaces the firmware through physical attack. Careful thought and study of recent attacks (Devil's Ivy and Perisai) must be done.

Threat #2: Device masquerading – An attacker creates a digital twin of the real device and jams or blocks transmission from the real device to inject false media streams into the system.

- Mitigation: Device identity must be used to set up mutually authenticated streams from the collection peripherals to the NVR VMS system; additionally the managed switch should perform access control on all connected devices. Physical and logical protection of the device's identity credentials prevents an adversary from stealing credentials and creating an evil digital twin. Storage of a device's unique identity credentials within a TEE is required to prevent the use of a digital twin to masquerade as the real device.

Threat #3: Permanent denial of service (PDoS) attacks – An attacker is able to inject a firmware update or critical operating system update that damages the hardware of the device or takes the device offline requiring depot-level service to repair the device.

- Mitigation: All updates and changes to the device require a signed update package that cryptographically verifies against a secured trust anchor on the device. No changes to the software, and especially the firmware, can be made without a signed package update command that comes from a trusted, authenticated source. Additionally, software and firmware updates must be protected against rollback attacks, where an adversary installs validly signed but older software versions that install an old security vulnerability onto the device. Rollback attacks must be prevented by using a protected value to store the software version number for the currently installed software/firmware, and this must be verified against the integrity-protected software version found in the signed software update package.

Threat #4: Unauthorized access to surveillance data – An attacker gains access to surveillance footage that includes private or confidential information to which that attacker should not have access.

- Mitigation: Proper access control for all surveillance footage is required. Best practice is to encrypt such footage and provide access control on the cryptographic keys. This ensures that all copies of the footage are equally protected, including backups. This of course shifts the burden of access control to the keys themselves. Proper key storage should include hardware-based protection with two-factor authentication to access the keys. Since backups are encrypted, the backup storage of keys becomes an issue. Having cold or warm sites with hardware security modules (HSM) that are unlocked with smartcards or other hardware tokens is best practice.

Standards – Regulatory and Industry

There are two primary industry standards organized around IP cameras and DSS: ONVIF and PSIA.[21] ONVIF (Open Network Video Interface Forum) was formed in 2008 as a nonprofit industry organization to define an interoperable interface standard for IP cameras allowing better interoperability between different manufacturers. ONVIF was originally formed by Axis Communications, Bosch Security Systems, and Sony Corp, but now has over 480 members. ONVIF has defined four profiles for video cameras (Profiles S, G, Q, and T)[22]; however, as shown in Figure 6-18, necessary security features are not yet mandatory in many profiles.

---

[21]IFSEC Global. 2014, November 23. ONVIF and PSIA: Guide to Standards in Video Surveillance. `www.ifsecglobal.com/video-surveillance/guide-to-standards-in-video-surveillance-onvif-v-psia/`

[22]Profile categories C and A are reserved for access control devices, like door locks.

Features		Profiles											
		G		Q		S		T		C		A	
		Device	Client	Device	Client	Device	Client	Device	Client	Device	Client	Device	Client
General													
System Settings		M	C	M	C	M	C	M	C	M	C	M	C
User Authentication	WS-Username Token					M	M						
	Digest Authentication	M	M	M	M	O	M	M	M	M	M	M	M
User Handling		M	C	M	M	M	C	M	C	M	C	M	M
Query Services and Capabilities		M	M	M	M	M	M	M	M	M	M	M	M
Device Discovery		M	C	M	M	M	C	M	M	M	C	M	M
Default Access Policy						M							
Network Configuration		M	C	M	C	M	C	M	M	M	M	M	C
Zero Configuration				C	C	C	C						
Firmware Upgrade				C	C								
Backup and Restore				C	C								
TLS Configuration				C	C								
IP Address Filtering						C	C			C	C		
NTP						C	C	C	C	M	C		
Automatic IP Assignment				C	C								
Media Profile Configuration						M	C	M	C				
Media Transport	RTP/UDP	M	M			M		M					
	RTP/RTSP/HTTP/TCP	M	M			M		M					
							M¹		M¹				
	RTP/RTSP/HTTPS/TCP	C	C							C	C		
	RTP/RTSP/TCP/WebSocket									C	O		
	RTP/UDP Multicast					C	C	M	C				

Figure 6-18. *ONVIF general requirements by profile category*[23]

PSIA (Physical Security Interoperability Alliance) is another industry consortium formed in 2008 covering the interoperability of IP media devices, recording and content management for recorders and video analytics.[24] PSIA was founded by 20 member companies including Honeywell, GE Security, and Cisco, but adoption under this specification

---

[23]ONVIF. (2018). ONVIF Overview. www.onvif.org/wp-content/uploads/2018/10/ONVIF_Profile_Feature_overview_v2-2.pdf

[24]Honeywell. (2014). IP Video Standards. www.security.honeywell.com/-/media//Security/Resources/PDF/News%20and%20events/White%20papers/IP_Video_Standards%20pdf

has stalled with the last publication from this body in 2010. Although there are still many cameras and devices on the market carrying PSIA compliance, PSIA is not considered a leading force in the industry.

Of all the driving forces for security in IP cameras, GDPR and the California Data Privacy Law in the United States are the main concerns. According to the European Data Protection Supervisor (EDPS),[25] surveillance footage can be used to identify people directly or indirectly and therefore falls within the GDPR regulations. The EDPS provides guidelines[26] to maintain compliance in digital surveillance systems, and much of this guidance focuses on policy, proper notifications through signage, and careful site planning and configuration. EDPS recommended protections cover data in transit (prevent transmissions from interception), data at rest (restriction on access to stored media, including backups), and access control, but these controls must follow the recommendations resulting from a threat analysis. Of all these issues, access control becomes the most difficult and requires good key management that is based in hardware-protected key storage and roots-of-trust. Compliance with the California law should follow similar guidance.

HIPAA (Health Insurance Portability and Accountability Act) may also be applicable in the medical field, relating to building surveillance systems used in hospitals and medical facilities, which must comply with the added burden of inference correlation between a person captured in a video feed within a medical facility and a person's medical treatment privacy.

---

[25]https://edps.europa.eu/data-protection/data-protection/
reference-library/video-surveillance_en
[26]https://edps.europa.eu/sites/edp/files/publication/10-03-17_video-
surveillance_guidelines_en.pdf

Summary

IoT security in the current fragmented ecosystem requires a completely different mindset. This includes leveraging the common Intel security building blocks and accelerators such as Movidius and Intel (Altera) FPGA solutions. It is feasible to maintain a baseline of security capabilities and add the domain-specific features on the top to make the security solution complete for deployment. In some cases, the solution may include a heterogeneous architecture with assets from Intel SoC and accelerators such as FPGA/Movidius. We have seen how the retail Solution domain is influenced by the PCI DSS standard and how this standard can be met with compliance on Intel product–based devices. We have also seen how the Transportation Solutions domain is changing with the connected vehicle concept and the plethora of threats looming over this domain. The specific requirements of TSD can be met using Intel security technologies. Industrial and Digital Surveillance System have their unique robustness and mandatory standards for compliance. Only a subset of IoT verticals are covered in this chapter, but most of these concepts apply readily to the medical field, gaming, print imaging, and so on.

APPENDIX

Conclusion

The world's most massive living organism[1] is named *Pando,* Latin for "I spread out." It is a quaking aspen clonal colony in south-central Utah in the United States located at the western edge of the Colorado Plateau in the Fishlake National Forest. It has a shared root system that is an estimated 80,000 years old,[2] making it one of the oldest living organisms as well as being the most massive. The colony of individual male trees has identical genetic markers due to one of its reproductive strategies, sending up stems cloned from its massive underground root system. The frequent intense forest fires that sweep through the colony trigger radicle stem growth that become saplings and eventually replacement trees for those consumed by forest fires.

Pando might very well be a reasonable metaphor for understanding security in the context of the Internet of Things. Even though malware, like forest fires, may compromise individual devices and services, hardware-roots-of-trust remain insulated from the effects of attack. Root-of-trust building blocks focus on securely restarting devices and services that allow automated resumption and continued operation of the Internet of Things colony.

---

[1]Grant, Michael C. (October 1993). "The Trembling Giant." Discover. Vol. 14 no. 10. Chicago. pp. 82–89. Retrieved 8 May 2008.

[2]"Quaking Aspen." Bryce Canyon National Park. U.S. National Park Service. February 24, 2015. Retrieved 17 November 2018.

© The Author(s) 2020
S. Cheruvu et al., *Demystifying Internet of Things Security,*
https://doi.org/10.1007/978-1-4842-2896-8

In the era of personal computing, the computer *virus* was the predominant term borrowed from biology. It seemed to adequately characterize computer security challenges. The antivirus scan and computer emergency response processes that counter viral attacks follow a strategy summarized as detect, contain, and correct. Detection improves with constant profile updates used by antivirus scanners. Containment is achieved through various techniques to quarantine software, services, and devices. Vulnerabilities are corrected by installing patches and software updates that also resist future attacks. Detect-contain-correct has been a major focus for security practitioners since the first PCs were connected to the Internet. However, these response processes required significant manual intervention that insufficiently scale when billions of new nodes are added to the Internet of Things.

In the era of IoT, *Pando* may be the more appropriate security paradigm where the focus turns to hardware-roots-of-trust that become the building blocks for resilient security. Automated recovery and re-instantiation of trustworthy IoT endpoints and services follows an outbreak. Pando-style security mechanisms are still in their infancy as IoT evolution transitions from its first phase of massive connectivity growth to its second and third phases of smarter autonomous systems.

In this book, we looked at the economics of constrained devices and its impact on security, the role of IoT frameworks in enabling interoperability, improved developer experiences, and complexity hiding; we reviewed currently available hardware security capabilities and their role as hardware-roots-of-trust. We also described some of the challenges facing system software, virtualization, and software frameworks when trying to use hardware security capabilities and expose those security services to the various software layers above them. Attestation was highlighted as a way for peer nodes to evaluate trustworthiness characteristics of hardware security capabilities. We saw how an increase in connectivity options leads to increased complexity in gateways, hubs, routers, and other networking infrastructure as constrained endpoints continue to implement narrow slices of connection technology. We also saw how system design objectives can lead to security, safety, availability, and usability trade-offs and how vertically aligned components, software, and operations rely on the continued preservation of vertical boundaries in light of technology that breaks through many of the historical technological and physical barriers.

In particular, we want to highlight several core security concepts and ideas that contradict conventional thinking when taken in light of very large-scale IoT deployments.

Economics of Constrained Roots-of-Trust

In Chapter 1 we described the economics and impact of scaling security down to constrained devices which constitute the vast majority of connected devices in the IoT ecosystem. The traditional expectation that approximately 5–10% of device resources being security-related becomes inverted where, in many cases, a majority of resources are security functionality focused. This is motivated by root-of-trust security capabilities that anticipate interoperable trusted behaviors designed to initialize, boot, discover, provision, configure, and decommission IoT devices without human involvement. Devices lacking these capabilities simply will not be allowed to connect.

IoT Frameworks – Necessary Complexity

In Chapter 2 we observed how IoT frameworks achieve the multifaceted goal of enabling broad connectivity, improving device manageability, simplifying distributed application development and operation while promising increased interoperability. Unfortunately, interoperability ethos isn't universally shared among framework providers as some vendors pursue proprietary IoT strategies and others are overeager to create a multitude of similar but different framework standards that further dilute the promise of interoperability. We further observed that IoT framework standards almost universally ignore specifying secure binding of security functionality that incorporates hardware-roots-of-trust technology to framework layers that would ensure framework layers are not easily overtaken by malware interposers.

Hardware Security – More Than a Toolbox

In Chapter 3 we walked through an array of hardware security technologies available for integration into IoT solutions. We explained essential protections for identity, initialization, storage, and execution require hardware-roots-of-trust that are secure by design. This principle should be common to all secure IoT platforms. We also characterized attacks on IoT platforms observing that attack pathology often follows a transition from applications to user mode, user mode to kernel mode, kernel mode to pre-OS boot loader, and pre-OS to hardware. Ultimately, hardware is the last line of defense. Hardware is also the first point of recovery when rebuilding a clean system. Consequently, hardware security should be where the most care should be applied to ensure robust predictable behavior. We showed how HW security elements can be used by upper layers to implement defense-in-depth strategies that enable layered approach to attack mitigation and resilient recovery.

IOT Software – Building Blocks with Glue

In Chapter 4 we considered the role software plays in securing IoT solutions and showed some of the ways popular system software and applications approach implementation of security features. We also motivated the need for hardware security integration and observed that integration is often nontrivial requiring adaptation and rework on behalf of firmware and software developers. For example, a Trusted Execution Environment (TEE) such as Intel SGX anticipates modularizing application software so that security relevant operations are performed within a secure enclave. System software may require modification to remove unnecessary features that add exploit risk and prohibit operation inside of a more secure virtual machine. We took a tour through multiple OSs and how they expose HW security features and described criteria for securely implementing and enabling solutions that build on top of hardware security mechanisms that act like security glue that holds the software layers together.

Ethernet TSN – Everybody's Common Choice?

In Chapter 5 we described a host of communications technologies that will be employed to one extent or another in the broad IoT landscape. The reality is many IoT endpoints will employ multiple communications technologies based on cost, improved flexibility, and interoperability all the while realizing the diverse security implications. The IEEE has standardized dozens of use cases and applications involving interoperation between disparate IoT protocols. Nevertheless, complexity for complexity's sake isn't justifiable as the IoT industry will inevitably select a few connectivity technologies that broadly satisfy requirements unique to IoT; in other words, the industry will find everybody's second choice technology. Before the Internet Protocol (IP),[3] every major computer vendor had a local area network solution, most of which didn't interoperate. IP became everybody's second choice option since supporting every possible combination of vendor proprietary solutions was intractable. We anticipate a second convergence phase of connectivity technologies will occur for the Internet of Things. Our focus on Ethernet TSN plus IPv6 as our first choice to replace fieldbus-based

---

[3]Information Sciences Institute, University of Southern California, "Internet Protocol DARPA Internet Program Protocol Specification," September 1981. IETF RFC791. https://tools.ietf.org/html/rfc791

solutions is in anticipation of the eventual consolidation of the fragmented state of brownfield IoT. We think brownfield IoT will regard TSN as a popular second choice.

Security MVP – The Champion Within a Fractured IoT Ecosystem

In Chapter 6 we broadened the view of vertical applications addressed by IoT to include any industry informed by "smart" devices. Each of these industries has different security requirements due to the nature of the information handled and to meet regulatory and industry standard bodies' requirements. An overview was provided of the different verticals and associated security requirements. IoT ecosystem is fragmented by nature with multiple verticals, but at the end of the day, we need a common set of HW/SW building blocks and augmenting accelerators to meet the domain unique requirements. We discussed technology layering characteristics where layered security functionality needs to be rooted in hardware where a security minimum viable platform (MVP) defines a core set of security ingredients that are by and large common across all nodes participating in the larger IoT system. Systems architects stand a better chance at designing secure IoT systems when the MVP set of hardware security capabilities is available for implementation of security enforcement points rather than relying on a mix of options that span the continuum of cyber and physical ingredients.

The Way Forward

The journey to demystify IoT Security doesn't end with this book. We anticipate there remains a huge scaling problem where the key to realizing secure IoT operation is anchored in autonomous response and recovery in the face of attacks. A "pragmatic" security-minded industry recognizes that heterogeneous networks constructed using devices having different HW and SW architectures, components, and capabilities are likely to coexist for the foreseeable future as some devices are expected to remain in deployment for nearly 30 years. Nevertheless, all devices need to be reachable and serviceable or reliably disabled and excluded. Given the IoT continues to be a target for attack and compromise, defense-in-depth layering supported by robust hardware security capabilities is essential. The security community refers to this as hardware-roots-of-trust, we think of it as a Pando security layer that isn't easily compromised and resiliently restarts in the face of attack.

We've presented a perspective to trusted computing that is intrinsic to a device and is recognizable to other IoT devices; looking ahead we anticipate distributed trust will become commonplace where trust may be distributed across millions of devices. Blockchain[4] technology might be a good example, where a consensus of participant devices may determine whether an individual device is configured with minimum viable root-of-trust capabilities. For more information about blockchain, see the Hyperledger Project,[5] a Linux Foundation open source effort, and these additional references.[6, 7, 8]

---

[4]Wikipedia, "blockchain" (as of this publication date). https://en.wikipedia.org/wiki/Blockchain

[5]www.hyperledger.org

[6]Khwaja Shaik, "Why blockchain and IoT are best friends", January 12, 2018. www.ibm.com/blogs/blockchain/2018/01/why-blockchain-and-iot-are-best-friends/

[7]Postscapes – A list of projects and companies, "Blockchains and the IoT," January 5, 2019. www.postscapes.com/blockchains-and-the-internet-of-things/

[8]Phillip J. Windley, Ph.D., Chair Sovrin Foundation, "Identity, Sovrin, and the Internet of Things," July 27, 2017. https://blog.sovrin.org/identity-sovrin-and-the-internet-of-things-8ef911fa715d

Security combined with artificial intelligence (AI)[9, 10, 11] and machine learning (ML)[12, 13] is another area ripe for innovation where Intel is conducting research.[14] Post-quantum cryptography[15] and resilient computing[16] are additional areas of technical exploration that are out of scope for this book that nevertheless promise impactful *Pando* security advances.

---

[9]Intel Artificial Intelligence Overview. `www.intel.com/content/www/us/en/analytics/artificial-intelligence/overview.html`

[10]Torsten George, Security Week, "The Role of Artificial Intelligence in Cyber Security," January 11, 2017. `www.securityweek.com/role-artificial-intelligence-cyber-security`

[11]Justin Jett, Threat Post, "Security and Artificial Intelligence: Hype vs. Reality," August 23, 2018. `https://threatpost.com/security-and-artificial-intelligence-hype-vs-reality/136837/`

[12]Jason Knight, Intel AI Products Group blog, "The Importance of Systems in Machine Learning," February 15, 2018. `www.intel.ai/systems-machine-learning/#gs.4FOjLznH`

[13]MIT Technology Review Insights/Research, "Machine Learning-driven analytics: Key to digital transformation," 2018. `www.intel.com/content/www/us/en/analytics/mit-machine-learning-advanced-analytics-key-to-transformation.html`

[14]Georgia Tech Institute for Information Security & Privacy, "Georgia Tech Launches New Research on the Security of Machine-Learning Systems," Oct 31, 2016. `www.iisp.gatech.edu/georgia-tech-launches-new-research-security-machine-learning-systems`

[15]Simona Samardjiska, Digital Security Group Radbound University, RIOT Summit 2017, "Post Quantum Cryptography for the IoT." `https://riot-os.org/files/RIOT-Summit-2017-slides/3-4-Security-session-Simona.pdf`

[16]Kemal A. Delic, Ubiquity, Publications of the ACM, "On Resilience of IoT Systems" The Internet of Things Symposium, February 2016. `https://ubiquity.acm.org/article.cfm?id=2822885`

Index

A

Access control lists (ACLs), 59
Access control policy (ACL), 74
Access point (AP), 376
ACRN™
    architecture diagram, 265
    connectivity-automotive
        CAN bus, 268
    DM applications, 266
    para-virtualized
        architecture, 265
    pSEED and vSEEDs, 271
    RPMB flash block, 270
        CSE, 271
        real-time and power
        management controls, 271
    secure boot flow, 267
    security feature, 270
    service VM, 266
    SOS kernel, 267
    system security features,
        272–276
    TEE implementation, 269
Air-gap security, 3, 4
AllJoyn security, 81
AllSeen Alliance, 78–81

B

Application and service layer
    management (ASM), 98
Application-level language
    frameworks
    Android devices, 331, 332
    architectural model, 329
    EdgeX Foundry, 333–335
    hardware-based
        security, 330
    Java, 331, 332
    JavaScript, 330
    NodeJS/Sails, 331
    security features, 335, 336
Authenticated Code Module
    (ACM), 192

Bill of materials (BOM), 33
Blockchain technology, 469
Bluetooth Low Energy
    (BLE), 383, 384
Bluetooth operates, 383
    advantage of, 385
    BLE, 383, 384
    fundamental security
        measures, 386

© The Author(s) 2020
S. Cheruvu et al., *Demystifying Internet of Things Security*,
https://doi.org/10.1007/978-1-4842-2896-8

Printed in the United States
By Bookmasters